*For Jacqueline and Rebecca,
women of courage and conscience*

Patriotic Treason
John Brown and the Soul of America

Evan Carton

University of Nebraska Press
Lincoln

© 2006 by Evan Carton
All rights reserved
Manufactured in the United States of America
∞
First Nebraska paperback printing: 2009

Originally published by Free Press,
a Division of Simon & Schuster Inc.

Library of Congress Cataloging-in-Publication Data
Carton, Evan.
Patriotic treason: John Brown and the
soul of America / Evan Carton.
p. cm.
Originally published by Free Press, a Division of
Simon & Schuster Inc., in 2006.
Includes bibliographical references and index.
ISBN 978-0-8032-1946-5 (pbk.: alk. paper)
1. Brown, John, 1800–1859. 2. Abolitionists—Biography.
3. Antislavery movements—History—19th century.
I. Title. II. Title: John Brown and the soul of America.
E451.C37 2009
973.7'116092—dc22
[B]   2008048470

CONTENTS

AUTHOR'S NOTE ix

PROLOGUE The Dawn's Early Light 1

ONE Founding Fathers 13

TWO A Firm Foothold at Home 33

THREE The Great and Foul Stain 53

FOUR Going Down to Tarshish 71

FIVE Crossing the Line 89

SIX The Slave Law of the Land 113

SEVEN To Answer the End of My Being 139

EIGHT Blood and Remission 167

NINE Marked Men 195

TEN Bringing Forth a New Nation 221

ELEVEN An Extended Family 249

TWELVE Abolishing Slavery in Virginia 277

THIRTEEN A Settlement of the Question 315

EPILOGUE The Unfinished American Revolution 341

SOURCE NOTES 347

ACKNOWLEDGMENTS 373

INDEX 375

AUTHOR'S NOTE

For drama, controversy, and historical impact, the life of John Brown exceeds that of any other private citizen of the United States. If American patriotism is defined as unqualified commitment to the nation's founding religious and political ideals—a commitment both to live by them and to die for them—then Brown may count as one of America's first patriots, though he was not born until 1800 and was hanged for treason in 1859. Many nineteenth-century Americans, white and black, revered him; many others despised him. In the twentieth century, however, most academic historians sought to diminish Brown's importance, reducing him to a caricature or a footnote in the civic imaginations of ordinary Americans.

"John Brown is the stone in the historians' shoe," novelist and essayist Truman Nelson wrote in *The Nation* in 1957, a century after Brown set in motion his campaign to free four million slaves—a campaign that, from a military standpoint, began and ended with his raid on the U.S. arsenal at Harpers Ferry at the head of an interracial army of twenty-one men and boys. "They cannot ignore him, but they try to choke him off in defaming parentheses." Nelson's image of the historians' Brown as a stone—uncomfortable, immovable, unassimilated—echoes Brown's portrayal in Stephen Vincent Benét's 1928 Pulitzer-Prize-winning poem, *John Brown's Body*, and anticipates Brown's 1979 representation by biographer Stephen Oates. "He was a stone. / A stone eroded to a cutting edge," Benét writes of his title character. He was "God's stone in the pool of slavery," Oates echoes.

John Brown was not a stone but a man of deep, varied, and sometimes conflicting capacities: for reason and faith, practicality and idealism, harshness and tenderness, isolation and intimacy, blindness, vision,

Author's Note

transformation. He was a man, most significantly, who understood race, religion, and revolution—as these tangled legacies of America's early history had come down to his generation—to be the shaping conditions of his life and the nation's life: and to confer inescapable demands on both. In my epilogue, "The Unfinished American Revolution," I offer some reasons why Civil War historians have so often been hobbled by Brown and have scaled down the irritant to pebble-size dimensions by labeling him a fanatic or a failure. The aim of this book, however, is not to give reasons but to tell the timely true story of Brown's life, his extraordinary family and friendships, and his country.

Since the 1970s, Brown's portrait has been better painted and his place in American history reassessed in several valuable biographies and one fine novel, Russell Banks's *Cloudsplitter*. But historical novels select episodes and invent or alter characters and circumstances to achieve their creative designs, while scholarly convention limits the ability of biographers to dramatize the thoughts and feelings, the lived experience, of historical actors. Accordingly, even in such detailed and admiring nonfiction accounts as David Reynolds's recent *John Brown, Abolitionist*, which appeared as I was completing this manuscript, Brown remains somewhat abstract and alien—an icon rather than a pebble, but still a stone.

This book is a work of nonfiction. Every scene, circumstance, action, and person I represent here is drawn in accordance with the available historical record. But there are crucial moments and passages in the historical story of John Brown to which the available record provides only a map, not a key. To enter into these moments and passages, to understand them more intimately, and to convey their living drama, I sometimes visualize the undescribed sensory and emotional particulars and imagine the unpreserved words, thoughts, and motives that animated them. In these instances, I derive the voices, ideas, and feelings of the historical actors as closely as possible from surviving letters and from contemporary third-person accounts of their character and style.

Author's Note

In July of 1846, the writer and naturalist Henry David Thoreau was arrested and jailed in Concord, Massachusetts, for refusing to pay his $1.50 poll tax. Thoreau committed his act of civil disobedience to protest his country's first foreign imperialist campaign, the Mexican War, and its ever more extensive, brutal, and complacent use of black slave labor at home. Thoreau also meant his gesture to challenge the idea that government was a great impersonal machine the operations of which individual citizens could not affect and were not responsible for. Peaceful mass resistance by a citizenry that refused to accept its government's commission of unconscionable acts in its name could stop the machine and achieve a bloodless revolution, he argued in his greatest essay, "Civil Disobedience." Yet: "Even suppose blood should flow. Is there not a sort of blood shed when the conscience is wounded? Through this wound a man's real manhood and immortality flow out, and he bleeds to an everlasting death. I see this blood flowing now."

Fourteen years later, during a memorial service at John Brown's gravesite on July 4, 1860, Thoreau returned to this theme of the life and death of conscience in recalling his first thought upon learning of Brown's execution. "Of all the men who were said to be my contemporaries, it seemed to me that John Brown was the only one who *had not died*." This book tells the story of John Brown, of where he lived and what he lived for, and of why–though his body molders–he lives on.

PROLOGUE

The Dawn's Early Light

"Was John Brown simply an episode, or was he an eternal truth?"
—W. E. B. DuBois

Lieutenant J. E. B. Stuart of the First United States Cavalry crossed the yard of the Harpers Ferry armory and approached the thick oak door of the engine house under a flag of truce. He felt eyes on his back. In the gray first light of the raw morning of October 18, 1859, Stuart could make out the muzzles of two rifles protruding from gun holes that appeared to have been hastily chiseled through the engine house wall. He doubted that he had much to fear from the incompetent band of northerners and negroes trapped in the small building in front of him, fanatical haters of the southern system of labor that was protected by the country's laws and enshrined in its traditions. He was at greater risk, he thought wryly, from the unsteady hands and judgment of his fellow Virginians who perched on the railroad trestle and the water tower and in every window of the hotel to his rear.

Drawn by the chilling news that white men in league with blacks had overrun the armory at Harpers Ferry and taken possession of its hundred thousand rifles and muskets, local militia companies and curious citizens from across the region had rushed to the snug commercial town throughout the preceding day and night. Harpers Ferry, Virginia, nestled at the tip of the peninsula bounded by the converging Shenandoah and Potomac rivers. Their churning waters formed a gateway to the Shenandoah Valley, which unfolded to the south. From its main street, lined with shops and government offices, the town ascended into the lush foothills of the Blue Ridge, finally reaching the Bolivar Heights plateau. Tidy and scenic as a Swiss mountain village, Harpers Ferry seemed an idyll of quiet and peace, but it was not–at least, not this morning. Stuart estimated that two thousand citizens–frenzied, sleepless, intoxicated, and armed–thronged doorways, windows, and rooftops and lined both riverbanks, surrounding the armory complex. The wall and the high arched doors of the engine house were already pocked and splintered by their buckshot and pistol balls. It was not the watery sun struggling to crest the soaring Maryland Heights that warmed his cheek and neck as he advanced but those grim stares, hot with outrage, heavy with fear.

Only the appraisal of one pair of eyes, however, mattered to the twenty-six-year-old Stuart. Those belonged to Colonel Robert E. Lee, the superintendent of West Point during Stuart's term there as a cadet five years before and, by sheer good fortune, his commanding officer again today in the business of suppressing these traitors.

Lee surveyed his messenger's progress from a patch of raised ground thirty yards away. He wore civilian clothes, but his bearing and his calm, steady gaze were sufficient signs of his authority. On leave from his Texas command, Lee had been summoned less than twenty hours ago to an emergency meeting at the White House and dispatched by President Buchanan to put down an astonishing traitorous attack on one of the United States military's principal installations.

The institution of slavery had been a matter of contention between representatives of the northern and southern states since the nation's founding. But in the 1850s the bitterness and violence reached unprecedented levels. The reasons were many. The founding fathers, devoted to the immediate task of securing the young country's economic and political viability and protecting it against threats from outside, had taken steps to defuse and defer the internal debate over slavery. Most had assumed that slavery was a temporary feature of the American social and economic landscape, a necessary evil that would gradually diminish. In 1808, Congress did outlaw the transatlantic slave trade, limiting the slave population to natural increase alone. Yet the population of enslaved blacks continued to grow, as did the reliance of the southern economy upon slavery. In 1820, Congress passed the Missouri Compromise, which—excepting the new slave state of Missouri—limited the institution's future spread to territories below that state's southern border. But in the 1830s and 1840s, economic instability and waves of job-seeking European immigrants led to heightened concern that slavery was depressing wages and limiting opportunity for whites.

During these same decades, the southern cotton economy expanded in scope and profitability, producing a new generation of political leaders, whose unapologetic commitment to slavery and growing power in Washington prompted some northern politicians to take a more active antislavery stance. Industrialization in the north ushered in an era of religious revival and social reform movements, which increased moral opposition to slavery among churchgoers and intellectuals. Most significant, however, was the opening of vast new western territories, which brought slaveholding and antislavery interests and populations into direct competition for land recently cleared of Indians or won from Mexico by the U.S. military. This situation was made more explosive by the passage in the early 1850s of a series of acts that repealed the Missouri Compromise and allowed western settlers to decide the legality or illegality of slavery in their territories by direct popular vote. The most dramatic and violent such contest, the battle for "bleeding Kansas" between 1855 and 1858, had at first promised a victory for proslavery forces but now seemed likely to be resolved in favor of the free state settler majority, though Kansas would not officially gain statehood for another two years.

For southerners, the loss of Kansas as a field for slavery's expansion was bitter. Yet they had made recent gains as well. The Fugitive Slave Law of 1850 confirmed the principle that slaves remained property even if they escaped to free states and forbade any citizen, on pain of criminal prosecution, to obstruct their capture. Even more decisively, the Supreme Court's Dred Scott decision of 1857 proclaimed that slaves could be taken and resettled by their masters anywhere in the country without gaining standing to petition for freedom under any state law. Slaves remained slaves, no matter what the laws of the state in which they resided said. Moreover, the decision stipulated that all blacks were barred from American citizenship and any rights that might pertain to citizens. As Chief Justice Roger Taney wrote, expressing the majority opinion of a court that was packed with southerners and included five justices from slaveholding families, the Constitution held blacks to be "unfit to associate with the white race, either in social or political relations, and so far inferior that they had no rights which the white man was bound to respect."

In 1859, passions remained high. On both sides of the Mason-Dixon line, prophets of doom and advocates of disunion were plentiful, as they had been for years. Yet many expected the old sectional strife to find a new equilibrium or at least to enter into another phase of compromise and uneasy truce.

A calculated attack on the venerable state of Virginia and on a U.S. government facility just fifty-five miles from Washington itself would change all that.

By Monday afternoon, October 17, when Lee embarked for Harpers Ferry at the head of a detachment of federal troops, panic gripped the nation's capital. Frantic early intelligence, conveyed by telegraph, horseback, and rumor, put the number of white and black conspirators as high as seven hundred. Reaching his destination at midnight and taking command of the U.S. artillery and marine companies as well as the numerous local militias on the scene, Lee determined that these reports were wildly exaggerated. Several insurgents lay dead in the armory yard and in the river, shot by townspeople and militiamen. Two more, one critically wounded, were being held in the Wager House hotel. The remaining handful appeared to be holed up in a single room with the hostages they'd taken at the beginning of the raid.

By chance, J. E. B. Stuart also had been visiting in Washington the day before and answered the president's call. Two hours after their arrival at Harpers Ferry, Colonel Lee assigned him the responsibility of conveying the surrender ultimatum at dawn. If the insurrectionists refused it, Stuart had orders to step away from the door and wave his cap. Upon that signal, Lieutenant Israel Green of the Washington-based U.S. Marines would lead an immediate attack.

Out of respect for local sentiment, Lee had first offered the honor of this assault on the engine house to the assembled volunteer units from the surrounding towns, but their leaders had declined it. Stuart thought it just as well. Had these Jefferson County men deserved the assignment, they would have overwhelmed the invaders and taken back the town and the armory before federal troops had arrived. Instead, they had apparently spent the previous afternoon and evening drinking and raging in the Galt House saloon, firing from cover into the armory yard and engine house, and disfiguring the corpses of the enemy they managed to kill. Stuart recalled with disgust the spectacle that he and Colonel Lee had encountered as they crossed the railroad bridge over the Potomac and entered the town the night before. In the shallows below, grotesquely illuminated by the torches of milling lookers-on, lay the body of a young man, his clothes shredded, entrails exposed, and face almost obliterated by the force of countless bullets. A few yards beyond on the bank were the remains of an older mulatto, similarly mutilated; in addition his ears had been sliced off and carried away as souvenirs.

From his observation post, Lee watched Stuart deliver the demand for unconditional surrender to the insurrection's leader, Isaac Smith.

Stuart reached the door and executed his commission. "Mr. Smith," he called. "I carry a message for you from Colonel Robert E. Lee, commander of the United States troops assembled here on order of the president." For a moment there was no response. Then Stuart heard the creak of an iron bar being lifted from its latch, and as the door inched open, the sound of someone within moaning or crying in pain. Then a rifle barrel was stuck through the opening and held an inch from his head by a man who remained partly concealed behind the door. Peering into the far corner of the engine house, Stuart could see ten or twelve persons seated on the floor. These were the hostages, who seemed to include several slaves, huddled near their masters. Not far from this group, along the back wall, lay two blood-soaked young men. Another insurgent, apparently unwounded, crouched beside them.

Stuart unfolded the letter Lee had written and began to read it aloud. The man with the rifle came more fully into the opening and interrupted him. "Lieutenant, if you please," he said mildly but authoritatively. "I am a capable reader." The man who had leased a nearby farm three months ago under the name Isaac Smith held out his hand for the paper.

Lee's missive to the raiders was blunt. "Colonel Lee represents to them, in all frankness, that it is impossible for them to escape; that the armory is surrounded on all sides by troops; and that if he is compelled to take them by force he cannot answer for their safety."

As Smith read, Stuart studied his adversary. His height was above average, five feet ten or eleven inches. Slightly hunched shoulders made him seem shorter but did not diminish the impression of energy and sinewy strength that his lean frame conveyed. Smith's iron-gray hair was brushed back off a high forehead. He had a sharp Roman nose and a thin, determined mouth above an angular jaw that was little softened by the short white beard that covered it. His deep-set blue eyes were clear and penetrating. The townspeople had called him an old man, but it was only the bent back and the short white beard that suggested advanced age. He was weather-beaten, certainly, but in a way that reminded the lieutenant of some of those Yankee farmers he'd observed on his rides in the countryside around West Point, men who both managed their properties and worked them winter and summer, acquiring features so craggy and expressions so impassive that a stranger might fix their years at seventy or at forty with equal chance of accuracy. Yes, that was exactly his type. Perhaps he had seen this very man along the Hudson.

The moment Smith raised his eyes, Stuart knew him. They *had* met before, not in New York but in Kansas Territory more than three years ago. He had been clean-shaven then. And then, as now, he'd held prisoners. This was John Brown, the abolitionist radical who had made the Kansas conflict so long and bloody. Osawatomie Brown, the murderer who had dragged five of his neighbors out of their beds at midnight and hacked them to death—or directed his sons to do it—with no reason or provocation other than that the victims were proslavery men. Captain John Brown of the Kansas Liberty Guard he had called himself on that afternoon in June of 1856 when he handed over Missouri militia captain Henry Clay Pate and twenty-five of Pate's men to Colonel Edwin Sumner's company of United States dragoons, in which Stuart then served. The Missourians had crossed into Kansas to apprehend the old man and his sons, only to surrender themselves to Brown's band of nine at the infamous Battle of Black Jack. Old John Brown, horse thief and man stealer, had last surfaced almost a year ago after raiding three plantations in Missouri and absconding with eleven slaves. Two and a half months and a thousand miles later, eluding posses all the way and making a mockery of the presidential bounty on his head, Brown had deposited his stolen cargo in Canada.

But now he was caught.

"Communicate to Colonel Lee that his terms are unacceptable," Brown began. "I am willing to retreat and abandon my purpose at the armory, but only if all my men, living or dead, are delivered to me and we are allowed to cross the Potomac bridge, taking our arms, ammunition, and prisoners with us to guarantee our safe passage. The colonel has my assurance that the prisoners will be set at liberty as soon as we reach the hills on the Maryland side."

Stuart considered turning away and making the signal without another word. Instead, he responded, "I know you, sir. We had business of this sort together in Kansas. You are Osawatomie Brown."

"I am afraid I cannot return the compliment," Brown replied. "As you see, I have aged, and my memory has grown imperfect. I am enfeebled, too, by not having eaten or slept for two days and distracted by the loss of several of my young men here to assassins' bullets, including some of my own family."

"Assassins?" Stuart challenged. "You are the ones who have invaded and terrorized this peaceful community, imprisoned, robbed, and murdered its citizens, and treasonously assaulted a United States armory."

"We have intended injury to no one, and I am quite certain that my men have only fired in self-defense at those who have attacked us. Those were the strict instructions I gave them."

"The bodies of the railway baggage master and of Mr. Beckham, the mayor of this town, which I have seen, belie you. Both were unarmed when they were killed." Stuart paused when he saw Brown's clear eyes cloud slightly. "Thousands have gathered here, Mr. Brown," he continued, "and they are justly aroused against you. But if you surrender now without further violence, Colonel Lee will keep you in safety pending orders from President Buchanan as to your transport and prosecution."

"If your report is true, Lieutenant, I am very sorry to hear it. Every man's life is dear to him, and it is a crime against God and humanity to take a life needlessly. I assure you that nothing was further from our intention. I believe that Colonel Washington, whom we have detained here, will vouch for my respect and care for our prisoners. It was for their protection, more than our own, that we retreated to the engine house, and no threat or harm has been offered them, even after my own son Watson and another of my men were shot down like dogs when I sent them out to negotiate terms of peace under the same flag of truce that has brought you here uninjured. I have sought neither vengeance nor gain. I came to this place in response to the cry of the distressed, with the single purpose of liberating my fellow human beings who are in bondage in Virginia."

Stuart had grown increasingly impatient as Brown spoke. "How acute your ear must be, Mr. Brown," he snapped, "to hear Virginia's distress from so far away. And what made you suppose that this imagined cry from a sovereign state not your own was addressed particularly to you?" Instantly regretting his loss of composure, the lieutenant added, "But I will not debate with you, sir. Will you surrender and spare these hostages from risk of harm, or do you choose to be overrun?"

As Brown did not immediately reply, a stately middle-aged man rose from the cluster of prisoners at the rear of the engine house. He was Colonel Lewis Washington, great-grandnephew of the first president, a gentleman farmer who owned property on the Bolivar Heights between Harpers Ferry and Charlestown. Speaking directly to Stuart, Washington confirmed that he and the other prisoners had been treated well during the ordeal of the last thirty hours and requested that Lee himself come into the engine house to discuss terms for their release.

Washington felt that a respectful understanding of sorts had developed between Brown and himself and that he and Colonel Lee together might persuade the man to listen to reason now. Excepting the captivity itself, the principal indignities he had suffered were the initial invasion of his home two nights ago by six of Brown's followers and their demand, as stipulated by Brown, that he place his family's most precious heirloom into the hands of one of the negroes among them. This was a ceremonial sword, a gift of Frederick the Great to his ancestor, General Washington. Brown had worn the sword at his waist all the previous day, only unbuckling it and setting it atop the fire engine when he went to sit by his sons during the night.

Washington, his neighbor John Allstadt, and their slaves had been taken to the armory by their captors in Washington's own carriage and farm wagon. On his arrival, Brown had greeted him pleasantly, almost deferentially. From that moment on, what Washington found most curious in the whole extraordinary business was Brown's seeming compulsion to be thought well of by the very men whose liberty he had infringed and property appropriated. Before the town had become a shooting gallery late the previous morning, Brown had insisted on sending one of the captured armory guards across the street to the Wager House to arrange for the delivery of a breakfast sufficient for all of his prisoners. And throughout the day, as the townspeople and neighboring militias gathered, blocking every possible exit route and raining bullets into the armory compound, Brown had seemed more concerned to defend his motives and tactics to Washington and Allstadt than to improve his deteriorating position. He appeared not to regard the fact that he'd kidnapped these gentlemen at gunpoint, held them hostage, and proposed to arm their servants as any sort of barrier to philosophical dialogue with them. Nor did he see any reason why, under such circumstances, his patient arguments from history and scripture might not bring them around to his view.

Brown had continued these arguments into the night, even as his two sons lay dying, the one he called Oliver repeatedly begging to be shot and put out of his misery.

"You will get over it," said Brown, and resumed his efforts to school his captives in the sufferings of blacks and the duty of Christians. Washington had wondered what kind of a man could so steel himself to the present agony of his own flesh and blood while he discoursed so passionately about the distant tribulations of strangers. Now Oliver's body lay cold against the wall next to his brother Watson, who still breathed.

John Brown did not hear Washington ask Stuart if Colonel Lee would come negotiate in person or Stuart's response that there would be no negotiation. The lieutenant's sarcastic request to know why he thought slavery was his personal business had thrown him into a momentary reverie. Slavery simply was his business and had been from as far back as he could remember. His own stern father's first and constant lesson to his children was that they must fear God and hate slavery, and Brown had always understood this to be one lesson, not two. The path of righteousness, he had been taught, must be walked, not merely proclaimed. Every man must find out that path in his own place and time. In his, it was resistance to slavery.

Not only the cry but the very heartbeat of the oppressed slave had long been addressed to him. He had heard it as a nineteen-year-old tanner in Hudson, Ohio, when a young fugitive, the first of many runaway slaves who would stop at Brown's station on the Underground Railroad, took momentary refuge in the cabin that he shared with his foster brother, Levi Blakeslee. Terrified by the voices of approaching strangers, whom he mistook for slave catchers, the runaway had clambered out the window at the rear of the cabin, leaving a half-full saucer of milk on the table and the warm imprints of his fingers on the uneaten bread. When the danger had passed, Brown discovered the fugitive's hiding place behind the woodpile, a spot to which he felt himself directed by the audible pounding of the negro's heart.

That was the second time he was called. The first was a decade earlier. His mother had died in 1808, when he was eight, and John still pined after her, resisting the efforts of his father's new wife to replace her in his affections. Just as he reached adolescence, the second war with Britain broke out and gave him the opportunity to put some distance between himself and the family circle from which he felt estranged. His father, a tanner, shoemaker, and cattle breeder in Ohio's Western Reserve, had a contract to supply beef to the American troops fighting along the Great Lakes. John learned the route and then volunteered to drive the cattle alone to a point on the supply line in Michigan. Arriving safely with his herd, more than a hundred miles from his home, he lodged for a week with a U.S. marshal, who treated him like a favorite nephew, giving him presents, praising his cleverness and conversation, and rehearsing young Brown's wilderness exploits at dinner to entertain his friends. But this attention and esteem, so much desired by the lonely child, was made bitter to him by a shocking contrast.

In this gentleman's household lived a negro serving boy. John sought his companionship, and across the divide of race and circumstance, the two quickly became friends. Though John was the hero of the hour, the blunt honesty and habit of critical self-scrutiny that his father had always demanded of him led him to recognize that the black child, a year younger than he, was his superior. He surpassed John in agility, in aptitude, in generosity, and surely in the fortitude with which he bore the loss of his family. Yet the same kind host who showered the white boy with gifts and praise bestowed on the black only poor clothing, meager food, and ridicule. And when the last guest had left the very dinner at which he had been celebrated, John watched in horror as the marshal casually took an iron shovel from the fireplace and beat his friend across the head and shoulders for some trivial lack of promptness or precision in his service at the table. Long after he had gone to his warm bed, John imagined he still heard the boy's muffled sobs.

For years after that, he would return in meditation to the wretched, hopeless condition of slave children, who could depend on neither mother nor father to protect and provide for them. Sometimes he even posed the question to himself whether these children had a caring father in God.

"For the last time, Mr. Brown," Stuart barked, "will you surrender now without conditions?"

Brown's eyes found him. "I have told you my conditions, Lieutenant. Failing to have them met, my men and I are prepared to sell our lives dearly." Brown's face had regained its granite calm.

Stuart stepped back out of the doorway, lifted his cap, and swung it over his head. The engine house door slammed shut and the bar clanged back into place as the soldiers of Lieutenant Green's detail charged. Three marines attempted to shatter the door with sledgehammers, the others waiting behind them with bayonets at the ready. Colonel Lee had ordered a bayonet attack in the hope of minimizing injuries to the prisoners. When the sledgehammers failed, Green instructed his men to use as a battering ram a heavy ladder that had been brought out into the armory yard.

The first marine to enter was shot and killed by one of the four remaining raiders with Brown in the engine house who were still capable of putting up a fight. Brown himself knelt beside his two sons as the troops rushed in, holding a rifle in one hand and feeling Watson's feeble pulse with the other. Two of Brown's men–Watson's brother-in-law Dauphin Thompson, and Jeremiah Goldsmith Anderson, grandson of a Virginia slaveholding family–were quickly bayoneted to death. The others–Edwin Coppoc, one of the two Quaker Coppoc brothers to fight with Brown, and the escaped slave Shields Green–were able to surrender. As Lieutenant Israel Green accompanied his troops into the engine house, Colonel Washington, whom he knew, greeted him and identified the kneeling man a few feet away.

"This is Osawatomie."

In his haste to leave the capital the afternoon before, Green had neglected to exchange his dress sword for a regulation battle saber. Armed with a weapon better suited for show than for use, he nonetheless sprang at the rising Brown, aiming a death blow at his enemy's midsection. The light blade caught Brown at the waist but struck something hard–Brown's belt or hip bone. The old man was knocked backward, but Green's sword was bent double and useless for a second thrust. Taking the weapon in both hands and using it as a cudgel, Lieutenant Green brought down blow after blow on Brown's skull, bruising and cutting his head, neck, and face in many places. When it was clear that Brown was unconscious or dead, Green desisted.

Had Israel Green struck him a few inches higher or lower, or had he been carrying the heavier sword designed for mortal combat, John Brown and his attempt to begin the forcible abolition of slavery with a volunteer army of twenty-one men and boys might have been simply an episode. But Brown recovered from his wounds and lived for six more weeks before he was hung by the state of Virginia for the crimes of treason to the commonwealth, murder, and conspiring with slaves to rebel. By the time of his death, on December 2, 1859, Brown's written and spoken words had set the United States on a path of radical and painful transformation. A path, as Brown viewed it, of renewal and fulfillment of the nation's founding promise.

It is a path we travel still.

CHAPTER ONE

Founding Fathers

*"If a tax on tea justified revolution,
did not the souls of men and women?"*
–William Lloyd Garrison

GEORGE LUTHER STEARNS was cold. He had been cold, it seemed, every moment since the Wednesday in mid-October when Boston newspapers reported that John Brown of Osawatomie had been captured in Virginia while attempting a bold, strange, doomed assault on the federal armory at Harpers Ferry. The discovery of a trunk full of papers by U.S. troops at a farmhouse across the Potomac in Maryland implicated leading northeastern industrialists, philanthropists, physicians, and even ministers in Brown's plot. The following week, Stearns shivered as he stared at the incriminating private correspondence of three of his fellow secret committee members that the *New York Herald* had published under the banner headline THE EXPOSURE OF THE NIGGER-WORSHIPPING INSURRECTIONISTS. Four months later, on February 24, 1860, the Massachusetts millionaire sat at the witness table in the Senate hearings room of the Capitol Building in Washington. He was still cold.

James Mason of Virginia, chair of the special Senate investigation of John Brown's objectives and accomplices, called the session to order. Next to Mason, author of the 1850 Fugitive Slave Law, sat Senator Jefferson Davis of Mississippi. Proslavery Indiana Senator Graham Fitch and two members of the minority Republican Party, Vermont's Jacob Collamer and James Doolittle of Wisconsin, filled out the Senate committee.

Stearns asked that he be allowed to read a prepared statement. He was not used to speaking in public, let alone to being interrogated, he told the senators, and he wished to offer them a clear, accurate, and condensed account of his dealings with John Brown. After some consultation, the committee granted his request. Stearns read for an hour and a half, gradually relaxing as he droned on.

He really had little to worry about, he told himself. Nothing specific could be proved, because he and the others had not known and had not wished to know the exact details of Brown's abolitionist operation in the south. Stearns doubted whether any of the senators besides Davis even wanted to force the criminal prosecution of prominent citizens of the north whose only provable offense was harboring antislavery sentiments and raising money to defend the right of the majority of free white settlers in Kansas to keep slavery out of their territory. Mason feared a sympathetic backlash that might drive more voters into the Republican ranks later this year if it appeared that the southerners were persecuting innocent men for the crime of a handful of frontier fanatics and negroes who had already been captured and executed. And the committee's two Republicans were all too willing to find that no respectable citizen of the north would carry humane antislavery sentiments, such as those their party professed, to such a lawless and repugnant extreme as knowingly to support an action like Brown's.

The interrogation that followed Stearns's opening remarks proceeded with little drama for ninety more minutes before Senator Collamer brought it to a close.

"Now," he asked, in a tone that announced they were finally getting to the heart of the matter, "did you ever, before that took place, have any intimation that that was contemplated to be done, intended to be done by him?"

"No, sir," Stearns replied. "I never supposed that he contemplated anything like what occurred at Harpers Ferry."

"Then I ask you, do you disapprove of such a transaction as that at Harpers Ferry?"

"I should have disapproved of it if I had known it," said the raid's principal funder and arms supplier.

The session was adjourned and the senators took a hasty leave, all except Mason, who stayed to review the transcript with the committee stenographer. Stearns had gathered his papers and was free to go. Yet he hesitated, remembering a winter afternoon three years ago in his parlor in Medford. Tears had welled in his wife Mary's eyes as their visitor recounted his family's sufferings in Kansas in the cause of freedom. Henry, his young son, had tugged at Stearns's sleeve, whispering a request for permission to give Captain Brown his pocket money to relieve some poor little boy in the territories. This recollection quickly gave way to the image of the small, unpainted farmhouse and adjoining family graveyard in the Adirondacks that Stearns had visited just three weeks ago. A procession of orphaned Brown girls and widowed women had greeted him there with modest embraces and brave smiles. They passed before him again now: quiet, solemn Mary Brown; the teenage widows of Oliver and Watson; several younger Brown sisters, the littlest no more than six; and Brown's eldest daughter and red-haired family scribe, thirty-year-old Ruth Thompson, who had written to his Mary inviting them to come. It would be a comfort to the entire family, Ruth had said, to be better acquainted with such warm friends and admirers of her father.

Brown's friend cleared his throat loudly. When Mason looked up, Stearns said that he had misspoken in answer to Senator Collamer's last question. "May I correct the record?" he asked. Mason stared at him for a moment, then nodded, and asked the stenographer to read back Senator Collamer's last question and take Stearns's amended answer.

"Then I ask you, do you disapprove of such a transaction as that at Harpers Ferry?" the stenographer recited.

Stearns took a breath. "I should have disapproved of it if I had known of it," he replied, "but I have since changed my opinion. I believe John Brown to be the representative man of this century, as Washington was of the last."

George Washington died on his plantation at Mount Vernon on December 14, 1799, days from the turn of the new century. Few Americans doubted that his resolute leadership alone had sustained their army through the dark years of the Revolutionary War and that his force of character as president had seen the country safely through its critical first decade. More than the Constitution itself, it was the childless Washington who had brought forth a nation out of a jumble of colonies and competing factions that had been united at first by little more than their common resentment of British political and economic control. Washington's fatherhood of the country was proclaimed by each of his many eulogists and by none more emphatically than the Constitution's principal draftsman. "Americans!" cried Gouverneur Morris of New York. "He had no child–but you!"

Within a few months of Washington's death, "Parson" Weems, Episcopal priest and itinerant bookseller, was peddling a pamphlet of his own composition designed to celebrate the hero's private virtues as well as his public deeds in a language that common people and even children could understand. Mason Locke "Parson" Weems steadily added material to his *Life of Washington* until by 1809 it had grown into a substantial completed book. By 1825, more than twenty-nine editions were in circulation. The cult of Washington, who stood at the head of an emerging pantheon of revered Founding Fathers, soon became a kind of national civic religion that served both a political and a psychological purpose. Politically it helped give form and character to the fledgling patriotism of early Americans, personalizing their sense of attachment to the country and to one another. Psychologically the cult of Washington and the Founders conferred on the next generation of Americans a filial obligation to preserve the Fathers' legacy by protecting what they had achieved and seeking to advance the principles they had held dear.

For John Brown, born in 1800, five months after Washington's death and just as the first version of Weems's *Life of Washington* began to circulate, the sense of a personal Revolutionary legacy was strong. His grandfather and namesake, Captain John Brown, had commanded a regiment in Washington's army, dying early in the war of the dysentery that contaminated food and water spread among the troops. In 1857, while visiting cousins in his family's native town of Canton, Connecticut, Brown came upon the original tombstone of this grandfather leaning against a wall by the roadside. Asking and receiving permission from his kin to take the displaced memorial back to his home at North Elba, he resolved to add an inscription commemorating his son Frederick, who had been executed by a proslavery vigilante in Kansas the previous year.

"That stone," said Brown to the Connecticut storekeeper with whom he was riding when he discovered it, "formerly marked the grave of my grandfather, who died fighting for the liberties of his country. My son has just been murdered in the same cause in Kansas, and the government applauded the murderer. This stone shall bear his name also." Later it would bear Brown's own.

Above all others, the word that proclaimed the American legacy was "liberty." Liberty named the Fathers' crowning accomplishment and their most closely guarded right. Liberty also anchored the loftiest and most familiar sentences of America's sacred founding documents: "We hold these truths to be self-evident, that all men are created equal, that they are endowed by their Creator with certain unalienable Rights, that among these are Life, Liberty, and the pursuit of Happiness," the Declaration of Independence pronounced. The preamble to the Constitution added, "We the people of the United States, in order to form a more perfect Union, establish justice, insure domestic tranquility, provide for the common defense, promote the general welfare, and secure the blessings of liberty to ourselves and our posterity, do ordain and establish this Constitution for the United States of America."

Liberty was the Founding Fathers' gift and their heirs' responsibility, and everyone knew it. Everyone also knew what liberty's symbolic and practical opposite was, though neither the Declaration of Independence nor the Constitution spoke its name. "Is life so dear, or peace so sweet," Patrick Henry famously demanded, urging his fellow Virginians to overcome their cautious arguments and psychological taboos against armed revolt, "as to be purchased at the price of chains and slavery? I know not what course others may take, but as for me, give me liberty or give me death!" As the slaveholding Henry's call for freedom unwittingly disclosed, America's noble thesis was bound to a degraded antithesis. Slavery falsified the new nation's self-evident truths and deformed its more perfect union.

At the outset of the War of Independence, slavery existed and was lawful in all of the thirteen colonies. Yet its incompatibility with the precept of liberty and the rhetoric of the Revolution had become apparent to most American leaders. "To contend for liberty and to deny that blessing to others involves an inconsistency not to be excused," wrote New York's John Jay. Abigail Adams of Massachusetts, in a letter to her husband, John, put it more bluntly. "It always appeared a most iniquitous Scheme to me—fight ourselves for what we are daily robbing and plundering from those who have as good a right to freedom as we have." And Virginia's Thomas Jefferson, though a slaveholder himself, brooded on how an American could "inflict on his fellow men, a bondage, one hour of which is fraught with more misery, than ages of that which he rose in rebellion to oppose."

Such inconsistency led the seven original northern states—which, in 1790, contained fewer than fifty thousand of the country's approximately seven hundred thousand slaves—to take steps to end slavery soon after the nation was established. When Congress outlawed the international slave trade in 1808, many white Americans assumed that slavery would gradually diminish throughout the country, that the African population itself would decline, and that eventually the remnant of former slaves and their descendants would either be resettled elsewhere or accommodated in the United States as a small, segregated laboring class. Instead, the numbers of blacks in bondage increased to two million in 1830, two and a half million in 1840, more than three million in 1850, and nearly four million when John Brown marched on Harpers Ferry in 1859.

Still, "Liberty" remained America's watchword, and in the first three decades of the nineteenth century, most Americans came to declare and exercise it without any of the personal discomfort or consciousness of national hypocrisy that Jay, Adams, and Jefferson had expressed. Slavery persisted, but the virtue of liberty seemed to have escaped its shadow. The legacy of the Founding Fathers was to be honored and preserved by seeing to it that the United States prospered, and that required enterprise, vigilant attention to one's private affairs at home, and advancement of the country's status and prerogatives in the community of nations. In pursuit of these ends, Americans supported territorial expansion, fought for maritime security and free access to world trade in the War of 1812, and became a strikingly litigious people in defense of their personal economic rights.

As the U.S. economy grew and slavery grew with it, Americans began to abandon the Founders' belief that the problem was temporary. Instead, many came to view it as insoluble. The sons and grandsons of the Revolutionary generation rationalized this view by asserting that the true American political legacy was balance and practical compromise, not emancipation. The Founders compromised on the issue of slavery for the sake of unity, and their descendants were obliged to do likewise. In the south, as the acquisition of the Louisiana territories vastly increased the plantation economy's scale and the invention of the cotton gin and other new textile-processing technologies vastly increased its profitability, expressions of concern about the practice or duration of slavery became less and less welcome. Though northern mills, manufacturers, and shippers also profited from the raw materials that slave labor cheaply provided, most northerners regarded slavery as a southern problem, an unfortunate vestige of a premodern age, maintained by a less enlightened population. In addition, there was racism, which the French social analyst Alexis de Tocqueville found, in his 1831 tour of the United States, to be more virulent in the north and northwest than in the south.

"The prejudice of race," he wrote, "appears to be stronger in the states that have abolished slavery than in those where it still exists; and nowhere is it so intolerant as in those states where servitude has never been known."

These causes of complacency about the institution of slavery in the early nineteenth century found support in the belief in a benign and progressive Providence that the Founding Fathers bequeathed to the political and intellectual elites who followed them. In the Declaration's first sentence, Jefferson asserts that it is "the Laws of Nature and Nature's God" that entitle the American people to assume a separate and equal station among the powers of the earth. For Jefferson, the Creator is not a God who works his will through decisive contests between good and evil but one who governs through natural laws and processes that are clarified and fulfilled "in the course of human events." Humankind inhabits a providential design, Enlightenment intellectuals contended, a complex and evolving physical, social, and moral environment whose workings might be gleaned and purposes gradually advanced by the application of reason.

This design was inherently benevolent, and the task of human beings was to live in harmony with it. Close observation of the physical universe and behavior in accordance with its laws could ensure a peaceful state, one in which evolutionary transformations rather than revolutionary ones would take place. Only on rare occasions and in response to unnatural provocations would "the Laws of Nature" authorize radical breaks. The persistence of slavery did not present such an occasion. For Jefferson, nature's dictates in regard to the status of blacks were at best ambiguous. In his *Notes on the State of Virginia,* written nine years after the Declaration of Independence, Jefferson argued that though white prejudices and injuries had played a role in limiting blacks' development, they did not account for or negate "the real distinctions which nature has made." Africans were not created equal but "inferior to the whites in the endowments both of body and mind." Jefferson concluded with a rhetorical question. "Will not a lover of natural history, then, one who views the gradations in all the races of animals with the eye of philosophy, excuse an effort to keep those in the department of man as distinct as nature has formed them?"

Like most children of the post-Revolutionary generation, John Brown imbibed a pious respect for the nation's founders. But by the circumstances of his birth, region, and training, Brown also inherited another American patrimony: an intense religiosity.

The Browns traced their American origins to a seventeenth-century English Puritan, Peter Brown, one of the original Pilgrims who stepped off the Mayflower onto Plymouth Rock in 1620 determined to establish a religious and civic community in the New World that would advance the kingdom of God. Followers of the stern precepts of Reformation theologian John Calvin, the Puritan settlers of New England worshipped a demanding God whose eternal character stood revealed in both testaments of the Bible. Theirs was the God who chastened the Israelites for forty years in the desert before deeming them worthy of deliverance in Canaan, who later sacrificed his only son to redeem humankind, and who might justly require great sacrifices of his faithful as well.

Calvinism was a rigorous form of Protestantism that entailed a challenging synthesis of emotion and intellect and of private and civic religious practice. The believing Calvinist conducted a lifelong spiritual inquiry consisting of three interrelated components: to study the Bible to better understand God's glory and God's requirements; to study himself to assess whether he genuinely felt that glory and dutifully strove to fulfill those requirements; and to study his social relations and worldly circumstances to determine where they were unrighteous and what he could do to rectify them. By their diligence in these religious exercises, Calvinists readied themselves for salvation, though no efforts of their own could ensure it.

Calvinists understood God to be both personal and infinite, but they did not construe those qualities in the more comforting ways that later Protestant sects often would. God was personal in the sense that his hand was actively involved in the affairs of individual lives but not in the sense that he could be known intimately or familiarly or would ever reveal himself, except indirectly through Scripture. God was infinite in the sense that he was everywhere and that every occurrence was—in ways and for reasons that were often mysterious to human beings—part of his plan, but this infiniteness did not mean he was all-accepting or all-forgiving. On the contrary, Calvinism insisted on a God who was at once punitive and loving, punitive *because* loving.

By the early nineteenth century, Calvinism had been eclipsed by newer Protestant denominations—Methodists, Baptists, Unitarians, and others—that offered an array of less stark theologies. If the original Calvinist synthesis held firm anywhere in John Brown's America, however, it was in the region of central Connecticut where Brown was born, a few miles from the birthplace of Calvinism's greatest eighteenth-century expositor, Jonathan Edwards. At least for the faithful of Connecticut and western Massachusetts, Edwards and his followers had successfully parried one of the principal thrusts of Calvinism's opponents, the charge that Calvinism limits or denies the free will of human beings. Demonstrating their belief in individual moral accountability, the nineteenth-century Edwardsean or Consistent Calvinists adopted the Puritan conception of life as a trial or test in which the individual approached or fell away from union with God. Within the course of a human life and the bounds of human understanding, this union could never be complete or certain. But through rigorous attention to the Bible, spiritual introspection, and an active commitment to righteousness, God's creatures might come to appreciate, as Edwards put it, that "their interest must be viewed as one with God's interest."

Nothing was more urgent than the pursuit of such oneness with God. In their determination to serve God's interest, however, Brown's seventeenth-century New England forefathers had often perpetrated terrible errors and self-deceptions. The burning of Indian villages, the persecution of Quakers, the execution of twenty-one suspected witches at Salem—all of these deeds, though largely motivated by worldly fears and desires, were done in the name of God. Opposition to negro slavery, on the other hand, had played little part in the early Puritans' commitment to righteousness, nor did the majority of their Congregationalist descendants in Brown's time embrace abolitionist sentiments, let alone antiracist ones.

How, then, did John Brown come to equate God's interest with the interests of the enslaved and divine truth with the truth of racial equality? Like most human beliefs, these were the products of no single cause or instant, yet Brown's association of religious reverence with antislavery commitment begins in his relationship with his father, Owen Brown.

Owen Brown's earliest childhood memory was the departure of his father's militia company to engage the British in New York in the summer of 1776. A kindly neighbor, John Fast, seeing that Captain Brown had had to abandon his farm with much work undone, sent over his slave Sam to help Mrs. Brown and her ten children. Five-year-old Owen attached himself to the black man, riding on his back as he plowed. But Sam had contracted pleurisy and worked only a few days for the Browns before returning to his cabin on Mr. Fast's property and dying. Owen mourned at his funeral, the first he had ever attended. A few weeks later he mourned for his father, who had also fallen ill and died away from home.

The link between Revolutionary heritage, the plight of slaves, and Christian faith and obligation was forged for Owen Brown in late adolescence. Sent out by his struggling mother to live with a series of relatives and friends, Owen eventually found refuge and tutelage in the home of the town's new Congregational minister, Jeremiah Hallock.

In 1791, Reverend Hallock received a copy of a sermon recently preached by his New Haven colleague, the younger Jonathan Edwards, son of the legendary theologian and a distinguished minister in his own right. Entitled "The Injustice and Impolicy of the Slave Trade and of the Slavery of the Africans," Edwards's sermon took as its text perhaps the most famous verse in Christian scripture, chapter 7, verse 12 of The

Gospel According to St. Matthew. "Therefore all things whatsoever that men should do to you, do ye even so to them; for this is the law and the prophets." Upon this teaching of Jesus, Edwards quickly built to the following crescendo of questions. "Should we be willing, that the Africans or any other nation should purchase us, our wives and children, transport us into Africa and there sell us into perpetual and absolute slavery? Should we be willing, that they by large bribes and offers of a gainful traffic, should entice our neighbors to kidnap and sell us to them, and that they should hold in perpetual and cruel bondage, not only ourselves, but our posterity through all generations? Yet why is it not as right for them to treat us in this manner, as it is for us to treat them in the same manner?"

It is a truth clearly demonstrable from both reason and revelation, as well as from the principle defended in the late War of Independence, Edwards concluded, that opposing slavery is "a duty which we owe to mankind, to ourselves, and to God too. It is but doing as we would that men should do to us."

Owen Brown read Reverend Hallock's copy of this sermon and declared himself an abolitionist. Years later, his son, stumping through Massachusetts, Connecticut, New York, Pennsylvania, and Ohio in an effort to gather money, arms, and recruits for a patriotic war against slavery, would tell his audiences, "I believe in the Golden Rule and the Declaration of Independence. I think they both mean the same thing."

Owen Brown would become one of the most prosperous and influential citizens of Hudson, Ohio, where he settled with his family when his son John was five years old. A successful tanner, cattle breeder, and land speculator, Squire Brown (as he came to be called) also served his community as justice of the peace, county commissioner, and one of the founders and trustees of two Ohio colleges, Western Reserve and Oberlin. Owen Brown was also a devout Calvinist. His brief autobiography, written at age seventy-eight, begins with the sentence, "My life has been of little worth, mostly filled up with vanity."

John Brown idolized his father. As a boy, however, Brown longed for more of the stern and busy Owen's regard; as an adult, he often wondered whether he merited it. To some degree, Brown's insecurity was the portion of every child born into a religious family in colonial and early republican America. Parents' first responsibility, instructed no less an authority than Cotton Mather, was not to love their children but to "give an account of the souls that belong unto their family." Because young children could and did sicken and die at any time, they must be made aware of their mortality and taught to prepare themselves for salvation as soon as they were capable of speech and understanding. What was required for their redemption was discipline, even if parents were as pained to administer it as children to bear it. Accordingly, when the children who had grown past infancy were disobedient or untruthful, Owen ventured conscientiously out beyond the patch of cleared land around his cabin and cut from a low branch of one of the encircling trees a "limber persuader" that either he or his young wife, Ruth, would apply to the bottom or thighs of the offender. Proverbs taught that "he that spareth his rod hateth his son: but he that loveth him chasteneth him betimes." This, after all, was how God shepherded all his children when they strayed, not out of cruelty but to return them to the fold before they were lost.

By 1807, Owen and Ruth Brown were responsible for six young souls. The eldest was a foster child, Levi Blakeslee, whom the couple took in after two sons of their own had died, one at two years old and the other at birth. Anna was born in 1798 and survived infancy, to her parents' great relief and delight. John was born two years later, on May 9, 1800, the Browns' first healthy son. But he was not to be doted on for long. Salmon arrived when he was two, Oliver when he was four, and then Frederick when he was six, a year after the family had moved from Torrington, Connecticut, to the village of Hudson, Ohio, in a region where Indians still substantially outnumbered white settlers.

Brown described his early life on the frontier in a third-person account of his boyhood that he wrote more than fifty years later to keep a promise he'd made to George Stearns's son Henry on that January afternoon in 1857 when the boy emptied his savings into Brown's hand. His most vivid recollections were of solitary wanderings in the woods around the tiny settlement, of hours spent hanging about the edges of the Seneca, Ottawa, and Chippewa camps that still dotted the territory in spite of the government treaties that required these tribes to relocate further west, and of his intense attachments to fleeting "earthly treasures." A brilliant and cherished yellow marble, given him by an Indian boy, was somehow lost "beyond recovery," a "wound," Brown recalled, that "took years to heal." A pet squirrel that he had captured and trained wandered away or was killed, and "for a year or two John was *in mourning.*" In after years, Brown told Henry Stearns, he would come to recognize in these experiences at ages six and seven "the beginning of a severe but much needed course of discipline" in accepting and surviving loss.

Hudson Township was officially incorporated in 1802. By the time the Browns arrived, three years later, the Calvinistic Congregational Church of Hudson had been erected on the south green. Fewer than a dozen families, one of them that of Owen Brown's father-in-law, Reverend Gideon Mills, resided in the village of Hudson when Owen came out alone to clear the ground and begin construction of his house in 1804. He would return to the unfinished one-room cabin in July of 1805, accompanied by his wife and children.

Aided by his eleven-year-old foster son, Levi, Owen Brown set to work weatherproofing the cabin, hanging a door in its open entryway, and filling its empty window holes with sliding wooden slats. Trees had to be cut and then cleared, along with stumps and rocks as well, from the land where corn, wheat, potatoes, turnips, and onions were to be planted. After these tasks were completed, Owen began to build a tannery on Brandywine Creek. Its completion would enable him to recommence the trades he had practiced in Connecticut: shoemaker, tanner, and leather worker. Once Owen's tannery was established, John watched him dress deerskins and other animal hides, observing the process intently and committing it to memory so that he could do exactly as his father did. He was delighted when Owen made him a pair of buckskin breeches with a single leather strap worn over the shoulder to hold them up out of one of the first skins he tanned at Hudson.

But John's most closely held earthly treasure was his mother. Though her own sphere of work was immense and there were three children younger than John to care for, Ruth Brown found time to teach her eldest son his letters and the words in the hymnal. A reverend's pious daughter, Ruth abandoned herself in holy music. It was her clear, sweet voice that enveloped John when the family sang. And sometimes, when Ruth joined in the mothers' prayer meetings or visiting rounds that were winter-evening customs in the township, he would be bundled into the straw-lined box of the ox sled along with his younger siblings, and his mother would gather them all to her and spread thick quilts filled with woolen batting over the whole family for the ride through the snow.

In December of 1808, in childbirth for the eighth time, Ruth Brown weakened, delivered a distressed and short-lived infant, and died a few hours later. Owen had loved her since they first met and thought of their marriage as "the beginning of days with me." To him, her death seemed the end of days. "All my earthly prospects appeared to be blasted," Owen Brown wrote four decades later. So it seemed, as well, to his eight-year-old son. Looking to his father for solace and direction, John saw a man paralyzed, almost catatonic with grief. Even had Owen thought to try to speak words of comfort to his children, he could not have done so. He had always been afflicted by a painful stutter that slowed and clotted his speech. Only in prayer and song were his facial muscles relieved of tension and his words granted free passage. Now, motionless on a three-legged stool at the bedside of his dead wife, with his tiny cold daughter wrapped in a blanket on a pallet near the hearth and his living children whimpering in the room's corners, Owen felt words and fluids rising in his throat but could not move his lips at all. After a while, he bolted up and out of the cabin, willing his legs to carry him through the wind-whipped snow to David Hudson's three-story, Federal-style clapboard house.

When the township chairman and founder opened his door to Owen Brown, he feared the solid, respectable tanner had become deranged, so agitated was his manner and incomprehensible his speech. At last, Hudson made out the reason for Owen's distress and the purpose of his call. He needed a place to bury his wife. There was no graveyard in the village. Hudson arranged for a local property owner with whom the Browns had traveled from Connecticut to donate a nearby spot of land for a cemetery. Owen buried Ruth and their unnamed infant there. Then he settled back into his depression. Neighbors came in with meals for the children.

Throughout the winter of 1808, the Browns trudged into the icy wind to stand at Ruth's lonely grave and stare at the inscription on her tombstone.

> SACRED TO THE
> MEMORY OF
> RUTH, WIFE OF
> OWEN BROWN
> WHO DIED DEC. 13, 1808
> IN THE 37 YEAR OF
> HER AGE
> *She was a delightful child,*
> *A sprightly youth, a Loving wife,*
> *A Tender parent, a Kind neighbor*
> *and an Exemplary christian.*
> *Sweet is the memory of the Just.*

But the text contained an error. The phrase "delightful child" had been mistakenly carved where "dutiful child" had been intended. Owen pulled himself out of his lassitude and ordered the correction. "Dutiful" was gouged in deeper, bolder letters over the place where "delightful" had been inscribed.

Within a year, Owen, following custom and necessity, remarried. Yet his son John felt his own loss to be "complete & permanent." The Westminster Catechism, from which their stepmother Sally Root now schooled Ruth's children in religious obligation, taught that God in his infinite wisdom justly decrees "whatsoever comes to pass" and demands of his creatures humble and reverent submission to his will. But John would not so mildly subordinate his memory of his delightful mother to his duty to respect and obey his father's new wife. Instead, he enlisted Salmon in acts of petty defiance and occasionally in dangerous pranks against twenty-year-old Sally. Reluctantly, mournfully, Owen prepared the necessary limber persuaders and thrashed him.

As time passed, the father's affection for his son and the son's need for his father began to win back John's obedience. At school he continued rowdy and restless. Yet when working with Owen at the tannery or with the livestock, John marshaled his precocious powers of observation and concentration and quickly made himself a skilled apprentice. Even as he sought his father's company and took pleasure in his increasing usefulness to him, though, John preserved a space of physical independence, usually in strenuous forest rambles, in which he struggled to cultivate or at least simulate the emotional self-possession that he felt he lacked. He was large and strong for his age. By early adolescence, he had nearly reached his full size of five feet ten inches and one hundred and forty-five pounds and was able to make the cattle-driving journey that culminated in his traumatic stay with the slaveholding U.S. marshal.

Brown would date his personal abolitionist convictions from this experience, when he stood helpless witness to his host's shovel-wielding assault on his friend and perceived that skin color alone made the difference between the marshal's extravagant esteem for him and gratuitous brutality toward the at least equally worthy black boy. John sensed too how different in motive and spirit was this master's vicious and unjust chastisement from the correction that his own father sometimes imposed on him. The horror of slavery, as he felt it then, was that it imposed on the slave a state of orphanhood that really was complete and permanent. Such, he wrote to Henry Stearns, was "the wretched, hopeless condition, of *Fatherless & Motherless* slave *children:* for such children have neither Fathers or Mothers to protect & provide for them." But this was not *his* condition, despite his vain and self-pitying brooding. He might be motherless–although only to the extent that he rebuffed all of Sally Root's efforts to be a mother to him–but he had a providing father here on earth and a protecting Heavenly Father in whom he had too little trusted.

Returning to Hudson, John applied himself even more zealously to his tasks at the tannery: drawing and carrying bucket after bucket of water from Brandywine Creek in which to soak and soften the cured animal skins before the process of scraping, or "beaming," began; scraping away the hair and tissue from calf skins and sheep pelts; preparing the strong lime solution to loosen the remaining hair on the tougher cowhides; climbing up into the tannery loft with the processed hides and suspending the smooth, tanned leather on drying poles. And he began to read works of classical and modern history lent to him by a neighbor, making his way by candlelight through Plutarch's *Lives,* Thucydides on the Peloponnesian War, accounts of Oliver Cromwell and the English Revolution, Weems's *Life of Washington,* and selections from Franklin's *Poor Richard's Almanac.*

He also discovered the Bible. From earliest childhood, John had been taught to fear God and keep his commandments, but he had been too rebellious to feel the former steadily, and too troubled to do the latter regularly. Bitterness and confusion had so clouded his thoughts during Sunday church services that he had harbored serious doubts about the state and future of his soul. Owen Brown had officially joined the church just three months before Ruth's death, a coincidence from which his son had derived no comfort. But now the boy found himself hungrily absorbing the Bible's teachings, even memorizing its verses and taking on their cadences as easily and precisely as he acquired the skills and formulae of his father's tanning trade.

Much of what he read, particularly the Old Testament's story of the Exodus of the Israelites from Egypt, resonated with a new spiritual and political drama that was beginning to involve the Western Reserve directly. At the end of the War of 1812, soldiers from western Virginia and the border states between north and south, such as Kentucky, returned home from duty on the Great Lakes. Some brought stories of scenes they had witnessed in British Canada, and these stories soon began to circulate among the slaves in their communities. A haven of freedom lay just beyond the United States' northern border, the slaves began to whisper. This Canaan was accessible by various routes, including water passage on one of the numerous tributaries of the Ohio River and overland travel through the new Ohio communities, some of whose leading citizens were rumored to hold strong antislavery views. There was new reason, too, for slaves in the northernmost slaveholding states to consider taking the terrifying step of abandoning everything and everyone they knew and risking death by starvation, exposure, drowning, or human violence to follow the north star. Cotton was enthroned as the primary business of the deep south and southwest, where the expansion and systematization of plantation production was well under way. Slaves who lived north of this region were becoming far more valuable as commodities than as laborers and understood that sooner or later they were likely to be sold.

The abolitionism of the small minority of northerners who opposed slavery on principle had been sentimental and theoretical until this moment. Now the opportunity arose for some to put it into practice. Assisted by Owen Brown, David Hudson established one of the earliest fugitive slave stations of what would later be called the Underground Railroad. Bible verses that John committed to memory confirmed his father's courage and righteousness. "If any man say, I love God, and hateth his brother, he is a liar: for he that loveth not his brother whom he hath seen, how can he love God whom he hath not seen?" "Verily I say unto you, Inasmuch as ye did it not to one of the least of these, ye did it not to me." "Ye shall not respect persons in judgment; but ye shall hear the small as well as the great; ye shall not be afraid of the face of man; for the judgment is God's."

On March 31, 1816, John Brown, now nearly sixteen, appeared before the entire congregation of the Calvinistic Congregational Church of Hudson to seek admission to church membership in his own right. His neighbors saw a settled, mature, accomplished young man, much changed from the restless, troubled boy many of them remembered. The new minister, Mr. Hanford, conducted the religious examination and found it satisfactory. Then the deacons deliberated, prayed over their decision, and approved John Brown's application. In fact, so impressed were they that John was invited to become the young children's teacher in the Sunday school.

But his new appetite for study and public recognition as a Christian fueled greater ambitions. John chose instead to strike out on his own path, one his father could scarcely disapprove. He appealed to Owen to send him to school in the east, so that he could prepare for college and a career in the ministry. Owen agreed, and John and fourteen-year-old Salmon, alternately riding and walking behind the one horse their father had given them to sell in Connecticut to pay for their schooling, headed back to Torrington. They were greeted there by Jeremiah Hallock, their father's old minister, who sent them on to Plainfield, Massachusetts, where his brother, the Reverend Moses Hallock, ran a private preparatory academy.

Brown's fellow students at Plainfield were two to six years younger than he was. Though no one knew the Bible as thoroughly as John or was more determined to succeed, he lacked formal instruction in grammar, arithmetic, Latin, and Greek, all required for college admission.

Many long, anxious nights spent squinting at the impenetrable Greek and Latin exercises that tripped off the tongues of boys half his size only impaired his vision. He was patient and self-controlled but quickly perceived that he was considered the earnest oaf, the oversized child of the wilderness who had foolishly assumed his classmates would be impressed by the smooth, hard square of leather that he had tanned himself and brought along to resole his boots with and by the string-thin strips of tanned sheepskin that he gave them to pull on, assuring them that it was too strong to break.

One afternoon, spying a strip of Brown's sheepskin on the big table in the kitchen where his students wrote their lessons, Mr. Hallock strode across the room and playfully snatched it up. In an instant, he had wrapped its ends around his forefingers and pulled it taut between his fists. All the students stared up at the master and then at Brown, who had raised his head slowly and was looking into the teacher's eyes.

"I shall snap it," said Mr. Hallock, with a patronizing smile at Brown and a wink at his young son Heman, who was watching from the doorway. He waited for the young man to protest. "I shall snap it," he said again, with a note of warning this time. Not a word or motion from Brown. Just his clear, calm gray eyes gazing into those of the minister. Hallock jerked his fists apart, brought them together and jerked them again. Then he strained for a long moment, using his arms and chest in the effort to break Brown's trivial handiwork. Then he tossed the unsnapped sheepskin down, darted his eyes around the table, and turned away. Heman Hallock remembered for the rest of his life "the very marked yet kind immovableness of the young man's face, on seeing father's defeat."

CHAPTER TWO

A Firm Foothold at Home

"It is a source of the utmost comfort to feel that I retain a warm place in the sympathies, affections, and confidence of my own most familiar acquaintances, my family: . . . *a man can hardly get into difficulties too big to be surmounted if he has a firm foothold at home."*
—John Brown

THERE WAS A PARTICULAR WAY, a right way, of going about each thing there was to do, he thought. There was a way it must be done if you were going to do it—if you were worthy of doing it—at all.

Six months after journeying east to school, the two Brown brothers began the five-hundred-mile return trek to Hudson. Walking with swift, stiff-legged strides, his heels absorbing the brunt of each step's concussion and his hands clasped behind him, John Brown did not move like a sixteen-year-old boy with the spring sun rising over his shoulder and no place to be anytime soon. He looked like a man absorbed by a single thought. In the first flush of his faith, in his secret longing to be learned, Brown had imagined for himself a religious vocation. He had construed the chorus of approval with which the deacons of the little Hudson church had greeted his membership examination as his call to "Come up unto the Lord." But he had not been properly prepared. The academic demands at Plainfield Academy—and later at Morris Academy in Litchfield, Connecticut, where Mr. Hallock had thought the Brown boys might fit in better—had proved too much, and now they were on their way home.

Still, Brown could say to himself and to his father that he had spared no effort to improve himself. Even after the eye inflammation had dashed any hope he might have had of making satisfactory progress in Greek and Latin, and the recession brought on by the "cold summer" of 1816–"eighteen-hundred-and-froze-to-death," as the farmers named that devastating year–had deprived Owen of the means to support his sons' education for another term, Brown had continued to persevere. There was a right way and a wrong way, whether or not success was likely. It was to teach this to Salmon that Brown took on the responsibility of chastising his younger brother when the boy flouted Morris Academy's rules and Mr. Vaill, the young assistant master there, declined to discipline him.

"Mr Vaill," Brown had appealed to the teacher without effect, before flogging Salmon himself later that day, "if Salmon had done the thing at home, father would have punished him. I know he would expect you to punish him now for doing this–and if you don't, I shall." When you committed yourself to doing each thing, however hard or unpleasant, in the way it should be done, you made yourself and others stronger, like the strip of expertly tanned sheepskin that Mr. Hallock could not snap.

Owen greeted his returning sons without a tinge of reproach, the warmth of his welcome tempered only by his customary paternal dignity and reserve. For Salmon, the boys' time in the east had been a fine interlude, though most of the stories with which he regaled his younger siblings concerned their trials and adventures on the long return journey. Brown said little. For him, the very thing that gave Salmon so much pleasure–the fact that they were home–was a reproach. Now seventeen, Brown resumed his place in his father's ever more crowded household and in the tannery, but he had grown estranged. In the evening, he felt more like a boarder; during the workday, like a servant.

Though he had failed as a scholar, the serious young man with his encyclopedic command of the Bible was still regarded highly by Hudson's minister, Mr. Hanford. Once again, Brown was invited to teach the young children's Sunday school class. Here was a position of respect and command, at least in the eyes of Brown's prize student, a stocky five-year-old named Lora Case, whose family had purchased the old Thompson cabin a couple of miles south of town. Case admired his first Bible teacher throughout his life, wrote him a letter of support forty-two years later when Brown was awaiting execution in the Charleston jail, and received in return Brown's last letter, written on the morning of December 2, 1859, an hour before he was hanged.

"May you ever prove yourself equal to the high estimate I have placed on you," wrote Brown to his former pupil, sounding like a headmaster at a graduation exercise. "Pure and undefiled religion before God & the Father is as I understand it an *active* (not a dormant) *principle*."

Brown's immediate basis for esteeming Case was the strong antislavery sentiment that his townsman's letter to him had expressed, but the original source of that high estimate was the young Lora Case's perfect memorization of the Bible chapter with which Brown chose to commence his Sunday school curriculum. "Children, obey your parents in the Lord: for this is right," begins Chapter 6 of Paul's Epistle to the Ephesians, which then moves to the parallel case of servants, who are likewise instructed to "be obedient to them that are *your* masters according to the flesh." But in both instances, the apostle promptly clarifies that masters according to the flesh derive their worldly authority from their own obedience to a higher one, in whose eyes persons young and old, poor and rich, are equal. "And, ye fathers, provoke not your children to wrath: but bring them up in the nurture and admonition of the Lord. . . . And, ye masters, do the same things unto them, forbearing threatening: knowing that your Master also is in heaven; neither is there any respect of persons with him."

Ephesians 6 spoke to John Brown at seventeen: a dutiful son and apprentice who longed to be his own master, a believer who had begun to cast about for a means beyond the ministry of acting on his faith. Abruptly shifting from a sermon on passive obedience to a religious call to arms, Ephesians 6 also fired the Sunday school teacher's vague aspiration to bolder initiatives. "Finally, my brethren, be strong in the Lord, and in the power of his might. Put on the whole armor of God, that ye may be able to stand against the wiles of the devil. For we wrestle not against flesh and blood, but against principalities, against powers, against the rulers of the darkness of this world, against spiritual wickedness in high places. Wherefore take unto you the whole armor of God, that ye may be able to withstand in the evil day, and having done all, to stand."

Owen Brown's tanning and cattle businesses prospered. He purchased a tract of land that included several lush hillside acres two miles north of Hudson, perfect for pasturing his growing herds, and built a larger tannery on it. To his sons Levi Blakeslee and John, Owen proposed that they live on the property, manage the new tannery, and oversee the cattle, leaving him free to pursue his land investments and civic projects. The young men eagerly agreed. Now it was John Brown's turn to clear the ground on which he would construct his cabin, to select, fell, and trim the timber for its walls. Now he and his brother split and planed the logs for their door and floorboards, packing clay mortar into the crevices between their large fireplace cobblestones and wooden wedges surrounded by mud into each space in the cabin walls. When, in the spring of 1819, the new house hosted its first fugitive slave, Brown felt for the first time since his return from Connecticut that his own adult life was truly launched.

Trusting to instinct, rumor, and luck in the contacts with whites that happenstance or desperation made it impossible for him to avoid, the runaway could not exactly be said to have *chosen* the young tanner as his Hudson conductor. Still, it was John Brown's home, not his father's or David Hudson's, to which Providence had directed this black man, and it was Brown who gave him provisions and protection and helped arrange for his safe transport one station closer to Canada. So vividly and often did Brown tell his children the story of the fugitive slave with the thunderous heartbeat that his eldest son, John Jr., "remembered" it later in his life as an episode in his own childhood.

Once again, a pattern of physical labor that he knew intimately and performed well gave shape and satisfaction to his days. In the new tannery, he held the responsibility of determining exactly how each task would be done. With Levi planning to marry and move to Wadsworth, thirty miles to the southwest, Brown took charge of the journeymen and apprentices they had begun to hire. The brisk business of the tannery and the care of his father's cattle soon left him with little time for cooking and cleaning, domestic chores that he also enjoyed and approached no less meticulously than he did the tanning. After consulting with their father, Levi and John hired the widow of their late neighbor Amos Lusk to come daily to the cabin to prepare meals, do the washing, and spin and sew for them and for their employees. Sometimes Mrs. Lusk brought along her eighteen-year-old daughter Dianthe to assist her.

John Brown could not name or explain the emotional turmoil that young women evoked in him. Instinctively he concealed this turmoil beneath a bashful silence and an impassive expression that girls might have taken for gloominess or pride had he lingered long enough in their company to be taken for anything at all. He would have been different had his mother lived. Somehow—he was not sure how but he felt it was so—she would have smoothed the path for him between the sexes. She would have been his natural connection to the world of women. Brown thought these things but broke off such meditations before they took him any deeper into regions of confusion and pain. Whatever Ruth's presence might have meant to him, her absence was the chasm that her adolescent son imposed, and that he longed and feared to cross, between women and himself.

It helped that Dianthe Lusk was quiet, industrious, and "remarkably plain." Brown did not indulge in small talk. He practiced no sociable entertainments beyond arm wrestling and philosophical debate. He could neither dance a step nor play cards. While he admired neatness and cleanliness of attire and person and was even judged "tasty," or fastidious, in his own dress, Brown's Puritan aesthetic and his Franklinian frugality combined to condemn deliberate attention to fashion or self-adornment as wasteful and vain. Beyond these barriers to youthful flirtation and romance, the peculiar quality of Brown's desire itself checked him from satisfying it frivolously on a woman of superficial attractiveness. The great loss of his mother on which this desire was founded demanded that he fulfill it but not cheaply. His union must be sacred.

Brown did not linger at home after the midday meal on days when Dianthe was there but returned as usual to his business. He conversed politely yet sparingly with her, touching on practical matters in direct and vaguely formal language and neutral tones. If his speech and manner were not awkward, neither did they appear avid. Yet day after day, Brown observed the girl's dignified passage to and from his cabin and the combination of efficiency and meditative abstraction with which she went about her labors in it. Her habits pleased him. He was somehow drawn to her as well by her fatherlessness, by the loss of comfort and place that she and her family had suffered at the death of Amos Lusk.

Brown had heard that Dianthe often went alone to a place in the woods to pray. One day, surveying a grove of oaks for suitable bark for tannin, he discovered her. She was singing, sweetly and freely, a familiar selection from the hymnal.

> Blow ye the trumpet, blow
> The gladly solemn sound;
> Let all the nations know,
> To earth's remotest bound.
> The year of jubilee is come;
> The year of jubilee is come;
> Return ye ransomed sinners, home.
>
> Ye slaves of sin and hell,
> Your liberty receive,
> And safe in Jesus dwell
> And blessed in Jesus live.
> The year of jubilee is come;
> The year of jubilee is come;
> Return ye ransomed sinners, home.

Jubilee. Leviticus 25. The year when the lost are found, the debtors released, the guilty forgiven, the slaves freed. "And ye shall hallow the fiftieth year, and proclaim liberty throughout *all* the land unto all the inhabitants thereof: it shall be a jubilee unto you; and ye shall return every man unto his possession and ye shall return every man unto his family."

Dianthe did not detect him through the summer foliage. For Brown, her unconscious performance was both moving and sensuous. Soon afterward, he spoke to his father of his feelings for the daughter of Captain Lusk and asked his advice. Owen did not think it too soon for his son to marry. Brown then approached Dianthe. Though deeply devout, she had not yet sought church membership. He bade her do so. On August 2, 1819, Dianthe appeared before the deacons of the Calvinistic Congregational Church and passed her spiritual examination. She was formally admitted to the church three weeks later, and that same month she and Brown became engaged. On June 21, 1820, with Levi now settled in Wadsworth, they were married.

Milton Lusk boycotted his sister's wedding. Three years Brown's junior, Milton was his antithesis in personality, a young man of modest ambition and enterprise and easygoing religious practices. Because he boarded in town with the family of David Hudson, Milton's opportunities to see his mother diminished once she began to keep house and cook at the Brown cabin and tannery, two miles distant. But what pained him more was his perception that Dianthe, too, was being drawn away from him and into the orbit of John Brown. His elder sister was the one who had comforted and sustained him five years earlier when their father had died. Milton called her "my guardian angel." Now he took to visiting her and his mother at Brown's cabin on Sunday afternoons, partly because he was free that day and partly because he knew that Brown, still in his teens himself, kept the Sabbath as strictly and imperiously as some Old Testament patriarch, requiring that every member of his household, down to the lowliest apprentice in the tannery, observe it as well in communal worship, religious reading, and silent meditation. After a few of these Sunday visits, Brown asked him to come in the future on a different day of the week. Milton never returned. Within a year, his sister was Mrs. John Brown. Four months later, she was carrying Brown's child.

Decades later, Brown and an associate were discussing the character of a well-meaning but weakly committed antislavery colleague when Brown produced a large pocket compass, unscrewed its brass lid, and placed the instrument on the table. Pointing to its shivering needle, he dryly rendered his assessment of the man in question. "You see that needle; it wobbles about and is mighty unsteady, but *it wants to point to the north*." What repelled Milton Lusk about John Brown and what would repel some others but powerfully attract many more throughout Brown's life was his aura of implacable steadiness–his almost preternatural absence of wobble. By some measures, this steadiness was more apparent than real, an aura, not a genuine achievement. Wandering, vacillation, chance, failure, regret, self-condemnation–all of these, over the span of Brown's years and in the recesses of his consciousness, were his familiars. Yet when men and women observed him, they saw a man who aligned–or thought he could align–his current enterprise, whatever it was, and his every habit and conviction along some mental magnetic meridian. A man whose belief in an absolute north, and whose acceptance of what he took to be the human duty to seek it, was so implicit and unwavering as to make him magnetic as well.

His marriage with Dianthe, Brown rejoiced, was blessed with fruitfulness. In July of 1821, Dianthe gave birth to a healthy son. Like his father, young John Jr. soon displayed an intense, willful personality. Eighteen months later, mild and dreamy Jason was born, followed in November 1824, by a rugged, red-haired boy whom Brown named Owen in honor of his own father. His business was also increasing, along with his reputation for honesty and for a kind of unhurried meticulousness that made him seem to his Hudson neighbors a man older than they knew him to be. He hewed conscientiously, sometimes inflexibly, to a particular way to do each thing, as if there were only one right way to do it and no other. His tanned leather, for example, must dry completely before he would sell it. His business was in leather, not water, he explained, and no customer of his would be charged for the weight of moisture—a policy that both annoyed and grudgingly impressed customers who had come ten miles for five pounds of sole leather only to be instructed to return a day or two later so as to be sure to get their five pounds' worth in leather alone.

At home, Brown insisted that a blessing be asked before any child or employee of his broke bread. His children recited from the Westminster Catechism every Sunday night before repeating the Ten Commandments and receiving and discussing their father's weekly Bible lesson. Particular feats of memory, piety, and intellect won the Brown children quiet nods of paternal approval, which they sought and cherished like trophies. But Brown also possessed a severity of judgment that his children quickly learned to recognize in the arched eyebrows and staccato "Tut! Tut!" with which he would greet certain sorts of verbal performance: the boastful exaggeration, the white lie, the indulgent complaint, the poor excuse. Sometimes his gray eyes might twinkle or the corners of his thin mouth turn puckishly upward as he uttered these warning syllables. But even if Brown's children read signs of suppressed amusement in their father's expression, when they heard the syllables in his distinctive, metallic tenor, the young orators stopped in midsentence and reconsidered their story or tone, lest they risk subjection to the limber persuader.

Brown also assumed the duty and the authority of moral supervision and discipline for the growing numbers of journeyman and apprentices who worked and lodged at the tannery. The men ate and worshipped with his family and joined in their conversation. Brown subscribed to several newspapers and circulated them among his workers, encouraging—even expecting—them to acquire the habit of reading and to broaden their knowledge of the issues of the day.

When a breach of honesty or respect occurred among them, his severity proceeded from the same sense of obligation with which he punished his children. James Foreman, who came to work for Brown in the year of his marriage and was his close associate for more than a decade, recalled the occasion in 1824 when a fine, valuable calfskin disappeared from the tannery. Brown suspected a particular apprentice of having taken it, a young man whom he judged "rather opposed to good order and religious habits," but had no concrete basis on which to accuse him. When the apprentice's brother visited him at the tannery, though, Brown saw an opportunity to test his hunch about the identity of the thief. Speculating that this visitor would be the means of smuggling the skin off his property, he ordered two trusted journeymen to conceal themselves in the bunkroom and watch the suspect's brother when he prepared to leave. They apprehended the man as he was packing the stolen article.

After sending the brother away, Brown closeted himself with the thief for a long time. The young man had sinned against God and imperiled his immortal soul, Brown told him, by coveting and stealing what belonged to his neighbor. He had also broken the law of the state, for which Brown might have him arrested as a criminal. And if fear of God's and man's laws failed to move him, his employer added, he should consider the offense he had committed against every other man in the tannery by casting suspicion on them all. Before Brown had concluded his lecture, the apprentice was weeping like a child. Brown told him he would not prosecute him for the theft so long as he agreed to remain at the tannery and submit to correction for his misdeed there. The correction that he devised and enforced was social ostracism, a ban on all civil communication with one who had damaged and devalued his community. For two months, the apprentice continued to labor and take meals with the others, but no one looked at him, no one spoke to him. Tools were put within his reach at the tannery and dishes passed to his place at the table by silent men with averted eyes who never touched his hand. "I think a worse punishment could not have been set upon a poor human being than this was to him," James Foreman later wrote. "But it reformed him and he afterward became a useful man."

That same year, having earned and saved enough to house his wife and children more comfortably, Brown tore down the log cabin that he and Levi Blakeslee had built and hired carpenters to erect a better house on the site. The Browns stayed in the tannery while construction was under way before moving into their spacious two-story clapboard home. Its elegance enhanced by a coat of white paint, the house was further warmed for the Browns by a midnight opportunity to receive and assist a fleeing slave couple. While Dianthe fixed supper for the fugitives and Brown arranged for their concealment and transport, four-year-old John Jr. awoke, wandered downstairs, and was scooped up and kissed by the grateful black woman sitting in the parlor. These were the first people of color whom the child had seen, and as soon as he could politely escape, he hurried to rub the woman's pigment from his face, believing that the contact would otherwise "'crock' me, like mother's kettle."

Despite the fine house, the solid business, the Railroad work, and the status in the community that all three had begun to bring him, John Brown was restless. Including John's five small half brothers and sisters, and not counting Levi in Wadsworth and Salmon studying law in Pittsburgh, nine children of Owen Brown now resided in the town that their father had helped build. It was Owen's tannery that his eldest son managed, and the vigorous Owen was and would be Hudson's Squire Brown for years to come. In fact, as his eldest son was building his new house, Owen was helping David Hudson persuade the presbyteries of the Western Reserve that the college that everyone agreed was needed in the region, for which several towns were competing, should be established in Hudson. In January 1825, the decision was made, substantially aided by the impressive sum of $7,142 that the town's leaders had solicited in local pledges for the school's construction and maintenance. Western Reserve College would be located in Hudson, and Owen Brown would join David Hudson and Heman Oviatt as building commissioners and members of the board of trustees. John Brown's father was once again the trailblazer, the pioneer.

An opportunity to plough his own field arose in the fall of 1825. Though Ohio's Reserve was by now well settled, a nearby portion of the old Northwest Territory remained largely wilderness. The region of northwestern Pennsylvania bounded by Ohio to the west, by New York to the northeast, and rising north to the shore of Lake Erie was heavily wooded and amply supplied with water and game. Land was cheap, and there was abundant hemlock and oak, the bark of which is rich in tannin. Brown toured Crawford County and selected a two-hundred-acre tract of land twelve miles east of the county seat of Meadville. The property, some eighty miles from Hudson, cost him seventy-five cents an acre. Crawford County did not yet produce enough beef cattle to yield an adequate supply of hides for tanning. But Brown had a plan to turn that liability into an asset. He would also become an importer and broker of livestock. He formed a partnership with Seth Thompson, a cousin of his father's by marriage, who lived in Hartford, Ohio, near the Ohio-Pennsylvania line. Thompson would supply cattle to Brown, who would sell the stock in Crawford County, where there was high demand. When the animals were slaughtered by the buyers in Brown's neighborhood, he would get the hides, tan them, and send much of the leather back to Thompson for sale in more populous eastern Ohio.

With the assistance of James Foreman, who had decided to relocate with his boss, Brown cleared five acres of forest and built a two-story log house with a large stone fireplace at each end. The decision to strike out on his own tapped an explosive energy source. He prepared his new home and tannery with such intensity and speed that he became a topic of lively conversation among his handful of neighbors before he even met them. The white clapboard house in Hudson, not yet two years old, was sold, and Brown brought Dianthe and their three young sons to live in the freshly cut double-log cabin among the twenty-five scattered families of Randolph township, a place name as yet untethered to any of the usual anchors of place—roads, stores, church, school. The stone foundation and ground floor and outsized twenty-six-by-fifty-foot dimensions of the new arrival's eighteen-vat tannery, however, proclaimed a faith in Randolph's solidity that the other inhabitants promptly reciprocated with faith in John Brown's.

By the end of 1826, Brown's tannery employed a dozen men. Having taught himself surveying from Abel Flint's *System of Geometry and Trigonometry Together with a Treatise on Surveying*, one of the first books he ever purchased, Brown also was enlisted by his neighbors to map out roads for the growing community. And one evening a week, at the nearby village of Guys Mills, Brown led a characteristically robust and memorable singing class. "I wonder that any roof timbers remained after our singing of anthems. I have longed for John Brown's anthems ever since," recalled Estelle Thomson, who was his student at age fifteen.

John Brown's tannery in Richmond Township, Pennsylvania, built in 1826. (LIBRARY OF CONGRESS)

Partly through Brown's efforts, a viable town was established along the state road east of Meadville. Brown became its first postmaster, receiving his presidential appointment on January 7, 1828, in one of John Quincy Adams's last official acts as president. The town was soon rechristened Richmond, its post office was a shelf in Brown's kitchen, and when letters had gathered for neighbors on outlying farms, he rode out along a wide-arching mail route to deliver them. Of these local residents, and of each new settler in Richmond, Brown wished to know three things, and asked his questions directly at the first opportunity. Were they observers of the Sabbath? Were they antislavery? Did they support common, or publicly funded, schools?

Before the community was prosperous or densely populated enough to have a public school, Brown arranged with Thomas Delamater, a like-mindedly progressive neighbor who lived four miles away, to begin a cooperative home school for the young children of both their families and any others who wished to attend. In the winter, Brown employed a teacher and boarded Delamater's school-age children at his house; in the summer, the school and the children moved to the Delamater cabin. The day at the Browns began before dawn with Brown's distribution of a Bible to each member of his extended household for family prayer and scriptural recitation, one or two verses per person until the chapter was complete. In the day's waning hours, the children might join Brown and his tannery workers in the yard for athletic exercises or tests of strength: footraces, leaping contests, rope pulls, arm-wrestling matches. On long winter evenings, after supper and prayers, family members and journeymen sat or sprawled around the roaring fire in the combination kitchen and living room, reading, mending clothes, and listening to or taking part in organized debates on questions such as whether Washington or Napoleon was the superior general and whether human beings, taken collectively, were fulfilling the end for which they were created. Brown loved staging such debates, which he valued for the mental and moral exercise they afforded. Later he would hold them while hiding in Kansas swamps with his Free State volunteers from the vigilante posses that had been sent from Missouri to kill him and while training with his young men in Iowa for their raid on Harpers Ferry.

For Brown, debate was a vehicle for self-improvement, an arena for testing and honing ideas and arguments. It was also a way for him to satisfy his growing passion for rhetoric. There was a fount of power, of mystery and mastery combined, in words. The Bible had taught him this long ago. But as he had enlarged his reading and added to his library—the sermons of Jonathan Edwards, the sayings of Franklin, Aesop's *Fables,* Bunyan's *Pilgrim's Progress*—that power had come to seem available for use as well as for appreciation. To express an idea in a phrase that resounded in the ear and in the heart, to turn an everyday occurrence into a parable that expanded in the mind to reveal a universal law—these were the gifts that the authors on Brown's shelves had in common, however different their personalities and purposes. When language animated men, changed their course, moved them to action, what was it but the word made flesh?

During the evening debates and in his instruction of his children, Brown tried out the store of pithy and resonant phrases that he regularly culled and adapted from his reading. In addition to Biblical quotes and allusions, so seamlessly stitched into his conversation as to appear part of its natural fabric, Brown borrowed practical proverbs from Franklin's Poor Richard. "A continual dropping will wear a stone." "God helps those who help themselves." "A ploughman on his legs is higher than a gentleman on his knees." From Reformation theologian Richard Baxter's *The Saint's Everlasting Rest,* he gleaned: "Christianity is not a sedentary profession" and "sitting still will lose you heaven, as well as if you run from it." Such calls to action often became Brown family mantras. "What you intend to be tomorrow," he would say and later write to his children, "be today." At their bedtime, Brown would call for "my babies" and have the younger ones recite the couplet that he taught them all as soon as they could understand it: "Count that day lost, whose low descending sun / Views from thy hand no worthy action done." Then, one at a time, he would sing each to sleep with the same hymn, "Blow ye the trumpet, blow."

In Richmond, John Brown was the head of the Brown family and one of the community elders in public respect and influence if not in years. People in Crawford County, James Foreman noticed, had begun to express their satisfaction with a new resident by saying that he promised to be "as enterprising and honest as John Brown, and as useful to the county." By the age of twenty-eight, Brown was well established: a civic leader, an important local employer, and father of five. Dianthe had become pregnant again shortly after their resettlement in Pennsylvania and given birth to a fourth son, Frederick, in January of 1827. Brown's first daughter, named Ruth after his mother, had followed two years later. But Brown neither trusted prosperity nor rested easily with it. In childhood, intense attachments and grievous losses—of keepsakes, pets, and a mother—had placed him in "the School of *adversity*," as he put it. A part of him still felt at home only there. Like many people whose early experiences prompt them to develop strong defense mechanisms, Brown embraced comfort warily lest it weaken his ability to withstand life's next blow. As a Calvinist, too, he had been schooled to profess his unworthiness of the blessings God bestowed upon him. Mostly, however, Brown felt restless when things were going smoothly. Success bred routine, which bred complacency and stasis. Sitting still would surely lose a man heaven. For ambition, adversity was the more fertile field.

"Business is not brisk but perhaps as good as is best." So wrote Brown at age thirty to his father. Over the next quarter of a century, his correspondence would repeatedly express such suspicion of too avid a pursuit of wealth. "I trust that getting or losing money does not entirely engross our attention; but I am sensible that it occupies quite too large a share in it." "The general aspect of our worldly affairs is favorable. Hope we do not entirely forget God." "We have in this part of the country the strongest proofs that the great majority have made gold their *hope*, their *only hope*." For all his citations of the wisdom of Franklin, early America's entrepreneurial guru, Brown was an ambivalent businessman who recognized his society's tendency—and his own susceptibility—to pursue material ends and exalt material values above all others. The ultimate product of this exclusive devotion to economic considerations, he well knew, was slavery.

Far from the gradual demise that many of his father's generation had predicted for it, the institution had grown larger and stronger as cotton planters turned ever more fantastic profits from a commodity that new technologies processed quickly and cheaply and that expanding international markets insatiably demanded. And what had he done about it? Nothing. Of course, he aided the few slaves who escaped north along the route up through Pittsburgh and Meadville, housing them in the secret room he had built in his barn before sending them on toward Buffalo. But these occasional actions, however energetic and potentially dangerous, seemed paltry in relation to his daily labors for no greater cause than his own and his family's support. And in light of slavery's entrenchment and expansion, he sometimes wondered whether his own small efforts toward its overthrow were like trying to empty a swollen river by the thimbleful as rain continued to fall. So when he wrote to his father in the spring of 1830 that business was "as good as is best" and that his family was healthy, except for the youngest children who were somewhat afflicted with whooping cough, Brown was unable to report his entire satisfaction with these circumstances or to muster the appropriate thankfulness for them. For this inability he chastised himself. "I feel that I ought to expect God's judgment when his mercies do not awaken more of my love and gratitude, and zeal for his honor."

A judgment was not long in coming. Brown's youngest son, three-year-old Frederick, had never been strong. As young Owen and even little Ruth recovered from their coughs, Fred's condition worsened. He became feverish, listless. By the fall, Dianthe was big with her sixth child. In the tannery, Brown was distracted by vague forebodings. Breaking off work, he would cross the path to the house with quick, nervous strides to monitor the older children's studies and assure himself that Fred still breathed. If he found Dianthe exhausted or indisposed, he would stay, worrying and praying as he fed the kitchen fire. Standing over the huge iron caldron, he would stir the bubbling cornmeal mush that left a half-inch crust in the pot, then spoon some into a bowl, mix it with cream, and take it to his wife in her bed, before calling the children to prayers and supper. At night, Brown sat up with his declining son, rocking him in front of the fire, rubbing his flaccid limbs when he had chills, holding water to his lips and a cool damp towel against his neck and forehead when he burned with fever. After the boy finally succumbed to sleep, Brown often would go outside to stand still and breathe deeply in the cold. On clear nights, he traced the constellations. Their majesty calmed him. Sometimes he watched them for hours. He needed little sleep.

On December 31, 1830, Dianthe gave birth to another baby boy. It was a difficult birth, from which she recovered slowly. Early in the new year, Brown himself fell ill with the ague, a sickness producing intermittent malarial symptoms—fits of shivering, fever, night sweats, and general bodily weakness—that would incapacitate him at intervals throughout the rest of his life. His business was also faltering, and recently he had lost the services of his longtime employee James Foreman, who had married, started a family, and resolved to farm on his own. To recognize and reward the loyalty of the man who had moved with him from Ohio and helped him reestablish his business in Richmond, Brown made Foreman a gift of 116 acres of land, in spite of the delicacy of his own finances. Without Foreman, and able to afford fewer journeymen, Brown began to require longer hours at the tannery of ten-year-old John Jr., whom he had been training to assist him there.

John Brown Jr. was a spirited and headstrong boy, as Brown himself had been. The father took pride in his eldest son but also knew it was his duty to discipline him, both for John's own future welfare and as an example to his younger sons of the diligence and obedience that he expected of them all. Brown had assigned John Jr. shifts in the tannery's grinding mill. John's job was to shovel tanbark into the mill and to make sure that the old blind horse that was harnessed to the grinder kept circling the chute, thus turning the mechanism that reduced the bark to powder. It was tedious work, and John often shirked it, sneaking out to play with Jason and Owen or daydreaming at the tannery window. Several times Brown discovered John in his indolence. Finally he spoke with his son in his characteristic corrective mode that combined rebuke and Socratic dialogue. Did John understand why his father needed a good supply of ground bark? Did he believe that he was cultivating a habit of faithful industry by working in this manner? Had he not often heard and even recited the scripture from Ephesians about serving "not with eyeservice" but "from the heart"? When these admonitions failed to mend the boy's conduct, Brown devised an account book in which John's faults or debits—disobeying mother, telling a lie, unfaithfulness at work—were each assigned a certain number of lashes, which could be cancelled by credits earned by his acts of obedience and diligence. One Sunday after the morning service, Brown quietly informed John Jr. that his account was hopelessly overdrawn. The time had arrived for a reckoning.

Father and son walked together from the house to the tannery and climbed the ladder to its second floor, where the tanned skins hung on hooks to dry. Brown carried the pocket-sized account book—coarse, grainy squares of paper stitched together along their left edge—in which John's liabilities had been tallied in pencil. John carried a long blue-beech switch, already peeled, that his father had handed him in silence. In the tannery's finishing room, they sat side by side on a bench-high stack of cured hides. Holding the book before them, Brown reviewed the entries in John's debit column one by one, reciting the circumstances of each offense in calm, methodical detail. After each recitation, he looked into his son's eyes and asked him whether the account was fair. Did John wish to offer any amendment? Any explanation? Any unrecorded worthy actions to help balance his ledger? The boy at first responded with half-hearted attempts to cast his conduct in a less unfavorable light, attempts that led to discussions in which his offered excuses and extenuations were agreed, in the end, to be poor ones. In the latter stages of the audit, John Jr. responded to his father's questions only with mournful shakes of his head and a steady flow of tears.

"Is a reckoning justified, then, John?" asked Brown at last.

"Yes, Father."

John Jr. stood in front of the hides and bent over them. His forearms rested on the top of the pile, supporting his weight. He clenched his fists against the coming pain. His brain had not yet registered the high, thin whistle when he felt the first sting of the beech switch. He gritted his teeth as more strokes fell on his buttocks and thighs. Six. Seven. Eight. His thin trousers did little to cushion the blows, but he was thankful that Father had not asked him to remove them. He wondered if they would be torn and need mending. Then he realized that the strokes had stopped at eight. He had been due twenty-five. He turned, dry-eyed, and looked back over his shoulder. His father had put the switch down and was removing the worn, shiny high-collared coat in which he had preached the morning's sermon. Brown folded the jacket carefully and proceeded to unbutton and remove his white linen shirt, laying it on top of the coat. Picking up the switch, he told John to rise and handed it to him. Then he knelt and bent his bare back over the hides.

"Seventeen more lashes are due, John," he said, "and I will take them myself. I am your father, and it is on me that blame must fall for failing to teach you your duties."

Grief and guilt rose in John Jr., and he begged his father to let him bear the full amount himself, but Brown was resolute.

"When you know that I suffer in body as well as in mind for your faults, perhaps you will learn to be more careful," he said. "Now, lay it on, John." The boy burst into choking sobs, but when the command was repeated, applied the switch reluctantly to his father's back. "Harder! harder! harder!" Brown instructed him. Beads of blood from the cutting tip of the switch trickled down his back when Brown raised himself from the floor once his son had delivered the final stroke. "After that," John Jr. concluded his last retelling of the story sixty years later, "nothing could ever persuade me that my father could possibly do anything wrong."

The four daughters of John Brown who lived to maturity likewise would idolize their father. Of the six younger sons who escaped childhood mortality, three to die violently in their twenties in the family's war against slavery, only Owen shared John Jr.'s belief—or determination to believe—in his father's infallibility. All the boys occasionally bridled at Brown's requirement of orderliness, rolling their eyes at each fresh repetition of his detailed instructions on the correct method of performing every little task. Some of his sons, particularly gentle, sensitive Jason, feared the harshness of Brown's punishments, though they recognized the dispassion with which he administered them and marveled at the capacity for personal tenderness that matched and mingled with their father's opposing gift for impersonal severity. In adulthood, several of Brown's sons argued with him about his tactics in Kansas and at Harpers Ferry. All would fall away from his strict religious practices, from his confidence in the truth of the Bible, and even from his faith in God. But none of John Brown's children ever grew alienated from their father, nor he from them, and not one abandoned the cause of abolition and racial equality that he championed.

CHAPTER THREE

THE GREAT AND FOUL STAIN

> *"Slavery is the great and foul stain upon the North American Union, and it is a contemplation worthy of the most exalted soul whether its total abolition is or is not practicable; if practicable by what means may it be effected, and if a choice of means be within the scope of the subject, what would accomplish it at the smallest cost of human sufferance.... The subject is vast in its compass, awful in its prospects, sublime and beautiful in its issue. A life devoted to it would be nobly spent or sacrificed."*
> –John Quincy Adams

On January 1, 1831, John Brown attended to his family in his home in western Pennsylvania, absorbed by private hopes and fears. Through the swaddling clothes of his newborn son he could feel the child's fast, sturdy heartbeat. It steadied his own as he sat watching by Dianthe's bedside. The approach of dawn at last revealed to him the comforting outline of his sleeping wife. On the other side of the wall, little Frederick, now desperately ill, sucked in a shallow, raspy breath. Brown wondered whether they would be called upon to return Fred to God before his fourth birthday, a week away, and whether the strong infant in his arms had been given them to recompense them for their loss. Three months later, four-year-old Fred would die, the first of twelve children that Brown would lose to illness, accident, or violence before his execution. The Browns assigned their new son his departed brother's name.

On that same New Year's Day, with little advance notice and no paid subscribers, the first issue of a four-page weekly newspaper appeared in Boston. Cheaply printed in the garret apartment of its publisher, editor, writer, and typesetter, *The Liberator* embodied an ambition out of all proportion to its humble appearance and to the circumstances of the obscure young man who fathered it.

William Lloyd Garrison was twenty-five when he launched the publication that precipitated a national abolitionist movement, a movement that would later ambivalently claim and disclaim John Brown as its most militant partisan. Slight, bald, pale, bespectacled, and fearless, Garrison was the child of an alcoholic seaman who had deserted his family in his son's youth, leaving them to survive on table scraps placed in pails behind the houses of the wealthy merchants and shipowners of Newburyport, Massachusetts. With little formal schooling, he was indentured to a printer at thirteen and used the seven years of his apprenticeship to become a skilled writer and publicist as well as an editor and compositor of the writings of others. Brief newspaper editing stints followed in Newburyport, Boston, Bennington, and Baltimore. During the last of these assignments, Garrison witnessed for the first time the everyday brutalities of the slave trade: the dealers' rough, immodest inspections of black bodies displayed for auction, the forcible separation of wailing families, the lines of shackled slaves being driven to the harbor. The young journalist once sheltered a slave who had been lacerated from neck to buttocks for loading a wagon too slowly. Garrison counted and recorded the man's thirty-seven bleeding wounds. He decided that slavery must end immediately and unconditionally and embarked on a speaking tour to rally popular support. The results were not encouraging.

In every northern town that he visited, Garrison encountered "contempt more bitter, opposition more active, detraction more relentless, prejudice more stubborn, and apathy more frozen, than among slave holders themselves." But he would not be dissuaded. "I determined, at every hazard, to lift up the standard of emancipation in the eyes of the nation, *within sight of Bunker Hill and in the birth place of liberty*," Garrison wrote in *The Liberator*'s first issue, promising not to put that standard down until "every chain be broken, and every bondman set free!" "Let southern oppressors tremble–let their secret abettors tremble–let their northern apologists tremble," the self-described emancipator continued. "I am in earnest–I will not equivocate–I will not excuse–I will not retreat a single inch–AND I WILL BE HEARD."

At first, *The Liberator* was purchased mainly by negro residents of Massachusetts. But soon, the efforts of free black sailors, who carried stacks of the paper for distribution in their ports of call, made Garrison's voice audible in cities up and down the Atlantic coast. Its eloquence, relentlessness, and moral confidence made *The Liberator* notorious. Within three years, Garrison had organized first the New England Anti-Slavery Society and then the American Anti-Slavery Society, with chapters throughout the northern states. Within five, he was the target of resolutions in southern state legislatures and municipal councils offering rewards for his apprehension. Even in Boston, a mob stripped him nearly naked and tried to hang him on the city common. Legislation was proposed to Congress by President Andrew Jackson to bar "unconstitutional and wicked" publications such as Garrison's from the U.S. mail in order to suppress their "inflammatory appeals" to "the passions of the slaves."

In fact, *The Liberator*'s appeal was directed not to the passions of slaves but to the moral and religious sensibilities of free white Christians. Emancipation would come about, Garrison wrote in July of 1831, when sufficient numbers of whites "discard their criminal prejudices, their timorous fears, and their paralyzing doubts" and come "to feel that two millions of their brothers and sisters are groaning under the thraldom of slavery." This self-reformation, he continued, must provide the foundation for a Christian campaign to overwhelm slavery by righteous example, practical incentives, and above all nonviolent persuasion. Garrison proposed "to scatter tracts like rain-drops over the land," to hire "active and eloquent agents to plead the cause constantly," to offer premiums "to encourage planters to cultivate their lands by freemen," and to teach blacks trades to help them support themselves and "recover their lost rights."

What Garrison discovered in his antislavery barnstorming, however, was that racial prejudice and fear and doubt that blacks and whites could or should live together in freedom were nearly universal among white Americans in 1830. Disapproval of slavery on moral or economic grounds by no means implied approval of the prospect of educated and vocationally competitive blacks living side by side with whites and claiming the rights of citizens. For antislavery whites, the rightful place for free people of color and the place for them to "recover their lost rights" was Africa. If it proved impractical to transport them there, a home for them might be found in South America or on a Caribbean island but not in the United States.

Before the formation of the antislavery societies of the early 1830s, the only national political organization that directly addressed itself to the question of black-white relations was the American Colonization Society. Founded in Washington, D. C., in December 1816, at a convention chaired by Kentucky congressman and Speaker of the House of Representatives Henry Clay, the American Colonization Society was officially neutral on the issue of slavery. Its mission was to repatriate free negroes in Africa. This was a mission that appealed to both northerners and southerners, who typically represented it and often believed it to be humane and philanthropic. As Elias Caldwell, whom Clay credited with the original idea for the Colonization Society, put it in his speech to the 1816 convention: "The more you improve the condition of these people, the more you cultivate their minds, the more miserable you make them in their present state. You give them a higher relish for those privileges which they can never attain, and turn what we intend for a blessing into a curse." Returned to Africa, however, as Clay himself contentedly mused in an 1827 speech that celebrated ten years of the Society's efforts, "they would be in the midst of their friends, and their kindred, at home, though born in a foreign land, and elevated above the natives of the country, as much as they are degraded here." There was, moreover, "a peculiar, a moral fitness, in restoring them to the land of their fathers." In recompense for "the evils and sufferings which we had been the innocent cause of inflicting upon the inhabitants of Africa, we can transmit to her the blessings of our arts, our civilization, and our religion."

Clay's sunny image of African repatriation concealed the facts. So poorly chosen and prepared were the locations on the west coast of Africa to which Colonization Society and U.S. government agents first brought negro colonists in 1820 and 1821 that large numbers sickened and died within weeks of their arrival. And despite the negotiations with local tribal leaders that resulted in the purchase and establishment of Liberia in 1822 as a permanent colony for the resettlement of American blacks, the colonists there had been repeatedly attacked by the very friends and kindred who were supposed to submit gratefully to the superiority that generations of exposure to white arts, civilization, and religion had conferred upon the newcomers.

For many of the ministers and other moral critics of slavery who supported the American Colonization Society, the Liberian settlement was not just an imagined haven for free blacks or a beacon for benighted Africa. It was, they hoped, the key to the gradual and voluntary manumission of America's slave population. Responsible slaveholders would be more willing to free their slaves and urge their neighbors to do the same, it was argued, if they knew there was a place to send them where they could pose no burden, threat, or offense to white Americans. But those blacks who were bold enough to publicly oppose colonization insisted that this argument was misguided and that the logic of colonizing free blacks actually supported slavery. Beneath the idea that colonization was the solution to America's racial problem, they pointed out, lay the conviction that blacks could never become fully accepted and enfranchised United States citizens. Clay and the other colonization spokesmen might dress up the Society's motives in the rhetoric of humanitarianism, but in the end their position that free blacks should be resettled because they were burdensome, offensive, dangerous, inferior, or simply alien to white America reinforced the rationale and the prejudice of those who defended slavery itself.

Colonization also served slaveholders practically. As more northern blacks were resettled in Africa, fewer would remain to serve as allies of the enslaved or as examples of the possibility of negro freedom and self-sufficiency in the United States. And if, as Caldwell advised, the Society particularly targeted for colonization those freedmen whose minds were most cultivated and who possessed "a higher relish" for the rights and opportunities of citizenship, then the very individuals most likely to prompt other blacks to aspire to those rights and opportunities would conveniently disappear from the scene.

Throughout the antebellum period, most free blacks opposed the Liberia option and the other colonization schemes that were advanced by white politicians, clergymen, and social reformers, and sometimes by black leaders as well. Beginning with the three thousand who gathered at Bethel Church in Philadelphia to denounce the American Colonization Society less than a month after its establishment, anticolonization blacks repeatedly asserted that America was their birthplace and home. They had taken up arms in 1776 to help win American independence and again in 1812 to help preserve it, blacks pointed out, and they supported themselves and contributed to the nation's economy in spite of all obstacles. In short, they were Americans and deserved to be accepted as such.

Nonetheless, thousands did emigrate in the four decades between the founding of Liberia and the start of the Civil War, and many thousands more considered it. At least at moments, the prospect of starting over somewhere, anywhere, outside the United States was a powerful temptation and a subject of lively debate for black communities throughout the north. The reason colonization drew black volunteers and advocates despite its racist premises was simple. The social, political, and economic conditions of life for most free American blacks were oppressive and grew worse each decade between 1820 and 1860. As slavery became more systematically enforced and vociferously championed in the south, so blacks in the north were increasingly stripped of civil rights and economic opportunity and subjected to insult, social indignity, and physical attack.

By 1830, only about thirty-five hundred blacks remained enslaved in the north. Abolition and gradual emancipation acts in the original northern states–Pennsylvania, New Jersey, Connecticut, Massachusetts, New Hampshire, New York, and Rhode Island–and bans on slavery in the state constitutions of Vermont, Ohio, Indiana, Illinois, and Maine had reduced the population of northern blacks in bondage from fifty thousand at the nation's founding. Yet in state after state, emancipation frequently was coupled with provisions to legislate black disfranchisement, prevent black immigration, and even encourage black departure. After the admission of Maine to statehood in 1820, blacks were constitutionally denied the vote in every new state that entered the Union until the end of the Civil War. Meanwhile, the states that had previously granted voting rights to free negroes in the early years of the Republic were busy rescinding them outright, restricting them through imposition of property qualifications, or turning a blind eye to the formal and informal ways that local communities obstructed or intimidated blacks from coming to the polls. As a result, by 1840, ninety-three percent of the north's free black population had been legally or effectively disfranchised. Most black children throughout the north were excluded from public education, though some states grudgingly allocated funds for negro schools. Many states prohibited blacks from testifying in legal cases involving whites, and only Massachusetts impaneled black jurors. Public spaces, conveyances, eating places, and cultural institutions were either strictly segregated or entirely off limits to blacks by force of law or custom.

Until the late 1820s, free blacks commonly found employment as artisans, tradesmen, and public works laborers in northern cities. But the influx of hundreds of thousands of Irish, German, and Scandinavian immigrants soon drove blacks out of all but the most menial occupations. The new white Americans often invoked racial solidarity to claim their political and economic rights and surmount their religious, cultural, and linguistic differences from the established population. As America industrialized, white workingmen's associations were formed. Association members were instructed to shut off their machines and throw down their tools if any employer brought a black worker onto the factory or shop floor. The workingmen's journal, *National Trades' Union*, regularly disparaged blacks as unfit for skilled labor, and in 1830, Ohio's Mechanical Association publicly tried and censured its president for helping a young black man learn a trade. In 1834, white Philadelphians, enraged that some negroes still had jobs in a season of high unemployment, attacked the city's black neighborhood, clubbing and stoning residents, destroying homes and churches, and forcing hundreds to flee.

Ohio, Pennsylvania, Indiana, Illinois—these free states shared a border with states in which slavery thrived. Such border states, especially their southern regions, had statutes and populations that were especially hostile to free blacks. White communities in these areas worried that the availability of nearby slave labor would limit their economic opportunities and depress their wages. And if large numbers of southern negroes were suddenly released from their bondage, border state inhabitants feared that their cities and towns would be inundated, especially if they were already home to established communities of welcoming freedmen. These states and municipalities began to take measures to discourage nonresident blacks from entering and even to encourage free black residents to depart.

Ohio's Black Laws had been on the books since the first decade of the nineteenth century. But such provisions as the one that demanded a five hundred dollar bond to guarantee the good behavior of any negro who entered the state and the one that required each black Ohioan to possess a court document that certified his status as a freedman had rarely been enforced. In 1829, however, Cincinnati's city fathers responded to the growth of their black population by informing black residents that they had thirty days to either comply with these statutes or leave. When black leaders sought more time, white mobs went on a rampage. Half of Cincinnati's approximately twenty-two hundred free blacks fled to Canada.

To resettle elsewhere in the Union was becoming more and more difficult, as state after northern state restricted negro immigration. Legislators promoted these restrictions by raising the specter that without them their states would be overrun by ex-slaves cast off by their owners when the value of their labor sank below the cost of their upkeep. Illinois, for one, Senator Stephen Douglas insisted, would not become "an asylum for all the old and decrepit and broken-down negroes that may emigrate or be sent to it." And when one state passed restrictive legislation, others felt obliged for their own protection to follow suit.

The result was a vicious spiral. The increasingly backbreaking and spirit-destroying labor regime of King Cotton in the south motivated more slaves to attempt escape, and those who succeeded swelled black populations in the north. Growing free and fugitive black communities heightened white economic and social anxieties, leading to antiblack legislation and deepening popular prejudice. Greater legal restrictions and social animosity closed most of the avenues by which northern blacks might demonstrate their economic and civic capabilities. Their consequent impoverishment and isolation proved to racists that negroes were naturally inferior and unsuited for a place in modern American society.

To many whites, including some who genuinely sympathized with blacks and wished them well, colonization seemed the only recourse. From its founding to the eve of the Civil War, the American Colonization Society included among its members leading citizens of every region, elected officials of every political party, ministers of every denomination. Its officers were often senators (such as Daniel Webster,

Stephen Douglas, William Seward, and Edward Everett), Supreme Court Justices (such as John Marshall and Roger Taney), and even presidents James Madison and Andrew Jackson.

The years of the Jackson presidency, 1829 through 1837, have been said to mark the rise of the common man in America. These were also the years in which America officially established the supremacy of the white man. Of course, racial consciousness and discrimination long predated Jackson's election. But in this period, immigration, westward expansion, and the intensifying debate about slavery prompted more categorical definitions and defenses of who had rights in and to the land and who did not. It was the shared claim of whiteness, not language or custom or heritage, that allowed Dutchmen, Irishmen, Germans, Frenchmen and Swedes to come together with Englishmen and Scots as fellow Americans. Whiteness was the basis of commonality in the formation of the American common man. It conferred entitlement to manufacturing jobs and commercial opportunities in the north and to land in the west. Practical applications of the doctrine of white supremacy went far beyond southern defenses of slavery. Northerners also drew on the doctrine in their arguments for keeping or driving blacks out of their communities.

Moving beyond the negro issue, the federal government officially confirmed that America was reserved for whites in the first major achievement of the Jackson administration, the Indian Removal Act. The projects of removing Indians to the other side of the Mississippi and of returning free blacks to Africa shared the aim of clearing the geographic and economic field for the American common man. Andrew Jackson, an officer of the American Colonization Society and a legendary Indian fighter, supported both initiatives. Shortly before Jackson took office, the state of Georgia had passed laws appropriating for development lands guaranteed to the Cherokee Indians by federal treaty. The tribe appealed to the authorities in Washington, arguing that states could not nullify a U.S. government treaty. Politicians and businessmen throughout the south and land speculators across the country eagerly awaited the new administration's initiative to settle the issue. At stake was much more than the disputed property in Georgia. Twenty-five million acres of valuable land in several southern states were held and inhabited by Creeks, Choctaws, Chickasaws, and Seminoles as well as Cherokees. Mississippi, Alabama, and Georgia felt no more pressing political objective than the freeing of this land for white settlement. Expanding populations in these states and elsewhere already were infringing on native domains and rights with the tacit approval or active support of local officials. But any systematic evacuation of the tribes required federal sanction and enforcement. Jackson did not disappoint his supporters.

Once installed in office in 1829, the president made it clear that he would not protect Georgia's Cherokees or insist that any state honor Indian treaties that the U.S. government had signed in the past. Alabama and Mississippi immediately seized Choctaw and Chickasaw holdings within their borders. The next year, Jackson submitted his Indian Removal Act to Congress, a bill that was sure to be bitterly controversial not only for the opposition it would draw from benevolent societies, Indian sympathizers, and lady reformers but also because many northern representatives saw it as a measure clearly designed to provide land for slavery's expansion and to increase the south's political muscle. After much negotiation, amendment, and presidential coercion, the bill passed with substantial support from northeastern Democrats.

Even over those regions of the country in which Indians and blacks were scarce, a thickening climate of intolerance began to settle. Indian tribes had left western Pennsylvania before John Brown had moved his family there, but the ample game to be found in the woods between Meadville and Richmond still attracted small parties of Indian hunters. Each winter, a few braves rode down from Canada and western New York and camped for several weeks along the banks of French Creek. Occasionally they would approach the Brown farmhouse to exchange a piece of handicraft or some fresh woodcock, snipe, or speckled trout for feed for their ponies. For Brown, these annual native hunting parties recalled his childhood in frontier Hudson and the long wilderness rambles to surrounding Indian camps in which he had taken physical pride and emotional refuge. But as the unlovely spectacle of Indian removal elsewhere in the nation produced a growing popular disdain for native tribes and a guilty impatience for their disappearance from the precincts of white civilization, some Crawford County residents began to resent the seasonal trespassers.

One Sunday afternoon, Brown was reading his Bible by the fire, seven-year-old Jason sitting quietly at his side, when a band of riders clattered up and called for him to come out. Jason did not chafe with boredom, as his brothers John and Owen did, at the weekly day of enforced inactivity and religious reflection in the Brown household. He even welcomed Sunday's peacefulness. It was the day he felt closest to his father and least afraid of him. Jason remembered being whipped only once, for telling a lie when he was three or four years old, yet the idea of physical punishment loomed much larger in his mind than it did for his brothers, who more regularly earned and received it. Jason was and would remain as sensitive to the pain of other creatures, human and animal, as to his own. Throughout his youth, he would not eat game that he had seen shot, and he was likely to refuse the meat of a creature raised for slaughter if he had known the animal and still harbored an image of it alive. So when he accompanied his father out into the yard to see what the men on horseback wanted, Jason was alarmed by their air of hostility and display of weapons.

The posse's leader told Brown that they were going to drive out that pack of Indians at French Creek and that he should grab his gun and come along. Jason saw the man grin at his father, as if they were already boon companions. As if it were not Sunday. For two seconds, then three, Brown did not speak. Jason could tell how angry he was by the way he rocked slightly onto his heels, his neck and back stiffening.

At last, his father replied, his voice even, matter-of-fact, "I will have nothing to do with so mean an act. I would sooner take my gun and help drive you out of the country."

Jason saw confusion and panic in the eyes of the grown men, and for a moment they seemed to him like bad children that it had been father's duty to thrash. The indignation and bluster that his stinging words elicited from the men on horseback scarcely covered their nakedness. No one would be riding out to French Creek to chase off Indians this day.

Brown's strange fondness for Indians and blacks and his insensitivity to community feelings on matters pertaining to the inferior races began to prick some of his neighbors. Like other towns in the north, the Crawford County seat of Meadville and its surrounding villages were becoming less, not more, hospitable to blacks. Even in the Congregational Church of Meadville, to which Brown belonged, the tide of inhumanity appeared to be rising. Meadville's thousand residents included only a handful of blacks: the Joneses, the Curls, the Greens, the Cliffords, the Molsons–families headed by respectable if humble workers in the tailoring, barbering, and laundering trades. Yet some of the white subscribers had begun to grumble about the customary openness of worship services to these families and, against the vociferous objections of Brown and others, had made them feel unwelcome there. In protest, Brown organized a new Congregational Society in January of 1832. Services were held on the second floor of Brown's tannery in a large open space adorned at intervals by hides hung up to dry.

Though he participated in local skirmishes over racial prejudice and in occasional Underground Railroad work, Brown had no connection in the early 1830s to organized abolitionism. In his home town of Hudson, copies of *The Liberator* brought in from the east had galvanized Brown's family and many of his childhood friends, and by the spring of 1832, dramatic events had begun to unfold there. But any involvement Brown may have contemplated in the early campaigns of the abolitionist movement gave way that year to a debilitating bout of the ague and to the even more ominous realization that his wife's health was failing.

It was to Jason that Dianthe first confessed her premonition of death. He was her favorite, a child who shared her love for growing things and her quizzical air of abstraction, as if he was listening to the strains of a distant aria unheard by others. One day in the early spring, pregnant again for the seventh time, Dianthe took Jason along with her to plant fruit seeds in ground that some of Brown's tannery workers had spaded for a small orchard. As they knelt and smoothed the soil over some peach pits, Dianthe clutched her son's hand, and he saw she was silently crying.

"I am most sure," she told him, "that I shall never eat any of the peaches from these trees. I hope that you will live. But if neither of us does, the peaches will do *someone* some good." By summer, Dianthe had developed heart palpitations and was running a high fever. Brown tended to both house and tannery throughout the latter months of her pregnancy.

On August 7, labor commenced and Brown called in a physician to deliver the child and tend to the mother. The baby presented breech first, and the doctor was unable to turn or deliver him in time. He emerged stillborn. At first Dianthe's condition seemed to improve, but three nights later she was dying. "I thought I might go to rest on God's Sabbath," she whispered to her husband. Brown called the children in to say good-bye to their mother. Dianthe embraced each child. Taking Jason's hand, she haltingly recited a chapter of the Bible–the twelfth and last of Ecclesiastes–that the older boys knew well as one of their father's favorites.

"Remember now thy Creator in the days of thy youth," Dianthe began. She struggled through to the end. "Also *when* they shall be afraid of *that which is* high, and fears *shall be* in the way, and the almond tree shall flourish, and the grasshopper shall be a burden, and desire shall fail: because a man goeth to his long home, and the mourners go about the streets: Or ever the silver cord be loosed, or the golden bowl be broken, or the pitcher be broken at the fountain, or the wheel broken at the cistern. Then shall the dust return to the earth as it was: and the spirit shall return unto God who gave it."

By eleven that evening she was dead. For the second time in his life, Brown had lost the woman he loved most in the world. He buried his wife in her wedding dress alongside her stillborn child in a grave next to Frederick's. Then, like his father when Ruth died twenty-four years earlier, Brown went completely numb.

For days, he sat in his house, scarcely moving. The five children fended for themselves until James Foreman came and took them into his home. Soon Brown moved in with the Foremans as well, paying for his family's board. Once, John Jr. wandered past the Browns' empty dwelling and was alarmed to find his father lying facedown on Dianthe's grave, wailing in agony. The boy slipped away unnoticed and ran to tell his siblings the extraordinary, disturbing thing he had seen. They had never known their father to give vent to strong emotion.

Garrison understood from the start that his demand for immediate abolition would trigger powerful antagonistic emotions in many whites. To insist that all true lovers of liberty and believers in Jesus must raise a moral and spiritual cry in support of unconditional freedom for the slaves was to pose a radical challenge to prevailing sentiments. But Garrison shrewdly reminded his readers in *The Liberator*'s inaugural issue that the course he proposed was less radical and less frightening than the one that a negro shopkeeper named David Walker had endorsed in a pamphlet published in the same city a little more than a year before.

Finding its way into the hands of black residents and white authorities in cities all along the eastern seaboard, Walker's 1829 pamphlet, entitled *Appeal, in Four Articles, with a Preamble, to the Colored Citizens of the World, but in particular to Those of the U.S.,* examined four reasons why "we (colored people of these United States) are the most degraded, wretched, and abject set of beings that ever lived since the world began." Walker's reasons were slavery, the ignorance born of white tyranny and blacks' own servility and despair, the travesty of Christianity that whites preached to negroes to keep them docile, and the colonization doctrine. Each article seethed with contempt and rage. What most appalled white readers, however, prompting several southern mayors and governors to call for Walker's suppression and some of their constituents to call for his blood, was the fact that Walker was a literate, intelligent, and defiant black man who spoke directly to blacks and spoke of vengeance.

With God's help, Walker wrote, the ancient Israelites confronted their enslavers, and the Egyptians suffered for their crimes. Before long, the slaves of the modern world, especially those of the United States, would do the same. "Let our enemies go on with their butcheries, and at once fill up their cup. Never make an attempt to gain our freedom or *natural right,* from under our cruel oppressors and murderers, until you see your way clear," he advised. But "when that hour arrives and you move, be not afraid or dismayed; for be you assured that Jesus Christ the King of heaven and of earth who is the God of justice and of armies will surely go before you. And those enemies who have for hundreds of years stolen our rights, and kept us ignorant of Him and His divine worship, he will remove."

Every dog must have its day, Walker reminded his black readers. "The American's is coming to an end."

Walker was dead when Garrison first brought out *The Liberator.* He had printed three editions of his pamphlet before he died, however, and its notoriety and effect on the south were still very much alive. Chronic fears of slave unrest, raised to acute anxiety by Walker's *Appeal,* had led to more stringent security provisions in many of the slaveholding states.

Stiffer penalties were imposed on anyone who taught a slave to read or disseminated antislavery literature. Assemblies of free negroes were outlawed and free black sailors from the north were quarantined in southern ports. Local and state militias, whose principal purpose was to intimidate slaves who might harbor thoughts of escape or revolt, increased in size. By 1831, Virginia's security force numbered over one hundred thousand men, nearly one-tenth of the population of the entire state.

Noting this climate of alarm, Garrison made a point in each of the first two issues of *The Liberator* to condemn "the spirit and tendency" of Walker's *Appeal* and to distinguish its program from his own. "*We* do not preach rebellion—no, but submission and peace," Garrison insisted, adding that "the possibility of a bloody insurrection at the South fills us with dismay." Yet it must be admitted, he wrote, that "if any people were ever justified in throwing off the yoke of their tyrants, the slaves are that people." America has a choice, Garrison plainly implied. Whites must either emancipate the slaves in the name of Christian love and duty and in a spirit of repentance and nonviolent reconciliation or face the prospect sooner or later of a potentially horrific race war.

The horror came sooner. Early in the morning of August 22, 1831, Nat Turner, a charismatic slave carpenter and preacher, assembled fifty black followers and led them in a two-day assault on the white population of Southampton County, Virginia. Fifty-five white men, women, and children were hacked, stabbed, and bludgeoned to death. Militias eventually suppressed the revolt, executing a hundred or more local negroes who had nothing to do with it in addition to the ones who did. In the immediate aftermath of the uprising, a serious discussion about the future of slavery ensued in the south. But Turner's actions, paradoxically, resulted in a newly decisive and aggressive affirmation of the slave system. Ultimately, the cost of losing two million unpaid laborers and the logistics of integrating blacks into southern society on other terms were too daunting to contemplate. For cotton planters, the issue was simpler. They ran a labor-intensive business that spent fifteen dollars per year to feed, clothe, and house an average worker and reaped twenty times that amount from each slave's work. Their profit was huge. They would never give it up.

Southern propagandists went on the attack. Slavery was no longer defended as a necessary evil; now it was heralded by figures such as

South Carolina favorite son and Jackson administration vice-president John C. Calhoun as "a positive good." The southern campaign to reconceive African slavery as one of America's virtues made the writings of Thomas Jefferson himself a target. Though he had owned slaves and believed in innate negro inferiority, Jefferson had harbored no illusions that slavery was anything other than an unjust exercise of power that brutalized and morally diminished both its victims and its perpetrators. More than forty years before David Walker composed his pamphlet, the author of the Declaration of Independence had gone so far as grimly to anticipate his vision of a divinely sanctioned and directed negro revolution. "I tremble for my country," Jefferson wrote, "when I reflect that God is just: that his justice cannot sleep forever: that considering numbers, nature, and natural means only, a revolution of the wheel of fortune, an exchange of situation, is among possible events: that it may become probable by supernatural interference! The Almighty has no attribute which can take side with us in such a contest."

The leading southern apologists of the 1830s contended, with all due respect, that Jefferson had badly misjudged the moral character of slavery and the feelings of slaves. In one of the most influential and widely circulated proslavery tracts of the period, *Review of the Debate in the Virginia Legislature*, College of William and Mary law professor Thomas R. Dew patronizingly observed that Jefferson's mistake was to assume that blacks felt what he would feel in their place. They did not, Dew argued. God gave whites and blacks different needs, capacities, and personalities. In consequence, Dew claimed, the negro slave "may indeed be happier than we are, and have his ambition too,–but his ambition is to excel all his fellow slaves in the performance of his servile duties–to please and gratify his master–and to command the praise of all who witness his exertions." Jefferson was mistaken, too, in characterizing the master-slave relationship as antagonistic, let alone depraved. While it could not be denied that unkind masters existed, just as unkind fathers did, as a rule the bond between a master and his slave was nearly as affectionate and mutually valued as that between husband and wife, parent and child, brother and sister. "We have no hesitation in affirming, that throughout the whole slave holding country, the slaves of a good master are his warmest, most constant, and most devoted friends."

This personal affection and mutuality of support between master and slave, as Calhoun and later talented proslavery theorists such as George Fitzhugh were quick to point out, stood in sharp contrast to the northern factory owner's complete lack of relation and responsibility to his anonymous, alienated "wage slaves." "There is and always has been in an advanced stage of wealth and civilization, a conflict between labor and capital," said Calhoun in an 1837 speech on the Senate floor. But in the south, he continued, the domestic intimacy between capitalists and their laborers has largely alleviated this conflict, "which explains why it is that the political condition of the slaveholding States has been so much more stable and quiet than that of the North." Nat Turner, according to slavery's apologists, was a gloomy and superstitious madman who had fancied himself religiously inspired and managed to delude negroes even more weak-minded than he into committing purposeless mayhem.

As for slavery's consistency with Christianity, one could scour the whole of the New Testament and "find not one single passage at all calculated to disturb the conscience of an honest slave holder."

Slavery was practical, defensible, even admirable. And it was here to stay.

CHAPTER FOUR

Going Down to Tarshish

> *"Now the word of the Lord came unto Jonah the son of Amittai, saying, Arise, go to Nineveh, that great city, and cry against it; for their wickedness is come up before me. But Jonah rose up to flee unto Tarshish from the presence of the Lord."*
> —The Bible, King James Version

For months, Brown dwelt in the shadow of Dianthe's loss, clutching his agony to him. His children suffered from his pain, as did his business. Not until late in 1832 did he resume his direction of the tannery and his importation and sale of blooded bulls from Ohio. Eventually he brought his children back from the Foreman farm to his empty house.

Early in 1833, Brown's neighbor Thomas Delamater suggested that the widower employ one of the daughters of a relative of his to cook and clean. Brown hired the eldest and a few weeks later asked if she had a sister who could come in to do the spinning and sewing.

Mary Ann, the younger daughter of blacksmith Charles Day, was large-boned, modest, and industrious. She had a stolidity, an air of physical and emotional resilience, that Dianthe had lacked. Brown was drawn to her yet said nothing. Instead, one spring afternoon, he wrote out a formal proposal of marriage and dropped it into her apron pocket. Mary told her daughters years later that she was too overcome to read the letter that day. She slept with it under her pillow, its seal still unbroken. Brown and Mary Ann Day were married one month before the first anniversary of Dianthe's death. Brown was thirty-three; Mary had just turned seventeen. Ten months later, on May 11, 1834, Mary gave birth to a daughter. Sarah was Brown's sixth living child, the first of thirteen that Mary would bear him.

The return of his domestic comforts renewed the restlessness and feelings of unworthiness that punctuated Brown's periods of absorption in life's common pursuits. He had always felt that he possessed a distinctive capacity to lead. But to what end? What service to God was he meant to perform? What duty did he shirk? Some years later, Brown confided to his father that he often regarded himself as a reluctant Jonah, neglecting the call to preach against the evil of the Ninevites. "I feel justly condemned as a most wicked and slothful servant; and the more so, as I have very seldom had any one refuse to listen when I earnestly called him to hear. I sometimes have dreadful reflections about having fled to go down to Tarshish."

Among his family and tannery employees, Brown lost no opportunity to decry the modern Nineveh that was slavery. Morning after morning, he prefaced his thanksgiving for the meal his household was about to receive with a scripturally inspired commentary on the subject. Standing at the end of the long table, speaking with his eyes closed, Brown catalogued the sufferings of the enslaved negroes in the south. It was their duty, he explained to his children, to do whatever they could to relieve these sufferings and help the slaves gain their freedom. It was their further duty to be respectful and kind to the negroes in their midst, who were often despised and poor through no fault of their own but through the ignorance and fear of some who called themselves Christians. "He that hath a bountiful eye shall be blessed; for he giveth of his bread to the poor," Brown quoted. But "whoso stoppeth his ear at the cry of the poor, he also shall cry himself, but shall not be heard." So insistent a refrain around the Brown family board were these sentiments and phrases that the boys would silently mouth them along with their father, often exchanging stealthy jabs and kicks beneath the table in the hope of drawing an audible response that might bring down wrath upon some unlucky sibling. But the lesson was learned.

There were wider spheres of action, however, than John Brown's breakfast table. Reports from his father and brothers in Ohio reminded Brown of that and made him feel his isolation and inadequacy more acutely. By the early 1830s, Hudson was already developing a reputation as a rabid abolition town. Days after the 1831 Nat Turner revolt, as unmitigated outrage and condemnation swept the country, the town's namesake and leading citizen had publicly thanked God for it. "The slaves have risen down in Virginia, and are fighting for their freedom as we did for ours," he announced. "I pray God they may get it."

That same year, a Western Reserve student, returning from vacation with his family in Massachusetts, brought back several issues of *The Liberator*. The college's senior professor and first president, Charles Storrs, read them and passed them on to his colleagues, Beriah Green and Elizur Wright. Soon all three were "immediatists"–advocates of immediate and unconditional emancipation with no compensation for slaveholders. By 1832, radicalized Western Reserve students and faculty were away delivering abolitionist lectures in towns throughout Ohio as often as they were in class. Between August and November of that year, Wright published a series of nine articles in the *Hudson Observer and Telegraph* in which he argued that those who contented themselves with supporting the gradual abolition of slavery–as most of the college's board of trustees did–were morally equivalent to those who would ask a serial murderer to give up his crime gradually and at his convenience. During these same months, Green, Western Reserve's professor of Sacred Literature, devoted his sermons in the college chapel to demonstrating that nothing short of a commitment to the slaves' immediate emancipation was consistent with faithfulness to Christian precepts.

Parents began to withdraw their sons from the college, and donors reneged on their pledges. When President Storrs sickened and died shortly after delivering a three-hour-long emancipation speech at a rally in the rain, the trustees took the opportunity to install a new, apolitical president whose charge was to turn the college's focus away from slavery and onto chemistry, astronomy, and medicine. Green and Wright both resigned, as did Western Reserve board member Owen Brown. Owen became the treasurer of the Anti-Slavery Society in the Western Reserve. Wright, a Hudson native and schoolmate of John Brown's, went to New York to serve as secretary of the American Anti-Slavery Society that William Lloyd Garrison had founded.

On a trip to Ohio in 1834, Brown saw copies of *The Liberator* for the first time. Later that year, Brown's younger brother Frederick visited Richmond, bringing with him the latest updates on the abolitionist firestorms that were raging in Ohio, especially in its educational institutions. The Lane Seminary in Cincinnati had been riven by a series of public debates on slavery and by irrepressible student antislavery activism, much as Western Reserve College had been in 1832 and 1833. The Oberlin Collegiate Institute, attracting faculty defectors from both Western Reserve and Lane, was reorganizing as a college officially dedicated to the antislavery cause. Owen Brown was actively involved in this effort and likely to sit on Oberlin's board.

Before he returned to Hudson, Frederick told Brown that the squire himself hoped to come soon to see his son and grandchildren. Reflecting on his brother's visit and anticipating his father's, Brown felt his own moral slothfulness keenly. Education was surely the key that would open minds and hearts to the antislavery cause. The powerful conversions of the students at Western Reserve and Lane gave ample proof of this proposition. Even better than to guide college boys from prejudice to principle, though, was to cultivate children's capacity for conscience and resolve at an early age. Brown took satisfaction in his own children's trained eyes and feelings for injustice. But it was not enough, Brown thought, for white children to be taught to act according to the principles set forth in the Declaration of Independence and in the Sermon on the Mount. Black children also must be prepared for a society organized on these principles. It was they, after all, who had most to gain by the birth of such a society and they whose demand for it, and whose demonstration of their readiness for it, would most effectively bring it about.

"Dear Brother," Brown wrote to Frederick in November. "Since you left me I have been trying to devise some means whereby I might do something in a practical way for my poor fellowmen who are in bondage, and having fully consulted the feelings of my wife and my three boys, we have agreed to get at least one negro boy or youth, and bring him up as we do our own—viz., give him a good English education, learn him what we can about the history of the world, about business, about general subjects, and, above all, to try to teach him the fear of God." To start a school for blacks, Brown continued, had been for him "a favorite theme of reflection for years." Now he felt the time and the place were right for such an enterprise, and he asked his brother to join him in it. "If the young blacks of our country could once become enlightened, it would most assuredly operate on slavery like firing powder confined in rock, and all slaveholders know it well."

This was John Brown's first written declaration of his commitment to action as an abolitionist. His proposed method is peaceful but his metaphor is militant. To educate fellow men in bondage, he asserts, is to rig slavery for demolition. Other white proponents of abolition in the early 1830s, as well as those who opposed it, also used imagery of explosion, but they typically deployed this metaphor to arouse fear, not hope. "When the molten rock bursts forth in a torrent of burning lava, it will overwhelm those who may be in its way, whether they had expected the explosion or not," wrote colonizationist Benjamin Silliman. Western Reserve's *Elyria Republican* expressed itself similarly in railing against Ohio churches that provided platforms for abolitionist speakers. "What would be said by a congregation sitting upon a powder magazine, should a mad man approach, torch in hand, to ignite the mine which could scatter them in atoms to the four winds of heaven?" Like Brown, such editorialists imagine slavery's sudden demise as a volcanic upheaval, yet Brown differs sharply from them in contemplating such a prospect with equanimity and hope.

The intensity of Brown's conviction and the moral clarity of his cause led him to overestimate the strength of those in his community who shared it and the readiness of others to be won to it. This characteristic mistake of the idealist, the purist, was one he would make again. Ignoring such episodes in recent Crawford County history as the opposition to black attendance in Meadville's Congregational Church and his own showdown with his Indian-hunting neighbors, Brown assured Frederick that "no powerful opposition influence" was likely to manifest itself and that "should there be any, I believe the settlement might be so effected in future as to have almost the whole influence of the place in favor of such a school." Moreover, he optimistically went on, the laws of Pennsylvania allowed the inhabitants of any township to raise a tax "for the purpose of common schools, which any child may have access to by application." Not only would Richmond's citizens tolerate negro education, Brown maintained; they'd tax themselves to fund it.

Had Brown's plan gone forward, his neighbors more likely would have responded as Prudence Crandall's did in the quiet village of Canterbury, Connecticut. The Quaker schoolmistress of a successful private boarding school for girls, Crandall received application from a negro family in 1832 and admitted their daughter. Most of her white students withdrew. Crandall traveled to meet with Garrison and other abolitionist leaders, and returned home to open a new "High School for young colored Ladies and Misses." Emergency town meetings followed. Canterbury and Connecticut, the townspeople cried, must be prevented from becoming "the Liberia of America." Miss Crandall must be foiled in her absurd and disgusting attempt "to foist upon the community a new species of gentility, in the shape of sable belles." Town selectman Andrew T. Judson promised, "that nigger school shall never be allowed in Canterbury, nor in any town in this State." Crandall persisted, opening her school in April of 1833 with students from free black communities throughout the northeast. Within a month, the Connecticut legislature passed a law prohibiting private schools from enrolling or instructing any negro who was not already a state resident. Crandall sustained her school for more than a year while she fought the legislation in the courts. Meanwhile, neighbors filled her well with manure, the local physician refused to treat her students, storekeepers refused to sell her supplies, and her school building was stoned and set afire. In September of 1834, Crandall gave up, closed the school, and left the state.

In April of 1835, Brown put his house and tannery up for sale to raise cash for a move back to Ohio. After living for a decade in Crawford County and contributing significantly to its development, the Richmond postmaster, tanner, cattle broker, and church officer was pulling up stakes. No single factor adequately explains Brown's sudden decision to leave Pennsylvania. Nothing had come of his idea of starting a negro school in the five months since he had proposed it to his brother. Business was slow. Brown missed his siblings, who still lived in the Western Reserve, and wanted his children to form closer relations with their relatives. At age thirty-five, after a decade of civic leadership in his own right, he no longer needed to steer quite so clear of Owen Brown's shadow. Moreover, Brown had received an offer from Zenas B. Kent, one of the wealthiest men in Ohio, to open and operate a new tannery in the promising commercial town of Franklin on the Cuyahoga River, less than ten miles from Hudson. Kent proposed to finance the entire project; Brown, for his part, would provide the management and expertise.

The business relationship with Kent was strained from the start. Expecting the tannery to be completed within a few weeks of his arrival in May, Brown arranged for hides to be shipped to Franklin for curing.

The skins sat in storage. Kent questioned some of the building expenses and meddled with Brown's design specifications, causing long delays. The tannery still was not operational in October, when Mary gave birth to another child, a boy, to whom Brown gave the old family name Salmon. By November, Brown's patience and finances were depleted. Abruptly he informed Kent that he wanted out. Tired of Brown's challenges to the authority of his money, the old financier happily dissolved their agreement. Kent's attention already had turned to a more lucrative scheme.

Earlier in 1835, work had begun on a new waterway long in the planning: the Pennsylvania-Ohio Canal. The east-west canal would bisect the Western Reserve, linking the already operational Ohio-Lake Erie canal, which connected Akron to the Great Lakes, to the Ohio River at its source in Pittsburgh, where the Allegheny and the Monongahela converged. The canal's potential economic impact on the Reserve was enormous. Once it was completed, products and raw materials could be shipped into and out of the region along a continuous network of waterways that extended from central Ohio to cities on the Atlantic coast and from the northern lakes down, via the Ohio's flow into the Mississippi, through the southern states to the Gulf of Mexico. Franklin's position on the Cuyahoga, a few miles east of Akron and along the canal route to Pittsburgh, made it a perfect site for factories and general commercial development, so long as enough water power could be concentrated there to give it the advantage over the other nearby villages that were fiercely competing to become the area's new industrial metropolis.

Zenas Kent was in a position to help Franklin gain that advantage. On behalf of the recently formed Franklin Land Company, of which he was a director, Kent negotiated a contract with the Pennsylvania-Ohio Canal Company providing for a series of dams and spillways that would concentrate the power of the Cuyahoga at Franklin. The Franklin Land Company had already made speculative land purchases of almost $150,000, half of it paid to Kent himself, to obtain a near monopoly on the property along the Cuyahoga's banks that the deal with Pennsylvania-Ohio Canal now seemed to ensure would be prime mill and factory sites. As a Franklin Land director, Kent stood to realize another windfall profit, either through the company's sale piecemeal of industrial and residential lots on speculation or through its development of the entire tract and its control of the new settlement of Franklin Mills once the canal was finished and the boom began.

John Brown, on the other hand, found himself living in a rented house in a new town, with little money, no land, and no means of supporting his wife and six children. Harnessing a team of oxen, he went to work digging a section of the canal that would make Kent and his fellow investors richer. An important local businessman, employer, and public figure at twenty-eight, Brown at thirty-five was a day laborer. As he hauled the wagonloads of mud from the deepening trench that would become the canal, Brown's folly rankled and his pride bristled. All around him, the talk was of the spectacular land prices that those with land to sell would soon be able to command. An acre that had sold for twenty dollars just a year ago, it was predicted, could fetch as high as seven hundred and fifty a year hence. Throughout the area, farmers who had eked out a living for decades by the sweat of their brow now fancied themselves future real estate tycoons. Those without land looked for opportunities to buy some on speculation. These opportunities were enhanced by the lax banking practices and government regulation of the day and by the fact that promissory notes, scrip, securities on other property, and locally printed paper money were all negotiable and indeed made up the principal currency for land purchases. As the grim, wasted year of 1835 drew to a close, Brown saw and seized a chance to redeem it.

He persuaded a local farmer, Frederick Haymaker, to sell him close to a hundred acres of prime land near Franklin Mills that the Franklin Land Company had not yet gobbled up. Brown borrowed money from his brother for the mercifully small down payment to which Haymaker had agreed. In January of 1836, he moved his family into the big, comfortable farmhouse that stood on his new property. Next he offered his old partner Seth Thompson a 50 percent share in "Brown and Thompson's Addition to Franklin Village," which would become a commercial subdivision of Franklin Mills. Thompson bought in for seven thousand dollars, three thousand in cash and the remainder in promissory notes payable over four years. Brown used part of the ready money from Thompson to reduce his debt to Haymaker and repay his brother. With the rest, he made a down payment on a second farm and farmhouse, just outside of Hudson.

As an independent real estate developer and the owner of two farms, Brown was again a man of stature. Though he was without capital or collateral, both his properties having been bought entirely on credit, and his development company had yet to make a cash sale on a single lot, Brown's reputation and prospects enabled him to find six guarantors for a new six thousand dollar loan from the Western Reserve Bank of Warren. With this money he purchased a third tract, part rolling pasture and part heavily timbered woods, called Westlands.

Many years later, John Brown Jr. would say that his father became a land speculator with the intention of making a large sum of money quickly so that he could turn his full attention to the antislavery cause and leave his family provided for if he died in it. Perhaps so. Or perhaps, like thousands of other Americans of the time, he was simply lured by the siren song of untold riches just over the horizon and the sight of so many of his fellows listening and following raptly.

Brown was not active in the abolitionist cause in the mid-1830s. He did become acquainted with some of the free black families in Franklin, however, and offered employment to one negro couple, the man assisting Brown and his sons with the farm work while his wife helped Mary inside the house. It was with this couple and community, and not with the new white neighbors on whose good offices his business prospects in the area might depend, that John Brown publicly aligned himself one notable evening in the summer of 1836.

The Browns had joined the Franklin Congregational Church earlier that year and rented a good family pew near the front of the meeting house. On this occasion, the Browns' church was the site of a marathon interdenominational revival service led by a renowned visiting preacher. The house was packed to hear the revivalist, Mr. Avery, preach four consecutive sermons from the text in Isaiah, "Cast ye up, cast ye up, prepare the way, take up the stumbling block out of the way of my people."

During the afternoon sermon, Brown noticed that the little group of Franklin's free blacks had been seated apart at the rear of the church, some behind a wood stove that obstructed their view of the preacher. As the sermon continued, different emotions arose in Brown from those awakened in the other congregants. "Take up the stumbling block out of the way of my people." Could God have signified the verse's meaning any more plainly today?

There was a break between the afternoon and evening sessions, after which white visitors from other towns and religious societies were seated throughout the congregation while Franklin's blacks were again placed by the stove. As Mr. Avery took up his theme once more, John Brown stood. His high, flat, metallic voice overrode the opening words of the sermon.

"A discrimination has been made," Brown pronounced, "an unChristian discrimination. Our colored neighbors and fellow worshippers have been made to sit at the back of this meeting house, scarcely within sight or hearing of the preaching of the word of God." Mr. Avery cast his eyes left and right helplessly. The congregation waited, hushed. "Take up the stumbling block out of the way of my people," Brown quoted, allowing a note of sarcasm into his voice. Then, turning to his family, he said evenly, "Come with me, children, Mary."

Silently the Browns filed up the aisle toward the exit. None seemed in the least confused or embarrassed—not Mary, carrying her infant son, or the three adolescent boys, or seven-year-old Ruth, guiding her brother Fred with one arm and cradling two-year-old Sarah in the other. Brown approached the door, but he did not go out. Instead, he bent and exchanged some whispered words with several of the negroes sitting there. Somehow, this white man had established a bond of trust with the blacks of Franklin in the few months of his residence there. As one, they rose and followed Brown down the aisle, where he seated them in his pew before rejoining his wife and children, who had taken the empty chairs around the stove.

According to Zenas Kent's son Marvin, who did not mean it as a compliment, "Brown saw everything large, and felt himself the equal of anything." As a social reformer, Brown was equal to the admonishments of the deacons who visited his house the day after the revival meeting, sending them away, as John Jr. told the story, "with new views of Christian duty." As a businessman, he was less well prepared to respond to the challenge that the federal government posed to his speculative empire later that summer.

The Jackson administration was at last becoming concerned about the myriad paper currencies and unsecured notes with which land was being purchased and prices inflated. On July 11, 1836, it issued the Specie Circular, which informed state and local banks that the United States government considered only gold and silver specie to be valuable and would accept no other forms of payment for government lands. The banks immediately tightened credit, land sales screeched to a halt, prices plummeted. Under these circumstances, Brown and Thompson's Addition to Franklin Village, on whose rapid development Brown had depended for both his livelihood and his loan payments, would have to be deferred. Closing the Haymaker house, Brown moved his family back to nearby Hudson, where he recommenced his old tanning business on a smaller scale.

The new year brought the Panic of 1837, the first full-blown crash of America's young commercial economy. The gold and silver specie with which the government had hoped to replenish its coffers through the sale of federal lands did not materialize. Banks called in their loans. Businesses failed by the thousand. One hundred million dollars of wealth evaporated in New York alone. Nine-tenths of the nation's factories and manufacturing plants shut down; nearly two-thirds of its clerks and salesmen lost their jobs. Widespread despair and anger gave rise to numerous suicides and to more frequent outbreaks of random violence against available scapegoats.

The editor of the St. Louis *Times,* a northern-born Garrisonian and Presbyterian minister named Elijah Lovejoy, had penned a vigorous protest against one such act of violence in which a mob had accosted a black man and set him on fire. Soon after Lovejoy's editorial appeared, a larger mob destroyed his office and home, terrorizing his wife in the process. Lovejoy left St. Louis but resettled only a few miles away in Alton, a town on the east bank of the Mississippi River in the free state of Illinois. There he launched a new antislavery newspaper, the Alton *Observer.* Citizens of his adopted community threw his printing press into the river. The town depended on the business of their slaveholding neighbors across the river, it was argued, and these neighbors would take their trade elsewhere if Alton allowed the troublemaking Lovejoy a platform for his radical views.

Twice more during the ensuing year, Lovejoy's press was destroyed. Each time he obtained a new one. Newspapers throughout the country began to follow the Lovejoy saga unfolding in Alton. In late September of 1837, Lovejoy's house was stoned. Defiantly he helped organize the Illinois State Anti-Slavery Society the next month. On November 2, Alton's town leaders met in committee and issued a formal report instructing Lovejoy to stop publishing the *Observer* and leave town immediately or face dire consequences. Lovejoy publicly refused, announcing that he stood "prepared freely to offer up my all in the service of God." Five days later, he was murdered.

Western Reserve College had been quiet since the departure of its abolitionist faculty and students four years earlier. But when news of Lovejoy's death reached Hudson, Laurens Hickok, a professor who had shown little previous interest in politics, abruptly cancelled his classes. Mounting a horse, Hickok rode through Hudson and the surrounding settlements, spreading word of Lovejoy's death and inviting everyone he encountered to a memorial prayer meeting at the church the next evening. At the meeting, near the conclusion of a long, impassioned speech, the converted Hickok declared, "The crisis has come. The question before the American citizens is no longer alone 'Can the slaves be made free?' but 'Are we free, or are we slaves under Southern mob law?'"

When the speechmaking subsided, Owen Brown rose and offered a long, tearful prayer, appealing for strength and guidance and asking that the case before them soon be carried "to the Court of Heaven for a decision." At the back of the hall, John Brown took in the final strains of his father's benediction. In the brief space of silence that followed it, he stood, with his right hand stiffly raised, as if heaven's court had already convened. Then, according to two neighbors in attendance, Emily Metcalf and Brown's old Bible student Lora Case, he said, "I pledge myself, with God's help, that I will devote my life to increasing hostility to slavery."

By the standard of his later words and deeds, this first public statement of Brown's antislavery mission is modest and subdued. Rhetorically, the sentence lacks flair, and the life goal it sets–to increase hostility to slavery–is humble, cautious. Years later, Edward Brown gave a different account of the oath sworn by his half brother. In this version, Brown's hesitant cadences and even his invocation of God's help disappear, replaced by the bold announcement of a radical purpose, delivered in a periodic sentence with three stacked phrases rising to a dramatic crescendo. "Here before God, in the presence of these witnesses, I consecrate my life to the destruction of slavery." This is how

Osawatomie Brown of Kansas and Harpers Ferry would have put it. But on November 9, 1837, John Brown was not yet that man.

In the Hudson Congregational Church that evening, Brown found respite from thoughts of his business failures and the pending lawsuit against him for the six thousand dollar bank loan he could not repay. When he made his pledge, heads nodded in approval. This gratified him. It was his habit, since childhood, to represent to others that he was the equal of anything. He needed them to believe it and needed to believe it himself. Often he did. But lately his plans had come to nothing, perhaps because they were not the plans he was meant to make. With God's help, however, he might at least devote himself, as Garrison and Lovejoy had done, to increasing hostility toward slavery. Consecrating his life to its destruction was still beyond him.

Publicly, John Brown's 1837 antislavery pledge was a promise for the future. Privately, it was also his confession to vanity and covetousness in the recent past. It did not absolve him. During the late winter and early spring of 1836, Brown had abandoned his Franklinian ethic of frugality, diligent labor, and economic independence. He had purchased three farms with bank loans, promissory notes, and funds supplied by friends for which his expectations were his only collateral. For these few months, getting money had entirely engrossed his attention. He had made gold his hope. The wages of this sin were the material, psychological, and moral burdens of poverty and debt that he would bear for the rest of his life.

Nationwide, the economic and social effects of the Panic of 1837 were profound and long-lasting. For seven lean years, joblessness remained high and wages and prices low. In 1843, farmers were forced to sell their crops more cheaply than ever in the country's history. Bankrupt merchants and industrialists were the norm. In New York state, according to social reformer Albert Brisbane, whose assessment of the capitalists' troubles was tinged with moral satisfaction, "scarcely a dozen men" between Albany and Buffalo remained solvent. What had led the nation's banks to overextend themselves so disastrously and to implement a credit system so lax and inflationary that it not only accommodated but even encouraged wild speculation? Simple greed, answered the reformers, but a few added that what stoked that greed was "the rich plunder" northern financiers, manufacturers, merchants, and shippers stood to realize if southern cotton production could be increased to a level that allowed them "the means of clothing the whole world." So wrote the secretary of the American Anti-Slavery Society, John Brown's old schoolmate Elizur Wright, in the Society's 1837 annual report.

In the depressed post-Panic economy, many thousands of indebted white Americans found themselves unable to repay or extend their loans. For them, life under the conditions of the free market and the claims of their creditors began to feel like a form of bondage. *New York Tribune* editor Horace Greeley made the comparison explicit. "I would rather be a convict in a State prison, a slave in a rice-swamp, than to pass through life under the harrow of debt." John Brown owed money that he did not have on all of his land holdings. Payments were due on the Haymaker property and on the Westlands farm. Seth Thompson was demanding some tangible equity in Brown & Thompson's Addition to Franklin Village, which Brown could not yet provide. More humiliating still was the $5,260 loss that Captain Heman Oviatt had suffered on his behalf when the Western Reserve Bank sued Brown in 1837 to recover the six thousand dollar short-term loan it had made him in 1836. Judgment in the case had been rendered against Oviatt, the only one of the six endorsers of Brown's promissory note who had assets sufficient for the court to attach. Brown vowed that he would promptly repay his family's old friend and neighbor, but only the completion of the suspended Pennsylvania-Ohio Canal, followed by the brisk cash sale of the carefully surveyed industrial lots in his Addition to Franklin Village, afforded him any hope of meeting this obligation and all of his others.

After two years in Hudson, the Brown family moved back to the Haymaker farm in Franklin. There was hopeful news that construction of the canal was about to resume, but it produced no spike of interest in Brown's and Thompson's commercial property. Brown again needed work. His family numbered eleven, with a twelfth on the way. In addition to the five living children from his marriage to Dianthe, Mary had by now blessed him with four more—Sarah in 1834, Watson in 1835, Salmon in 1836, Charles in 1837—and was pregnant with Oliver, whom she would bear in March of 1839.

In November of 1838, Brown returned to the labor of his boyhood: cattle-driving. With several hundred head from herds belonging to Owen Brown, Heman Oviatt, and Seth Thompson, he set out for Connecticut, where cattle were in short supply. It gratified him that Oviatt and Thompson, the men his investments had exposed to financial loss, still entrusted him with valuable stock and the negotiation of their sale. Even more comforting for Brown were the natural stimuli of the drive: the deep scent and rumble of the herd, the wind and rain on his face, the steady percussive thud of his mare's hooves on the road beneath him. For three years, he had lived in a world of notes, deeds, blueprints, and summonses. That world was not behind him. When he reached New England, Brown intended to persuade some eastern banking establishment that a man of his reputation, holdings, and prospects was a safe bet for the large loan he needed to hold onto his farms until Ohio land values recovered. Still, it was a temporary relief to exchange paper plans and prospects for animals and weather—creations and reminders of God.

John Brown's first business trip to the east lasted nearly three months and succeeded in every respect but one. The cattle fetched good prices. In fact, Tertius Wadsworth and Joseph Wells, two Connecticut cattle brokers who purchased some of Brown's stock, were so impressed by its quality and by Brown's claim that he could regularly deliver other herds to sell on the eastern market that they offered him a partnership in their company. If Brown made a second drive, Wadsworth & Wells would not only buy more of his cattle but also would make him their western purchase agent, advancing him cash to obtain new stock in Ohio and western Pennsylvania. Before his return home in February of 1839, Brown also fulfilled his childhood desire to become a shepherd. In West Hartford, he purchased from Samuel Whitman thirteen certified full-blooded Saxony sheep, four ewes and nine bucks, whose sires he proudly traced back for two generations.

What Brown failed to do on his trip east in the winter of 1838 to 1839 was to secure a loan. If he could not soon raise the money to make the overdue payments on his properties, he would lose them all. Back at the Haymaker farm in February, Brown worked restlessly alongside his elder sons, eighteen-year-old John, sixteen-year-old Jason, and fourteen-year-old Owen. In the evenings he sang to the smaller children and to his twenty-two-year-old wife, whose fifth pregnancy was nearing its term. But the shadow of failure hung darkly over these domestic routines and pleasures.

Late one night, Brown sat staring into the fire, his Bible open on his lap. The younger children had been asleep for more than an hour, and John Fayette, a young black theology graduate of Western Reserve College who roomed with the Browns, had just said his good-nights and gone upstairs. John Jr., Jason, and Owen remained awake, reading in the light from the open kitchen fireplace. Mary sat with her husband and stepsons, mending a child's torn frock.

Brown's eyes returned to his book and scanned the familiar phrases of Job lamenting his losses. "Oh that I were as in months past, as in the days when God preserved me; When his candle shined upon my head, and when by his light I walked through darkness." As he continued to read, Brown found himself condemned rather than comforted by Job's protestations of righteousness, which spoke to him of obligations unfulfilled. "I was a father to the poor: and the cause which I knew not I searched out. And I brake the jaws of the wicked, and plucked the spoil out of his teeth."

Closing the Bible, Brown rose and began to speak to the others of the evils of slavery. The topic was familiar to everyone present, but tonight there was an urgency and a note of plaintiveness in Brown's voice that his sons had not heard before. He spoke for a long time, drawing images from stories in the antislavery press to dramatize slavery's horrors and its victims' helplessness–images of black children who were bought and sold for money by men who tore them screaming out of their mothers' arms and of negro men who were branded with hot irons like cattle and hunted and shot like wolves if they tried to run away. Slavery was nothing but the most diabolical and cowardly form of warfare that human beings had devised, Brown told his family. It was war of the strong on the weak, war on women and children as well as on men, war to kill the soul before the body. Nonresistants such as Mr. Garrison, he continued, could never bring this unholy war to an end. Those who wielded words alone could never end it. Only force could end slavery–force brought by white men as well as black who were willing to take up arms against it and, if necessary, die in the fight. He knew it to be his duty, Brown told his wife and sons, to make war on slavery. He had known this for some time, and tonight he wished to assure those nearest to him that it was a duty he intended to perform.

Whether his family felt it to be their duty too, only each one of them could say.

Brown paused. "Who among you," he continued, "is willing to make common cause with me to do all in our power to break the jaws of the wicked and pluck the spoil out of his teeth?" His gaze swept across the faces of his hushed auditors. "Are you, Mary?" he asked, looking imploringly into his young wife's wide eyes.

"Yes, Husband."

"Are you, John?"

"Yes, Father."

"Are you, Jason?"

"Yes, Father."

"Are you, Owen?"

"Yes, Father."

After the last affirmation, Brown nodded and sank abruptly to his knees. The boys exchanged glances, startled. Brown always prayed standing, with slightly inclined head and lowered eyes, his hands resting on the edge of a table or gripping the back of a chair. He had never knelt to pray before.

In a moment, Mary had lowered herself gingerly off her chair. Lifting and cradling her belly with her hands, she knelt beside Brown. The others followed.

CHAPTER FIVE

Crossing the Line

> "The most interesting part of my visit to Springfield, was a private interview with Mr. Brown, Mr. Van Rensellaer, and Mr. Washington. The first of these, though a white gentleman, is in sympathy, a black man, and is as deeply interested in our cause, as though his own soul had been pierced with the iron of slavery."
> –Frederick Douglass

IN THE MORNING, Brown's debts were still with him, and he once again addressed himself to the matter of averting bankruptcy. His efforts to secure a loan in the Reserve, however, continued fruitless. Remaining with his family in Franklin through Oliver's birth and Mary's recovery from her labor, Brown assembled another herd and set out on a second cattle drive at the end of March. This time, he was determined, he would convince a New York or Boston banker of his worthiness. Seven or eight thousand dollars, even as little as five, would keep him solvent and his family housed until his investments or the cattle brokerage in which he was about to become a partner began to pay off. Then it would not be long before he could raise his sights from the daily pursuit of money and fix them firmly on the higher cause of the slave.

In May, Brown believed he had secured a loan from a Boston bank. On the first of June, he traveled to receive the draft but was told there was a delay. The money would be sent to him in Hartford, where he was staying, within two weeks. He went back and waited, filling part of the empty time by conversing with George Kellogg, agent for the New England Woolen Company, about breeds of sheep and grades of wool. Kellogg was taken with Brown's knowledge of the business and discussed employing him as a buyer for New England Woolen. On June

12, Brown's loan still had not arrived, and he admitted in a letter to Mary and the children, "I am now somewhat in fear that I shall fail of getting the money I expected on the loan. Should that be the will of Providence, I know of no other way but we must consider ourselves very poor; for our debts must be paid, if paid at a sacrifice. Should that happen (though it may not), I hope God, who is rich in mercy, will grant us grace to conform to our circumstances with cheerfulness and true resignation."

When he wrote these lines, however, Brown could not yet confess to his family that he was a hypocrite who lacked the very virtue of humble resignation that he piously commended to them. A few days earlier, expecting the loan—willing the loan—to come at any time, he had averted foreclosure on his beautiful Westlands farm by paying the balance due with money that Wadsworth and Wells had advanced him to purchase cattle. He would square the cattle brokerage account, he told himself, as soon as the loan arrived, and no one's interest would suffer. By the middle of the month, there was still no loan, and Brown's partners had discovered his misappropriation of their funds and were threatening to press charges. To placate the cattle brokers, Brown turned over to them twenty-eight hundred dollars that he had just received from George Kellogg to buy wool and pledged to restore the balance of their funds in thirty days, within which time the draft from Boston must certainly come. Then he started back to Ohio to wait with his family either for the money or for exposure as a bankrupt and a criminal.

Twenty-two years before, he had walked the very same road, returning home from Connecticut feeling humiliated, mocked, a failure. But now he would have to stand ashamed not only before his father but in the eyes of his wife and children as well. In a letter he sent them from the road, Brown begged—as directly as he was capable of begging—to be welcomed with sympathy and continued familial regard. "I have left no stone unturned to place my affairs in a more settled and comfortable shape," he reported, "and now should I, after all my sacrifice of body and mind, be compelled to return a very poor man, how would my family receive me?" He was not yet able to convey, even indirectly, that rectitude was one of the stones he had turned, and principle something else he had sacrificed in his attempt to retain his worldly possessions.

The loan never came. In August, Brown fully confessed to George Kellogg his "abuse of the confidence of those whom I esteem," signing his letter "Unworthily yours." By mid-September, an Ohio court had attached his assets and appointed a trustee to oversee their liquidation. Brown wrote again to Kellogg, informing him of this development and advising that he "present a claim of sufficient amount abundantly to cover interest and every species of damage and disappointment." The settlement of claims and selling off of property that followed was relentless and torturously slow. In June of 1840, the Browns' furniture, farm implements, and livestock were sold at auction. The family again left the Haymaker farmhouse, forced to move back to Hudson, where Brown returned to tanning.

In October, a man named Daniel C. Gaylord, who had acquired from an intermediary one of the postdated promissory notes that Seth Thompson had given Brown in payment for his share of the Franklin Mills property, won a judgment against Brown for $1,202.28 in the Ohio State Supreme Court. The court directed that Brown's Westlands farm be put up for auction and that Gaylord be paid from the proceeds. Though he had signed the note, rendering it negotiable and himself responsible for its payment, Brown contended that Gaylord had obtained it fraudulently. Residents of Hudson and the surrounding area took Brown's side in this dispute. On the day of the auction, no one would bid on his farm with the exception of Amos Chamberlain, a man whom Brown had known and liked since childhood and considered a friend. Chamberlain bought Westlands for $1,681, less than a fourth of its value. Brown begged him not to demand the farm, proposing that he accept instead a security for what he had paid. Despite his current troubles, Brown assured Chamberlain, he had friends who remained willing to act as his guarantor. After what Westlands had cost him, to see it taken for so little was devastating. In his foolish passion to retain it, Brown had already squandered the respect of Wadsworth, Wells, and Kellogg and the business opportunities they had offered. Now the property's auction at such a ruinous price would deprive him even of the means to repay his honest creditors from its sale.

Chamberlain ignored Brown's entreaties and, in the spring of 1841, prepared to take possession. Outraged and desperate, Brown vowed to resist eviction and holed up in a shed on the property with his three eldest sons and some rusty muskets. Yet his tannery could not be neglected, and the county sheriff found and arrested him there. Clad in the stained red undershirt that he wore while scraping his hides at the beaming table, Brown was escorted to the Akron jail. The Brown boys surrendered and joined their father in custody. Once in possession of his farm, Chamberlain dropped his charges against them.

It took more than a year longer before Brown was officially declared bankrupt. His last property, the Hudson farm where Mary and the nine youngest children were living, was auctioned off. The family was forced to vacate. They moved to nearby Richfield, into a log cabin they rented from Captain Oviatt, who had agreed to employ Brown as a shepherd and breeder. As the large family began to adjust to its new circumstances, five-year-old Charles fell sick with what soon proved to be dysentery. Nine-year-old Sarah, two-year-old Peter, and the infant Austin also succumbed to the infection. Within three weeks, all four children were dead.

To John Jr., away studying at a vocational school, his father wrote: "In our sore affliction there is still some comfort. Sarah (like your Mother) during her sickness discovered great composure of mind, and patience, together with strong assurance of meeting God in Paradise. We fondly hope that she is not disappointed. They were all children towards whom perhaps we might have felt a little partial but they all now lie in a little row together." Brown had dug the row alone at twilight, sobbing–as Sarah had never done–as he drew to a close. During the short lives of the three sons he buried, Brown had crossed the line between entrepreneur and bankrupt and between public repute and public degradation. All the Browns had crossed the line between proud autonomy and humble dependence on the goodwill of others. These passages were intensely painful. Yet they also helped clear the Brown family's path across the color line.

"As soon as circumstances would enable him he began to be a practical *Shepherd*," Brown wrote of himself in the autobiographical letter that he sent to twelve-year-old Henry Stearns as he started to recruit volunteers to raid Harpers Ferry. To be a shepherd, he continued, was both "a calling for which *in early life* he had a kind of *enthusiastic*

longing" and one that "bid fair to afford him the means of carrying out his greatest or principal object."

For more than a decade, beginning with his ill-fated trips to Connecticut in 1838 and 1839, Brown, along with each of Dianthe's sons, would be employed as buyer, seller, herder and driver of cattle and sheep or as dealer in wool. Brown believed that the shepherd's life was especially conducive "to reading and some thought," and it was while he lived this life that he read and thought most about slavery and formulated his strategies to defeat it. But reading and thinking were not "the means of carrying out his greatest or principal object" that a shepherd's calling afforded Brown. Nor was his claim in the letter to Henry Stearns merely metaphorical, a fanciful association between his care for animals and his care for the herded and driven portion of his fellow men.

The means Brown referred to were the opportunities that his travels provided him to assist fugitive slaves and build alliances with black antislavery activists. The practical shepherd was, in fact, a double agent. His official rounds–transporting herds, meeting with associates, assessing stock and markets–gave him both occasion and cover to conduct his other business. That business was to familiarize himself with black communities in the northeast and to cultivate friendships with the increasing number of outspoken blacks who in their pulpits, newspapers, and antislavery congresses were beginning to advocate a more politically active and resistant abolitionism than the mainstream antislavery movement preached or favored. As Brown crisscrossed Ohio, New York, Connecticut, and Massachusetts, and as he sought and achieved hardier and better-yielding stock by crossing the blood lines of breeds of sheep or cattle, he made it his business, too, to cross the color line that categorically divided white America from black America.

Virtually alone among nineteenth century white Americans, John Brown managed not only to free himself of the pervasive and supposedly scientifically respectable white supremacism of his time but also to develop personal relationships with black people that were sustained, intimate, trusting, and egalitarian. In these relations, he was joined by every member of his family–from his wife, Mary, to the children of both his marriages, and even to his son- and daughters-in-law. No white family before the Civil War ever lived in such communion and solidarity with African Americans—at work, at worship, at meals, at war—as did the Browns. None would pay a higher a price or pay it more willingly for their commitment to black people's freedom.

By the late 1830s, black and white communities throughout the north had established more than five hundred local antislavery societies devoted, at least in principle, to immediate abolition. For a while, the growing antislavery movement in the north remained unified under the leadership of William Lloyd Garrison and the American Anti-Slavery Society. Blacks played a crucial role in sustaining this unity, as they had done in initiating an organized abolitionist movement and promoting Garrison to lead it in the first place. Four hundred of the four hundred and fifty subscribers to *The Liberator* in its first year were black. By 1833, over one thousand paying black subscribers supported Garrison's newspaper and, for the next five years, blacks comprised the majority of its sales agents. Embracing Garrison's efforts, black leaders generally were united in their adoption of a moderate antislavery rhetoric that disavowed violence, avoided or de-emphasized the issue of northern racism so as not to alienate white allies, and endorsed the Garrisonian principle that slavery must be opposed and overcome by moral suasion alone.

In Garrison's mind, slavery and the institutions that supported or tolerated it had come to symbolize the general presence of evil in the world. When enough people were persuaded to come out of evil, slavery would end. In the meantime, those who sought the good must exemplify the good by preaching against evil in all its guises and by separating themselves from any society or practice that it tainted. This meant spurning the churches, because all denominations included slaveholders and their supporters. It meant washing one's hands of the corruption and compromise of organized politics and political parties. Since all violence only added to the sum of evil in the world, it meant absolute pacifism, no matter what the circumstances. Since women were also oppressed, it meant demanding women's rights as well as freedom for slaves. Eventually, the Garrisonian quest for pure goodness led to a call for national disunion. The northern states should form their own nation, letting the slaveholding south go its own way and take the

United States Constitution—which Garrison regarded as a proslavery document—with it.

Elizur Wright was among the earliest white abolitionists to express frustration with Garrison's new "perfectionism," which seemed to him not only a political distraction from the antislavery movement but also a mental distraction on the part of its leader. "I have no more hope from him in the future," Wright confided to Beriah Green, his former faculty colleague at Western Reserve, "than I have for the inmates of Bedlam in general. His guns are all turned inward, and he is thundering away with his grape shot to the muzzle, at the *mice & chipmunks.*" Nonetheless, most of the movement's national leaders and local chapters remained loyal to Garrison and to his fundamental principle of non-interference with slavery by legislative pressure, physical resistance, or any means besides moral argument.

The methods and limitations of Garrisonian abolitionism reflected the movement's reasonable public relations concerns. Still an embattled minority in the north, white antislavery activists believed that the ultimate triumph of their cause depended on the gradual conversion of their neighbors to it. For them to rail against northern prejudice and the plight of free blacks in their own communities or to encourage slave revolt would only alienate the moderate whites whose support they hoped to enlist. But it was not only strategy that wedded most white abolitionists to peaceful moral appeal and made them willing patiently to await the blessing of Providence on their efforts. Intellectually, religiously, their opposition to slavery was genuine, even fervent. Yet slavery remained for them an abstraction, an emblem of evil rather than a lived human experience. Black people remained an abstraction, too, a collective object of pity and, inevitably, of condescension. For white antislavery activists, abolitionism was a campaign to save others: to save an alien race that suffering, simplicity, or natural passivity rendered helpless, to save the souls of slaveholders from eternal corruption by greed. It was not, however, a struggle to save themselves.

Black abolitionists observed and connected the various limitations of their white colleagues. It was no surprise, they suggested, that an antislavery movement whose leaders had failed to overcome their own racial biases was also excessively abstract, rhetorical, and patient with minimal or nonexistent results. "Prejudice must be killed or slavery will never be abolished," Theodore S. Wright told the 1837 New York State

Anti-Slavery Convention. "Abolitionists must annihilate in their own bosoms the cord of caste." This cord remained strong, however. The leadership of the American Anti-Slavery Society, for instance, was almost entirely white, although black contributions accounted for one-seventh of the society's annual budget. Black staff members of the Society, moreover, were assigned more of the menial tasks than their white counterparts and received about half the salary. Such indignities, combined with the movement's apparent stagnation at the end of the 1830s, prompted black abolitionists such as William J. Watkins to conclude that it was time "to hang out *our own shingle*." To take control of the struggle for their own liberation, many blacks had come to feel, was a psychological necessity as well as a practical one. Slavery and subordination diminished people, both in the eyes of their oppressors and in their own. The act of demanding respect and equality, even if these goals were not immediately achieved, was a means of reclaiming self-worth.

Blacks who had grown dissatisfied with the passivity of the abolitionist establishment and sought a more aggressive and self-reliant form of antislavery activism found inspiration in two highly publicized mutinies that occurred within two years of each other on slave transport ships off the U.S. coast. In 1839, a Mendi tribal chieftain named Cinque, one of a company of forty Africans illegally transported to Cuba by Spanish slave traders, led a bloody and successful revolt aboard the schooner *Amistad*. In 1841, an American black named Madison Washington carried out a similar mutiny on the *Creole*, a packet transporting nearly one hundred and fifty slaves from Virginia to New Orleans. Washington and his fellow freedom-fighters hijacked the ship and sailed it to the British Bahamas.

Among those who celebrated Cinque's and Washington's acts of resistance and self-liberation were two young New Yorkers, both escaped slaves. J. W. Loguen would go on to open a negro school in Syracuse. Henry Highland Garnet would be pastor of the Liberty Street Negro Presbyterian Church in Troy. Both would become leading figures among the black abolitionists of upstate and western New York, the most energetic and militant black community in the country. They would also become associates and confidantes of John Brown, whom they would recommend to their colleague Frederick Douglass as a man he should meet. "In speaking of him," Douglass recalled, "their voices would drop to a whisper, and what they said of him made me very eager to see and to know him."

Between the *Amistad* and the *Creole* mutinies, the schism within the abolitionist ranks resulted in the formation of the American and Foreign Anti-Slavery Society, a more radical counterpart of and a competitor to the Garrisonian American Anti-Slavery Society. Many blacks, especially the large contingent of New York antislavery activists, helped to establish and direct the new organization. In the same year, 1840, these New Yorkers called for a black state convention on the issue of voting rights. New York law enfranchised all white male citizens but withheld the vote from blacks unless they could prove they owned property worth at least $250, an injustice that Garnet assailed in the convention's most notable speech. For the next twenty-four years, Garnet led the negro suffrage struggle in New York. His speech to the 1843 national Convention of the Free People of Color, however, focused not on the vote but on slavery and revolution. In it, the Troy minister did not address the audience assembled before him in Buffalo but spoke directly "to the slaves of the United States of America."

Your friends in the north have failed you, Garnet told them. "If you would be free in this generation, here is your only hope. However much you and all of us may desire it, there is not much hope of Redemption without the shedding of blood. If you must bleed, let it all come at once—rather, *die freemen, than live to be slaves*." For American slaves, he continued, "it is impossible, like the children of Israel, to make a grand Exodus from the land of bondage. The Pharaohs are on both sides of the blood-red waters!" Therefore, he concluded, "Let your motto be Resistance! Resistance! Resistance!"

By a margin of one vote, the delegates to the 1843 Buffalo Convention resolved to suppress Garnet's speech. It would not be published. It would not be mentioned in the official minutes. Frederick Douglass attended this convention and voted with the majority against Garnet's militancy. A rising star on the antislavery lecture circuit, Douglass had only recently begun his career in abolitionism and at the time of the convention was an employee of the American Anti-Slavery Society and a Garrison protégé. A few years later, John

Brown would play a role in his radicalization. Though Brown could not have read Garnet's speech until some time afterward, he heard of Garnet and sought him out. As he told Douglass at their first meeting in February of 1848, he had been watching and waiting for "some true men" to rise from out of slavery, black men willing to stand up against it, violently, if need be. Garnet's confrontational spirit spoke to Brown, as did the religious sensibility that led the black minister to invoke the story of Exodus and to associate slave redemption with slave revolt.

The Christianity that white Europeans had taught to the Africans they brought to the Americas was the Christianity of loving your enemy, of turning the other cheek, and of heavenly reward for earthly suffering. But as slaves and former slaves began to hear, read, and preach the Word for themselves, they discovered in it a theology not just of consolation but of liberation. Jesus was the special ally and deliverer of the oppressed poor, not the powerful rich. And in the Old Testament, they found slaves freed from bondage in Egypt by a God who worked through human leaders that He selected from among the slaves themselves. The Unitarians and other liberal Christians who made up the majority of white abolitionists saw slavery as an affront to the general moral principles and spiritual ideals of their religion. But they did not understand Thomas Jefferson's Revolutionary War slogan, "Resistance to tyrants is obedience to God," to describe a practical religious obligation. It was a useful phrase for linking the unpopular antislavery cause to the hallowed Revolutionary one, but hardly any abolitionist took it as a direct injunction, as it was for Moses, when God's voice in the burning bush instructed him to return to Egypt and rescue his people from the Pharaoh.

For the Calvinist John Brown, however, the Old Testament stories were living guides to understanding and conduct in the present. What these scriptures told him was that God acted in history and demanded active assistance from those who had chosen him. They also told him that the struggle for liberation, whether of a people from bondage or an individual from sin, was the story of life itself and that everyone's soul was at stake in it. As it was for many black but few white Americans in the 1840s, Christianity for Brown was a liberation theology, one that required powerful faith and—when the moment was right—power politics. God had saved the Israelites when the mighty tribe of Amalek attacked them in the desert, but only after Joshua had fought from dawn until dark, while Moses provided inspiration by standing on a hill nearby and holding his weary arms outstretched throughout the battle. Accordingly, when Brown moved to Springfield, Massachusetts, in 1846 and began to worship and sometimes preach at its black church, his message to the congregation of freedmen and fugitives was not to bear their cross with humility and patience but to "trust in God and keep their powder dry."

By 1845, three years after his bankruptcy, John Brown was one of the most successful breeders of sheep and respected authorities on the cleaning and grading of wool in the United States. Under Brown's care, Heman Oviatt's flock had flourished. In 1843, the Saxonies that he had purchased, cross-bred, and raised for the old captain won prizes at county fairs throughout the Western Reserve for their size, strength, and quality of fleece. Late that same year, Brown was approached by Colonel Simon Perkins, an Akron capitalist and owner of one of the largest and finest flocks in Ohio. In exchange for Brown's labor and expertise in the care and improvement of his fifteen hundred sheep and the preparation of their fleece for market, Perkins would supply all the feed and the shelter for wintering and divide with Brown their annual profit on the sale of wool and stock. He would also house the Brown family in the most comfortable quarters they had ever known, a roomy cottage on Perkins Hill in the countryside outside town, close to the colonel's own mansion. For Brown, the partnership represented not only opportunity but also vindication. Sharing the news with John Jr., he noted the striking reversal that brought a family "three of whom were but recently in Akron jail" into close and trusting association with Akron's leading citizen. It proved, he wrote triumphantly, that "our industrious and steady efforts to maintain our integrity and our character have not been wholly overlooked."

Brown exhibited the 1844 Perkins and Brown spring clip, or season's shearing, at shows in New York City and Boston and won gold medals in both cities. "Mr. Brown's wool has ever been of the highest character since he first brought it here, but this year it has amazed us," wrote Massachusetts textile manufacturer Samuel Lawrence to Perkins back in Ohio. "Your flock is now superior to any in old Spain, and there is no reason why it should not surpass the Germans." L. A. Morrell, author of a popular guide to sheep husbandry entitled *American Shepherd*, wrote of another exhibitor's fleece that "with the exception of Messrs. Perkins & Brown's wool, I have never seen wool so perfectly clean. His process is the same as that of Perkins & Brown, which they should favor the public with a knowledge of." Soon Brown was receiving invitations to inspect and certify the quality of other flocks and to address wool growers' conventions. Between 1845 and 1848, no fewer than fourteen articles in the *Ohio Cultivator*, several of them reprinted in the Chicago journal *Prairie Farmer* and in agricultural publications in other states, contained admiring descriptions of Brown's methods, speeches, and efforts to unite growers in producing higher quality American wool and extracting better prices from eastern manufacturers.

Brown's travels as breeder, inspector, and wool merchant in the 1840s regularly took him to Washington County, in the southwest corner of Pennsylvania, and south into western Virginia. Crossing the Ohio River on his return from these trips, Brown would carry the latest business information from the large growers in the area and some new additions to Oviatt's, and later Perkins's, flock. Often he also transported a party of fugitive slaves. In Pennsylvania, he usually stayed with Matthew McKeever, whose house was a well-known Underground Railroad station for slaves fleeing plantations in Kentucky and the interior of Virginia. When pursuit or betrayal did not seem imminent, Brown delivered the runaways he had transported from Virginia or the Pennsylvania stations to other Ohio conductors, who arranged for their final passage to Lake Erie and across to Canada. When there was danger, he brought the blacks home, concealing them in his house and barn for days or weeks at a time. Colonel Perkins's wife already disdained the rowdy, common Brown boys whom her husband's arrangement with their father had brought virtually to her doorstep. The constant presence of smuggled negroes in the neighborhood—or her constant suspicion of their presence—was almost more than she could bear. "He was always concerning himself with Negroes," she recalled later, "often having several hidden at once about his place." Charles S. S. Griffing, a colleague of Brown's in the Ohio Underground Railroad of the 1840s, agreed with Mrs. Perkins's assessment, though he cast it as a tribute. "He had a consuming idea in life, and that was to free the black man. He had no other aim."

Shepherding, however, was no mere cover for Brown. After the collapse of his grandiose designs as a real estate developer, after his humiliation as a beggar for loans and a petitioner for bankruptcy, physical labor under a canopy of sky and amidst the purity of animals renewed him and often contented him. Pursuing "the same calling that the old patriarchs followed," as he put it in a letter to his children, Brown found his talents and temperament well suited to it. He could tell every sheep in his flock apart, he claimed, sheep looking, to an attentive eye, "about as much alike as men do." He read and tested and observed to determine the most effective cure for sheep grubs and other parasites. And on winter nights, while the rest of his family slept, Brown walked out among the flock, scooping up the weakest of the young lambs if they appeared to be in distress from the cold, and carrying them to the kitchen. There he revived the creatures by immersing them gradually in a tub of hot water, drying their limbs with a flannel cloth, and spoon-feeding them warm milk. At dawn, his wife and children were likely to find him sitting with his back to the fire, a delighted audience of one, watching lambs gambol and skitter across the room.

Managing the Perkins flock, however, did not restore Brown to a pastoral existence so much as it gave him a deeper understanding of the vagaries and injustices of a market economy. Small wool growers, whether in Ohio, Virginia, or upstate New York, shared a common disadvantage. Their distance from the operations of the big northeastern manufacturers who bought their wool, and their lack of bargaining power to set the price of their clips, put them at the mercy of itinerant purchase agents for particular mills, who visited them after each shearing season and offered a flat price per pound for their yields. This system not only deprived the growers of a share in the textile manufacturers' profit on the sale of their finer quality products; it also discouraged them from seeking to improve their breeds or even clean their wool properly. But growers had few other options. They could accept the offered bulk price for their wool (which the manufacturers would later sort and grade themselves), try to sell it locally—and usually end up getting even less per pound, or watch their harvest rot.

The solution was obvious to Brown: collective bargaining. The growers could command fair prices by consigning all their wool to an agent of their own and empowering him to sort it, grade it, and sell it to manufacturers from a central depot at rates that were tied to quality. Once the sorted wool had been sold, each member of the association would receive a payment based on the average grade of the wool in his clip minus the cost of transport, storage, fire insurance, and sales commission. Manufacturers would have to pay higher prices for fine wool, but they would gain the convenience of buying in bulk and at the correct grade for the particular woolen goods they produced.

Growers from eight states endorsed Brown's idea and urged him to carry it through. Perkins agreed. In the spring of 1846, a circular announced Perkins & Brown's opening of an office in Springfield, Massachusetts, "for receiving wool of growers and holders, and for grading and selling the same for cash at its real value." Typically for a John Brown collaboration, labor and management fell solely on his shoulders.

Leaving Mary and the younger children in Akron, Brown moved to Springfield in June to commence the new operation, taking John Jr. and Jason along to assist him. Within a few months, his rented warehouse near the train station overflowed with wool. A single shipment could present five thousand pounds to unload, sort into one of the nine different quality grades in Brown's system of classification, store, and try to sell. Meticulous records had to be maintained of the different amounts and qualities of individual clients' contributions to the collective supply, and correspondence with the growers was a time-consuming daily task. It could also be a maddening one. While their leverage with the manufacturers depended on presenting a united front and releasing their finer grades only for higher unit prices, the growers were accustomed to receiving at least partial payment upon shipment of their wool. Many could not afford to wait and demanded advances against future sales, to provide which Brown established a line of credit at Agwam Bank. Others pressed him to move their wool more quickly by discounting it below the set prices for the grades into which it had been sorted. "Their calls are incessant," Brown complained to Perkins before six months were out, "and how to avoid sacrificing their wool, & yet relieve them, calls for all the tact I am master of."

Brown assured the manufacturers who visited his warehouse that any wool they bought from him would be clean, reasonably priced, and exactly the quality advertised. But none would be sold ungraded. In another departure from common practice, he would sell only for cash on delivery. The mill owners promptly resolved to ruin him. They snapped up the poorer quality wool that Brown priced low and bought Brown's higher grades only when they could purchase fine wool nowhere else. Otherwise, they were willing to pay Brown's competitors more than he was asking, correctly judging that financial necessity would break Brown's growers before this tactic broke them. For good measure, they bribed a man named Flint, whom Brown had hired as a sorter, to spy on the Perkins & Brown operation from the inside and provide them with information about the state of its finances and the growers' desperation.

In spite of everything, Brown sustained the Springfield enterprise for almost four years, moving an average of 130,000 pounds of wool annually. Had he been a different man, he might have approached the manufacturers more flexibly, acclimated them to their new business relations with the growers more gradually, demonstrated the mutual benefits of these relations more patiently, and imposed a looser grading and pricing system that buyers were more likely to tolerate. He might even have made a lot of money. But compromising or moderating an action that he believed to be justified had never been John Brown's strong suit.

Brown stuck with the Springfield venture as long as he did partly out of obligation to Simon Perkins and the growers that Perkins & Brown represented and partly because he had other business in town. For the first time in his life, the small-town frontier tanner and abolitionist now lived among significant numbers of black men and women. Of course, whites in Springfield did not actually live among negroes, whose residences and businesses were clustered in two small districts known as Hayti and Jamaica. But a white man who was interested in the experiences, ideas, and political attitudes of blacks might educate himself here, if he was capable of winning black people's trust, by spending time in their neighborhoods and worshipping with them at their church.

Though a newcomer to the city, Brown quickly won that trust. It was not simply his outspoken hostility to slavery and support of negro rights in the north that enabled him to cross an invisible threshold of intimacy over which few whites ever passed. Other white abolitionists shared Brown's general principles and sympathies. It was the utter lack of discomfort he displayed as a minority of one in black environments, the way he simply assumed an equal footing in his personal interactions with blacks, a footing grounded nowhere but in his assumption of it. Neither condescending nor excessively solicitous, Brown's manner in his exchanges with blacks about religion, politics, slavery, and resistance was the manner of a man who took it as a given that he and his interlocutors were both creations of a God who was no respecter of persons.

Brown dispatched John Jr. and Jason to seek out black men to work in the Perkins & Brown depot. Preferred credentials for employment went beyond aptitude and good character. Brown wanted men who were ready to be mobilized to attack the institution of slavery. One prospective fighter whom John Jr. and Jason recommended to their father was twenty-nine-year-old Thomas Thomas, who had been born a slave in Maryland in 1817 and through extraordinary enterprise managed to acquire enough money to buy his own freedom.

Thomas accepted Brown's offer of a job in the warehouse and asked what time he should report the next morning. Work commenced at seven, Brown responded, but there was a private conversation he wished to have with Thomas if he would come earlier. At 5:30 A.M., Thomas arrived to find Brown waiting for him. What the wool merchant wanted to discuss with his new warehouse porter was the practical destruction of slavery. His own plan for achieving this end was to deploy armed bands at intervals along the Virginia Appalachians to stage lightning emancipation raids on the plantations in the valleys below and then disappear back into the mountains. Liberated women and children would be sent on to the north, while the men would be urged to join the insurgents in taking the campaign, and the destabilization of the slave economy, ever further south.

Before dawn and again after business concluded for the night, the office of Perkins & Brown housed black men in animated conversation about the evils of slavery in the south and prejudice in the north. Even during the work day, the company bookkeeper later recalled, John Brown and his eldest son often huddled in the counting room, examining the slavery question for hours on end. In some way, Brown believed, though he could not say exactly how, the unintended move to Springfield, the daily pressures and frustrations of his dealings with

This photograph was taken by black photographer Augustus Washington, to whom Brown was introduced by black associates in Springfield, Massachusetts. A striking detail of the image is the contrast between the white right hand that Brown raises as if to take a pledge and the dark left hand with which he grips the banner inscribed with the tiny initials SPW. The "Subterranean Pass Way" was another name for the Underground Railroad.
(WEST VIRGINIA STATE ARCHIVES)

Thomas Thomas (left), John Brown's employee at the Perkins & Brown wool depot, in the doorway of the Springfield restaurant that he owned in later life.
(CONNECTICUT VALLEY HISTORICAL MUSEUM)

Frederick Douglass.
(WEST VIRGINIA STATE ARCHIVES)

growers and manufacturers, and the long separation from Mary and the children were all part of a providential design. They were necessary steps along a path he had yet to discern toward the fulfillment of his pledge and destiny to help bring slavery to an end.

Though busy with the demands of the wool cooperative, and gratified by his expanding circle of abolitionist friends and associates, Brown missed his family back in Ohio. In September, Mary had given birth to a daughter, whom she named Sarah after their first child, who had died in the dysentery outbreak three years before. Brown had not yet seen the new baby. He also worried that the other children's religious education was suffering in his absence. His elder sons, to his dismay, no longer attended church with him. Fierce in their hatred of slavery, they did not share the religious foundation of his commitment to oppose it or his faith that God would soon bless human efforts to abolish it. Brown suspected that the younger boys—Watson, Salmon, and Oliver—were also falling away. The painful tidings that he received on November 7, 1846, brought his feelings of loneliness and guilt to a head.

Seventeen-year-old Ruth, serving as family cook and housekeeper while Mary recovered from her tenth childbirth, had dropped a caldron of boiling water that she was removing from the fire. Amelia, a toddler, whom the family called Kitty, was scalded as she played on the kitchen floor. She died of her burns. In his return letter to "My Dear Afflicted Wife and Children," Brown professed himself "utterly unable to give any expression of my feelings on hearing of the dreadful news" and lamented that "I do not feel at liberty" to come immediately home. "I trust," he added, "that none of you will feel disposed to cast an unreasonable blame on my dear Ruth on account of the dreadful trial we are called to suffer; for if the want of proper care in each & all of us has not been attended with fatal consequences it is of no thanks to us. If I had a right sense of my habitual neglect of my family's Eternal interests, I should probably go crazy."

Sending Jason, with his gift for empathy and healing, back to Ohio in his stead, Brown wrote again to Mary alone. His mind, he assured her, was "more than ever filled with the thoughts of home, of my wife & my children," and when the day arrived that presented him with a chance to return, "I shall be awake to greet the earliest dawn, if not its *midnight birth*." In the meantime, he urged Mary to hold fast with him to their faith, "notwithstanding God has chastised us often, & sore," and to their purpose. "I have sailed over a somewhat stormy sea for nearly half a century, & have experienced enough to teach me thoroughly that I may most reasonably buckle up & be prepared for the tempest. Mary, let us try to maintain a cheerful self command while we are tossing up & down, & let our motto still be Action, Action."

The course of action that Brown had revealed to Thomas Thomas, however, would require careful planning and influential black partners. By the end of 1846, Brown had identified Frederick Douglass as such a partner. There was no man he more fervently wished to meet. Six years before, Douglass had been an anonymous fugitive, recently escaped from Maryland and resettled in New Bedford, Massachusetts, where he had abandoned his given surname, Bailey, and begun calling himself Johnson, and then Douglass. Though he and his wife Anna struggled to support their two infant children on his earnings as a day laborer in the shipyards and her sewing piecework, Douglass nonetheless put aside money to purchase a subscription to *The Liberator*. He began to attend local antislavery meetings, often rising to speak himself, and soon was invited to testify about slavery from the pulpit of the New Bedford Zion Methodist Church. In August of 1841, Douglass took a three-day holiday from the shipyard to attend the Massachusetts Anti-Slavery Society convention in Nantucket. A prominent member of the Society, William C. Coffin, recognized him there. Coffin had happened to visit the negro church in New Bedford on a day when Douglass was speaking to his fellow parishioners. Seeing him at the convention, the white social reformer invited the handsome, well-spoken, twenty-three-year-old mulatto fugitive to say a few words to it.

Douglass's knees shook as he stood before an audience of five hundred that included William Lloyd Garrison and many of the country's other leading abolitionists. But his mind and his voice had been in constant training for this moment ever since the day Fred Bailey began to cajole and bribe and trick white women and children into teaching him to read and write. His speech enraptured the crowd.

When Douglass finished, Garrison vaulted onto the stage and shouted, "Have we been listening to a thing, a piece of property, or a man?" "A man! A man!" the crowd cried out in unison. Within a year, Douglass would become a full-time employee of the American Anti-Slavery Society and the most famous negro orator in the country. But in his subsequent work with and for Garrison, Douglass often felt less like his own man than like the American Anti-Slavery Society's prize exhibit. "Tell your story, Frederick," Garrison would whisper to him, as he stepped onto the platform to speak. "Let us have the facts," others would advise, at the same time urging him to mix in "a little of the plantation speech" to refute the skeptics and ill-wishers who cited his large vocabulary, perfect grammar, and cultivated standard English as evidence that he had never been a slave.

With increased fame and influence, Douglass became freer to move beyond personal testimony in his lectures and speak as he liked. Still, he did not set the American Anti-Slavery Society agenda and had come to disagree with Garrison on some of its tactics. Garrison's attacks on the church, the sabbath, and the Bible's divine inspiration troubled Douglass and seemed to him needlessly divisive. Like other black abolitionists, he also worried that the disunion with slaveholders that Garrisonians advocated, if ever actually achieved, would not create irresistible pressure for emancipation but only abandon southern blacks to permanent bondage. Though he continued publicly to support the Society's restriction of antislavery activism to moral suasion and its categorical opposition to violence, Douglass had begun to chafe under these constraints. As John Brown would recognize, it was not in Douglass's nature to turn the other cheek.

They met for the first time early in 1848. Douglass, who had recently broken with Garrison and was publishing his own newspaper, *The North Star,* in Rochester, New York, had come to Springfield to lecture. Brown attended in the company of two black friends, Thomas Van Rennselaer and Augustus Washington. By this time, Brown had reconciled himself to an extended stay in Springfield, found a house to rent, and sent for his family. There was "a peculiar music" in the word "home," he had written to Mary back in Ohio the year before, but after a time the word alone had ceased to soothe him.

Douglass began his long friendship with the Browns on his second visit to Springfield that fall, when Brown invited him to have supper with his family and stay the night. The men met at the wool merchant's office and walked together to his house. The confident authority of

Brown's speech, combined with the wool depot's size and prominent location, led Douglass to expect an entirely different residence from the one at which they arrived. It was a small wooden house, closely bordered by other such dwellings, most of them containing the large, cramped families of day laborers and factory workers. Inside, the furniture was plain and sparse, almost to destitution. The character of the inhabitants was also surprising to Douglass, pleasantly so. All of the Browns, from the grown sons down to the little girls, received him expectantly, familiarly, naturally, as if the occasion of a black dinner companion and lodger were a matter of great interest to everyone in the family but of no particular novelty or social awkwardness to anyone.

The simple but abundant meal of beef soup, cabbage, and potatoes was brought to and from the table by Mary and children of both sexes. "They were evidently used to it," Douglass wrote of the evening, "and had no thought of any impropriety or degradation in being their own servants." The family was also used to lively conversation at the table and to teasing banter from which no one, not even Brown, was exempt. But when the subject was social injustice or moral duty, Douglass noted, Brown's utterances seemed to rise to another plane, lifted by the current of the others' heightened attention and reverence. "His arguments, which I ventured at some points to oppose, seemed to convince all; his appeals touched all, and his will impressed all," Douglass recalled. "Certainly I never felt myself in the presence of a stronger religious influence than while in this man's house."

After the meal had been cleared away, the family members took themselves to other rooms, leaving Douglass and Brown at the table in the kitchen. As he conversed with his host about his paper, *The North Star,* and the women's rights convention at Seneca Falls that he had attended in July, Douglass could hear the scraping of chairs and some fragments of quiet conversation from the adjoining parlor and floorboards creaking under the feet of children preparing for bed above. An older female voice sharply called out, "Annie," an instant before a little girl in nightclothes rustled in and stood holding Brown's sleeve as he finished the sentence he was saying. "What is it, Annie?" Brown asked, turning to her. "Trumpets," she answered impatiently, as though her reason for interrupting them should have been obvious. "Ruth will sing it to you tonight," Brown said, patting her shoulder and turning her toward the door.

As Annie trudged away, Brown stood and came around the table to seat himself next to Douglass. He had a plan to liberate the slaves, he told his guest, and he had invited Douglass to his house to ask his assistance in it.

The plan depended on black men who were willing to fight alongside whites for their freedom, Brown said. Once, he had wondered whether there were enough such men, but now he saw them rising in every direction. Then he described to Douglass the campaign he had previously laid out to Thomas Thomas: a series of surprise freedom raids by teams of men operating from strongholds in the Appalachians. The idea was to render slave property insecure up and down Virginia, driving slavery ever further south and reducing the price and profitability of slaves until the entire system collapsed.

Even as he offered reasoned objections, Douglass wondered why it was that this grand design, proposed to him by a little-known middle-aged white man who lived in a house poorer than his own, did not seem more unreasonable. The first few raids might free some slaves, he conceded, but soon the slaveholders would band together to hunt Brown and his men out of the mountains with bloodhounds or starve them out by cutting their supply lines. Whatever the outcome, Brown countered, the very fact of negroes carrying arms in such a cause would be a kind of liberation, for it would give them a sense of their manhood. No people could have self-respect or be respected by others, he said, who would not fight for their own freedom. As for the possible loss of his own life in the fight against slavery, he could think of no better use for it. There was a silence that Douglass finally filled with words that he already disbelieved.

"Perhaps we might convert the slaveholder by more peaceful means," he said.

"No," Brown almost shouted. "I know their proud hearts. They will never be induced to give up their slaves until they feel a big stick about their heads."

Douglass was silent. Once or twice before, since his arrival in the north, well-meaning white men had professed to him their willingness, if need be, to lay down their life for the slave. These declarations were meant, he knew, as gestures of equality and solidarity between the white man and the black, but they always struck him as affected and obsequious. "You see, I am choosing to enter the valley of the shadow of death where you noble, suffering negroes live all the time." This white man, however, was not appealing for his favor or his forgiveness when he spoke about attacking slavery and possibly dying in the process. Strange, too, Douglass realized, was his response to Brown's statements about negro self-respect and slaveholders' proud hearts. Listening to a white man who had spent his life in the north tell him that he knew about negroes and slaveholders, Douglass, a black man who had lived with slaveholders for twenty years, perceived no condescension and took no offense. When Brown spoke about winning self-respect by fighting for freedom and about stubborn pride in status and possession, he was simply saying what he knew not about negroes and slaveholders alone but about men and about himself. Douglass knew the same things, had often thought them, even written them.

The day he liberated himself from slavery was not the day in 1838 when, with borrowed identity papers and in the guise of a seaman, he had boarded a train in Baltimore, then a steamer in Wilmington, and stepped onto the pier in Philadelphia a new man. It had occurred four years earlier, when he was sixteen.

To break his independent spirit, his master had hired him out for a year to Edward Covey, a farmer and professional slave breaker. Covey had beaten him for the slightest infraction, finally almost kicking him to death one summer day when Douglass had collapsed from heat exhaustion while threshing wheat and was unable to obey Covey's command to rise and return to work. The next time Covey advanced on him, Douglass grabbed his assailant by the throat and made him understand that from then on, "the white man who expected to succeed in whipping, must also succeed in killing me." Having felt the stick about his head, Covey never touched him again. As for Douglass, "I felt as I never felt before. It was a glorious resurrection, from the tomb of slavery, to the heaven of freedom. My long-crushed spirit rose, cowardice departed, bold defiance took its place; and I now resolved that, however long I might remain a slave in form, the day had passed forever when I could be a slave in fact."

Douglass and Brown talked for hours, the reciprocity of their conversation growing as the night advanced toward morning. Sitting at John Brown's table, plotting physical resistance, Douglass felt again the exultation, the redemptive defiance, of half a life ago. After that evening in Springfield, he knew that the violent enslavement of millions would require violence to overcome. Gradually he allowed this knowledge that he shared with Brown to enter his public speech. "My utterances became more and more tinged by the color of this man's strong impressions." But Brown had not taught him something new. He had only given voice to what Douglass had learned at sixteen and had never really forgotten throughout all the moral suasion he had practiced since. The color of Brown's impressions recalled and reaffirmed for him the color of his own.

CHAPTER SIX

The Slave Law of the Land

"This filthy enactment was made in the nineteenth century by people who could read and write. I will not obey it, by God."
—Ralph Waldo Emerson

I<small>N THE MORNING</small>, after the men had shaken hands and Douglass had boarded his train, Brown returned to the wool depot. It would require all his patience to confront the stack of unanswered letters from growers in need of cash. A greater account awaited settlement, and to Brown, that settlement seemed more imminent than ever before.

He stood at the edge of the Jordan, Brown felt, among a gathering vanguard of bold black men–Garnet, Loguen, Douglass, Thomas, Van Rensellaer, Willis Hodges. Soon they would start their circuit around slavery's fortress, preparing the blast that with God's help would bring down its walls, like Jericho. It was possible, of course, that those walls would collapse about their own heads, burying them in the rubble. When he spoke of his plan to his black friends, as he had last night to Douglass, there was always a silent moment in which the specter of their own destruction gripped them. They were men like any others. Their lives were dear to them, dearer still for the struggle it had cost them to gain the simple chance to live lives of their own at all. A chance to own their labor, to cleave to their wives, to raise their children, rights that white men took for granted. But the price of free lives in the north, for those blacks whose exceptional efforts and talents had won them more than bare subsistence, was a self-confinement of the spirit. To protect their personal safety and their private gains, they must suppress their rage at the daily indignities they endured. Even more difficult for men of conscience, they must go about their business under the constant burden of knowing that millions still languished in bondage. Acquiring the ability to tolerate this burden or shed it–to water one's own garden while others perished in the desert just beyond–was how free negroes in the north imitated whites. Brown knew from his own experience how tempting a bargain this was and exulted in the evidence that ever larger numbers of black leaders were resolving to refuse it. His black colleagues recognized the depth of his resolve to refuse it as well and accepted him as one of their own.

One measure of that acceptance was the article of Brown's that Hodges and Van Rennselaer, editors of the black newspaper *The Ram's Horn*, had printed earlier in 1848. The piece appears to be a memoir, written by a free negro who identifies himself only as Sambo, of a life misspent in the pursuit of trivial objects and status symbols. Popular novels, fashionable clothing, fine tobacco, hired horses and carriages–such are the things that Sambo has consumed or coveted in the self-hating hope that possessing them would make him "but little inferior to some of the whites." Sambo claims at the outset that though he has "committed a few mistakes in the course of a long life," he always has made "a seasonable discovery of my errors & quick perception of the true course." Yet, as each new paragraph confesses another "small mistake" or "trifling error," immediately followed by the complacent refrain, "I can see in a twink where I missed it," the article reveals itself to be a satire in the style of some of Ben Franklin's pieces of topical wit but with a harder edge. The target of "Sambo's Mistakes" is its first-person narrator, Sambo himself, who never fully grasps the enormity of his degradation. Its author, as *The Ram's Horn*'s editors knew, was John Brown.

Among themselves, the more radical black abolitionists of the late 1840s were beginning to criticize what they saw as the materialism, conformity, and submissiveness of those northern blacks who steered clear of politics. What made "Sambo's Mistakes" remarkable was not its content but the fact that black editors welcomed such criticism from a white man and gave it a public forum. Hodges and Van Rennselaer trusted Brown and approved the aim of his satire: to anger or shame more blacks into taking a militant stand. The opening sentence of the article's last paragraph makes that aim explicit. "Another trifling error of my life has been that I have always expected to secure the favour of the whites by tamely submitting to every species of indignity, contempt, & wrong instead of nobly resisting their brutal aggressions from principle

& taking my place as a man & assuming the responsibilities of a man, a citizen, a husband, a father, a brother, a neighbor, a friend as God requires of everyone (if his neighbor will allow him to do it)."

Soon after writing these words, Brown spied an opportunity to conclude his double life, a chance to devote all his energies to helping blacks practice what Sambo preached. In the northernmost reaches of New York, where the peaks of the Adirondacks rise above Lake Placid and the Saranacs, millionaire abolitionist Gerrit Smith owned 120,000 acres of land. Smith's fortune and his vast land holdings had been inherited from his father, Peter Smith, who with his business partner, John Jacob Astor, got rich in the last decade of the eighteenth century by buying furs in the region's declining Indian settlements and selling them in its advancing white towns. Growing up in a mansion, attended by slaves, in a town–Peterboro–that his father had named for himself, Gerrit Smith became an ardent abolitionist and a philanthropist eager to use a portion of his unearned wealth to help freedmen overcome prejudice and poverty in his home state.

In 1846, Smith devised a plan to provide three thousand black men with an independent livelihood and possibly with the means to meet New York's $250 property requirement for negro enfranchisement. To each applicant approved by the committee of black leaders that he had appointed to recommend worthy recipients, Smith would sign over forty acres of the 120,000-acre tract that stretched across Franklin, Essex, and Hamilton counties. In the wilds of northern New York, these men and their families might then establish self-sufficient black farming communities. If the communities succeeded, each farmer's improved land would yield him not only sustenance but also suffrage. By the summer of 1847, Smith's Adirondack experiment was home to a small cluster of settlers, new property owners, some of whom had recently been considered property themselves.

J. W. Loguen visited the area and interviewed some of the first blacks to arrive for an article that Douglass published in *The North Star* on March 24, 1848. Loguen praised the quality of the land but warned grantees about the efforts of hostile white residents to discourage them from settling and to cheat them out of their tracts. Unfamiliar with the region and coming mainly from domestic and commercial occupations in urban environments, the holders of Smith's deeds were easy marks. Dishonest local guides charged them exorbitant amounts to lead them on circuitous routes to their property. Sham surveyors informed them that the land they had been given was uninhabitable and then offered a few dollars to take it off their hands. Many blacks who managed to build shelters and begin to farm were being gouged by local merchants when they tried to buy tools and supplies. And then there was the cold, unlike anything that most of the new settlers had ever known.

Two weeks after Loguen's article ran, John Brown presented himself at Gerrit Smith's home and told the philanthropist that he was determined to see his experiment succeed. If Smith was willing to sell him land adjoining the settlement on terms he could afford, Brown proposed, he would move his large family there and do what he could to help the other colonists prosper. He was a trained surveyor; he would make sure that the tracts were properly delineated. He was an experienced farmer and a prize-winning sheep and cattle breeder who could show his neighbors how to enhance their crops and stock. And he and his sons would see to it that white officials and businessmen thought twice before they tried to cheat or intimidate the people that many of the locals referred to as "Smith niggers." Although his current business was a wool depot in Springfield, Brown expressed his intention to get out of it soon. "I am something of a pioneer," he concluded. "I grew up among the woods and wild Indians of Ohio, and am used to the climate and the way of life that your colony find so trying."

Sitting across from Smith in the millionaire's study, Brown was acutely conscious of all that he had not accomplished. Nearly fifty, he was as landless as the black beneficiaries of Gerrit Smith's generosity, and his family's future was nearly as insecure. Within the past year his two eldest sons had married. Jason had not returned to Springfield after going back to Ohio when Kitty died, and only Brown's earnest entreaties to help him manage the wool business a little longer had kept John Jr. and his bride from settling immediately in the Western Reserve as well. He had nothing to give his grown boys and nothing to hold them with, except the oath that they had taken together in the kitchen of the Haymaker house–John, Jason, Owen, Mary, and himself–to make war on slavery. But almost a decade had passed. The house was lost, the oath still unfulfilled. For all his resolutions to attend to a higher good, he repeatedly had let himself become distracted. To Mary he had confessed the previous year to feeling "considerable regret by turns that I have lived so many years, & have in reality done so very little to increase the amount of human happiness." Throwing in his lot with the colony at North Elba, known to its residents as Timbucto, was a chance to do much more, while providing his family with a fresh start and a permanent home. It was also a chance to expand his circle of intrepid black men, men who might at last help him make good on his promise to break slavery's jaws.

Smith was impressed and agreed to sell Brown a 244-acre tract on a plateau three miles from Lake Placid for one dollar an acre, payable over time. Before he could even contemplate taking possession of this property, however, Brown had to extricate himself from the wool business in a way that fulfilled his obligations to Perkins and the western growers. With a three-hundred-thousand-pound inventory in the Springfield warehouse, growers clamoring for payment, and a substantial debt owed to the Agwam Bank, Brown's task was enormous. Together, he and John Jr. wrestled with it throughout the spring and summer. To make matters worse, Brown was incapacitated for most of July and August by a severe and persistent case of the ague. Recovering, he decided to leave his son in charge so that he could visit Timbucto, meet the settlers, inspect his land, and arrange to lease a nearby cabin to accommodate his family when they arrived next spring until he and the boys were able to clear their own tract and build on it.

 Traveling north through western Massachusetts and Vermont, Brown crossed into New York and continued up the eastern shore of Lake George to Ticonderoga and along the western edge of Lake Champlain to Westport, before turning west across the Keene Valley and up again into the Sentinel Range to North Elba. He encountered few other people, but as he climbed, God's presence was palpable to him: in the clarity of the icy mountain streams, the breathtaking depths of the gorges, the aromas of cedar, spruce, hemlock, and balsam that spiced the autumn air. Standing for the first time on his allotment, Brown looked north to the forty-five-hundred-foot summit of Whiteface Mountain looming above him and knew at once that this was where he wished to be buried. "I like to live in a country where everything you see reminds one of Omnipotence," he remarked to his family after their move to North Elba the following year. When winter set in, the other Browns declared themselves less enamored. "Father's New Palestine" would have made a fine promised land for a colony of Norwegians, Jason jibed, though he had to admit that the place did reveal "the truth of Scripture where it says, 'who can stand before his cold?'"

In addition to the sublimity of the scene, Brown admired the industry and character of the Timbucto settlers whom he met that fall, though he recognized that the community was struggling to establish itself against long odds. Upon his return to Springfield in late October, he arranged to ship five barrels of pork and five of flour to distribute among the colonists. The staples would help sustain them through the long winter and reduce their need to purchase food at inflated prices from the white storekeepers who wanted them gone. Along with the pork and flour Brown sent letters of encouragement. Through whatever privation or injustice they might suffer, he urged them to remember "the vast importance of sustaining the very best character for honesty, truth, industry, and faithfulness. I hope every one will be determined," Brown wrote, "to not merely conduct [themselves] as well as the whites, but to set them an example in all things." As he had done fourteen years earlier, when he assured his brother Frederick that the citizens of Richmond, Pennsylvania, would support a negro school, Brown assumed that demonstrable black virtue and achievement would command white respect. No intervening disappointment or disillusionment had undermined his expectation that what should be would be. Unafflicted by racism's irrationality, he habitually underestimated its power and depth.

Early in 1849, a French clothing manufacturer purchased several bales of Perkins & Brown's premium grade wool. For Brown, this was evidence that the quality of his product and the professionalism of his operation had at last overcome the European prejudice that held American wool to be inferior. It was also the solution to the problem of how to liquidate his inventory on favorable terms, conclude his three-year detour into the brokerage business without exposure to a recurrence of the lawsuits that had bankrupted him a decade before, and free himself for the move to North Elba. If American manufacturers were paying more for fine wool in Europe in order to break John Brown at home, he would take as much of his competitively priced stock across the ocean as his growers would allow and sell it there to European mill owners for its fair value. Persuading Perkins and most of the firm's suppliers of the merits of this plan, Brown contracted for the summer delivery of two hundred thousand pounds of wool to the London brokers William C. Pickersgill & Company. From Pickersgill he collected an advance against the sale, an amount well below the 50 percent of the wool's estimated value that he requested but sufficient to provide partial payments to the individual growers whose wool would be shipped and to finance Brown's own voyage in August. By early May, he had completed his arrangements. Now he could devote the first part of the summer to taking his family to the mountain.

The Browns' departure from Springfield in mid-May was somber. Eleven-month-old Ellen had been tubercular throughout the winter. In the painful last days of her illness, she was only peaceful when her father held her and walked with her. She died in his arms three weeks before her first birthday, the eighth child Brown had lost. John Jr. stayed in town to manage the business in Brown's absence. Twenty-six-year-old Jason and eighteen-year-old Fred were employed as shepherds on one of Simon Perkins's farms in Akron. That left nine Browns to ride on the wagon, wedged between boxes of clothing and the family's furniture, or walk beside the lone ox that pulled it. Mary, ill but characteristically stoical, sat in a chair that Brown had lashed down in the front of the wagon bed. Dianthe's third son, Owen, and only daughter, Ruth, tended the five young children of their father and stepmother–Watson, Salmon, Oliver, Annie, and Sarah–during the 225-mile journey.

Eager to arrive and conscious of the short time he would have in North Elba before his scheduled departure for Europe, Brown set a pace that tested the endurance of both his ox and his family. At Westport, while Mary and the children rested for the final push through the mountains, he judged that the overloaded wagon was too heavy a burden for the ox to pull across the steep, winding Adirondack trails. Inquiring in town about horses that he might purchase, Brown happened upon a black man who had often navigated these trails and was preparing to move to Timbucto himself. Impressed with the man's knowledge of the region and inwardly delighted by his name, Thomas Jefferson, Brown bought a team and hired his new acquaintance as his teamster.

The rest of the Browns were equally delighted by the care and skill with which Mr. Jefferson transported them, guiding the wagon over rough terrain more gently than Brown had done over smooth. Brown's spirits were high as he scooped gleaming white pebbles for Annie and Sarah from a streambed and challenged Watson, Salmon, and Oliver to inhale the air and name each tree whose fragrance mingled in it.

They were not dampened by the bare adequacy of the rented cabin at which they at last arrived. The largest of its four rooms would serve as a combined kitchen, dining room, and parlor. Adjacent to this was a supply pantry. For sleep, the nine Browns would have to distribute themselves into two cramped bedrooms and a low-roofed attic, accessible by ladder and big enough to hold up to four beds side by side. "It is small," Brown admitted to his weary family, "but the main thing is, all keep good-natured." The next day, a young escaped slave named Cyrus appeared at the cabin door. Brown had been kind to Cyrus in Springfield and found him occasional work at the wool depot. Soon after the Browns' departure, the lonely boy had impulsively followed them. He became the tenth member of the Brown household at North Elba.

Assisted by his three younger brothers and Cyrus, Owen commenced the management of the farm, planting crops of potatoes, carrots, turnips, rutabagas, and oats. Brown once again made the rounds of the Timbucto settlers he had met the previous fall. They had numbered about one hundred then, but not all of these had stayed through the winter. Brown surveyed each grantee's property, resolving uncertainties of boundary and title that some of the white residents of the area had tried to exploit. In one case, by the threat of a lawsuit, he restored a land deed to a Timbucto settler who had lost it in a swindle. He quickly formed a close friendship with Lyman Epps, the most determined of the Timbucto grantees and the colony's unofficial leader. Also a native of Connecticut, the devout yet fiercely independent Epps was a man very much like himself. In the evening, Brown enjoyed visiting his neighbor to discuss politics or the Bible, often tussling playfully with his host's young children or bouncing them on his knee as he conversed

Lyman Epps in old age. Epps was one of the leading settlers and Brown's closest friend in the Timbucto community in North Elba, New York. (WEST VIRGINIA STATE ARCHIVES)

with their father. A decade later, Lyman Epps and his three children stood over Brown's black walnut coffin and led off the funeral service for him at North Elba, their clear voices sending the strains of "Blow Ye the Trumpet" slicing through the December air.

In the summer of 1849, however, Epps and the other Timbucto colonists were focused not on revolution but on survival. To those whose circumstances were most precarious, Brown gave farming assistance, food, and paid work when he could afford it. He hired the recently widowed Mrs. Reed to help Mary and Ruth cook and keep house for his large family. And he continued to employ Thomas Jefferson, one of whose jobs was to steer the family wagon safely over the mountain roads toward Canada on nights when new fugitives lay covered in its bed and Brown and Owen perched on its sides holding rifles and staring into the darkness.

One afternoon in late June, Brown and Jefferson returned from overnight Railroad business to encounter three sunburnt, mosquito-bitten gentlemen reclining in the grass beside the Brown cabin. Richard Henry Dana Jr., a leading Boston attorney and the famed author of *Two Years Before the Mast,* an account of his travels as a common seaman during a long break from his studies at Harvard, had come to the Adirondacks to hunt, fish, and camp with two of his friends. On the previous morning's hike, however, Dana's party had lost its way. The men wandered all day and night without finding food, water, or their campsite. Finally stumbling out of the woods after twenty-four hours, they spied a cultivated field and a cabin at the end of it. Ruth had taken them in and served them so much milk and bread that she began to fear they would hurt themselves before they quenched their thirst and satisfied their hunger. She urged them to nap upstairs and then join the family for a proper dinner when her father returned.

Dana had helped found a new political party the year before, the Free Soil Party, dedicated to keeping slavery out of the vast western territories that defeated Mexico had signed over to the United States at the end of the Mexican War. Five years later, he would vigorously but unsuccessfully represent the slave Anthony Burns in Boston's most notorious capitulation to the Fugitive Slave Law. But despite his antislavery credentials, Dana was unprepared for the democracy of the Brown family dinner table. As he would later write, he and his friends joined "Mr. and Mrs. Brown, and their large family of children, with the hired men and women, including three Negroes, all at the table together." Even more striking to him was that Brown called the black adults "by their surnames, with the prefixes of Mr. and Mrs." and "introduced us to them in due form, 'Mr. Dana, Mr. Jefferson,' etc." Though the company was unusual, Dana was pleasantly surprised as well with the conversation of his backcountry host. "We found him well informed on most subjects, especially in the natural sciences. He had books, and evidently made a diligent use of them."

In August, Brown left Owen in charge of the North Elba farm and traveled to London to conclude the affairs of the wool brokerage. To his surprise, he found that Pickersgill & Company had not yet displayed or offered any of the Perkins & Brown wool. The brokers told him they had deemed it best to introduce it at their mid-September sale. There was nothing for him to do until then.

John Brown was an inquisitive and observant man, but his temperament was ill suited to tourism, and he had no experience as a vacationer. He required an immediate objective and was given to restlessness and brooding without one. In Europe, however, with time on his hands, he had little choice but to assume the role of man of the world. He made hasty rounds of Paris, Brussels, and Hamburg, but had less to say about these metropolises in the letter he wrote to John Jr. than he did about the English livestock he had inspected. "Horses, as seen at Liverpool and London, and through the fine country betwixt these places, will bear no comparison with those of our Northern states," he pronounced, while conceding that "their hogs are generally good, and mutton-sheep are almost everywhere as fat as pork." John Jr. sent the letter on to Mary, scrawling in its margin an affectionate deadpan barb: "You will see that he does not design to stop to write much poetry among the old castle ruins of that country." The one European landmark that Brown made sure to visit was the battlefield of Waterloo. Surveying this historic ground, the wool merchant recalled the positions and strategies of Napoleon and Wellington from the books he had read, assessed the command decisions they had made, and envisioned the ones he would make when his great battle arrived.

Back in London, Brown learned that prices for the finer grades of wool had risen in America in the month since he had sailed. He passed an uneasy hour. If he failed here, if the representatives of the large

British manufacturers did not buy, Perkins & Brown would emerge from the venture in a financial position much worse than the one that drove him to take the gamble and bring the wool over in the first place. But they would certainly buy, Brown told himself. The British were rational businessmen. They would see the quality of his wool, the logic of his gradations, the fairness of his asking prices, and they would buy. The main thing was to keep his dignity. He would not be bullied or condescended to. And he would not plead, he thought, coloring at the memory of himself in another commercial capital ten years ago, appealing at every Boston banker's door for the loan that would save his land business and retiring gratefully, hopefully, with the scraps of vague promises they threw to him.

The British manufacturers disliked John Brown. His manner, like his long-tailed brown suit, was neither a gentleman's nor a tradesman's but some odd hybrid of the two. He was certainly eager, they observed, perhaps even a little too eager for their favor and their business. But at the same time, there was nothing of the tradesman's deference in his tone as he stood before his fleeces explaining in excessive detail the origins and virtues of each. Indeed, the set of his features as he spoke and the steadiness of the gaze that he locked on the buyers gathered around his bales conveyed a hint of arrogance, an impression that Brown confirmed by his boast that he could feel a snip of wool in the dark and tell the breed of sheep and region it came from. The American acted as if his wool were not just a product for sale but a testament to his personal expertise and a tangible proof of the equality of American growers to any in the world. Accept the commodity, and you accepted these propositions with it.

One of the men in the circle decided to take Brown up on his challenge. "What do you make of this, then?" he asked, handing over a ball of fluffy white fibers. Brown rolled the sample between his fingers quickly and declared, "Gentlemen, if you have any machinery that will work up dogs' hair, I would advise you to put this into it." Had he laughed with them, had he shown his audience that he enjoyed the joke and recognized in himself the imperiousness that had provoked it, Brown might have won them over. But his face was expressionless as he rendered his judgment and handed back the poodle hair. The American was not a fool, the buyers concluded, but he was bound to be a rogue. Everyone knew, after all, that Yankee growers and dealers failed to clean their wool properly and deliberately inserted sticks, leaves, and filth into the center of their bales to increase their weight.

Normally, prospective wool buyers examined only a few of the outer fleeces in each bale, but Brown's bales were torn open and subjected to an inspection so thorough and rough that he feared that any rejected ones would be too damaged for later sale. He reddened with indignation as the probe proceeded and then reddened more deeply with shame. At the outset of Perkins & Brown's wool cooperative, in meeting after meeting with the growers, Brown had emphasized that every fleece sent to the Springfield depot must be meticulously washed and cleaned of foreign matter if his gradations of the wool and assignment of higher prices to the better grades were to have any credibility with manufacturers. He and his workers at Springfield had double-checked as much as they could of the hundreds of thousands of pounds of wool they received. But some of the growers had been lazy or dishonest. Worse, in his rush to deliver the bulk of his remaining wool to Pickersgill in time to settle his family in North Elba before the sale, he had been negligent. Deep inside several of Brown's highly graded bales, the British buyers had exposed coarse, unwashed wool and fleeces caked with excrement. The men yanked the offending fleeces loose and shook them in the swindling American's face. Brown stood silently before them, too humiliated and too proud to attempt any explanation or excuse. After a while, the buyers dropped the evidence at his feet and walked away.

While John Brown was taking his wool to England in the hope of concluding his brokerage business without ruinous loss, tens of thousands of adventurers from the United States and countries around the globe were rushing in the opposite direction to strike it rich in California. The vast, lush California territory, with its heavily timbered coastal mountains and alluvial farmland, was the jewel of the 525,000-square-mile tract of land that Mexico had surrendered to the United States in February of 1848 at the village of Guadalupe Hidalgo, where representatives of the two countries signed the peace treaty that ended what the Americans called the Mexican War. The acquisition of California–along with the other southwestern lands that would later form all or part of the states of Nevada, Utah, Colorado, Arizona, and New Mexico—had been the war's motive as well as its spoil. The quarrel over Texas's southwestern boundary that had triggered the fighting in 1846 was a convenient pretext for war but not a sufficient cause.

Months before President Polk ordered Major General Zachary Taylor to advance from his station on the Nueces River to confront Mexican forces along the Rio Grande, the United States had offered Mexico twenty-five million dollars for the land that would give it an unbroken domain over the entire territory between the Atlantic and the Pacific coasts. Mexico had refused to sell. From the standpoint of the expansionist United States administration and press, Mexico's hold on California was simply obstructive, even perverse. Mexico could make little better use of the land than could the Indians, and its claim on it was almost as ridiculous. The Mexican government was too weak to control, let alone to develop, a province so distant from its capital. But the United States, with its rapidly expanding industrial base and waves of new immigrants, was poised to populate and improve this alluring territory. Since the early 1840s, American pioneers and speculators had been staking claims and establishing small settlements in California, mainly in the north, where Mexican communities were sparse. What California needed now, urged the *Illinois State Register* and dozens of other Democratic Party organs, was the political and economic organization that only the United States could provide.

With annexation, the *Register* predicted, "myriads of enterprising Americans would flock to its rich and inviting prairies; the hum of Anglo-American industry would be heard in its valleys; cities would rise upon its plains and sea-coast, and the resources and wealth of the nation be increased in an incalculable degree." It was time now for Americans to fulfill the role that *Democratic Review* editor John O'Sullivan had defined in an 1845 editorial that supplied the watchword of American expansionism for the rest of the century. It was "our manifest destiny," O'Sullivan wrote, "to overspread the continent allotted by Providence for the free development of our yearly multiplying millions." Congress agreed. "We must march from Texas straight to the Pacific Ocean, and be bounded only by its roaring wave," one Maryland representative intoned on the House floor. "It is the destiny of the white race, it is the destiny of the Anglo-Saxon race."

The United States had owned California for almost a year when the gold rush began in earnest, shortly after the December, 1848, State of the Union message, in which the president encouraged American migration by trumpeting recent prospecting strikes in the Sierra Nevada foothills. But Congress had been slow to make any formal provision for a territorial government, let alone for a process leading to California statehood. The main reason for its inaction was the bitter and paralyzing division that the acquisition of the Mexican lands had created in American halls of power over whether the destiny of the Anglo-Saxon race on the Pacific coast included the right to bring and own slaves there.

The issue of slavery had been central to the United States-Mexican conflict from the beginning. Mexico had outlawed the practice shortly after winning its independence from Spain in 1821, but the American colony that the new Mexican government authorized Moses Austin to establish in Texas in that same year drew slaveholders from neighboring Arkansas and Louisiana, eager to plant new cotton fields in soil that had not been depleted by the nutrient-stealing crop. The determination of Texans to protect slavery from the Mexican government's repeated threats to eliminate it helped spur their independence movement; the determination of northern representatives to protect the congressional balance of power against the admission of an enormous new slave state kept independent Texas out of the union for nine years. Many in the north viewed the 1846 outbreak of the Mexican War, one year after Texas became the twenty-eighth state and fifteenth slave state, as the latest and boldest plot by the slave power to extend its territory and influence. In Concord, Henry David Thoreau refused to pay his tax bill in protest and spent a night in jail before his aunt cleared the debt and freed him to return to his cabin on Walden Pond. Indeed, some of the south's more zealous champions, envisioning a hemispheric slave economy under United States control, urged the slaveholding Kentuckian Polk to annex all Mexico, not just its northwestern provinces. While this ambition was not politically or militarily viable, southern planters and their delegates in Washington more realistically set their sights on acquiring California for slavery. Northern leaders resolved to block any such outcome.

The seventy-seven thousand people who flocked to California in 1849, quadrupling the territory's 1848 population, settled the question that had stalemated the politicians. In March of 1848, two months before Sacramento storekeeper Sam Brannan ambled into San Francisco with a fistful of gold and a fantastic story that shut down the town by sending every able-bodied man in it scurrying to the Sierras, the *California Star* had written that slavery should be barred from the territory because its presence "would make it disreputable for the white man to labor for his bread, and it would thus drive off to other homes the only class of emigrants California wishes to see, the sober and industrious middle class of society." The discovery of gold eliminated underpopulation as a concern and sober respectability as an option. It also made the antislavery argument concrete and irresistible. As one of the delegates to the September, 1849, Constitutional Convention in Monterey put it, "The causes which exclude slavery from California lie in a nutshell. All there are diggers, and free white diggers won't dig with slaves.... That is the upshot of the whole business." The white new Californians, clustered in hundreds of mining camps and in the swollen towns that now supported the digging economy, already faced conflicts with competing Mexican miners, with the Indians their settlements had displaced, and with other foreigners whom the dream of wealth had drawn. They would not tolerate African slaves in their state as well, they decided, as they began to write their state constitution in Monterey at the very moment that John Brown was being humiliated by British wool buyers. Instead, they demanded immediate enfranchisement as the thirty-first state and sixteenth free state, a status that would provide the established executive, legislative, and judicial structures they needed to secure their rights and the territory's wealth.

As the nation reached the century's midpoint, the slaveholding interest found itself in a position nearly identical to the one that confronted its antislavery opponents exactly three decades earlier. In 1820, with slave states and free states evenly divided at eleven apiece, the inhabitants of another fertile and geographically crucial territory had petitioned for admission to the Union. Missouri was the strategic and economic heart of the land acquired from France in the Louisiana Purchase, just as California would be of the land ceded by Mexico. Rich in mineral and agricultural resources, Missouri was watered by three important rivers—the Missouri, the Illinois, and the majestic Mississippi—and situated at the hub of the commercial transport system that these waterways provided. The Missouri territory was a coveted field for western expansion that lay on a direct line west from such free states as Illinois, Indiana, Ohio, and Pennsylvania. But slaveholding southern settlers had beaten the northerners to it and written a state constitution that protected chattel slavery.

The battle over Missouri statehood was the first great national conflict over the territorial expansion and political future of slavery in America and a sign of things to come. It ended in a compromise, deftly engineered by the slaveholding Kentucky congressman and Speaker of the House, Henry Clay. The north would accept Missouri's petition for statehood with legal slavery. In exchange, southern representatives would cease to block Maine's admission as a free state and would agree that no future slave state, with the exception of Missouri, could extend any further north than Missouri's southern boundary, the line of 36 degrees and 30 minutes north latitude. Fourteen congressmen from the more populous north voted with the unified southern delegation, and the Missouri Compromise passed by a narrow margin. The south hailed the Compromise as a smashing political victory. After the vote, Roanoke, Virginia, representative John Randolph, a manic opium addict with a piercing soprano voice, who liked to appear in the House chamber dressed for a fox hunt and attended by his dogs, ridiculed the half-baked antislavery men of the north who had capitulated to the more resolute and manly southern contingent. "They were scared at their own dough faces," the colorful and hypnotic Randolph cackled, "yes, they were scared at their own dough faces! We had them, and if we wanted three more, we could have had them." "Doughface" instantly entered the political lexicon as the standard term of contempt for northern politicians who did the south's bidding.

Now, in 1850, however, it was the south that faced the prospect that a large new state that it had sought and lost for its own economic expansion would tilt the senate's scales in favor of the north. The seventy-three-year-old Henry Clay again was summoned to cobble together a compromise. If sectional tensions over California and the other Mexican acquisitions were not eased, many feared, they would soon lead the country down the path of disunion. The Compromise of 1850 granted California's admission under a state constitution that outlawed slavery. It authorized settlers to organize the New Mexico and Utah territories that Mexico had also relinquished and empowered those settlers to decide whether to allow or ban slavery in their states when they formally petitioned for statehood. The element of the Compromise of 1850 that was most controversial in the north—and the one that southern representatives insisted on if there were to be compromise and peace at all—was the Fugitive Slave Act.

Over the two decades of its existence, the abolitionist movement had not prevented slaveholders from adding more than a million men and women to their inventory, for a total of three million in 1850. Nonetheless, the growth of antislavery sentiment in the north had encouraged slaves to try to escape. While only a small minority of white northerners would actively assist them, fewer still would take steps to apprehend the fugitives and return them to their owners. Fugitive slaves blended in among free northern blacks in every northern city, and local sheriffs' offices and courts made little effort to weed them out. The north's accommodation of thousands of escaped slaves outraged southerners not only because of the financial losses they suffered but also as a matter of principle. The protection of private property rights, they argued, was the country's founding commitment. Slaves were legal, constitutionally protected property. How could the slaveholding south remain party to a Union in which the citizens of the northern states did not respect its property rights, the legal system of the northern states did not enforce them, and the federal government did nothing to compel northern compliance with the law of the land?

The Fugitive Slave Act was the slaveholding interest's long-awaited instrument of compulsion. It provided for the appointment of fugitive slave commissioners throughout the north whose job was to receive claims from slaveholders or their agents on local black runaways. Commissioners were empowered to issue arrest warrants and, once the alleged slave was apprehended, to determine whether he or she was the person described in the southern court record or other identifying document that the owner's representative submitted as proof of ownership. Accused slaves had no right to present a defense. There were no juries. No judge in the regular court system could intervene or stay the extradition of a black who had been found by a fugitive slave commissioner to be an escaped slave. Commissioners received a fee of ten dollars for every black they returned to slavery and five dollars for each hearing in which they found insufficient proof that the detainee was the property claimed. Finally, the Fugitive Slave Act imposed steep fines and a term of imprisonment on anyone, white or black, who assisted a slave to escape or obstructed a slave's recapture.

Even those northerners who felt only a vague distaste for slavery that they had never acted upon recognized at once that passage of the Fugitive Slave Act would change their relation to the institution. Such northerners looked on the slave system as a distant wrong perpetrated by someone else, which had nothing to do with their communities or with them. Now they would have to look at it at close range; worse, they would be a part of it. Their local sheriffs and constables would be forced to spend their time chasing down some Mississippi cotton planter's runaway, perhaps a boy who had been driven to desperation by the beatings of a drunken master or a woman who was only trying to preserve her chastity from an overseer's predatory assault. Southern slave catchers and bounty hunters would invade their peaceful streets, lurk in the corners of their places of business, and perhaps even insist on worshipping in their churches while they were in town. Not in the south, but here in Philadelphia, Cleveland, and Boston, suspected slaves would receive only the barest mockery of the due legal process on which the north prided itself. Then every man, woman, and child in these cities would have to endure the repeated spectacle of negroes paraded in manacles and leg irons to their docks and railroad stations. And if they could not endure it and tried to interfere, the good citizens of the north themselves risked being branded and punished as criminals. In Massachusetts, such citizens looked to their beloved and powerful Senator Webster to denounce and dismantle this "bloodhound bill," as they called it, the evil brainchild of Virginia senator James Mason, and to persuade his northern colleagues to vote it down.

Daniel Webster was one of the most admired men in America and had been for almost forty years. A brilliant attorney and formidable legislator, Webster combined classical eloquence with savvy political and business sense. His mere presence in public was an event that drew crowds of gaping onlookers. Webster's commanding physique, noble carriage, legendary brows, cavernous eyes, and dark, handsome complexion were generally agreed to be marvels. But his most marvelous attribute was his voice–rich, deep, and especially thrilling in oration and debate, when it was the instrument of such rolling cadences and inspiring sentiments that schoolboys rushed to memorize them. "His wonderful organization, the perfection of his elocution, and all that thereto belongs,—voice, accent, intonation, attitude, manner, are such as one cannot hope to see again in a century," Ralph Waldo Emerson gushed in his journal, after hearing Webster speak at Concord in 1843. Webster had opposed the annexation of Texas and the Mexican War, and he had voted in favor of the failed Wilmot Proviso to ban the introduction of slavery in any of the territories acquired from Mexico. Surely, thought many of his admirers, he would not allow slavery to extend its ugly tentacles into Massachusetts itself. Rather, he would stand up against the Fugitive Slave Act and cut it down to size, as only Webster could do. For, as Emerson had written, "what is small, he shows as small, . . . and his words are like blows of an axe."

On March 7, 1850, Webster rose in the U.S. Senate chamber to speak on the proposed Compromise.

"Mr. President," he began, "I wish to speak today, not as a Massachusetts man, nor as a Northern man, but as an American." Continuing, Webster evoked the image of an American ship of state in imminent danger of foundering. "The imprisoned winds are let loose. The East, the North, and the stormy South combine to throw the whole sea into commotion." With respect to the cause of this commotion, the vehement sectional disagreement over slavery, Webster professed to see both sides. Any American committed to his country's preservation must see both sides, he argued. "There are thousands of religious men, with consciences as tender as any of their brethren at the north, who do not see the unlawfulness of slavery," Webster pronounced. Differently situated men, he observed, naturally will have different perceptions of truth and duty. The people who endanger the peace, however, are those zealots who are "disposed to mount upon some particular duty, as upon a war-horse, and to drive furiously on and upon and over all other duties that may stand in the way." These perfectionists think they can "deal with morals as with mathematics," he thundered. "If their perspicacious vision enables them to detect a spot on the face of the sun, they think that a good reason why the sun should be struck down from heaven." Descending from his rhetorical height, Webster came to the crux of the matter: on the issue of fugitive slaves, the south was right and the north was wrong. "There has been found at the North, among individuals and among legislators," Webster admitted, "a disinclination to perform fully their constitutional duties in regard to the return of persons bound to service who have escaped into the free States." Insisting that there were no legitimate "excuses, evasions, escapes from this constitutional obligation," Daniel Webster threw his weight behind the Fugitive Slave Act.

With his support, this bill, along with the other parts of the Compromise of 1850, was passed into law. Bankers, businessmen, and political moderates throughout the north applauded Webster's courage and hosted banquets in his honor. For New England's liberal intellectuals, though, Webster's defection was almost as traumatic a blow as the fact that slave law would now be enforced throughout the land. A day after the senator's fateful speech, Massachusetts congressman and educational reformer Horace Mann wrote to his wife, "Webster is a fallen star! Lucifer descended from Heaven." And a year later, after northern blacks had begun to be arrested and returned to slavery, Emerson heard Webster deliver a patriotic speech about America's blessing of liberty and bitterly remarked, "The word *liberty* in the mouth of Mr. Webster sounds like the word *love* in the mouth of a courtezan."

In Springfield again, after his return from England at the end of October 1849, John Brown spent a spiritless week sifting through the unsold wool and shattered finances of the firm of Perkins & Brown. Then he retreated to the isolation of the Adirondacks and the comfort of his family. Putting on a mask of confidence, he resumed his customary work on the farm and advice to everyone else about theirs.

Winter was coming on, and Brown could see the apprehension and gloom in the faces of his black neighbors at Timbucto. Many could barely produce enough food on their land to sustain their families through the frozen months, let alone to sell for money to pay their property tax. The colony was not growing but diminishing, and Brown had done little to prevent its decline. Nor was he likely to do much in the years ahead. Once he had settled the company's affairs in Springfield as best he could, Simon Perkins wanted him to come back to

Akron and resume the care of his flock. He owed Perkins that much, Brown thought. Perkins had supplied the capital to launch their wool cooperative, and Perkins's fortune would be at stake were any of the threatened damage suits against Perkins & Brown to prove successful. The lawsuits would shackle him for years, as they had a decade ago. He, who had pledged to free the slaves, could not even free himself from bonds of his own making.

The Fugitive Slave Law, which took effect on September 18, 1850, renewed Brown's faith and energy. The new legal mechanism to apprehend escaped slaves in the north and deliver them to their masters may have seemed to Daniel Webster a mere spot on the face of the sun. But for Harriet Jacobs, a North Carolina slave hiding in New York City and the future author of the powerful memoir *Incidents in the Life of a Slave Girl*, it was "the beginning of a reign of terror to the colored population." Throughout the northern states, blacks prepared to abandon their homes and flee to Canada. More than twenty thousand did so.

Brown spent most of the year 1850 traveling up and down the Atlantic coast and inland to the Great Lakes, pleading with angry wool growers to accept their share of the cooperative's losses and forgo legal action against Perkins & Brown. When he returned to Springfield in November to complete his final audit and close the firm's office, he found his black friends in a state of confusion and despair. Many had been living freely there for a decade or more. Should they go and leave everything behind or risk staying? Men with families told him they were so anxious for their wives and children that they could not sleep. "I want all my family to imagine themselves in the same dreadful condition," Brown instructed, in the letter back to North Elba in which he described the scene. Still, he saw signs of a divine plan in the new law's very abomination. "It now seems," he wrote to Mary, "that the fugitive slave law was to be the means of making more abolitionists than all the lectures we have had for years. It really looks as if God had his hand in this wickedness also."

At Springfield's Free Church, the Reverend John Mars, himself the son of slaves, preached resistance. Quoting Christ's words to his disciples at the Last Supper, Mars advised that "he that hath no sword, let him sell his garments and buy one." Invited to speak at the Thanksgiving Day service, Brown echoed Mars's militance, telling the congregation, "Trust in God and keep your powder dry."

The Old Testament tells the story of Gideon, who saved his people from destruction with a small, brave force handpicked by the Lord. In it, the children of Israel had been overrun by the Midianites and driven into caves and dens in the mountains. Yet even there they were hunted down and began to believe that God had forsaken them. But God spoke to Gideon on Mount Gilead, instructing him to reduce his force to those who had no fear. Those fearless few alone should remain at Gilead and prepare to fight; to them God would deliver victory over the oppressors. This story now provided Brown with a blueprint for resistance to the Fugitive Slave Law. Assisted by Reverend Mars, Thomas Thomas, and the young runaway, Cyrus, who had returned from North Elba to Springfield with him, Brown built his first antislavery military organization, a mutual defense league to protect Springfield's blacks from apprehension as fugitive slaves. He named the group the United States League of Gileadites.

Though the Gileadite chapters that he hoped would spring up throughout the free states never materialized, the forty-four black men and women whose names appear at the bottom of the Springfield League's charter proved a formidable and enduring force. No slave ever was taken back from Springfield. In 1854, according to one report, a party of slave catchers did arrive in town with proofs of ownership for some of its residents. But city officials persuaded them that they would surely be killed if they tried to apprehend the negroes on their list, and the men took the evening train back to New York.

Brown's charter for the League began with a preamble entitled "Words of Advice," which opened with the proposition: "Nothing so charms the American people as personal bravery." Here was the argument he had made to Douglass nearly three years before. Whites would respect blacks when they fought for their independence, just as the British had only begun to respect the Americans when they proved they were willing to revolt. As usual, Brown ignored the likelihood that most Americans would be outraged and terrified, rather than charmed, by black violence against whites, even in self-defense. But he shrewdly recognized the human tendency to empathize more with an individual who dramatically symbolizes an injustice than with the anonymous masses who suffer the injustice every day. Recalling the *Amistad* case, and uncannily forecasting the effect of his own raid on Harpers Ferry and prosecution for treason nine years later, Brown continued, "The trial for life of one bold and to some extent successful man, for defending his rights in good earnest, would arouse more sympathy throughout the nation than the accumulated wrongs and sufferings of more than three millions of our submissive colored population."

The business of the Gileadites, however, was neither symbolism nor charm. Members of the society were to establish a surveillance and communications network capable of quickly alerting the entire force at the first sign of "any attack upon the rights of our people." They were to supply themselves with weapons and carry them concealed and ready at all times. If force proved necessary to save a fugitive from recapture, they should take care only to use it against the aggressors, but they must use it without hesitation or remorse. "Do not delay one moment after you are ready," Brown instructed; "you will lose all your resolution if you do. Let the first blow be the signal for all to engage; and when engaged do not do your work by halves."

Brown also advised the Gileadites to perform a deft maneuver designed to implicate and perhaps even to radicalize half-hearted white sympathizers. "After effecting a rescue, if you are assailed, go into the houses of your most prominent and influential white friends with your wives; and that will effectually fasten upon them the suspicion of being connected with you, and will compel them to make common cause with you, whether they would otherwise live up to their profession or not."

The black laborers, barbers, woodworkers, machine operators, waiters, and cooks who formed the Springfield branch of the United States League of Gileadites agreed to organize for the purpose and under the guidelines that Brown had sketched out. They resolved to stand by one another and to hang before giving any of their members or activities away. They resolved to elect no permanent officers until after some trial of courage and talent enabled them to discern who was most worthy to lead them. Finally, they resolved the following: "That as citizens of the United States of America we will ever be found true to the flag of our beloved country, always acting under it."

Rage may have risen in the throats of some of the Gileadites at this oath of allegiance to a country that did not recognize their citizenship and did not love them, a country that had enslaved them and now passed a law to reconfirm their enslavement, the very law that their organization was dedicated to oppose by force. But for Brown, this resolution was neither bitter nor absurd. In a way, it was a version of the same strategy and principle that he followed in urging blacks to take refuge in the homes of prominent white liberals after they had thwarted a state action that white legislators had authorized and white society allowed. The strategy enforced a commitment that was not one-sided but mutual. It challenged the timid liberal and the hypocritical country to measure up in deed to what they professed in word. It identified them not with their flawed performance but with their high ideals. In this invitation to America to be true to its flag and worthy of their love, the Gileadites and their founder were not traitors but patriots.

CHAPTER SEVEN

To Answer the End of My Being

"Dear Wife and Children, All—I am writing in our tent about twenty miles west of the Mississippi, to let you know that we are all in good health and how we get along. . . . The country through which we have traveled from Chicago has been mostly very good; the worst fault is want of living streams of water. With all the comforts we have along our journey, I think, could I hope in any other way to answer the end of my being, I would be quite content to be at North Elba."
—John Brown, en route to Kansas, September 4, 1855

J OHN BROWN JR. carefully broke the seal of the letter from Springfield, the second he had received from his father that week. It had been ten years since he had quit Brown's roof for the first time, to board with another Ohio farm family and teach at a country school a day's journey from Hudson. Now, in December of 1850, John Jr. was twenty-nine years old, three years married, and a property owner in his own right. But a letter from the old man still evoked in him mingled feelings of pride and unease, as if it were at once an affidavit of his equality and a notice of his truancy.

John Jr. still recalled the stinging response he had received to one of his earliest letters, in which he had confessed his disillusionment with teaching, his frustration with unruly and uninterested students, and his intention to quit at the end of the first term. "I think the situation in which you have been placed by Providence at this early period of your life will afford to yourself and others some little test of the sway you may be expected to exert over mind in after life," his father had sternly replied. If John Jr. failed to carry out the task he had set himself, if he could not go into a country school and "reduce it to good order, &

waken up the energies & the very soul of every rational being in it, yes of every mean, ill behaved, ill governed, snotty boy & girl," then where would he find the strength and resolve to meet the greater challenges that doubtless lay ahead? "If you run with footmen & they should weary you, how should you contend with horses?"

More times since than he could count, John Jr. had groaned under the burden of his father's certainty, his clarity of purpose. John Brown was the man who set a course and stuck to it, the man—as his sons knew better than anyone—who dispensed, rather than required, direction. That was why the recent change in their relationship, though it gratified John Jr., also troubled him. It was strange to offer his father advice, even stranger for his father to ask it of him so openly and earnestly as he had of late, as if he were willing, even comforted, to be directed.

John Jr. had done all he could to save Perkins & Brown. He had interrupted his courtship of Wealthy Hotchkiss in northeastern Ohio to help Brown open the Springfield office in 1846 and then returned with Wealthy after their marriage in the summer of 1847. More patient and less excitable than his father, John Jr. had gradually assumed much of the responsibility for the firm's books and correspondence, writing hundreds of receipts and letters to growers and recording the details of each transaction and communication in a daily ledger. When Brown moved his family to North Elba and then took the bulk of the Perkins & Brown inventory to England in the summer of 1849, John Jr. had stayed behind in Springfield and sold enough wool to reduce the company's debt to a few thousand dollars. Noting the rising prices in the United States and the warning signs that the London brokers were determined to undervalue the American import, he had even urged Brown to ship the wool back from England without attempting to sell it there. It gave him little pleasure that he had been right. In the fourteen months since the fiasco at Pickersgill and his father's return, John Jr. had watched Brown scurry from state to state in a hopeless quest to placate Perkins & Brown's aggrieved growers and creditors.

What his father feared most, John Jr. recognized, was not that the litigants in the six suits filed against the firm would win the forty-thousand-dollar cumulative judgment that they sought, but that he would lose, or had already lost, the respect and friendship of his partner, Simon Perkins. "He is a most noble-spirited man, to whom I feel most deeply indebted," Brown had written to his son, in the letter that

John Jr. had received three days earlier than the one he was opening now, "and no amount of money would atone to my feelings for the loss of confidence and cordiality on his part." Reading the new letter, John Jr. saw that his father had returned to this theme and to the appeal that he had made in the earlier one. Brown wanted his three sons in Ohio to be his ambassadors, to do everything in their power to retain or renew Perkins's good opinion of the Brown family. Jason and Frederick now worked for Perkins and lived on his land. John Jr.'s property was some miles distant from Akron, yet he served both Perkins and his father by his continuing consultation on the partnership's tangled accounts and his preparation of documents and testimony for its pending legal battles.

It was clear to John Jr. that the Browns had ceased to be partners or even employees in the eyes of the Perkins family. Holding John Brown entirely responsible for the failure of the Springfield venture, Mrs. Perkins in particular regarded the Brown family as bearers of a debt of servitude. She missed no opportunity to remind her husband of her view, and for all his "noble spirit," Perkins had been swayed by it. Recently, he had complained that Jason was not tending the flock as carefully as his father had done. He wanted his old shepherd back, and had communicated his desire to Brown, who had asked his eldest son what he thought of the idea.

John Jr.'s response was vigorously negative. The thought of his father living on the Perkins estate again produced in him a surge of filial defensiveness. Under present circumstances, such an arrangement would be an affront to his father's dignity, he argued, a "slavery of the soul." Or perhaps, John Jr. reflected, he was protecting his own independence, not John Brown's pride. He had put distance between himself and his father before, only to find their paths again converging.

It was remarkable, his father's letter began, how similar their thoughts were. "Indeed, your letter throughout is so much like what has often passed through my own mind, that were I not a little skeptical yet, I should conclude you had access to some of the knocking spirits." John Jr. smiled. His father was the kind of man who found it hard to express appreciation of his adult son's insight and counsel without mixing in some mockery for leavening. Here the object of his satire was John Jr.'s interest in the new sciences of mind and spirit that so many of America's and Europe's most up-to-date thinkers and experimenters were beginning to advance. The developing practices and doctrines of hypnosis and phrenology offered tools for revealing and improving the workings of human physiology, mentality, and character, tools as powerful for transforming man's interior landscape, many believed, as were those of modern industry for transforming the exterior one. Such practices and prospects intrigued John Jr., who had amassed a library of more than two hundred volumes that contained a number of recent books about them.

Earlier that year, he and Wealthy had moved to New York so that he could train in phrenology–identification of an individual's leading traits and potentialities through analysis of the contours of the skull–and other diagnostic and therapeutic methods at the well-known firm of Fowler and Wells. For a few months after he completed the program, until an inflammation of the throat forced him to seek other work, John Jr. had represented Fowler and Wells as a circuit lecturer on phrenology and health and a promoter of the books and pamphlets that the firm published on these topics.

His father doubted and distrusted phrenological claims of access to the springs of human spirit and behavior. He was more adamant in his opposition to any suggestion that direct revelations from the spirit world might be available to people living in post-biblical times. The Bible contained all the truth that God ever revealed or would reveal directly to men, he once remarked to John Jr. in Springfield, voicing Calvinism's uncompromising verdict on the subject. "The book has been sealed."

Nonetheless, on an 1847 trip to New York, Brown had allowed Orson Squire Fowler to conduct a phrenological examination of his skull and work up a reading of his personality from the results. John Jr. became attracted to phrenology in part because of the acuity of this characterization of his father. "You are very active, both physically and mentally," Fowler's report stated, "are positive in your likes and dislikes, 'go the whole figure or nothing' and want others to do the same." The shape of Brown's head also led Fowler to venture: "You can measure well by your eye and are annoyed if you see anything out of proportion, as not exactly plumb." The final paragraphs of the reading focused on Brown's independence and stubbornness. "You like to have your own way, and to think and act for yourself," Fowler concluded, "say just what you think, and most heartily despise hypocrisy and artificiality, yet you value the good opinion of others, though you would not stoop to gain applause."

Brown sympathized with his son on the illness that had ended his lecturing career, but it pleased him that John Jr. had rejoined his brothers Jason and Frederick in "the same calling that the old patriarchs followed." The image of those worshipful biblical shepherds, however, threw into stark relief his own patriarchal failure. Again, Brown felt, he had allowed business and worldly ambition to absorb him, while his children, whether by his inattention or as punishment for his sins, drifted from the faith of their fathers. "I will say but one more word on that score," begins the sentence that immediately follows his reference to the patriarchs, "and that is taken from their history: 'See that ye fall not out by the way,' and all will be exactly right in the end."

The Brown family moved back to Akron in March of 1851 after Simon Perkins made a personal visit to Springfield to request that Brown resume the management of his flock. Once the lawsuits were resolved and he had been able to put aside some money, Brown told his family, they would move back to North Elba. Twenty-two-year-old Ruth remained there. The previous fall she had married Henry Thompson, the eldest son of a large Adirondack farming family. Henry had promised to build a house for his in-laws on the land Brown had purchased from Gerrit Smith. It would be ready when they returned.

Seven male Browns comprised the bulk of the labor force on two of Simon Perkins's properties. Jason and Owen worked on a large farm in Tallmadge, a few miles to the east, while Frederick helped his father with the sheep and butchered the hogs on the Akron farm. Sixteen-year-old Watson, fifteen-year-old Salmon, and twelve-year-old Oliver tended the cows, calves, and crops. But Perkins's financial arrangement with Brown was less generous than it had been, and the family struggled to maintain the minimal trappings of respectability. Though old acquaintances and close relatives surrounded them in that part of the Reserve, they socialized little. "We don't like to ask people to visit us, we are living so poor," Mary once confided to a sister-in-law, while in January of 1852, Brown had to appeal to Ruth and Henry Thompson for the money to renew his subscription to *Frederick Douglass's Paper.* "You have been very kind in helping me," his letter concluded, "& I do not mean to make myself a burden."

The health of Brown's fourth son, and Dianthe's last child, Frederick, was another chronic family concern. Twenty-one in 1852, Frederick had suffered intermittently since his early teens from blinding headaches, fits of delirium, and episodes of compulsive behavior, most often an uncontrollable impulse to eat to the point of nausea. Boston physicians had attributed his condition to "an accumulation of blood on the brain" but offered little in the way of treatment. Between his poor turns, as his father called them, Frederick was as strong and lucid as any of the Brown children and participated fully in the family's occupations. Outdoor labor and simple, abstemious living, Brown believed, were Frederick's best protection against relapse. But he also tried to counter his son's excitability and tendency to depression by treating him more gently and less demandingly than the other boys. While he was still at Springfield, Brown had even delicately asked his father to do him the "particular favor" of approaching this grandson somewhat differently from Owen Brown's or his own custom. "Should my Frederick be with you any," Brown wrote to Owen, "be exceeding patient with him and get along by encouragement as much as possible."

At the end of April 1852, just as Frederick was recovering from another poor turn, Mary Brown bore her twelfth child, a dark-haired, dark-eyed son whom Brown described in a letter to Ruth and Henry as "the largest and strongest boy she ever had." Whooping cough had recently run its course in the Perkins family, and Brown's children contracted it. All recovered except the infant, who died in the third week of May. Brown had lost eight children before this unnamed son and had either openly grieved when they died or resignedly accepted God's will. This time he responded with barely suppressed fury. After completing the tiny coffin in the room where Mary still lay ill herself, he placed the infant's body in it, nailed the box shut, and carried it out to the yard, where he buried it without ceremony. Afterward, according to an appalled Mrs. Perkins, Brown drove his team of oxen over the grave, effacing all signs of it. Then he himself succumbed to an attack of fever and chills that debilitated him until late July.

If this episode marked a small, silent crisis in Brown's own faith, the crisis passed with his illness. When his fever had subsided, Brown wrote a series of letters to John Jr. and Ruth, again expressing his distress over the religious indifference of most of his adult and adolescent children. "My affections are too deep-rooted to be alienated from them," he assured, "but 'my gray hairs must go down in sorrow to the grave' unless the true God forgive their denial and rejection of him, and open their eyes."

In their departure from their father's living faith in God and hope of salvation in Christ, Brown's adolescent sons–Salmon, Watson, and Oliver–exceeded their older brothers. "After THOROUGH AND CANDID investigation," Brown wrote to John Jr. in bitter frustration, "they have discovered the Bible to be ALL a fiction!" To one degree or another, all the Brown boys rejected their father's scripture. Yet none failed to embrace the moral duty to resist slavery that he derived from it. Mary's sons succeeded Dianthe's as witnesses to the stealthy arrival of escaping slaves and auditors of the political conversations between their father and Frederick Douglass, who often stayed with the Browns when he lectured in Ohio. On starless nights, they sat beside Brown in the ox-drawn wagon, peering into the impenetrable foliage at the road's edge and listening to the rumble of the stacked furniture in the wagon bed and to the fast, shallow breathing of the negroes curled beneath it. The Browns transported fugitives from Kentucky into Ohio and from Ohio north into Michigan. Sometimes they carried them as far as Detroit, where an active and well-organized black abolitionist community arranged for their passage into Canada.

Among the leaders of this community was William Lambert, a tailor. Before he met Brown, Lambert had heard stories of the intense, inexhaustible Ohio farmer who had "brought hundreds of Negroes here in safety." Since some conductors had proved treacherous or counterfeit, however, Lambert and his colleagues had taken the precaution of devising an elaborate series of ritual signs and passwords into which only the most trusted white operators were initiated. One night in 1853, a sinewy white man, leading a party of twenty blacks, arrived at Lambert's station. The tailor surveyed him closely.

"Cross?" Lambert pronounced.

"Over," the man replied.

"Have you ever been on the Railroad?"

"I have been a short distance."

"Where did you start from?"

"The depot."

"Where did you stop?"

"At a place called Safety."

"Have you a brother there? I think I know him."

"I know you now. You traveled the road." The white man's face was impassive throughout this exchange, but his gray eyes gleamed as they met Lambert's.

The black man considered him a moment longer. "Are you John Brown, the John Brown I have heard about?" he asked. Before Brown could reply, he added, "You are. I know it, brother."

"Yes, brother, I am John Brown."

Senator Stephen A. Douglas of Illinois, one of the architects of the Compromise of 1850, believed in the manifest destiny of the United States to extend its domain of liberty and industry across North America. After his election to a second term in 1852, Douglas became the chairman of the Senate Committee on Territories, a position he planned to use to promote new opportunities for settlement and commerce—including the development of a transcontinental railroad—and to chart his own path to the presidency. Nicknamed the Little Giant for his combination of diminutive physical stature with prodigious charisma, Douglas had already helped bring about the territorial organization of the land ceded to the United States by Mexico at the end of the recent war. In 1853, he turned his attention to the northern reaches of the Louisiana Purchase, which Congress had yet to apportion.

These lands were the central plains of the continent, stretching west from Iowa and Missouri, and occupied only by Indians. Before the Mexican War and the California Gold Rush of the late 1840s, few Americans had even glimpsed the Nebraska and Kansas prairies. Those who had—traders in the Spanish southwest, soldiers assigned to remote frontier outposts, and missionaries—rarely intended to stay. As more wagons rumbled west along the Santa Fe and Oregon trails, however, over gentle rises carpeted with pale prairie flowers springing from the rich black loam, this fertile and beautiful country began to seem the next Promised Land. In December of 1853, Iowa Senator Augustus

Dodge submitted to Douglas's committee a bill to establish the territory and prospective state of Nebraska. Douglas promptly endorsed the proposal, remarking in a speech three days later, "The tide of emigration and civilization must be permitted to roll onward." But the Little Giant soon received a visit from Missouri Senator David Atchison, President of the Senate, who reminded his Illinois colleague that the fate of the Nebraska bill rested in the hands of the powerful southern voting bloc.

Aside from the flamboyance and ambition they shared, Atchison and Douglas made an odd couple. Standing six feet two inches tall and weighing two hundred pounds, the Kentucky-born Atchison cultivated an image of a tough-talking, hard-drinking, backslapping frontiersman. "Old Bourbon" to his friends, Atchison saw himself as a man of the people and understood that his people were slaveholders. Southerners had no more wish than other Americans to stem the westward tide of emigration and civilization, Atchison pointed out. What they objected to and would no longer abide was unfair restriction on their freedom of movement and legal property rights. If the Nebraska bill were passed under the current law, an Iowa farmer could stake a claim, move due west, and freely resettle in the new territory, bringing his entire family and all his property with him. But Atchison's slaveholding Missouri constituents could not, for the Nebraska territory lay north of the 36° 30' latitude established by the Missouri Compromise of 1820 as the northernmost boundary of future slaveholding states. That territory, Old Bourbon threatened, either would be opened to everyone or to no one.

Southerners had failed three years before to extend slavery to the new state of California. But the Compromise of 1850 did give them a legal and philosophical basis for the demands they now made that further territorial expansion involve the repeal of geographical restrictions on slavery. The 1850 legislation had organized the territories of New Mexico and Utah but had not prejudged the legality of slavery there, leaving it for future settlers of those regions to decide. Thus, Atchison and his supporters argued, the principle of popular sovereignty on the slavery question had been established in federal law. The residents of each newly formed territory should be able to vote on whether or not to include negroes among the legal and protected classes of private property in their state. What could be more democratic, more American, than that?

By late January of 1854, Douglas and Atchison had agreed on a substitute version of the Nebraska bill and taken it to President Pierce for his endorsement. Less than a year into his term, Franklin Pierce was a weak, southern-sympathizing New Hampshire Democrat, a compromise candidate who had been nominated on the thirty-fifth ballot of his party's deadlocked 1852 convention. Though fearful that the explicit repeal of the Missouri Compromise would unleash a new political tempest just as agitation over the Fugitive Slave Law was beginning to subside, Pierce bowed to the senators' pressure. The Kansas-Nebraska Act put forth by Douglas on January 23 divided the new territory into a northern and a southern portion: Nebraska would stretch westward from Iowa, and below it Kansas would share a border with Missouri. Most important, the bill stipulated that "all questions pertaining to Slavery in the territories and in the new States to be formed, are to be left to the decision of the people residing therein, through their appropriate representatives."

The Kansas-Nebraska Act–also known as the Squatter Sovereignty Act and the Organic Law of the territories–passed by a 37 to 14 margin in the Senate and a much narrower 113 to 100 vote in the House, where the populous northeastern states were more heavily represented. When President Pierce signed the bill into law on May 30, 1854, slaveholders and their advocates hailed the event as a momentous moral and practical victory. Slavery was no longer either stigmatized or contained by federal statute. The west was open to any political interest enterprising enough to place its supporters and impose its will there.

Southerners assumed that natural patterns of migration would result in Nebraska's settlement by northerners, who would doubtless prohibit slavery. Kansas, however, they considered their own. Missouri's planters and politicians especially were intent on establishing slavery in Kansas. Missourians owned eighty-seven thousand slaves in 1854, almost fifty million dollars' worth. But theirs was a border state, hemmed in, its leaders felt, by northerners hostile to their economy and way of life. Illinois lay to the east, Iowa to the north. If another free state were established on their western frontier, Missourians would be surrounded by abolitionists tempting their slaves to escape or encouraging them to murder their masters in their beds.

Determined not to let this happen, proslavery Missourians began to organize even before the Kansas-Nebraska Act was passed. Squatters' associations formed in the hemp- and tobacco-growing counties of western Missouri, Senator Atchison's political base. And throughout the spring of 1854, as the federal government forced treaties on the Otoes, the Delawares, the Kickapoos, the Shawnees, the Sacs, the Foxes, and the other tribes of the plains, moving them further west, Missouri residents crossed into Kansas Territory to claim new land for themselves and for slavery. Kansas's soil invited plantations and its climate was "peculiarly healthy to the negro," claimed B. F. Stringfellow, one of the leaders of the campaign. "Nature intended it for a slaveholding State."

Eli Thayer, an ambitious young Massachusetts entrepreneur, had a different idea. What if prominent northern capitalists were to form a corporation and invest large sums of money to develop Kansas? The money would not be used to buy land alone but actually to build towns, to seed a free commercial economy, and to transport and equip emigrants from the northeast to inhabit those towns and drive that economy. Here was a way to populate the territory with ready-made communities of antislavery settlers whose ever increasing numbers would both secure Kansas for freedom, under the terms of the Organic Law, and enhance the value of the corporation's land and commercial holdings there. Investors throughout the north purchased stock in Thayer's New England Emigrant Aid Company, which enlisted the services of Amos Lawrence, heir to the Lawrence family textile and railroad fortune, as its treasurer. Soon the first party of corporation-sponsored settlers was en route to Kansas, where they pitched tents on land that company funds and machinery would shortly transform into the bustling town of Lawrence, furnished with an array of shops and businesses, two newspapers, and a four-story stone building to which was assigned the provocative name The Free State Hotel.

After failing to block the Kansas-Nebraska Act's repeal of the Missouri Compromise, antislavery congressional leaders jumped on Thayer's bandwagon. Political and business interests throughout the north collaborated in establishing aid societies to assist citizens who were willing to emigrate to Kansas. Rallies were held and handbills posted, advertising for men ready to enlarge their prospects in the world and serve the nation at the same time by advancing the cause of free labor on the frontier. The north had a larger and more mobile population than the south, one swelled by the arrival of fresh land-hungry immigrants every day. It had more disposable capital to supply Kansas settlers with sawmills and other essential equipment for building new permanent communities. Even northern racism was a resource that could be tapped to motivate emigration. Under the terms of squatter sovereignty, a free white majority could vote to exclude from their state not only slaves but all negroes. If slavery's future in Kansas was to be staked on which region could establish its partisans there more quickly and in greater number, the north would play to win. "Come on, then, gentlemen of the slave states!" New York Senator William Seward goaded his southern colleagues. "Since there is no escaping your challenge, I accept it on the behalf of Freedom. We will engage in competition for the virgin soil of Kansas, and God give the victory to the side that is stronger in numbers, as it is in right."

At Simon Perkins's request, Brown continued to work for him throughout 1853. Early in 1854, the men finally agreed to conclude their business relations. The parting was amicable, and John Jr. was summoned to help settle accounts. His father was eager to move back to North Elba but was unable to sell his share of the previous year's harvest of wool and crops at high enough prices to finance an immediate departure. Realizing that he would miss the spring planting season, he decided to rent a small property in Akron and wait until 1855 to return to the Adirondacks. An extended visit from Ruth and her husband, Henry, reunited the entire Brown family for the first time in many years and somewhat eased Brown's longing for the mountains. With all his children near him, he was more conscious than ever how much time he had spent apart from them. North Elba, he thought, was the place for the family to start again, a place where there would be land and work for all of them. He hinted at this idea in a letter to John Jr. "I would like to have all my children settle within a few miles of each other and of me," Brown wrote, "but I cannot take the responsibility of advising you to make any *forced* move to change your location. Thousands have to regret that they did not let middling well alone."

The weather in Ohio that spring and summer seemed to conspire in Brown's plan to resettle his whole family in New York State. Day after day of scorching heat and no rain produced a devastating drought. Jason's ironic name for his small farm, The Rock, had never been more descriptive. Owen and Frederick, who had left Perkins's employ along with their father, had nothing to keep them in Akron. But the time had come for Brown's four eldest sons to make a plan of their own. It was John Jr. who proposed one to his brothers: Kansas. He had attended a lecture about the recently opened territory and returned with a pocketful of handbills. "The Climate is mild; atmosphere dry, the prairie winds tempering the intensity of the summer heat. Very little snow—no use for sleighs," they advertised. Horses, cattle, and mules were in short supply and fetched a premium, and 160-acre claims, once occupied and surveyed, were available for purchase at $1.25 per acre.

The decision was unanimous. Owen and Frederick would leave in the fall and travel overland, driving all the brothers' livestock. Seventeen-year-old Salmon, larger and bolder than Mary's eldest son, Watson, a year his senior, resolved to emigrate with his half brothers. John Jr. and Jason would sell their Ohio farms and follow in the spring with their wives and young children, traveling by steamer down the Ohio to Cairo, Illinois, then up the Mississippi to St. Louis and west on the Missouri to Kansas.

John Jr. invited his father to join them, suggesting that the entire family emigrate together. There was cheaper land, better soil, and a more temperate climate in Kansas than in North Elba, he argued. And they would not be forsaking the slaves by going. Helping to thwart the designs of the slave power on the new territory would do more for blacks in the long run than whatever comfort the Browns could give the ragged remnant of the Timbucto settlers by sharing their struggle for subsistence. Brown was uncertain. What of his hope to gather black recruits for the series of emancipation raids on southern plantations? What of his obligation to his black neighbors in North Elba?

In September of 1854, as Owen, Frederick, and Salmon prepared to depart, Brown dashed off letters to Gerrit Smith and Frederick Douglass, seeking their advice. He also wrote to Ruth and Henry in North Elba to ask what they wished him to do and to request that they find out how Lyman Epps and some of the other black farmers felt about the matter. "As I volunteered in their service," he reasoned, "they have a right to vote, as to the course I take." Douglass thought he should return to New York. Ruth hoped to have at least part of her family living near her, in the house that Henry had already begun to build for them. Divided in his sentiments, Brown at last bade his sons godspeed in Kansas but told them he would not be joining them there. In November, the three unmarried boys set out with eleven cows and three horses, including several animals that their father had given them, out of his settlement with Mr. Perkins, to increase their western herd.

That same month, Andrew Reeder, a proslavery Pennsylvania Democrat whom President Pierce had selected as governor of Kansas Territory, called the first territorial election. All voting-age white male residents were eligible to elect Kansas's delegate to Congress, the official who would represent the Territory's interests and ultimately present its petition for statehood in Washington. For the purposes of this election, Reeder announced, residency would be defined as "the actual dwelling or inhabiting in the Territory to the exclusion of any other present domicile or home, coupled with the present *bona fide* intention of remaining permanently for the same purpose." Though, in late 1854, legitimate settlers from Missouri outnumbered those who had emigrated from more distant states, proslavery leaders knew that many of these Missouri expatriates could not be counted on to support the Southern Rights candidate, J. W. Whitfield. The result of this ballot, they determined, was too important to leave to chance.

For months, these leaders had been taking steps to ensure that squatter sovereignty in Kansas would result in a slaveholding state. B. F. Stringfellow established one of many vigilante organizations dedicated to policing acceptable attitudes toward slavery in Missouri and to dissuading antislavery emigrants passing through the state from entering Kansas. Strangers in Missouri quickly learned to dread the question, Where are you from? Even if they lied, northerners' accents generally gave them away, leading to such episodes as the detaining of a Massachusetts emigrant on the charge of abolitionism, for which the man was publicly tried, sentenced to twenty-four lashes, whipped, and deposited on the Iowa border. Despite open threats and widespread harassment, people continued to flock to Kansas from the east.

"We will have difficulty with the Negro Heroes in Kansas," wrote Senator Atchison, two months before the delegate election, to the most powerful member of the president's cabinet, Secretary of War Jefferson Davis. "They are resolved to keep the Slave holder out, and our people are resolved to go in and take their 'Niggers' with them." Boasting to

Davis about the "almost universal applause" he had received for a speech in which he urged his fellow Missourians "to hang a Negro thief and Abolitionist without judge or jury," Old Bourbon predicted, "We will before six months rolls round have the Devil to pay in Kansas and in this State. We are organizing to meet their organization. We will be compelled to shoot, burn, & hang, but the thing will soon be over." Stringfellow's rhetoric outdid his mentor's. "I tell you to mark every scoundrel among you who is in the least tainted with abolitionism or free-soilism, and exterminate him," he told an audience at a rally in St. Joseph, Missouri, a river town on the Kansas border. Speaking on the eve of the Kansas balloting, Stringfellow, a lawyer, also had counsel for those who preferred to work through the political process. "I advise you, one and all, to enter every election district in Kansas," he thundered, "and vote at the point of the bowie knife and revolver."

On election day, November 29, 1854, more than seventeen hundred Missourians answered Stringfellow's call. Descending on the Kansas polling places, they terrorized and dismissed dutiful election officials, commandeered and stuffed ballot boxes, and prevented anyone suspected of free soil sentiments from voting. The proslavery candidate received 2,258 votes, almost ten times the number of his nearest competitor. Only Lawrence failed to deliver a Southern Rights majority. Though the blatant fraud and intimidation disgusted Governor Reeder, he certified the election result. Whitfield was likely to have won even without all the ineligible votes cast for him, the governor argued. Besides, the delegate to Congress would have little to do with the determination of Kansas's legal code and the character of its eventual state constitution. The responsibility for drafting those documents would fall to the territorial legislators from each district, who would be chosen at a new and more carefully monitored election the following spring.

In the meantime, more determined antislavery emigrants–Negro Heroes, in Senator Atchison's words–were on their way. With two brothers on horseback herding the cattle and the third driving the covered wagon, Owen, Frederick, and Salmon Brown reached Meredosia, in western Illinois, by December and spent the winter with the older boys' maternal uncle, Edward Lusk. In March of 1855, they resumed their trek, crossing the Mississippi above Hannibal and there entering Missouri. John Brown's younger half sister, Florilla, and her husband, Reverend Samuel Adair, had preceded them to Kansas to work as missionaries among the Indians. The Adairs settled at a place called Osawatomie, where Pottawatomie Creek flows into the Osage River, thirty-five miles southeast of Lawrence. The three Brown boys decided to stake claims nearby for themselves and for John Jr. and Jason, who were to meet them in late April or early May.

At Rochester, Pennsylvania, south of Pittsburgh on the Ohio River, the families of John Brown's two oldest sons embarked on the first of the three-legged river journey that would take them to Kansas. Wealthy and Ellen Brown warned their small boys, Johnny and Austin, to keep close by and stay out from under the feet of other passengers on the steamer's deck. Ellen, Jason's wife, also had an infant to look after. It was a relief to her that four-year-old Austin had his cousin to keep him occupied. Aside from their clothes and a few household items and family mementos of Wealthy's and Ellen's, the Browns' only freight consisted of the two men's prize possessions. John Jr. had crated his library, now numbering three hundred volumes. He had sent the bulk of the collection ahead to his Uncle Adair but kept one case full of his favorites near him. Jason had selected the hardiest of his fruit trees and grapevines and planted seedlings and cuttings in boxes. By careful transport and nurture, he hoped to preserve these samples—the beginnings of his Kansas orchard—for transplantation on his new farm.

As John Brown's five sons made their way west, five thousand armed Missourians, along with scattered bands of mercenaries organized and financed in other southern states, gathered on the Kansas border, poised to cross into the Territory to guarantee the election of a proslavery Kansas legislature. In February, Governor Reeder had conducted a territorial census that had set the number of eligible Kansas voters at 2,905. Three election officials were stationed at each polling place for the March 30 balloting with lists of the names of bona fide residents and instructions to administer a residency oath to each prospective voter. Anyone who refused to take the oath or whom they judged ineligible was to be denied a ballot. And no ballot box would be counted without an accompanying affidavit signed by the election monitors certifying that it contained only the votes of sworn and legal residents. Antislavery Kansans, who by now were a clear majority in a number of districts and probably in the Territory at large, organized for the March election, as they had not for the delegate election the previous November, and rallied behind clearly identified Free State candidates. None of these preparations made a difference.

The March vote was a repeat of the November one, except that the fraud was more massive and the intimidation more violent. On the night of the 29th, many election judges received visits at their homes from posses of drunken border ruffians, as the proslavery vigilantes had come to be known, informing them that they would be hung if they appeared for duty in the morning. Replacement officials for those who stayed away were elected by acclamation of the Missourians. In one district, the authorized election monitors barricaded the log cabin that served as a polling place to keep the invaders from stuffing the ballot box. The proslavery mob smashed the windows and began to dismantle the structure. Its leader, Samuel Jones, postmaster of Westport, Missouri, consulted his watch and told the officials that in exactly five minutes they would either have resigned and vacated the premises or be dead. Anti-slavery residents who tried to vote and candidates who vowed to protest the results were dissuaded by similar threats. At the end of the day, the winning proslavery candidates—many of whom lived in Missouri themselves—had received a total of 5,427 votes; 791 votes were cast for antislavery nominees. In the Free State stronghold of Lawrence, proslavery votes prevailed by a margin of three to one. A subsequent U.S. Senate investigation would conclude that only 1,310 votes had been legal out of the more than six thousand that were cast.

Free State partisans and election officials whose work the Missourians had obstructed flooded Governor Reeder's office with petitions demanding that he set aside the election results. Proslavery militants warned him that it would be unhealthy to do so. Reeder certified the votes in thirty-three of thirty-nine districts and called for new elections in May in the six whose results he overturned. The May balloting produced antislavery winners in five of these six contested districts, but when the bogus legislature, as it was popularly dubbed, met in July in the proslavery capital of Lecompton, its Southern Rights majority expelled them. The legislature then proceeded to enact what one of its members, writing in an Alabama newspaper, heralded as "laws more efficient to protect slave-property than any State in the Union." Any person who spoke, wrote, or acted in such a manner as aided or encouraged a slave to escape or rebel was guilty of a felony punishable by death. Any person who spoke, wrote, broadcast, or circulated opinions that might produce disorder or disaffection among the slaves in the Territory was guilty of a felony punishable by five years at hard labor. No person who held antislavery sentiments was eligible to serve on a jury in Kansas.

Reeder, who had wrangled with the new legislature over its procedures and its venue, was visiting his home in Easton, Pennsylvania, when this territorial slave code was passed. While there, he gave a speech in which he vented his frustration. "Kansas has been invaded by an organized army, armed to the teeth, who took possession of the ballot-boxes and made a legislature to suit themselves," the territorial governor pronounced.

In August, President Pierce dismissed him.

The recent election in Kansas and the protests of northern meddlers and Lawrence abolitionists dominated conversation in St. Louis when John Jr. and Jason arrived there with their families in April. Purchasing two small tents, a plough, some farming implements, and a hand-mill for grinding corn, the families loaded these items, along with their other possessions, onto the *New Lucy* for the three-hundred-mile steamer trip across the state. The water level was dangerously low at various points along the Missouri that season, making navigation difficult and dangerous. But the Browns could not afford stagecoach passage.

There had been cholera in St. Louis, and midway along the river several of the passengers began to fall ill. Young Austin Brown was stricken and, despite the family's efforts, rapidly grew feverish, became dehydrated, and died. The breaking of a rudder in low water near Waverly, seventy-five miles from the Kansas border, came almost as a relief to the panicked throng aboard the *New Lucy*. The passengers disembarked, the Browns to make arrangements to bury Austin in the town cemetery. It would be the next day before the rudder was fixed, and the captain promised to send notice to everyone of the steamer's departure time. John Jr. and Jason buried Austin that night by the light of a violent thunderstorm. A farmer whose land adjoined the dilapidated graveyard took pity on the drenched emigrants and offered them shelter in an upper room of his storehouse. Early the next morning, a slave brought the Browns bread and coffee. When they walked out to the steamboat landing shortly afterward, the *New Lucy* was gone.

Nearly prostrate with grief, Jason and Ellen allowed John Jr. and Wealthy to guide them to a stage depot, where the families used most of their remaining funds to pay for transport to Kansas by land. The stagecoach stopped along the way at several farmhouses, where the driver took his meals. At each, the Browns attempted to buy food, but when they spoke, the proprietors' expressions hardened. "We have nothing for you," they were told.

In early May, they at last reached Kansas Territory. Its rolling plains, dotted with milky wildflowers beneath an immense blue dome of sky, held comfort and hope for them after their bitter voyage. Even Jason and Ellen's deep gloom on account of their son's death and wilderness burial seemed lightened at moments by contemplation of this welcoming land. Recalling their first sight of Kansas, John Jr. wrote: "Her lovely prairies and wooded streams seemed to us indeed like a haven of rest." Rest, however, was not an immediate option. After a warm reunion with Owen, Fred, and Salmon and an approving survey of their five adjacent tracts northwest of Osawatomie, the Browns went to work. They pitched tents, dug trenches, constructed a makeshift corral for the cattle, and planned for the more permanent structures that would follow. They plowed ten acres for corn and another for garden vegetables: peas, squash, beans, cabbages, onions, lettuce, cucumbers, sweet potatoes, turnips, and water and musk melons.

At dusk, a few days after their arrival, they heard the clatter of horses' hooves. A party of Missourians, heavily armed, approached the Browns' cluster of tents. Its leader, the proslavery minister and militant, Reverend Martin White, claimed to be looking for stray cattle. But what he seemed more interested in discovering was whether these new settlers were "sound on the goose." In the southern idiom of the day, to be sound on the goose was to be right-thinking or sound on the slavery question—in other words, solidly proslavery. As the eldest brother and leader of the family in Kansas, John Jr. looked up and answered White with placid, combative, and reckless honesty. "We are Free State," he said, "and more than that, we are abolitionists."

Describing this first Brown family encounter with proslavery forces in Kansas, Jason recalled, "They rode away at once, and from that moment we were marked for destruction."

In Lawrence, Dr. Charles Robinson, agent for the New England Emigrant Aid Company, was leading the campaign against the border ruffians and the bogus legislature they had installed. A formal request for congressional intervention had been sent to Washington, and there was talk of holding new, unauthorized elections for a competing Free State territorial legislature, demanding that it be recognized as the true representative of the people of Kansas. Within two weeks of his arrival in the Territory, John Jr. met the antislavery leaders in Lawrence and judged that their talk and their organizing alone would not make Kansas free. The Pierce administration and the Senate were in the pocket of the southern bloc. Moreover, most of the new settlers who opposed slavery wanted only to be left alone. They were not abolitionists. They favored a free state only because they preferred neither to compete with slave labor nor to live near negroes. If staying on their claims in Kansas meant unending harassment by the hired Missourians, they would soon go elsewhere or make their peace with slavery. Even those who might be willing to put up a real fight had no means to do so. The Browns were better armed than most, though they possessed among them only two squirrel rifles, one old revolver, a useless little pocket pistol, and a single bowie knife.

On May 20, 1855, John Jr. sat in a tent on the family claim that he had christened Brown's Station and began to compose a long letter to his father. He wrote of Austin's death and Jason's and Ellen's continuing depression. He described the prairie, billowing in every direction "in vast, gently rounded waves, as though the Ocean once were here, and before retiring had taken pains to smooth her bed that not a rough spot might be seen." He observed that the land's capacity to support prosperity and health "much exceeds even my most sanguine expectations." Yet for all its promise, Kansas, he feared, was doomed without prompt, radical action on the part of its antislavery inhabitants.

"I tell you the truth," John Jr. wrote, "when I say that while the interest of despotism has secured to its cause hundreds and thousands of the meanest and most desperate of men, armed to the teeth with Revolvers, Bowie Knives, Rifles & Cannon—while they are not only thoroughly organized, but under pay from Slaveholders—the friends of freedom are not one fourth of them half armed, and as to Military Organization among them it nowhere exists in this territory." Not satisfied with their victory in the bogus election, the Missourians were said to be

John Brown never owned property or built a house for himself in Kansas, but sometimes stayed with his sister Florilla and brother-in-law Reverend Samuel Adair in their cabin in Osawatomie. (WEST VIRGINIA STATE ARCHIVES)

organizing a large militia "whose purpose is to drive out from the Territory every Anti slavery man they can find in it" and to do it "*now* while they can nip their opponents in the bud as it respects numbers and strength." The only remedy was for antislavery men to acquire arms, organize into military companies, and prove to themselves, to their assailants, and to the country that they were not the cowards the southerners took them for.

What Kansas lacked was a militant, equipped antislavery vanguard capable of shaming and rousing the "abject and cowardly spirit" of the Free State majority and offering righteous resistance to the Missourians as an alternative to fear. John Jr. and his brothers were ready to assume that role. "Here are 5 men of us who are not only anxious to fully prepare, but are thoroughly determined to fight." What they needed from their father was for him to persuade Gerrit Smith or another wealthy friend in the east to give or loan them money for the purchase of high-quality weapons for Kansas's defense–large Colt revolvers, the accurate, rapid-fire Sharps rifle, the long-range Minnie rifle.

"We need them," John Jr. wrote, "more than we do bread."

When his son's letter was posted, John Brown was in northern Illinois, looking to sell his remaining cattle profitably enough to finance his resettlement in North Elba with those of his family who had not gone west. The opening of Rockford's spring market was delayed, and there was little for Brown to do but wait and brood, for the headlines in the Ohio and Illinois papers screamed of the slave power's theft of Kansas and of the weak submission of Free State men. Writing to his sons in care of Samuel Adair, he equivocated about his decision to return to North Elba, worrying about how Free State settlers in Kansas were to get their land properly surveyed to protect it against Missouri claim-jumpers. Clearly, southern-sympathizing government surveyors could not be trusted to do an honest job of it. Yet the pull of North Elba remained strong, and in early June, Brown, Mary, and their children–all except Salmon in Kansas and Oliver, who had hired out for summer farmwork in Rockford–began the long trek from Akron to upstate New York.

Upon their arrival in North Elba late that month, Henry Thompson pulled his father-in-law aside. A letter had arrived for him, he said. It was John Jr.'s call to arms. And it was a month old.

Mary Brown had long known that when it was time for her husband to do his duty for the slaves, she must be ready to let him go. And she was. She had been letting him go throughout the twenty-two years of their marriage, often joining him later in the places he had gone first without her. She had moved with him eleven times and lived without him for months on end. But these were not the experiences that prepared her to bow her head in assent and say only, "God bless you there, and keep you well," when Brown showed her the letter from Kansas and said he would leave within the week. Mary had always been prepared to let him go, since she had never really thought of herself as having him in the first place. She had been a large, ordinary girl of sixteen, whose schooling was minimal and whose family and prospects were poor, when Rich-

The three eldest sons of Brown's first wife Dianthe–John Jr. (top left), Jason in old age (top right), and Owen (bottom left) and Mary's second son Salmon (bottom right) fought beside Brown in Kansas and all survived him. (JOHN JR, JASON & OWEN—— *L. OF C.*, SALMON—— *WVSA*)

mond's tanner and postmaster approached her as she sat at the spinning wheel in his house. He had rested one hand on her shoulder while with the other he dropped a letter into her lap, the first she had ever received addressed to herself alone. The hand on her shoulder had been gentle, but long after he had gone back to his work, his fingers seemed to grip her flesh there. It was the grip she would later know, lying beneath him, on nights when he was filled with hope or with doubt and upon his returns from selling wool, freeing negroes, contesting lawsuits. He held her, and she watched him, and held to that vision.

Over time, she had come to see him more clearly and critically. She saw his inconsistencies and his excesses. How he bathed his family in his regard, only to seem to forget them entirely for weeks at a time when a new project absorbed him, resuming his attentions afterward without hesitation or remark, as though they had strayed for no more than a moment. How he mustered meticulous rational arguments for each venture he pursued or action he took, concealing from himself how often these decisions were driven by impulse. How he turned the boys away from prayer and worship by imploring them at every turn to find God rather than allowing them to seek him in their own way. How he nursed his wife and children tenderly and expertly when they were too ill to leave their beds, then expected of them—as he did of himself—a level of energy and resiliency that they often fell ill again trying to demonstrate.

Once, she had left him. It was six years ago, just after their first move to North Elba. She was sick, but Brown had taken little notice, throwing himself into the affairs of the negro settlers at Timbucto and then departing just as abruptly to take his wool to England. The sick headaches, swollen glands, and digestive troubles that had plagued Mary in Springfield only worsened in the lonely Adirondack woods, and Mary had told her husband that she thought Dr. Ruggles's hydrotherapy clinic back in Northampton, Massachusetts, might help her. Brown had dismissed the idea. He did not believe in such newfangled medicine, even when administered by a fearless black Railroad conductor, antislavery pamphleteer, and self-educated physician whom he knew and admired. But as soon as Brown had gone, Mary disobeyed his wishes, left the children in Ruth's care, and journeyed to the Water Cure establishment. For three months, a period that extended several

Mary Anne Day married the widower John Brown in 1833, when she was seventeen. Mary Brown bore thirteen children between 1834 and 1854, seven of whom died in childhood of illness or accident and two of whom were killed at Harpers Ferry.
(WEST VIRGINIA STATE ARCHIVES)

weeks beyond her husband's return, she stayed, following Dr. Ruggles's hydrotherapy and diet regimen and walking the clinic's grounds in the company of distinguished women abolitionists such as Lucy Stone and Sojourner Truth. In her conversations with these women, Mary Brown often found herself voicing her husband's thoughts and expressions. The sensation was a pleasant one.

For all the children she had borne him, it was his words, more than his arms, that held her. In words that had once been foreign to her, John Brown had given her a better home than any of the houses in which they had lived. The words were grand and spacious, and she shared them, though they were often addressed to purposes that took him from her. At other times, though, his words were directed to her alone. When his letters arrived, addressed "Dear Wife and Children, All," Mary would read them first, scanning the general news and instructions they contained. Then with her sewing scissors, she would cut out the lines in which he spoke particularly to her, placing these fragments in a box of her own things before relinquishing the rest of the letter to the family. The words and her children were enough.

On June 26, Brown traveled to Syracuse, where Gerrit Smith was presiding at the first convention of an interracial political party, the Radical Abolitionists. Delegates wept as Brown read John Jr.'s letter aloud; sixty dollars was raised to arm the Browns in Kansas. Brown went on to Springfield to buy guns and solicit more donations. Returning to North Elba in early July, he instructed eighteen-year-old Watson to manage the new farm and care for his mother and three young sisters: eleven-year-old Annie, eight-year-old Sarah, and nine-month-old Ellen, to whom the Browns had given the name of the baby that died in Springfield six years before. The neighboring Thompson boys, Ruth's brothers-in-law, would lend a hand, and Douglass, who had been at the Syracuse convention, had offered to send provisions if the family should find themselves in need when winter set in. After making these minimal arrangements for his family's care, Brown walked over to the house where Ruth and Henry lived with their first child and asked his daughter if he could take her husband with him.

Ruth held a special place in Brown's affections. She was his first daughter, his living reminder of Dianthe. Alone among his older children, moreover, the spirit of religion was strong in her. For her part, Ruth adored her father. It had been his complete and immediate forgiveness, his loving acceptance of her in the grief they shared, that permitted Ruth to overcome her guilt for Amelia's death. Without that, she could not have let herself fall in love with Henry when she met him less than three years later. For Henry Thompson, a serious young farmer of twenty-seven, the arrival of the Browns in North Elba in 1849 brought him not only Ruth, his wife, but an image of a life more purposeful and a faith more alive than any he had encountered before. Henry and his father-in-law quickly adopted one another as father and son. If it was the duty of the Browns to sacrifice, it was the duty of Henry Thompson as well.

The leave-taking was emotional. Only Ellen was too young to understand that, this time, Brown was going to war.

Brown and Henry stopped at Hudson on their way west, visiting the elderly Owen Brown and canvassing antislavery friends in Ohio for additional funds and weapons. They met Oliver in Chicago, where they purchased a sturdy young horse for $120 and a wagon in which they placed their boxes of rifles, revolvers, and knives, covering them with Brown's surveying instruments and some innocent household furnishings. The three men made their way overland through Iowa, living sparsely on crackers, herring, and boiled eggs. At dawn, they shot prairie chickens for their breakfast. Brown's plan was to cross into north central Missouri and make their way down to the river near Waverly, where they would find the village cemetery and exhume Austin's body. No Brown should be laid to rest in the soil of a slave state. It would comfort Jason and Ellen as well, Brown thought, to have their boy near them.

At Brunswick, on the north bank of the Missouri, they stopped to wait for the ferry that would take them across the river to the place where Austin was buried. The town, the first they had entered in Missouri, was dirty and disorganized. Its most conspicuous building turned out, upon inspection, to be a slave pen. As the Browns waited with their wagon at the dock, they drew the attention of a local resident, an old man who wandered down to get a closer look at them.

"Where are you going?" the man asked them.

"Kansas," Brown answered.

"Where are you from?"

"New York."

The Missourian assessed the three travelers in turn, then genially observed, "You won't live to get there."

Brown met his gaze and overpowered it. "We are prepared," he replied, "not to die alone."

CHAPTER EIGHT

Blood and Remission

> *"I never had much doubt that Captain Brown was the author of the blow at Pottawatomie, for the reason that he was the only man who comprehended the situation and saw the absolute necessity of some such blow, and had the nerve to strike it."*
> –Charles Robinson, first governor of the state of Kansas

SIX WEEKS AFTER LEAVING CHICAGO, John Brown, Oliver Brown, and Henry Thompson entered Kansas Territory with a wagonload of arms. Battling a frigid autumn wind, they reached the family claim near Osawatomie on the morning of October 7. None was prepared for what they found.

In May, John Jr. had calculated that the family could live comfortably enough in tents until autumn. It was more important for the brothers to devote themselves to planting, growing, and harvesting sizable crops, thereby storing food for the winter, he had argued, rather than waste the summer building cabins, which they could do in October after the crops were in. Unseasonable cold, however, had spoiled much of the harvest, and as the Browns began to gather what remained they fell victim to a flu epidemic that had spread throughout the Territory. Soon they were too weak even to tend the garden or to round up the livestock, which wandered free and ate the half-grown corn. For the last month, the family had survived on dried apples, boiled potatoes, and thin johnnycakes.

This, then, was the sight that greeted John Brown that morning in October 1855: his five sons burning with fever on beds of soiled prairie grass in tents pitched in a muddy ravine, exposed to the slicing wind.

Taking charge, Brown dispatched Oliver to replenish the supply of firewood. Working around the prostrate bodies of his feverish older boys, he and Henry removed as much of their old bedding as they could, replacing it with what little fresh dry hay was available and with clean blankets from the bundles of supplies in the wagon. From the wagon, too, Brown took down the remaining jars of herring that had been a staple for Oliver, Henry, and himself en route, along with containers of tea and the cured pork and cornmeal that Salmon had asked him to bring to help tide the family over until the crops the brothers had planted that spring and summer were harvested. With the fires roaring again, Oliver and Henry scoured the cleared fields for any squash, beans, or pumpkins that the animals and the elements might have spared, while Brown prepared meat and corn mush and quantities of hot tea.

By evening, the beginnings of order had been restored. In the fading light, Brown took a shovel and climbed a little rise near the tents, accompanied by Oliver, Henry, and John Jr.'s wife and little boy, the only inhabitants of Brown's Station who had remained healthy. Heads bowed, the Browns stood close together as Austin's body was reinterred beneath a stand of cottonwood trees and the steady monotone of his grandfather's voice in prayer.

After Brown's patients had drifted off to sleep, Henry and Oliver helped him unload their own tent from the wagon and pitch it in the dark. Into it, the three men brought the other supplies they had carried across the Illinois and Missouri plains: extra clothing for Owen, an iron stove, Brown's surveying instruments, and the bulk of their cargo—the unmarked cases of rifles, revolvers, and ammunition. There was one other heavy, odd-sized crate that the men lifted off the wagon bed, carried inside, and covered with a blanket. Given to Brown in Akron by a retired military officer, Lucius V. Bierce, the crate was filled with short, thick army surplus broadswords, each emblazoned with an ornamental eagle on its blade. Hollow, and loaded with quicksilver that slid from the hilt to the point to increase the force of the blow when the upraised weapon was swung, these unwieldy but deadly swords were designed not to thrust but to slash and bludgeon.

Alternating shifts with Wealthy and the recovering Ellen, Brown nursed his sick sons. After a few days, and racing against the imminent full winter, he turned his attention to the construction of housing for the families of Jason and John Jr. Though both Oliver and Henry also fell ill and could offer little assistance, Brown succeeded in building two crude but functional wooden shelters. Salmon, who had almost died of bilious colic, was the first son to regain his health and helped his father with the hauling and the masonry required to outfit one of the cabins with a working hearth and chimney. At last, wrote Ellen Brown to her mother-in-law back in North Elba, "I can cook a meal without smoking my eyes almost out of my head." Brown also wrote regularly to Mary, commiserating with her about the upcoming winter that she would face without him "in that miserable Frosty region" where he had left her, but also reporting that on October 25 there had been as hard a freeze in Kansas as he had ever encountered anywhere. "Those here," Brown ironically ventured, "are not altogether in paradise."

His levity did not disguise or dissipate his guilt. Brown had traveled far from home before, leaving Mary and the children for weeks or months at a time. But his motive had been the conventional and socially irreproachable one of financial necessity or opportunity. The intention, if not the outcome, of these previous separations–the cattle drives and sheep-buying circuits, the quests for business loans, the establishment of the Springfield wool cooperative, the trip to Europe, the attendance of interminable trials in scattered American jurisdictions–had always been to provide for his family or to protect it. In each case, too, he could reasonably expect to return soon, and, with God's mercy, healthily, or to send for his dependents to join him. This time, their reunion could not be predicted and would be long in coming, if it came at all. He had left his wife and daughters isolated and unprovided for in a place they scarcely knew, left them in an unfinished house in a region whose winters were devastating. He had left Mary the comfort and labor of only one of her three boys, and none of his older sons. And he had left her and the girls by choice, choosing the interests of anonymous millions before those of his family.

But he could not have chosen otherwise. The hardships experienced by Mary and the girls surely paled beside the unmerited sufferings and strangled aspirations of the poorest and most cruelly despised of God's children. Who could compare his family's–or any white family's–destitution of comfort with the slave's destitution of freedom, of hope, even of family itself? Who could reserve his compassion for his own intimates alone, hardening his heart against the multitude in the wilderness? The teaching of the Gospels on this question was clear: "Whosoever will come after me, let him deny himself, and take up his cross, and follow me. For whosoever will save his life shall lose it." This cause, Brown had no doubt, was his cross, and this path his to follow, wherever it led.

Still, as he wrote to his wife and children on November 23, Brown "felt a great deal troubled" about their circumstances in North Elba. All the practical support he could offer was an idea for Watson about "a cheap ready way" to insulate their cabin. To Mary, he added: "May God abundantly reward all your sacrifices for the cause of humanity, and a thousandfold more compensate your lack of worldly connections!" It had long been his custom to end his letters home by commending to God's grace the family he had left behind there. But now the shadow of death hung over his familiar benediction. It was possible, even likely, Brown considered, that he would lose his life here to exposure, to illness, or to violence. "I think much, too, of your widowed state," he wrote, "and I sometimes allow myself to dream a little of again some time enjoying the comforts of home; but I do not dare to dream much."

Brown would see his wife again, but not for another year, and he would enjoy the comforts of home with his family in North Elba for only five or six weeks over the remaining four years of his life. He had seen his father Owen for what would turn out to be the last time that summer in Hudson. Eighty-four-year-old Owen Brown was worried for the safety of his two children and six grandsons in Kansas, and what he had observed during his son's visit in July only deepened his concern. In conversation, John had displayed "something of a warlike spirit," which the Squire had sternly cautioned him to contain except in the case of necessary self-defense. After Brown left Ohio, Owen had remained troubled enough to send a letter ahead to Osawatomie, counseling again that violence was only justified in defensive and not offensive action. It was important to be vigilant in distinguishing between the two, he added, since "the one sometimes runs into the other." Owen closed his letter, which Brown received in October, by admonishing his fifty-five-year-old son: "Plant no seeds that bear bitter fruit and if any spring up attend to them before they take root." In Kansas, however, the bitter seeds had taken root already—strewn, in John Brown's view, from the evil growth of slavery. He would bring them to their full fruition.

In early October 1855, two elections were held in Kansas Territory to appoint a new territorial delegate to Congress. The first of these elections, and the official one, took place on October 1. It was overseen by the "bogus" proslavery legislature that had been voted in the previous March by the invading Missourians. This election was boycotted by most antislavery settlers, who did not recognize the authority of the legislature and expected this vote to be fixed, as its predecessors had been. J. W. Whitfield, the Southern Rights delegate who had won the vote the previous November, was easily returned. On October 9, the recently organized Free State party held its own election. Heavily armed and just three days into his Kansas residency, John Brown took those of his sons strong enough to walk and traveled to Osawatomie village, ten miles east of the Brown claim, to guard the local polling place.

Since the new territorial governor, Wilson Shannon, had already certified the October 1 vote, proslavery forces saw no need to impede this legally inconsequential exercise, and the Browns returned home without a fight. But the October 9 election of Andrew Reeder, though legally void, was politically potent. For one thing, the Free State party immediately appealed to Congress and argued in the press that Reeder was the true choice of "the Sovereign People." For another, in the eyes of many northerners the nationally known Reeder—the former territorial governor who had been relieved of his duties by the president after his public protest against the fraudulent March election—was already a symbol of what firebrand Massachusetts senator Charles Sumner was soon to call "the crime against Kansas."

The position of the Pierce administration, however, and of its territorial servants, Governor Shannon and Samuel D. Lecompte, Chief Justice of the Federal Court in Kansas Territory, was that the members of the Free State party were the lawbreakers. These settlers regularly violated the territorial ordinances against antislavery speech and agitation. Moreover, they refused entirely to recognize the authority of the territorial legislature and rejected the constitution that it had voted to adopt. Instead, these abolitionists and tools of the Massachusetts and New York financiers had elected delegates to a constitutional convention of their own. This treasonable assembly met in Topeka on October 23 and, by mid-December, had drafted and ratified a competing constitution to the one that the federally certified legislature had produced.

It was only a matter of time before the powder keg that was Kansas Territory in 1855 exploded. On October 25, at a town called Doniphan some forty miles north of Lawrence, a sawmill owner named Samuel Collins was shot and killed by Patrick Laughlin, a neighbor whom Collins had accused of betraying a secret antislavery society. The location of the killing was remote from the places where the Free State party was most active—Lawrence, Topeka, and the Osawatomie region, seventy-five miles to the south—and its circumstances were muddy. The two men, who seem to have dueled, both fired and both were hit, with Laughlin sustaining serious wounds himself. Free State settlers took no retaliatory action, but the story of Collins's death passed from mouth to mouth and from town to town among them. A few weeks later, when the unarmed Ohioan Charles Dow received a chestful of buckshot at the hands of a native Virginian named Franklin Coleman, who then fled with his family into Missouri, there was no question in the minds of the Free Staters: the shooting of Dow was an explicit, barbaric example of what the slave power and its hired thugs had in store for any man in Kansas Territory who opposed slavery's expansion. After all, it was no more than what "Old Bourbon," Senator Atchison, and his sidekick Stringfellow had been urging upon their constituents, just across the Missouri line, for over a year.

The murdered Dow was a tenant of Free State partisan Jacob Branson, whose longstanding property dispute with the southerner Coleman was the original source of the conflict that led to Dow's death. Branson claimed that he possessed legal title to the land on which Coleman had built his house; a year before, he had tried, unsuccessfully, to evict Coleman from it. On the afternoon of November 26, five days after Dow was shot, Branson convened a meeting of Free State men at his home to determine what should be done. Though this was Hickory Point, a town twelve miles south of Lawrence in the Free State stronghold of Douglas County, the men knew that Dow's killer would never be brought to trial. Not only was Coleman in Missouri, but the appointed sheriff of Douglas County was Samuel Jones, one of the vigilante leaders who had forcibly hijacked the March election that brought the bogus legislature to power. Jones did not even live in Douglas County, but across the line in Westport, Missouri, where he continued to hold his old office of postmaster. Frustrated, Branson and his colleagues burned down Coleman's empty house and threatened several of his friends, one of whom sent a message to Sheriff Jones swearing out a warrant against Branson for disturbing the peace. Late that night, Jones gathered a posse and rousted Branson from his bed. When Branson's friends got wind of the arrest, they rallied and confronted the sheriff's posse at the Wakarusa Creek crossing, four miles south of Lawrence.

It was dark, cold, and well after midnight when the two parties of horsemen, each numbering about fifteen, faced off a few yards apart, weapons leveled. Jones identified himself as the sheriff of the county and demanded that Branson's friends clear a path. One of the rescuers replied that the only Jones they knew was a postmaster in Missouri. They were at a standoff. Branson sat uneasily on his horse, flanked by his captors. His friends suggested he simply ride over to their side of the crossing. Branson feared Jones's posse would shoot him if he tried. "Let them shoot and be damned," the leader of the Free State party, Samuel Wood, challenged. "We can shoot, too." Jones backed down. There would be no shooting, he said, and Branson and his rescuers galloped off.

Jones instantly understood that the loss of his prisoner to an ambush sprung by northern vigilantes could be converted to a great political victory. It was the revolutionaries in Lawrence who had obstructed a duly appointed officer of the law in the performance of his duties, holding him at gunpoint until he released a man he'd properly arrested on a sworn warrant. And it was to Lawrence that they'd hustled the fugitive for protection. Why bag Branson when Branson on the run would lead him to the far bigger prize of Lawrence itself? Within a few hours of the confrontation at the creek, Jones had notified Governor Shannon that antislavery fanatics were in "open rebellion" against the laws of the territory, that they were aided and abetted by the Free State party leadership and most of the population in Lawrence, and that it would take a force of three thousand men–composed partly of U. S. army troops, partly of Kansas territorial militiamen, and partly of loyal

Missourians willing to help–to subdue this town full of subversives and anarchists once and for all.

In Lawrence, Free State leaders anticipated the fallout of the Branson rescue and hastily prepared for a siege. Dividing into teams, the men worked around the clock, piling earth and stones into embankments to form a military perimeter, digging trenches and rifle pits, and constructing several circular earthwork fortresses at strategic locations in the town. Three coordinated teams alternated tasks: eight hours of digging and building; eight hours of standing guard or holding lanterns for the night workers; eight hours of rest. Then the cycle would begin again. Lawrence's women matched the men for industry. Turning a cabin near the Free State Hotel into a cartridge factory, they loaded powder and shot into capsules and stockpiled them for use in the Sharps carbines. Riders were dispatched to nearby Free State villages to muster companies of volunteers willing to pledge to come to Lawrence's aid. In Osawatomie, a twenty-man company was sworn into service. Its members named themselves the "Liberty Guards" and assigned their commanding officer the rank of captain, Captain John Brown.

Even as Lawrence prepared for war, its leading citizens began intense diplomatic efforts to avoid it. Within twenty-four hours of Jacob Branson's arrival in Lawrence, he and his rescuers were sent away. Branson, it was pointed out to Governor Shannon, did not live in Lawrence, was not taken from Sheriff Jones in Lawrence, and was not hiding in Lawrence, so what laws had Lawrence broken? Moreover, his whereabouts were not known in Lawrence, so how was Lawrence responsible for him? By the 4th of December, the Lawrence Committee of Safety had also sent messages to President Pierce and to Colonel E. V. Sumner, commander of the federal garrison at Leavenworth, requesting the aid of U.S. troops to defend law-abiding civilians against unwarranted attack by a force of as many as fifteen hundred heavily armed vigilante Missourians, who were now camped along the Wakarusa less than five miles away.

As he watched the swelling of the unruly, hard-drinking, abolitionist-hating "irregulars" whom Jones had assembled, Shannon began to worry. He, too, like the Lawrence Committee of Safety, had requested that federal troops be sent from Leavenworth, not to defend the town but to bring it to heel in a controlled and official way. But, though the southern-sympathizing Franklin Pierce had no intention of dispatching soldiers to defend an antislavery stronghold, neither was he eager to court general outrage in the north by turning federal guns on American citizens, even abolitionists. Colonel Sumner's orders from Washington were to do nothing. That vacuum left the Missourians unfettered. When Shannon visited their camp, his fears were confirmed. Fueled by whiskey, and straining under Jones's and Atchison's efforts to maintain discipline, the Missourians chafed to get on with the attack and reduce the den of the thieving abolitionists to rubble. To this end, one contingent had raided a U.S. arsenal, stolen three cannons, and dragged them into position around Lawrence.

Foreseeing a bloodbath and an escalation of hostilities into open civil war throughout the territory, Shannon frantically sought a negotiated settlement. Shuttling back and forth for two days between the Missourians' camp and the Free State leaders in Lawrence, the territorial governor persuaded both sides to sign an agreement. The citizens of Lawrence were officially absolved from responsibility in the Branson affair; in exchange they agreed to aid Sheriff Jones in appropriate legal action against Branson or any other lawbreaker in Douglas County. Shannon pronounced the crisis over and the law restored, thanked Jones's recruits for their service, and told them to go home.

John Brown and his Liberty Guards had arrived in Lawrence a day before the peace agreement was signed. To get there, they had to cross a little log bridge guarded by a patrol of Missourians. Brown's men, each carrying a Sharps rifle in his hands and displaying two large revolvers strapped at his waist, walked coolly toward the bridge without pausing or speaking. The Missourians tensed but, receiving no order from the patrol leader, allowed the Osawatomie company to pass in silence. A day earlier, a smaller and weaker contingent of Free State men had not been so fortunate. Thomas Barber and two other settlers living on claims near Lawrence were returning to their cabins from a meeting in the town when they were detained by a proslavery patrol that attempted to arrest and interrogate them. The men refused to cooperate, and Barber, who was unarmed, was shot.

For antislavery Kansans, Barber was the third in the pantheon of martyrs sacrificed that fall in the cause of freedom. Lawrence's leaders had his body laid out on a table in the unfinished Free State Hotel and displayed it to Governor Shannon when he came the next day to complete the settlement talks. Charles B. Stearns, Kansas correspondent for the *Anti-Slavery Standard,* witnessed the scene and on the spot abandoned his previous commitment to Garrisonian nonresistance. "Christ says, 'If a *man* smites thee on one cheek, turn to him the other also,'" Stearns wrote shortly afterward, "but after hearing the screams of the wife and mother of the murdered Barber, and witnessing his lifeless form locked in the cold embrace of death, for no other crime than because he was a Free State man, I made up my mind that our invaders were wild beasts." Yet, in spite of Free State outrage over Barber's killing and proslavery frustration at Governor Shannon's protection of Lawrence, the flimsy peace agreement held. Leaders on both sides concluded that it was simply too cold and too risky to violate it.

Only two men argued otherwise. Samuel Jones fumed that he had the men and the means to wipe out Lawrence, and if Shannon weren't such a waffling fool he would let him do it now rather than have to mobilize again to do it later. And in Lawrence, a still unknown middle-aged man, stoop-shouldered but vigorous and steady-voiced, climbed a makeshift platform to urge the antislavery forces to do more than just beg the invaders to leave in peace. Instead, John Brown volunteered to lead a dawn sniper attack on the Missourians' camp the next morning. He'd need only ten men, he said. Taking up widely spaced positions in the night along the camp's flank, his assault team would wait for a signal upon first light and then all fire at once upon the sleeping enemy. Men who fought for pay, sport, or plunder, Brown believed, were easily dissuaded. When they were firmly opposed, they discovered that they didn't have enough at stake to stand and die. The ruffians would panic and scramble back to Missouri, once and for all. Brown's recommendation of preemptive action, like Jones's, was rejected. But both accurately forecast that the war for eastern Kansas had not been averted, only delayed.

Snow fell almost continuously in Kansas for six weeks, and subzero prairie winds blew icy crystals up from the crusts of snowbanks and threw them into settlers' faces like tiny shards of glass. By the first of February in 1856, the ice on the Osage River at the Osawatomie settlement was nearly a foot thick under its blanket of snow. Brown sold his horse and wagon to buy food and supplies for his family. Eleven Browns crowded into the two shanties. Sometimes, Brown traveled the nine miles from his sons' claim to the home of his sister Florilla and her husband, Reverend Samuel Adair, who owned a well-built, warm, and spacious twelve-by-sixteen-foot cabin on the west side of the town of Osawatomie. The reverend was nearly as devoted to his father-in-law, Squire Owen, as Brown was himself, and wrote to him often that winter: "As for law here—every man to a great extent is his own.... We greatly need wholesale law and a righteous government. But as things are we may have bloody war before a government in Kansas is organized on a permanent basis."

Although it was too cold for military conflict, the political battle for Kansas intensified over the winter of 1855–56, both in the territory and in Washington, D.C. President Pierce fired the opening salvo when he announced in his State of the Union message on the last day of 1855 that the "fanatical devotion" of some northerners to the fate of "a relatively few Africans" was not only disturbing the peace in Kansas but provoking a conflict that might engulf the whole country. In Lawrence and Topeka, antislavery leaders had already written off the president as an enemy. They would take their case directly to Congress. On January 15, proceeding under the terms of the Topeka Constitution that Free State delegates had drafted the previous fall, antislavery Kansans elected their own governor—Lawrence's leading citizen, Charles Robinson—as well as territorial legislators. John Brown Jr. was voted in as the representative from Osawatomie, and signed the petition for statehood that the Free State faction submitted to Congress in March.

Congress was evenly and bitterly divided on the Kansas question. Many senators and representatives who were not strongly antislavery were nonetheless troubled by the official territorial government's flawed election and mob rule, and its support mainly by southern slaveholding interests rather than Kansas settlers. As far as President Pierce was concerned, however, the proslavery legislature had been duly constituted. His appointee, Wilson Shannon, not Charles Robinson, was Kansas's governor. Officially denouncing the Free State movement as "treasonable insurrection," Pierce now authorized Shannon to call up federal troops from Fort Riley and Fort Leavenworth whenever he deemed them necessary to enforce territorial law or suppress civil unrest. Republicans in Washington raged in speeches on the Senate floor that the president of the United States was the most tyrannical enemy of American self-rule since George III sent his redcoats to Boston to suppress the spirit of freedom.

Back in Kansas, war fever heightened again as the ground began to thaw. Nowhere was the tension greater than in the triangle formed by the meeting at Osawatomie of the southeast-running Osage River and the northeast-flowing Pottawatomie Creek. About nine miles upriver on the Osage, on a little tributary called Middle Creek, lay Brown's Station, where John Brown's sons had staked their claims. Six miles southeast of the Browns, a group of proslavery families lived along the Pottawatomie. Allen Wilkinson, a member of the recognized territorial legislature, and "Dutch" Henry Sherman and his brother William, who operated a tavern and proslavery meeting house, were the group's leading figures. A fourth activist in the cause, James Doyle, lived close by with his wife and three sons. On the half-cleared frontier road that ran between the Browns' claim and Dutch Henry's Crossing stood a general store owned by Theodore Weiner, an Austrian Jew who had emigrated to Texas and wandered north to claim land in Kansas. Weiner had owned slaves himself in Texas but favored a free Kansas and quarreled with his proslavery neighbors. Once, he and William Sherman had come to blows. After that, proslavery partisans began to linger menacingly around Weiner's store; sometimes, they handed his customers notices signed "Law and Order" that warned that Free State men who failed to leave the territory within thirty days would have their throats cut.

The Browns themselves had several run-ins with these proslavery neighbors as spring approached in 1856. James Doyle, encountering Henry Thompson on the road one day in March, thought to have some fun by haranguing him about the stupidity and insensibility of the colored people that abolitionists like the Browns were all worked up about. After a few minutes, Henry pointed to a scrawny mongrel at Doyle's feet. "Look here, old man," he said. "I know colored men that are as much smarter than you as you are smarter than that little dog." Doyle trembled and told Henry the time was coming when he'd pay for that insult. In April, a territorial court–presided over by an Alabaman, Sterling Cato, who had been appointed district judge–convened in Dutch Henry's tavern to issue arrest warrants for district residents who had violated laws against antislavery speech and refused to pay taxes to support the Lecompton government. Wilkinson acted as district attorney; Doyle was a juror, and his oldest son William served as bailiff. In a gesture of defiance, John Brown sent Salmon and Henry to stand outside Cato's courtroom, daring anyone to actually attempt to take them into custody. No one did.

The muscle-flexing of the proslavery forces that spring in Kansas, however, was no empty show. The president had unambiguously branded the Free Staters as traitors, and Secretary of War Jefferson Davis had given orders to Governor Shannon to suppress Free State political gatherings, which he referred to as "insurrectionary combinations" intent on "invasive aggression" in Kansas. More avidly than ever, proslavery men rushed to do their patriotic duty and support the federal government. If Free State settlers were guilty of "invasive aggression," then they must be opposed on two fronts: those already resident in Kansas must be driven out, and those en route kept out. To this end, Missourians locked down the three hundred miles of the Missouri River that flowed between St. Louis and Kansas City. Northerners who attempted river passage, or to cross through Missouri overland, in the spring of 1856 were routinely robbed, assaulted, and turned back by gangs of armed vigilantes. The same gangs also intercepted and destroyed mail and appropriated supplies intended for Kansans who lived in known Free State communities.

The westernmost railway destination outside of Missouri was Iowa City in eastern Iowa, a little over two hundred miles from Lawrence as the crow flies across northwestern Missouri. But northwestern Missouri, along with the entire stretch of Kansas-Missouri border marked by the river's jog north into Nebraska, was impassable for would-be Kansas immigrants. Their only choice was to add hundreds of miles to their journey by trekking due west through Iowa and into Nebraska, before turning south down a freshly blazed trail into Kansas.

For the first time, too, Missouri ruffians were joined by large numbers of men recruited from more distant slaveholding states. Major Jefferson Buford of Eufaula, Alabama, a lawyer, adventurer, and Indian fighter, led the campaign to recruit four hundred Alabamans, South Carolinians, and Georgians for irregular military service in the territory. Selling off some of his own slaves to begin a war chest, Buford gave speeches and took out newspaper ads throughout the south, publicly challenging other slaveholders to pledge the price of one or more of theirs to fund his operation. Private donations poured in. Other state militia and slave patrol officers, from Florida to Kentucky, formed companies to put down the Kansas insurrectionists. As spring advanced and the melting snow revealed the high prairie, receding toward the horizon in an infinite series of gold-green waves, dark patches of men began to appear and spread on its surface, like flocks of scavenging birds. Buford and the other southern commanders established their camps on Indian or federal lands surrounding the Free State communities of Lawrence, Topeka, and Osawatomie. Their troops, along with the Missourians, harassed settlers attempting to move between these towns or to bring in provisions. Occasionally, they would make night raids on the fields and barns of antislavery farmers, damaging crops and rustling horses and cattle.

As he performed several surveying jobs for Indian tribes south of the Kansas River who were struggling to protect their reserved lands against encroaching settlers and squatting vigilantes, John Brown witnessed the southern mobilization. Neither Shannon's territorial militia nor the federal troops attempted to clear the Indian lands of the illegal and growing camps of Missourians and other proslavery partisans. Nor did the influx into Kansas of mercenary, non-emigrating fighters from distant states—certainly more deserving of the tag "invasive aggression"—draw any warnings at all from the secretary of war. Brown viewed the government's inaction as part of a deliberate policy not just to deny tribal rights to the Indians but to provide the invaders with a nearby base from which to launch the upcoming assault on Free State Kansans. His surveying equipment gave him effective cover to spy on the slave power's forces. Running his lines directly through their camps, Brown counted on the southerners' assumption that he was a government surveyor, in the employ of President Pierce or Governor Shannon, and therefore likely to be "sound on the goose." James Doyle, he learned, regularly visited Major Buford to give him information about the strength and personnel of the Free State militias in the area. Indeed, it would not be long, Buford's men assured the old surveyor, before they wiped the territory clean of abolitionists, especially "those damned Browns." All they needed was a suitable provocation.

Sheriff Jones helped provide one. On April 19, 1856, he and a deputy rode into Lawrence to arrest S. N. Wood, the leader of the men who had ambushed him and ridden off with Jacob Branson five months before. A crowd of citizens surrounded the sheriff and thwarted Wood's arrest. A day later Jones returned with a posse and demanded that the people of Lawrence assist him in enforcing the law, as promised in the agreement that their leaders had signed in December. He was greeted again with insults and curses. Jones returned once again, on April 23, this time at the head of a column of U.S. dragoons, assigned to him by the governor. He took six prisoners, all men who had refused his order three days before to help him catch Wood. Wood himself remained at large. Jones camped outside of Lawrence that night, meaning to pursue his quarry again in the morning. Late that same evening, he was shot.

THE ABOLITIONISTS IN OPEN REBELLION—SHERIFF JONES MURDERED BY THE TRAITORS!!! screamed the headline in B. F. Stringfellow's newspaper, the *Squatter Sovereign*. In fact, Jones was not badly wounded and soon recovered, but reports of a fatal attack glutted the southern press long after Jones was once again leading the campaign to finish the job that he had wanted to do in December. The identity of Jones's assailant could not be determined, and many suspected a man who was known to hold a personal, rather than a political, grudge. But, on May 5, Chief Justice Lecompte convened a grand jury and charged it to return an indictment against any and all members of the Free State party, which he described as that "unlawful, and before unheard-of organization, that has been formed in our midst for the purpose of resisting the laws of the United States." Where there is evidence that particular individuals have resisted these laws, his charge continued, "then must you, under your oaths, find bills against such persons for high treason." If there is no evidence of actual lawbreaking but only of membership in an association formed for the purpose of resistance, "then must you still find bills for constructive treason, as the courts have decided that to constitute treason the blow need not be struck, but only the *intention* be made evident."

Since antislavery residents of Kansas were by law ineligible for jury service, Lecompte's grand jury promptly returned wholesale indictments for treason against known Free State party members. Additionally, jury foreman Owen C. Stewart reported that the two Lawrence newspapers and the Free State Hotel were themselves guilty of "constructive treason" and should be destroyed, the former for printing seditious material and the latter because its fortress-like structure "could only have been designed as a stronghold of resistance to law, thereby endangering the public safety, and encouraging rebellion and sedition in the country." To help him serve the writs of arrest that the court was preparing, the U.S. marshal for Kansas Territory, I. B. Donaldson, deputized the leaders of several bands of Missourians, including Franklin Coleman, the killer of Samuel Dow the previous November. Donaldson also issued a proclamation to drum up additional volunteers. "The law-abiding citizens of the territory," it read, "are commanded to be and appear at Lecompton, as soon as practicable, and in sufficient numbers for the execution of the law." This call for citizen deputies was announced and published not in Kansas but in Missouri.

Emboldened, proslavery companies stepped up their harassment and intimidation of travelers to and from Free State communities throughout the territory, and closed in on Lawrence. On May 11, Lawrence residents formed a citizens' committee to petition the governor, as they had done in December, to protect the town from what they called the unlawful force gathering around them. Shannon wrote back coldly the next day. The force to which they referred, he explained, was "the legally constituted posse of the United States Marshal and Sheriff of Douglas County," which had numerous legal writs of arrest to execute. If the people of Lawrence submitted to its authority and aided it in its work, there would be little trouble. "But so long as they keep up a military or armed organization to resist the territorial laws and the officers charged with their execution, I shall not interpose to save them from the legitimate consequences of their illegal acts."

Nine days later, on May 21, at the breaking of a bright, cloudless dawn, the people of Lawrence awoke to discover an army massed on Mount Oread, a majestic hill overlooking the town. Moments later the siege began. The eight-hundred-man posse descended on the town under banners that read "Southern Rights" and "The Supremacy of the White Race." Many of Lawrence's leaders had already slipped away to escape arrest under Lecompte's warrants. The remaining population surrendered without a fight. The offices of the *Kansas Free Press* and the *Herald of Freedom* were ransacked, their printing presses smashed, their type thrown into the river. The mob shot out windows and looted some houses but did not kill any of the unresisting citizens. In the afternoon, Sheriff Jones ordered cannon wheeled up in front of the Free State Hotel. The thick stone walls trembled but did not collapse under sustained bombardment. Jones again tried to raze this symbol of antislavery defiance by placing powder kegs inside it and lighting them. Window glass blew out, but still the hotel stood. Festive Missourians milling in the street began to chant, "Fire it." The hotel's roof, floors, staircases, and furniture were all wood. Fires were lit, and flames and smoke soon billowed from every window and enveloped the roof. The sheriff's face glowed. "This is the happiest day of my life," he pronounced.

The hotel was already in flames and Lawrence beyond help by the time the Pottawatomie settlement heard that the antislavery stronghold was under attack. John Brown Jr., at the head of a company of volunteers that called themselves the Pottawatomie Rifles, and his father, leading "a little company by ourselves" that consisted of his unmarried sons and son-in-law, immediately mobilized and marched toward Lawrence to assist in the town's defense. The two units totaled thirty-four men. They sent a runner to instruct two larger companies, the Marion Rifles and the Pomeroy Guards, both based a few miles to the southeast in Osawatomie, to meet them at a rendezvous point on the California Road. The men walked long into the night, slept a few hours, and resumed their march before dawn. Only two Osawatomie volunteers appeared at the meeting place. Still, the Browns pushed on. Before they reached Prairie City, more than twenty miles from Lawrence, they encountered a rider who reported the stunning news that the border ruffians had sacked the town and destroyed the Free State Hotel and newspaper offices. Lawrence had given up without a fight.

The men stopped, uncertain. Was there any point in going on? Should they return to their homes to protect them from roving bands of Missourians, emboldened by victory as well as whiskey, or from their own proslavery neighbors, who might now try to make good on their threats to drive them out once and for all? While they stood and debated in the dust alongside Ottawa Creek, another messenger approached and informed them that U.S. troops now policed what was left of Lawrence, having entered the town as the victorious southerners melted back into the Kansas countryside. There was nothing to do. John Jr.'s company decided to encamp for the night and see if any Osawatomie reinforcements or further news arrived. Brown's family platoon had no choice but to wait with them.

In Washington, D.C., on the same day that Sheriff Jones and the other proslavery leaders were massing their forces for the assault on Lawrence, the U.S. Senate's leading antislavery voice, Charles Sumner of Massachusetts, commenced a speech on the Senate floor. The crime against Kansas, bellowed the fiery Sumner, was no less than "the rape of a virgin territory, compelling it to the hateful embrace of slavery." Continuing, Sumner pointed at the empty seat of one of his staunchest adversaries, the aristocratic Senator A. P. Butler of South Carolina: "The Senator from South Carolina has read many books of chivalry, and believes himself a chivalrous knight, with sentiments of honor and courage. Of course he has chosen a mistress to whom he has made his vows, and who, though ugly to others, is always lovely to him; though polluted in the sight of the world, is chaste in his sight. I mean the harlot, Slavery." Two days later, Preston Brooks, a nephew of Senator Butler and himself a member of the House of Representatives, strolled into the Senate chamber. Sumner was seated, hunched over a sheaf of papers, his long legs crossed beneath an undersized desk. Brooks approached and, without warning, raised his polished, metal-tipped walking stick and delivered blow after savage blow to Sumner's head. Bloody and dazed, Sumner tried to rise but his knees were caught beneath the desk, which was bolted to the floor. With a desperate upward lurch, he wrenched one of the bolts loose and half stood, before losing consciousness under Brooks's continuing assault and slumping to the floor.

On May 23, other men had begun to gather in the Browns' camp at Ottawa Creek. Most were from Osawatomie, but a few had come from Lawrence. One of the latter had been in the ravaged town the previous evening, when a telegram had arrived bearing the news that Sumner had been caned by Preston Brooks and lay near death. "It seemed to be the finishing, decisive touch," Salmon Brown recalled, years later. Squatting in front of a small fire over which he was cooking breakfast for his sons and some of the other men, Brown announced to anyone who wished to listen: "Something *is going to be done now.* We must show by actual work that there are two sides to this thing, and that they cannot go on with impunity."

Three months earlier, Brown had appealed for congressional intervention to prevent the armed conflict that he believed would be forced upon Kansas's antislavery majority in the spring. Writing to his old Ohio representative, Joshua R. Giddings, he warned that President Pierce and Governor Shannon clearly intended to use the Missourians to help enforce "those Hellish enactments of the (so called) Kansas Legislature, absolutely abominated by a great majority of the inhabitants of the Territory." Continued resistance to the Missourians and to the bogus laws, he predicted, would eventually be met by the deployment of federal troops against that majority, the effect of which "will be to drive the people here either to submit to those Infernal enactments, or to assume what will be termed *treasonable grounds* by shooting down the poor soldiers of the country with whom they have no quarrel whatever. I ask in the name of Almighty God; I ask in the name of our venerated fore-fathers; I ask in the name of all that good or true men ever held dear; will Congress suffer us to be driven to such 'dire extremities'? *Will anything be done?*"

Congress would do all it could, Giddings had replied. He thought that Brown could count on a "supply of men and arms and money which will move forward to your relief as soon as the spring opens." He closed by remarking: "I may be mistaken, but I feel confident there will be no war in Kansas." Giddings had been mistaken. Or had he? War required opposing combatants, and the so-called Free State men had not engaged the enemy in combat. They had only bled and pleaded and fled and cowered, even as their capital was sacked.

Huddled around the stove in Jason's shanty that winter, the Browns had often debated among themselves whether antislavery Kansans would find the will to fight. Many Free State partisans hailed from southern and border states; these men, Brown wrote to his father in January, "are only half right in regard to slavery; and go for Negro and Mulatto exclusion." In this, though, they differed little from most of the northern emigrants, who wished neither to compete with black men for work nor to live among them. Their property was what most concerned them—as it concerned the New England Emigrant Aid Company, which owned most of Lawrence and employed its leaders. Now that Free State property in Kansas was at risk of total loss, what was to stop its owners from accepting any compromise or compliance with the slave power in order to save it?

And what of Brown's own family? Of their sacrifices? For what had Jason lost his first-born son, and Salmon and Oliver left their mother and sisters? For what had they hobbled through the winter, their toes cracked and black from frostbite? For what had Brown abandoned Mary? Thoughts of North Elba, he had written to her one subzero day in February, are "calculated to unman me." Henry suffered even more grievously his absence from Ruth, who was expecting their second child, conceived during her young husband's last week at home the previous summer. "It is a great trial to stay away from you," Henry had written to her in mid-April, "but I am here, and I feel have a sacrifice to make, a duty to perform." Soon afterward, news from North Elba heightened all the men's distress. The family had nearly depleted its winter store of food and had no immediate means of buying any, reported a letter from Ruth dated March 26. Brown responded the day he received it: "my heart is sorely grieved at your trials," he wrote, bidding his family to trust in God and promising to get some money to send to them as soon as he could. Emotion filled him, and for a moment he waxed poetic, but the cause was never far: "The trees begin to leave out a little, & the grass to grow—which we hope will soon come to visit you; and that *Green* may in some measure take the place of *Blue*. Can think of but little more to add but my earnest desire for your happiness; & the constant ringing in my ears of the despairing cry of Millions whose woes none but God knows."

The turmoil of the past few weeks had raised that ringing to a din. Even before the attack on Lawrence, the mobilization of the southern invaders on the edges of Kansas's Free State enclaves—with the full knowledge and support of the territory's governor, chief justice, and marshal, and of the president of the United States himself—had become so explicit in its threat and so corrupt in its intent that avowed nonviolent resisters were moved to militancy and rage. "Such a state of things as this maddens men and throws them back upon their own resources for redress," Samuel Adair wrote from Osawatomie to his father-in-law, Owen Brown, on May 16. "O, the depth of revenge in the human heart when the powers that should execute justice, not only connive at the wrong, but abet & help it on, & screen the offender. May Heaven grant us deliverance soon."

Owen was spared the discomfort this letter would have caused him, for he was dead when Adair wrote it. On Sunday the 19th, Brown's sister Florilla handed him a note just received from his half brother Jeremiah that contained the news. Owen Brown had been buried beside his beloved first wife Ruth on May 9, their eldest son's fifty-sixth birthday. A year before, he had advised his son not to plant the seeds of bitter fruit. But what fruit had John Brown ever harvested? His father had sown seeds of righteousness all his life and was now reaping his eternal reward. His father had acted. It was past time for the son to act as well. Staring into the iron skillet as the johnnycakes blistered, blinking in the rising smoke, Brown murmured the long familiar verse from the ninth chapter of Hebrews: "And almost all things are by the law purged with blood; and without the shedding of blood is no remission."

Slavery's champions in Kansas were not religious men, but they were superstitious ones. If they did not fear God's judgment in the hereafter, they might be made to fear the swift sword of retribution here and now. This Brown knew and here resolved. Those who sowed terror in seeming security and power would reap a terror beyond their imagining. And those who now quaked in terror would be emboldened, unified, liberated, like the Israelites of old, by the midnight descent of an angel of death upon their oppressors. A few deaths, terrible deaths, would suffice to demonstrate to every border ruffian and proslavery agitator that the idol he served could not protect him and that the threats he made against others would be visited upon himself. After such action, there would be no neutrality and no accommodation in Kansas. Either slavery or freedom would be decisively vanquished. Whichever ensued, the nation would be called upon to answer its defining question. That was what must be done. That was what he was going to do.

After breakfast, Brown asked for volunteers to go with him. John Jr., the ranking officer of the Pottawatomie Rifles, leapt to his feet in alarm. He strode over to within a foot of his father and looked him in the eye. "Father, I object to any of the men leaving," he said. "We are getting up here near the enemy and may need them." Three inches shorter than his son and fifty pounds lighter, Brown stood motionless in his battered straw hat, black neckerchief, and patched brown coat. He recognized that John Jr. could not join him in what he was about to do, that his eldest son's stature in the community of Free State settlers would be damaged if he participated directly. That it might be damaged regardless. Still, the work needed doing. Brown stepped away and looked to the others. Without hesitation, Owen, Frederick, Salmon, and Oliver Brown came to stand by him. So did Henry Thompson and the storekeeper Theodore Weiner. Brown had his killing team.

No one urged the remaining member of the family, Jason, to join the mission. Jason's deep aversion to violence and empathy for any creature who suffered it was legendary, and quietly indulged, among the Browns. For this sensitivity, Jason often referred to himself as the family coward, yet Brown believed that, under attack, Jason would fight as bravely as any of them. Frederick had taken the place closest to his father's side. He stood very still, awaiting direction, his expression bland and impassive. Brown looked up into the strapping young man's broad, handsome face. He had only just recovered from his latest poor spell, caused by the mental wound that his father could not locate and the doctors could not heal. Brown considered insisting that he remain behind, but there would be no disguising his motive for forbidding Fred to accompany him, and this insult to the boy's stability was as likely to upset it as allowing him to come. He would keep Fred close to him, but apart from the mission's actual work. Owen, Salmon, and Henry, he felt certain, were strong enough to do that work without flinching, and to live with it once it was done. The storekeeper Weiner, a reformed slaveholder himself, and the resentful victim of repeated harassment at the hands of the Sherman brothers and their friends, could also be relied upon. As for Oliver, in physical strength he exceeded all of his older brothers, and he was a more avid reader than Brown himself of all manner of antislavery literature—especially the sermons of Boston's radical minister Theodore Parker, a favorite of his father's as well. But Oliver was only seventeen. Whether, for all his zeal and bold talk, he would be able when the moment arrived to look in a man's eyes and strike him down, Brown did not know.

There was a grindstone in the Ottawa settlement. Brown and his sons wore at their waists the hollow army broadswords he had brought from Ohio. Now he ordered several of the boys to carry the swords to the grindstone and hone them razor-sharp. By the time they finished it was after noon. The little party gathered up their weapons, bedding, and cooking implements. No one asked Brown to lay out the particulars of his plan, but its general character was understood. Brown asked James Townsley, an antislavery settler who lived near the southern end of Pottawatomie Creek, if he would transport his men and their supplies back to the creek in the lumber wagon he had brought to the camp. Townsley agreed. Late on Friday afternoon the group of eight men set out.

Night had fallen by the time the party stopped and camped, a few hundred yards above the Pottawatomie and a little more than a mile downstream of Dutch Henry's Crossing, their destination. During the night, Townsley began to have second thoughts. Having taken the Browns where they wanted to go, he asked on Saturday morning if he could leave them and return to his home. Brown insisted that he stay.

From their campsite, it was a short walk through the trees along the creek's edge to the dwellings of Doyle and Wilkinson. The cluster of cabins that housed the Sherman brothers and their employees was just across the Pottawatomie. These were the chief local proslavery instigators–the men who pressed actions in the courts against antislavery settlers; the men who provided Buford and other ruffian invaders with information about the activities and vulnerabilities of their Free State neighbors; the men who were behind the "Law and Order" party and its cowardly leaflets inviting antislavery men to either clear out of Kansas or have their throats cut. These men would discover before the sun rose again that there was a price to pay–a terrible price–for the attempt to steal Kansas by force.

Lying prone in the tall grass, hidden from view, the men spoke little. The waiting was interminable. Only the altered shadows of the trees as the sun inched across the sky marked the passing of time. Brown pounded corn between small stones, then moistened it and rolled it into balls, which he cooked slowly among the coals of a small, nearly smokeless fire. Some of the men nibbled at the corn balls or chewed on dry beef. At intervals, their leader broke the silence with a few words of encouragement. They had a duty to perform, he said. However hard, it was necessary work. However their flesh and even their consciences might revolt from it, it was righteous work. And there was no one else to do it.

Not until the moon shone weakly in the cloudy sky did the eight men leave the wagon and horses. It was just after ten o'clock on Saturday night. Walking up the north bank of Pottawatomie Creek toward the proslavery settlement, they approached the Doyle cabin. There, Brown divided the company into three groups. Townsley and Frederick Brown were to stop about two hundred yards short of the cabin and stand guard on the rough wagon road. Weiner and Henry Thompson were assigned to continue down the road past Doyle's house and take up a post between it and the Wilkinson place a half mile further on. Brown, Owen, Salmon, and Oliver would approach James Doyle's door.

The guard detail had no sooner taken up its position than two of the Doyles' dogs leapt out of the brush and charged toward them, furiously barking. Frederick swung his broadsword down onto the neck of the lead dog, killing it instantly, and slashed at the other until it retreated howling into the woods. Brown and his other sons froze. If someone had heard the dogs and came to investigate, the men would have to force their way in. But, inside the cabin, all was silent.

His team waited a few minutes before Brown stepped to the door and rapped hard.

"What is it?" James Doyle's voice sleepily called.

"I am looking for Mr. Wilkinson's house," Brown responded. "Would you be kind enough to point out the way?"

When Doyle cracked the door, Brown shoved him back, and he and his three sons entered with drawn pistols and knives. Doyle's wife Mahala stood behind him, clutching a frightened little girl. From their beds in the room's far corner, Doyle's three sons arose in their nightclothes. Confiscating the Doyles' few small arms and knives, Brown announced that the father and sons were prisoners of the Northern Army and ordered them outside. Staring at this implacable old man in soiled clothes, a straw hat pulled down almost to his eyes, and an ominous black bandana tied loosely around his neck, Mahala Doyle alone seemed to understand what was happening. She begged him not to take her youngest son, who was only fourteen years old. Brown looked the boy over, nodded, and released him to his mother. Then Doyle, twenty-two-year-old William, and twenty-year-old Drury were led out into the night, with Mrs. Doyle sobbing and screaming at her husband that she had told him what all this was leading to and what trouble he was bringing down on his family. "Hush, mother, hush," Doyle said quietly, looking back at his wife over his shoulder as the muzzle of Brown's pistol against his ribs guided him out the door.

Owen, Salmon, and Oliver drew the swords from their scabbards as they marched the Doyles down the road in the direction of the Wilkinson house. After about a hundred yards, Brown stopped the procession. Without word or warning, Salmon raised his broadsword and began hacking at the neck and chest of James Doyle while, next to him, Owen slashed at William, the quicksilver whistling through his hollow weapon as it fell. The Doyles's hands and arms were sliced open as they futilely attempted to block the mortal blows. In seconds, their mangled bodies fell to the ground, spurting blood. Drury Doyle, however, yet lived. Oliver had been unable to strike. Seizing his chance, Drury broke into a stumbling run, but Salmon, having quickly dispatched the father, caught the younger son from behind and dropped him with three overhead slashes, cleaving his arms from his trunk and opening a deep wound in his head. Trembling and blood-spattered, Salmon walked back to the road where his father and brothers were standing, heads bowed, over the bodies of Doyle and his eldest son. Oliver was in shock. Owen was fighting back tears. After a moment, John Brown raised his pistol and fired a bullet into Doyle's forehead. The gunshot snapped the Brown boys out of their reveries. Their father ordered them to collect themselves, to go back down the road and get Townsley and Fred, and then to meet him and the others at the forward checkpoint on the way to Wilkinson's.

Brown proceeded on his own, joined Weiner and Henry Thompson, and let them know that the campaign had begun. When the others arrived, the sons who had been present at the Doyle killings stood guard with Townsley, while Frederick, Henry, and the shopkeeper went with Brown to the Wilkinson cabin. There, he knocked as before and inquired the way to Dutch Henry's. Wilkinson began to shout out directions from his bed, but Brown interrupted and asked him to come out and show him how to go. When Wilkinson objected that he could not easily find his clothes in the dark and that he could tell the travelers what they wanted to know just as well from within, Brown told him that they were the Northern Army, and that he was their prisoner. If he didn't open the door and surrender they would open it for him. Wilkinson surrendered and opened the door. He was instructed to dress and come with his captors. His wife was sick with the measles, Wilkinson protested, and asked Brown to let him stay with her until the morning when he could get a neighbor to come tend to her and the young children. Brown refused. After scouring the cabin for weapons, the party led Wilkinson out half-dressed and without allowing him to put on his boots. A few minutes later, Frederick was sent back to the cabin to take two saddles that Brown had seen inside. What were they going to do to her husband? Mrs. Wilkinson asked. Take him as prisoner to the camp, Frederick replied. Mrs. Wilkinson then asked Frederick to stay in the house to protect her and the children until the morning, and he said he was willing but that the others would not let him. During this conversation, at a little distance from the house, Weiner and Henry executed Wilkinson in the same manner that the Doyles had been killed.

Brown's party now crossed the Pottawatomie and approached Dutch Henry's Tavern on its south bank. Henry and William Sherman were not only dangerous men but massive ones, well over six feet tall, and the Browns were unsure in which of the dwellings surrounding the tavern they lived. It was now after midnight on Sunday morning. Leaving Townsley, Frederick, and Oliver to stand guard, the rest of the company approached a likely cabin. Brown leaned against its door to listen. Unbarred, the door swung open and the men crept into the structure. Brown and Owen, guns drawn, approached the bed in which a man, woman, and small child lay sleeping. The other raiders, swords in hand, discovered three more men asleep behind a curtain at the far side of the room. They woke the sleepers and informed them they were captives of the Northern Army.

The cabin's owner was not Henry Sherman but James Harris, who worked for him. Dutch Henry was out on the plains that night, Harris told Brown, searching for some lost cattle. William "Dutch Bill" Sherman, however, was one of the three visitors. Brown's men confiscated two rifles and a bowie knife that they found in the house and forced

Harris to saddle several horses, owned by Dutch Henry, that were stabled outside. One by one, they took Harris and his other two guests outside and interrogated them about their reasons for coming to the territory and the extent of their proslavery activities. Each of these men was returned to the cabin unharmed. Salmon and Owen stood guard over them while Brown escorted Dutch Bill down to the creek where the swords of Henry Thompson and Theodore Weiner split open his skull.

When it was over, Brown and his seven followers walked back to camp. Dutch Henry's horses followed behind them, loaded with saddles and weapons confiscated during the raid. After gaining a little distance from the scenes of the killings, and hearing no pursuers, the men stopped and knelt in the water of the Pottawatomie. They let it drench their clothes and run over their bloody hands and flushed faces; they let it rinse the gore from their swords. Owen walked off by himself and began to sob. The others looked down and waited a long time for him to regain control. Daylight was fast approaching when they reached their hideout. Townsley scanned the faces of the silent Browns. Owen's was now expressionless.

"There shall be no more work such as that," he said matter-of-factly, when Townsley caught his red-rimmed eye.

CHAPTER NINE

Marked Men

"If murder and assassination is the programme of the day, we are in favor of filling the bill. Let not the knives of the proslavery men be sheathed while there is one Abolitionist in the Territory."
– *The Leavenworth Herald,* June 4, 1856

JOHN BROWN JR. watched the sky's incremental lightening as he lay on the moist earth beside his sleeping brother Jason in the predawn hours of Saturday, May 24. "Jay?" he called, mechanically, as he had at intervals throughout the night, expecting no reply. Sixteen hours ago he had watched his other brothers and his father load their clumsy, old-fashioned broadswords into James Townsley's wagon. He had not closed his eyes since.

Jason could sleep because he did not allow himself to see what the old man planned to do, perhaps had done already. John Jr. could see nothing else. That he had borne, or would bear, no actual witness was one source of his distress. He should be with his father, John Jr. felt, but whether to stay his hand or to hold up his arms he could not decide.

Saturday morning dawned and passed, placid and glorious, with no word of his father's renegade company, or of new raids or mobilizations by proslavery forces that would give his Rifles a reason to move and a direction to go. In the afternoon, unable to stay still a moment longer, John Jr. saddled a horse and galloped off toward Lawrence at the head of a small scouting party. The ruffians had taken the town apart, intent not so much on destruction as on humiliation. Aside from random stretches of bullet-riddled walls and windows, the houses and businesses generally were intact. But their contents seemed to have been turned inside out. Even after two days of cleanup, the streets bore evidence of broken furniture, looted articles of clothing, and shredded pages of books and newspapers. The expressions of the federal troops now billeted in Lawrence said they were not responsible for this state of affairs and had no opinion about it; the demeanor of the residents said they were resigned. John Jr. did not know which attitude disgusted him more.

It was evening when he and his men began their return journey to the camp at Prairie City. Near midnight, they approached the town of Palmyra, a few miles from their destination. A light shone from a farmhouse window just before they crossed the Santa Fe Trail. It took a moment for John Jr. to get his bearings. This was the property of a man named Jones, a southerner who kept two young slaves. "Come with me," John Jr. shouted to his companions without turning to look at them, and charged toward the farmhouse. Dismounting, he threw his shoulder against the door, and burst into the kitchen with revolver drawn just as the startled Jones was rising from his chair by the fire, a Missouri newspaper held fanned across his chest like a shield. Though they were no less stunned than Jones, John Jr.'s men entered the room as well and stood behind him. The commotion roused Jones's wife, who soon appeared in her nightclothes. Jones demanded to know the intruders' business, adding that he had made no trouble and wanted none. John Jr. told the farmer that free labor was the law—the law of the people—in Kansas Territory, and that slaveholders must either leave or die. His rifle company, camped just to the south, was prepared to enforce this law, beginning tonight. "We give you just one hour to cross the Missouri line with your wife and what you can take in your wagon," he concluded. "But you cannot take your slaves. They are free."

Mrs. Jones was sent to fetch the negroes, an eighteen-year-old young woman and a fifteen-year-old boy, who in a few minutes were led in and presented to their liberators. They clutched small bundles of clothes and stared fixedly at John Jr., with expressions he could not read.

Back at camp, John Jr. woke his brother Jason. "We freed two," he said, his face blazing with excitement. "Don't you want to see them?" It took Jason a minute to shake off sleep, adjust his eyes to the torchlight, and make out the slim silhouettes of the black boy and girl standing perfectly still a few feet away. Until he did, he had no idea what his brother meant.

Seeing that Jason had now observed them, John Jr. turned to the young woman for affirmation. "Do you want to be free?" he asked her.

"Yes," she said, doubtfully.

"Well you *are* free," a triumphant John Jr. all but shouted, "free as air!"

Jason stood and approached the boy. He gently repeated his brother's question, receiving the same answer. He nodded, and paused. "Are you afraid?" he asked.

"As shore's yer born, I feel powerful skeerd like," the boy confessed.

The men sleeping nearby had awakened at the voices and demanded to know what the blacks were doing in the camp. When John Jr. told them, they confronted him angrily. They were fighting for a free white state, not to free slaves, they reminded him. "We are no nigger stealers."

Jason defended his brother. Would they have freedom only for themselves, condemning the broken remnants of the eleven or twelve tribes of red men around them to another removal and the black men to eternal bondage?

The men ignored him. Someone called for a vote to decide whether or not to return the negroes. An overwhelming majority voted in favor, and appointed a Kentuckian to make the delivery. He caught up with Jones and his wife as they approached the Missouri line, a little before dawn. Rejoining his fellows a few hours later, the man stared at John Jr. When he handed the slaves back to their owners, he reported, they were "wild with joy."

Not long afterward, a rider entered the camp with news from Pottawatomie Creek: Five proslavery men had been taken from their homes and hacked to death in the night. Old John Brown and his sons were the suspected killers. All the men in the company now cast accusing looks at Jason and John Jr. They had had enough of the Browns' leadership. Fearing that their farms and families would be targets of retaliation by the Missourians, the men decided to break camp and start for home. The Brown brothers followed in a daze.

The Rifles stopped for the night a few miles north of Brown's Station. Near midnight, twenty-four hours after their execution of the Doyles,

John Brown and his men crept into the new camp. Both John Jr. and Jason confronted their father. John Jr., who was on the verge of physical and emotional collapse, could not justify his family's action, but neither could he entirely repudiate it. Jason was more clear. "I think it was an uncalled for, wicked act," he told his father. Brown was stung, and for a moment turned away. Then he replied that, under the circumstances, the act was absolutely necessary, and that God would judge it differently from Jason. Jason walked away and began to interrogate Frederick, who wept as he protested that he could not tell his brother which of the young men in Brown's party had struck the actual blows.

On Monday morning, May 26, the main company continued south toward their homes, while Brown and his seven followers looked to establish a secure base in the woods where they could await the response to their raid and decide on their future course. Alien from both groups, Jason and John Jr. traveled together to their claims. Wealthy, Ellen, and the children had left. Assuming that their families had taken refuge with the Adairs in Osawatomie, and considering it too dangerous to remain at Brown's Station in any case, the men set off for their Aunt Florilla's cabin. They took an indirect route, hiding often from the government soldiers and ruffian posses whose numbers increased throughout the day. By late afternoon, every road in the area was choked with hunters looking for the Browns.

The brothers completed the journey in the dark, and Jason knocked softly at the door of the Adair cabin. Their uncle Samuel's voice demanded to know who was there. Jason told him. "Can't keep you here," came Adair's muffled reply. "Our lives are threatened. Every moment we expect to have our house burned over our heads." Jason whispered that he and John were alone and hungry, and that John was ill; he pleaded with his uncle to let them see their wives and sleep on the floor for just this night. Adair cracked the door open but continued to block it, rifle in hand. Their wives and children were safely housed with neighbors, he assured them, but he could not let the men in. Florilla appeared behind him and asked Jason whether he or John had had anything to do with the murders. Jason swore they did not. "Then you may stay," his aunt replied, placing a hand on her husband's shoulder, "but we risk our lives in keeping you." While she gave the Browns something to eat, Adair put down a mattress on the floor for them.

Lying awake in the dark, Jason told his relatives what he knew of the Pottawatomie killings.

Hours past midnight, hoof beats outside the cabin, followed by a sharp rap at the door, awoke the restless sleepers. It was Owen, seeking shelter until daybreak. He had been sent into Osawatomie by his father to gather donations of food and supplies for the men in the woods from the residents of the Free State town. Anxiety and outrage overcame the peace-loving Adair. "Get away," he shouted. "You are a vile murderer, a marked man!" There was a long silence. Then Owen shouted back, "I intend to *be* a marked man!" A moment later, they heard him ride off. No one slept much after that. Sometime before dawn, Florilla heard John Jr. say: "I feel that I am going insane."

In the morning, Samuel Adair circulated among his neighbors, discussing the threat to the town in the wake of the southern attack on Lawrence and the killings on Pottawatomie Creek. Beyond the fear they shared, the thirty families who resided in Osawatomie were divided in their response to Brown's action. Many felt that more than a year of unchecked and unanswered proslavery violence and intimidation had necessitated some such response, and that the town was safer now that several of its most belligerent local enemies had been removed and their associates warned. Others were appalled and angry. The town's connection with John Brown and his family, they insisted, made it a prime target for destruction by the Missourians. The angriest and most vociferous of this party, a man named Hughes, was talking of getting together a posse to arrest any of the Browns who might have taken refuge at the Adairs' cabin and turn them over to the territorial authorities as an earnest gesture of Osawatomie's peaceful intentions and respect for the law.

Learning of Hughes's plan, Adair hurried home to warn John Jr. and Jason. There was a ravine at the edge of his property, disguised by undergrowth, he suggested the brothers hide in. Traumatized by the events of the past seventy-two hours, nearly incoherent with sleeplessness, and fearful that he would be hung as a slave stealer under territorial law, John Jr. sought the oblivion of the ravine. Jason resolved instead to walk back toward Lawrence and surrender there, or along the road, to United States troops, of whom he would demand protection. This, he thought, was the safest course for both himself and John Jr., who were guilty of nothing, and the best way they could shield their families from retaliatory violence at the hands of the Missourians.

Not far from the spot where he had last seen his father, Jason was stopped by several dozen of the very men he had hoped to avoid. He did not recognize the company's leader, but Martin White—the spokesman for the party of Missourians who had ridden onto the Brown claim shortly after the brothers' arrival to see if the new settlers were "sound on the goose"—recognized him. "You are one of the very men we are looking for! Your name is Brown," White exulted. Someone yelled "Down with him!" and Jason heard the clicking of guns being cocked, but the Missourians were mounted and clustered around him; there was no vantage point from which any of them might shoot him without endangering one of their horses or comrades. White held up a hand, pronounced Jason their prisoner, and ordered him to hand over his revolver. When he had complied, White told him to move away from the horses and stand in the road out in front of the posse.

Jason knew that he would now be killed. What terrified him was the idea of torture, of bullet after bullet aimed to make his death slow and painful. "My name is Jason Brown," he proclaimed, as he backed away. "I am a Free State man, and what you call an abolitionist. I have never knowingly injured a human being. Now if you want my blood for that," he concluded, reaching the spot that White had indicated, and ripping open his shirt to reveal his pounding heart, "there is a mark for you." The southerners hesitated, baffled and impressed by this performance, and less eager to kill a man after such a display of gallantry. Several lowered their rifles, and lay them across their saddles. "We won't kill you now," White decided.

White's men drove Jason before their horses at a fast walk for several miles until they reached a store where other southern militia companies had congregated. In the proslavery town of Baptisteville, eight miles northeast of Osawatomie, Sterling Cato—the same territorial judge who had issued arrest warrants for the Browns in April—was prepared to convene a court to try captured Free State men on charges ranging from horse-stealing to treason to murder. The posse resolved to march Jason there, but he had become feverish and faint and had to be taken on horseback, arms bound behind him. Three hundred armed proslavery men, by Jason's estimate, thronged Baptisteville. Cries of "Swing him up" erupted, as word of his identity passed among them.

Then a group of men grabbed him, one of them swinging a bright new coil of hemp rope over his head, and forced him over to a nearby tree.

He was saved by a prominent local slaveowner and territorial judge named Jacobs, who intervened in a manner that Jason later said "changed my whole mind and life as to my feeling toward slaveholders." Judge Jacobs spoke sternly to the crowd, and took custody of Jason until his trial or delivery to federal authorities. For the following two days, the judge housed him, along with forty proslavery militiamen. All of them took their meals at the same table, joined by the widowed Mrs. Doyle, whom the Jacobs family had also taken in, and served by slaves.

On the 29th, another prisoner was led into the room where Jason was being held. John Jr. had wandered back to Adair's house after two days in the ravine. Disoriented and listless, he had been apprehended that morning by a U.S. Cavalry detachment assigned to assist Missouri militia captain and deputy marshal Henry Clay Pate in his search for the Browns. A native Virginian, Pate was both a leading proslavery combatant in Kansas and the correspondent on territorial affairs for the St. Louis *Republican*. He would die with J. E. B. Stuart, as colonel of the Fifth Virginia Cavalry, at the Battle of the Wilderness in May 1864.

The difficulty of gathering witnesses for legal prosecutions under the conditions of general turmoil that prevailed in the Territory prompted the authorities at Baptisteville to postpone the trials of John Jr. and Jason Brown and the other Free State captives. In the meantime, the horses of the mingled U.S. military and Missouri militia units bivouacked in the town had grazed off all the grass. Captain Thomas Wood, the commanding federal officer on the scene, decided to relocate his men and their prisoners to a camp on the outskirts of Osawatomie. Wood saw in John Jr., who had been charged with treason for his membership in the antislavery Topeka legislature, a symbol of the flagrant disrespect for governmental authority that had brought Kansas to the brink of anarchy. Further enraged and revolted by what he viewed as the prisoner's cowardly pretense of madness, Wood resolved to make an example of him.

Yanking John Jr. out of bed early on the morning of the 30th, the captain bound his upper arms with hard, thin cord, which he pulled tight behind his back until John Jr.'s elbows nearly touched. When the cavalry company set off on its seven-mile ride, all its prisoners were transported by wagon except John Jr., who was tied to a horse and forced to run in front of it to avoid being trampled. During the drive through Bull Creek, sharp yellow flints in the creek bed sliced through his worn, cheap boots, lacerating the soles of his feet. Upon his arrival at the Osawatomie campsite, a little more than a mile from the Adairs' cabin, he was chained with an ox-chain to the center pole of the guard tent. John Jr.'s arms were so swollen that the cords with which they remained bound had been entirely swallowed by discolored flesh. When Jason reached the tent, his brother was hallucinating. Imagining himself to be the company commander, he shouted an unending stream of military orders at his phantom subordinates as he hopped around the pole. Wood came in and ordered Jason to keep his brother quiet. When he could not do so, three troopers entered. One felled John Jr. with a blow to the jaw. The others beat and kicked him until he lost consciousness.

Henry Clay Pate did not accompany Captain Wood, and the Free State agitators he had helped to capture, on the trip back to Osawatomie. In Baptisteville, he witnessed the column's departure and took time from his own law enforcement duties to file a report that was published in the *Republican* and reprinted in the *Leavenworth Herald*. One of the abolitionist murderers, "who feigns to be crazy, has just left in charge of the dragoons," Pate wrote. "He is made to accompany them on foot at a pretty rapid gait of course, as the troops are mounted. His day's march will help the craziness, and perhaps cool down the fanaticism which has laid five innocent men in their graves." After sending in the story, he gathered his men and rode west toward the Marais des Cygnes, where it was rumored that the ringleader, old John Brown, was hiding.

As Pate set off to hunt the Brown gang, Governor Shannon reported to President Pierce on the "extraordinary state of excitement in this portion of the Territory." He had posted a five hundred dollar reward for Brown, dead or alive, and a hundred dollars for any of the other participants in the killings at Pottawatomie. "I hope the offenders may be brought to justice," Shannon concluded. "If so, it may allay to a great extent the excitement. Otherwise, I fear the consequences." For the next four months, however, until he left Kansas in early October, Brown and his men avoided capture. The very excitement their violence had produced proved one source of protection for them. As the early Kansas state historian, D. W. Wilder, put it: "Hitherto, murder had been an exclusive Southern privilege. The Yankee could 'argue' and make speeches; he did not dare to kill anybody." Brown's smashing of this psychological constraint and regional stereotype was a key component of Pottawatomie's impact. It was this, beyond the brutality of the deed itself or the reputation for military prowess and resolve that he would later earn at the battles of Black Jack and Osawatomie, that gave the fifty-six-year-old former shepherd and wool merchant an instant aura of invincibility and fearsome power. With much of the reciprocal violence that followed in Kansas Territory, Brown and his family had little to do. His shadow, however, hung over it all.

The *Border Times* of Westport, Missouri, was among the first publications to identify—and assist in aggravating—the new situation in Kansas. "Hundreds of the Free State men, who have committed no overt acts, but have only given countenance to those reckless murderers, assassins, and thieves, will of necessity share the same fate of their brethren," the paper editorialized in early June. "If civil war is to be the result of such a conflict, there cannot be, and will not be, any neutrals recognized. 'He that is not for us, is against us,' will of necessity be the motto." A less combative writer for an eastern paper agreed, lamenting that the "body of good citizens, once numerous in the territory, who sided with neither party but attended to their own affairs, regardless of the issue of the dispute, is not now to be found. Every man has been compelled to join one party or the other and to become active in its behalf."

As Brown had intended, to be neutral, to be unimplicated, to be regardless of the issue of negro slavery, was no longer possible in Kansas. The demands of the proslavery press for indiscriminate revenge in response to what it portrayed as the indiscriminate crime at Pottawatomie left the ambivalent Free State volunteer companies no choice but to mobilize, expand, and fight, sometimes preemptively, against the Missourians and Buford's southern forces. Polarized and mistrustful Kansas settlers on both sides of the conflict also confronted one another in skirmishes that, though rarely deadly, deployed theft, vandalism, and intimidation in the effort to demoralize and drive off their opponents. Free State settlers and militias began to avail themselves of the violent means that the proslavery men previously had monopolized. Once they did, their strategic advantage became evident. Among territorial residents, the Free Staters were a large majority, and of the two groups of organized combatants, they were the ones fighting for their homes. The proslavery fighters were mostly invaders and mercenaries, whose property and families were elsewhere. They had nothing to lose in Kansas but their lives.

Along Pottawatomie Creek, where antislavery and proslavery residents were closely intermingled, both factions responded to the Brown killings in complex ways. The initial dismay of Free State settlers was tempered by their relief at the removal of five of the authors of a neighborhood reign of terror. It was the Shermans and the Doyles who had assaulted the antislavery storekeeper Squire Morse in front of his small children, promising to kill him if he did not immediately abandon his property, and they and their friends were the ones who had cornered Mary Grant, the daughter of a family allied with the Browns, and threatened her with rape for helping Frederick Brown mold rifle bullets for Lawrence's defense. The relief of the antislavery households, however, was mixed with dread that they would be singled out for retaliation by the Missourians, or the Buford company camped just to the east.

While some proslavery settlers on the creek fled after the murders, others joined their antislavery neighbors at a meeting in which the factions formally resolved to make peace and "oppose all men who are so ultra in their views as to denounce men of opposite opinions." According to James Hanway, a young Pottawatomie resident who later became a prominent Kansas jurist and man of letters, the proslavery men who remained on the creek were "as desirous of peace as any class of the community." In the interest of peace, and self-protection, proslavery men on the Pottawatomie soon disassociated themselves from the nonresident southern forces that Sherman, Wilkinson, and the Doyles had served. Most of these settlers owned no slaves themselves and had left slaveholding states in search of the same opportunities for which their antislavery neighbors had left free ones. Though they might hold it to be a white man's right to own slaves if he could afford them, recent events had made it clear to many of the southern emigrants on the creek and elsewhere in the territory that a war over this issue in

Kansas jeopardized their interests rather than served them. After Brown's raid, wrote newspaper publisher and early territorial resident James Legate, "even the Pro-Slavery men were active in their opposition to the atrocities of the border ruffians, and did their full share in stopping them."

As the shock waves from the Pottawatomie killings rippled out across Kansas and the nation, the men at their epicenter sat in a small clearing produced by the fall of a giant oak in an ancient forest along Ottawa Creek, southwest of Prairie City. Ottawa Jones, a Christian Indian and friend of the Browns who lived at the mouth of Ottawa Creek with his white missionary wife, had supplied the band with molasses, which sustained them for several days. To each man, Brown rationed two spoonfuls twice a day, which they mixed with creek water and ginger. Before each meal, he insisted on having prayers and asking a blessing; afterward, they gave thanks to the Bountiful Giver. Owen, Salmon, and Oliver no more shared their father's piety now than they had before the events of the previous Sunday morning, but they inclined their heads more solemnly than was their custom as he spoke, and found their mouths shaping the familiar words, all the same. In the middle of one long silent afternoon, Oliver turned abruptly to Brown and asked: "Father, have you ever had the least doubt of the Christian religion?"

"No," Brown replied, "but I have doubted my own sincerity."

The company now numbered ten. O. A. Carpenter, who lived outside of Prairie City, and August Bondi, a friend and neighbor of Weiner's on the creek, had joined the eight participants in the Pottawatomie attacks. It was Carpenter who guided Brown and his followers to their camp site–a safe place, he promised, from which they could also readily monitor the movements of the Missourians and the government forces in the area and, if necessary, come to the aid of nearby Free State settlements. Owen returned from Osawatomie with disturbing news about John Jr., whom he had found cowering in some brush on Uncle Adair's land, nearly incoherent except for his clear refusal of Owen's offer to bring him back to the camp. But Owen also brought provisions, including flour and a side of pork. While the younger men slept, Brown kept watch and made bread by the fire. His sons and son-in-law offered to relieve him, but he told them there was no sense in it. They needed sleep, while he had always required very little. Once, Salmon awoke in the night and lay for a long time watching the curious man who was his father: cheerfully absorbed in his domestic occupation, Brown squatted before the campfire, hands covered in dough, a rifle close by his side.

On May 30, a Scottish journalist and gadfly covering Kansas affairs for the antislavery *Missouri Democrat* wandered into the woods near Ottawa Creek. James Redpath's horse had been stolen in Palmyra the night before by one of the search parties that had passed him on the road. Emerging from the underbrush onto the creek's bank, Redpath gasped to find himself face to face with a large, powerfully built man in a coarse blue shirt, pantaloons tucked into calf-high, red-topped boots, and a thick leather belt from which protruded the butts of several different-sized pistols and the handle of a large bowie knife. In one hand, the man still held the water pail that he had been filling in the stream when the Scotsman appeared a few feet away. "Don't fear," said Frederick Brown. "I have seen you in Lawrence and you are true."

Here was a man, Redpath felt at once, of heroic physique and bearing. But as he looked more closely, and as Frederick talked, Redpath revised his first impression. There was something wild and fragile about him—about his tangled hair, his gleaming eyes, and the torrent of his voice. He began to speak of the Pottawatomie affair as he and Redpath returned to the Brown camp, to ask the journalist what he'd heard of it, and to denounce the unfounded rumors circulated by his family's enemies that his father and brothers had been involved. So agitated did Frederick become in his protestations, that he crossed and recrossed the creek several times. Fearing they would become hopelessly lost, Redpath insisted they go the rest of the way in silence.

Sentries waved them on as they approached the campsite, where horses grazed beneath the trees and men rested on their saddle blankets. One lean man who appeared to be in his sixties, dressed in thin, worn trousers, a tattered shirt with rolled sleeves, and old boots from which his toes protruded, stood red-faced before the fire, turning pork on a spit. At supper, Redpath ventured to revisit the subject of Pottawatomie, but Brown, looking sadly at Frederick, said that this was not a topic on which his men were at liberty to communicate. Instead, the old man expounded on his military philosophy as it pertained to the battle for Kansas that had now begun. People misjudge, he asserted, when they think that bullies or naturally violent men make the best fighters. "Give me men of good principles, God-fearing men, men who respect themselves," Brown continued, with a sweep of the hand to indicate that such were the men who flanked him now, "and, with a dozen of them, I will oppose any hundreds such men as these Buford ruffians." Redpath surveyed the young men around the fire, who appeared to receive this information as matter-of-factly as their leader delivered it. Describing the scene in the biography of Brown that he wrote and published four years later, he wrote of this tiny untested army: "They were not earnest, but earnestness incarnate."

The next day, Samuel Shore, the captain of Prairie City's Free State militia, brought news to Brown's camp. Henry Clay Pate's company of Missourians, about sixty strong, was camped at Black Jack Springs, five miles east of Prairie City on the Santa Fe Trail. In the course of their search for the Brown party and other indicted antislavery men over the previous five days, Deputy Marshal Pate and his men had plundered Free State settlements, burned Brown's Station and Weiner's and Bondi's empty houses, and taken three men prisoner for whom they had no warrants, including a local doctor and minister. Fearful that the ruffians would overrun Prairie City if they were not confronted, Shore had tried to raise a sufficient force to attack them, but many of his Prairie City Rifles preferred to stay and defend their homes. If Brown would commit his party to the attack as well, Shore believed he could recruit enough others to put up a fight. Brown agreed and arranged to meet Shore and his men in town the next morning, a Sunday, at ten o'clock. He had heard that an itinerant preacher was leading a prayer meeting there, and he wanted to attend it.

On the morning of June 1, 1856, sporting what one of their number described as "ideas, suspicions, and memories of what had once been boots and hats," Brown and his men rode into Prairie City. After the service, Brown and Shore consulted. They would set off that night, leave their horses under Frederick's guard a mile from Pate's camp, and continue on foot through the scrub forest of Black Jack oaks that fringed the springs, taking their positions in the dark and attacking at dawn. To the nine men under Brown's command, Shore brought seventeen under his own, equipped with long-range Sharps rifles. The pistols and muskets that Brown and his company carried were effective only in close quarters.

Pate's scouts detected the approaching Free State force before first light, and rushed to warn the Missourian camp of the attack. Brown's and Shore's companies pursued them. At 6:00 A.M., the twenty-seven Free State men broke the tree line and stumbled out onto an exposed plateau. Several hundred yards in front of them, well within the range of the Sharps, Pate's forces squatted in the tall prairie grass. Behind them, four supply wagons had been drawn together to form a breastwork, and behind the wagons a deep ravine sloped down to the springs. The Missourians were well equipped and lay down heavy fire, which Shore's men returned. Their own weapons useless at this distance, Brown and his men made a slow loop to the left, hoping to gain a nearer, more protected position in the ravine on Pate's right flank. For hours, Pate's and Shore's companies exchanged Sharps rifle fire, holding each other at bay. The undermanned Prairie City contingent had the best of it, killing a handful of Missourians while suffering no fatalities themselves. But by midmorning, several of the Free State volunteers had been wounded and fallen back, several more had given up on the fight and crept away, and the seven who remained with Captain Shore had all but exhausted their ammunition. Meanwhile, Pate's men had taken cover behind their wagons. From this position they fired ineffectually at Shore's troops on the plain above them and at Brown's, who had secured the ravine below. Ignorant of the size of the Free State force or its depleted firepower, many of the Missourians began to desert. At each lull in the shooting, two or three more would dash to their horses–which were clustered together at the water's edge, not far from Brown's position–and gallop off to the east.

During one of these lulls, the remnant of Captain Shore's detachment joined Brown in the ravine. Now totaling seventeen, the entrenched Free State fighters considered their options. Four of Shore's men and two of Brown's had at last concluded that the battle was unwinnable and resolved to disperse. O. A. Carpenter and Henry Thompson were badly wounded and could no longer fight. Henry, hit in the side by a bullet that had followed the curve of his rib cage and lodged near his spine, had returned fire for an hour after he was shot before giving in to the pain and blood loss. By sheer intensity and force of personality, Brown persuaded the six men who had lost the will to continue not to retire altogether. Instead, they agreed to retreat to a spot protected from the Missourians' guns, though within sight of their horses, where their mission was to shoot as many of the horses and mules as they could. This would demoralize the enemy, Brown reasoned, as well as cut off his means of escape. After the plan was enacted, nine Free State men—including Captain Shore and John, Owen, Salmon, and Oliver Brown—were left to engage three times as many of Pate's. But the screams of terrified and dying horses paralyzed the ruffians.

From his distant post, Frederick could hear the faint report of rifle fire. He accepted his supporting role here, as he had at Pottawatomie, because he knew that illness lodged in his brain, even when he seemed most healthy, and that he could not trust himself under stress. It was a wordless compromise that Brown and his fragile son had struck together: Fred would not be stigmatized by exclusion from any of the family's work, and in return he would accept unquestioningly whatever small or protected share in that work his father assigned him. As Brown arranged, Fred had struck no blow on Pottawatomie Creek nor even witnessed the killings. But the trauma had brought on another of the young man's episodes. Brown had often wondered whether it was his mother's dying when he was still an infant that made Fred take everything so hard. Whatever the reason, Fred seemed to feel more deeply stained by those five deaths than the men whose swords and clothes the blood had spattered. Brown should have insisted that he stay behind with Jason and John Jr. When Fred's sickness was upon him, he was susceptible to fits of obsessive guilt and self-hatred of a different order entirely, it seemed to his father, than the consciousness of sin and dependence on a merciful God that was proper to every Christian. During the most severe of these fits, a few months before the brothers emigrated from Ohio, Fred had been tormented by unclean impulses that he had thought at last to suppress by attempting to castrate himself with a pocket knife. Brown nursed him until the wounds were healed and the crisis had passed.

Hours into the battle at Black Jack Springs, Frederick Brown suddenly mounted his brother Owen's fast pony and charged toward the battlefield, bursting onto the empty prairie in front of the Missourians' wagons soon after the rear guard of the Free State remnant had begun to shoot their horses. "Father," he shouted, "we have got them surrounded and have cut off their communications!" Holding a rifle aloft in triumph, Fred wheeled the pony back and forth across the rise as Pate's men fired at him in vain.

A moment later, two men from the Missouri camp appeared with their hands in the air, walking slowly toward the ravine and shouting for a cease-fire. One of them waved a white flag. Pate had earlier dispatched one of his troops to ride for reinforcements, but now he feared that another Free State unit had beaten them to the scene. Under the flag of truce, he hoped to discover his enemy's true strength and stall for time. Brown, to whose leadership the younger Captain Shore had deferred throughout the fight, advanced alone to meet the peace delegation. The man carrying the flag was one of Pate's prisoners. Brown asked the other, Pate's lieutenant W. B. Brockett, if he was the company commander. Told that he was not, Brown instructed: "Then stay with me and send your companion back to call the captain out; I will talk with him, and not with you."

Pate appeared and began to lecture Brown in an imperious tone. He was legally deputized by U.S. Marshal Donaldson, under the authority of the governor, to search out and apprehend indicted criminals and insurrectionists, he informed the ragged old man before him. Those who had obstructed him in his fulfillment of his duties . . .

Brown cut him off. "I understand exactly what you are, and do not wish to hear any more about it. Have you any proposition to make me?"

Flustered, Pate began again to invoke his legal authority. Again, Brown silenced him.

"Very well; I have one to make to you. You must surrender unconditionally." When Pate hesitated, Brown drew a revolver from his belt and raised the barrel to the Virginian's chest. The rifles of every fighter on both sides trained on the two principals standing exposed between them.

"Give the order," Brown commanded.

By nightfall, Brown's camp on Ottawa Creek was host to twenty-six captive Missourians, their weapons, horses, and wagons. Dr. Graham, one of the three prisoners whose release was secured by the Free

State forces, dressed and bound Henry Thompson's wound and oversaw the first days of his convalescence at Prairie City. The rest of Brown's men feasted on the ample provisions in Pate's wagons, from which they also prepared meals for their prisoners. Brown's sons inhaled their brave victory at Black Jack, the first proper combat any of them had known, as if it were a drug. They filled their lungs with it, opening the passageways that the grim work at Pottawatomie had clogged and choked.

That same evening an article of agreement on prisoner exchange was drafted and signed by Captains Brown and Shore on the Free State side and Captain Pate and Lieutenant Brockett for the Missourians. It called for each of Brown's captives to be exchanged "for one of those lately arrested near Stanton, Osawatomie, and Pottawatomie and so on, one of the former for one of the latter alternately until all are liberated." Brown had discovered that John Jr. and Jason were among the arrested Free State men, and the agreement stipulated that they be released in exchange for Pate and Brockett themselves. The transaction was to take place on a neutral site, at which all of the men slated for exchange were to be physically produced by their captors.

This prisoner exchange never occurred. The United States territorial government in Kansas could not have retained the least credibility had the one-paragraph plan been enacted. Yet the very existence of the document, and the circumstances that produced it, illustrated the untenable position into which John Brown's resistance had cast the Pierce and Shannon administrations. Jason, John Jr., and the other Free State detainees were not in the possession of Henry Clay Pate. They were held by the territorial militia and U.S. army units assigned to U.S. Marshal Donaldson to execute Judge Lecompte's arrest orders. But Brown's agreement with Pate plainly presumed what Pate steadfastly claimed: that he was a deputy marshal who thus retained some official authority to negotiate the fate of the men he had arrested, or whom, at the least, his colleagues would wish to ransom by their release. At the same time, Brown's possession of Pate and his "posse" revealed them to be what they were: not Kansas civil servants but Missouri ruffians who had indiscriminately plundered and vandalized the homes of antislavery settlers and taken hostages under the pretext of enforcing territorial law. The very notion of a prisoner exchange, and Pate's agreement to it, moreover, implied that both sets of captives were of equal status. Pate was not the officer of the law, obstructed in the performance of his duty, any more than John Jr. was the duly charged and apprehended criminal: both were prisoners of war.

Had Brown and Shore lost at Black Jack, the episode would have been represented as another treasonous attempt by abolitionist agitators to thwart the execution of the law in Kansas, like the shooting of Sheriff Jones. Instead, by instigating and winning the first military battle of the Kansas conflict, they dramatized the truth that many northerners and southerners recognized already but that government policy had until now obscured: that the settlement of Kansas was a war between irreconcilable claimants that threatened to become increasingly violent. Black Jack was national news, and the proslavery and antislavery press lost no time etching indelible battle lines in the public imagination. To some, Pate was the defender of southern rights, with both U.S. and Kansas law on his side, foully attacked by antislavery fanatics who tricked him into surrendering by abusing a flag of truce; to others, Brown was the modern-day Minuteman, the ordinary citizen-hero of old New England stock who stood up to organized tyranny and prevailed. The Democratic administration in Washington could not afford to be seen as embracing either of these positions, especially in an election year, so it adjusted its Kansas policy. Governor Shannon was now instructed to defuse the conflict. The policy of aggressive enforcement of the bogus laws and indictment of Free State leaders gave way to efforts to improve public relations as well as restore public peace by suppressing all nongovernmental military organizations equally.

Franklin Pierce's bungled management of the Kansas situation had already alienated both the northern and the southern leadership of his party and cost him any chance he might have had for nomination to a second term. In May, the Democratic nominating convention had met in Cincinnati and chosen James Buchanan, a moderate proslavery Pennsylvanian, as its presidential candidate. Buchanan's most formidable rival in the fall promised to be John C. Frémont, the favorite of the new Republican party, which had formed two years earlier specifically to oppose any expansion of slavery beyond its southern base. Running on the slogan, "Free soil, free labor, free speech, free men, Frémont," the Republican posed so strong a challenge in border states such as Buchanan's own Pennsylvania that, later that summer, President Pierce would seek to assist his party's nominee by replacing Shannon with

John Geary, a native Pennsylvanian himself and a man untainted by southern partisanship. In the immediate aftermath of Black Jack, though, Governor Shannon issued a stern proclamation "commanding all persons belonging to military companies unauthorized by law to disperse" or be forcibly dispersed by U.S. troops. To the president, Shannon reported that Captain Pate had ridden "at the head of an unauthorized company."

On June 5, two armed forces set out in the direction of John Brown's camp, one to release Pate and his men and the other to avenge them. Colonel Edwin Sumner, commander of the U.S. troops at Fort Leavenworth, led the smaller, official unit, charged by the governor to rescue Pate and disperse both the proslavery and the Free State fighters. The other unit came from Missouri. It was commanded by General J. W. Whitfield, the sitting Kansas congressional delegate, and its mission was to complete the job that Pate had botched. At more than two hundred men, the strength of Whitfield's company was four times that of Sumner's, but when they met on the road and Sumner read out his orders and firmly asserted his authority, Whitfield yielded. Sumner and his dragoons proceeded to locate the Free State militia, which had swelled to nearly one hundred and fifty men with the arrival of a Lawrence company under the command of Captain J. B. Abbott. But it was Brown who came forward to try to negotiate terms for a hostage exchange with Sumner and his attending officers, Major John Sedgwick and Lieutenant J. E. B. Stuart.

Sumner told the old man that he was not there to discuss prisoners or exchanges. His orders were to inform all present that their military assemblies were unauthorized and that they must disband immediately and return to their homes. Pate protested that he had been deputized and that Brown was a notorious outlaw whom Sumner should arrest. The colonel answered that he had spoken specifically about Pate with Governor Shannon, who had denied that the Missourian had any authority or official business in Kansas. The other part of Pate's communication Sumner ignored. Edwin Sumner was a conscientious career officer who was disgusted both with the general lawlessness in Kansas and with Shannon's entanglement of the U.S. military in a partisan political struggle. He was also a cousin of Massachusetts Senator Charles Sumner, who still clung tenuously to life after the beating he had suffered at the hands of Preston Brooks two weeks before. Had he not intercepted and deterred Whitfield's army on its way to attack Brown, or had he taken Brown into custody on suspicion of the Pottawatomie murders, American history might have unfolded differently. But Colonel Sumner chose to carry out his orders and nothing more. Brown and his men were free to go.

Violence flared in Kansas Territory throughout the summer and, intermittently, for more than two years afterward. But with the military now deployed as a neutral peacekeeping force and the Free State fighters steeled to match the Missourians' aggression, proslavery partisans could achieve no better than a stalemate. Stalemate also prevailed in Washington. The Senate and the president blocked a House initiative to admit Kansas to statehood without slavery under the Topeka Constitution, yet could not strong-arm the House into accepting Kansas's admission as a slave state under the constitution drafted at Lecompton by proslavery delegates. After his inauguration in 1857, President Buchanan would try for a year and a half to revive the Lecompton Constitution's fortunes and bring slavery to Kansas, but time was on the side of the ever-increasing Free State majority, and these efforts failed.

Jason Brown, held by U.S. troops at Lecompton, was released on June 22. The conspiracy charge against him was never prosecuted. John Jr. was detained at Leavenworth until August, when he too was released without a trial. During the latter months of his confinement, as he regained strength and sanity, his wife Wealthy boarded near the fort where he was held and was allowed to cook and care for him during the day. Throughout the remainder of June, Brown stayed close to Ottawa Creek, where most of the rest of his family in Kansas lay ill. Owen had fallen victim to a fever and intestinal virus that reduced him to nearly a skeleton. Henry, still recovering from his bullet wound, also suffered from a less severe case of the same ailment. And, shortly after the battle of Black Jack concluded, Salmon had accidentally discharged his rifle, depositing a bullet in his shoulder that ripped through muscle and left him with limited use of one arm. When Owen and Henry were well enough to travel, Brown planned to transport his boys by wagon north to Nebraska and then into Iowa, where they could complete their recovery under better conditions before heading home. Oliver, too, once the post-combat exhilaration had subsided, found himself weary of violence and ready to return to North Elba.

While his sons rested and healed in preparation for the journey, Brown led an expedition of Free State men to Topeka in early July to protect the Topeka legislature, then in session, from a threatened ruffian attack. On the way, he stopped at the Eastern House, a hotel in Lawrence, to visit with William Addison Phillips, Kansas correspondent for the *New York Tribune* and the leading antislavery journalist in the Territory. When he could get them, Brown was an avid reader of newspapers, and the examples of Garrison and the martyred Lovejoy, together with his personal connection to Frederick Douglass, had taught him the power of the press. In Kansas, Brown had come to realize that he was not only a political actor but a compelling story. In fact, as a story he might act even more effectively than he did as a man. Accordingly, he began to cultivate sympathetic journalists: James Redpath, Richard Hinton of the *Boston Traveller* and *Chicago Tribune*, and especially Phillips. His interest in these literate men was not exclusively strategic. On the frontier, they also provided him with audiences for his theories and partners for the sorts of homespun philosophical conversations he had always enjoyed.

At Phillips' hotel, Brown reminisced about his former life in Ohio, his experiences as a wool merchant, his trip to Europe. He invited the journalist to ride with him to Topeka that evening and continue their talk as they went. They rode side by side at the head of the column of volunteers, stopping near midnight for a supper of lumps of cornbread that Brown prepared by crushing kernels between stones, rolling the paste into balls, and cooking them in the campfire's embers. After the meal, Brown and Phillips placed their saddles on the ground for pillows. Gazing up into a majestic summer sky, Brown traced the constellations and their movements. The symmetry and harmony of God's plan is evident in the heavens, he remarked, but not among men, who preferred their own erratic and self-serving courses to conformity to divine principles. Slavery was the "sum all of villainies," Brown went on, because it was the purest expression of man's sacrifice of principle to advantage, whereas all great reforms in human history were the opposite. Like Christianity, reform represented the sacrifice of advantage to principle. Remembering this evening with Brown, Phillips wrote: "In his ordinary moods the man seemed so rigid, stern, and unimpressible when I first knew him that I never thought a poetic and impulsive nature lay behind that cold exterior." He was, Phillips concluded, "always an enigma, a strange compound of enthusiasm and cold, methodic stolidity–a volcano beneath a mountain of snow."

The slow, dusty trip north with his sons commenced a month later at the beginning of August. Henry and Owen lay in the bed of a covered wagon, pulled by a team of oxen. Lucius Mills, a cousin of the Browns, attended the invalids. Frederick and Salmon walked or rode alongside their father. Oliver and Henry's younger brother William Thompson–who had rushed to Kansas after hearing of Henry's injury at Black Jack–scouted for ruffian posses a distance ahead of the wagon or behind it, riding horses that they had "liberated" from service in Missouri. Jason had remained in Osawatomie with Ellen and their child. When John Jr. was released from prison, the two brothers and their wives planned to leave Kansas together, as they had entered it. For the time being, Jason wrote to his sister Ruth, he and his family were living in a little rail shed. He spent his days with the other men of the settlement, cutting hay that they expected to be burnt any day by a company of ninety or so Georgians who had recently returned to the area and were camped south of Pottawatomie Creek. The only thing preventing the attack, Jason speculated, was the southerners' fear that their father might be lurking somewhere nearby. "Old Captain Brown," he wrote wryly, "can now be raised from every prairie and thicket."

Violent conflict continued to rage in Kansas Territory, despite the efforts of an undermanned and thinly spread U.S. military to suppress it. In mid-August, Governor Shannon resigned. It was weeks before the arrival of his replacement, John Geary, which left Kansas temporarily in the hands of Lieutenant Governor Daniel Woodson, an open Southern-sympathizer. Proslavery leaders decided that this was their opportunity to recoup the losses their settlements and military encampments had suffered since June and perhaps to deal the abolitionists a decisive blow. Missouri companies remobilized along the border under the command of Mexican War veteran, Brigadier General John W. Reid. Coordinating with other southern units inside Kansas Territory, Reid planned to attack and burn the major Free State population centers, including Topeka and Lawrence, and beginning with "the Abolition fort and town of Osawatomie–the headquarters of Old Brown."

On the night of August 29, 1856, two small companies of Free State men positioned themselves on the north bank of the Osage River at the eastern edge of Osawatomie. John Brown, who had returned to Kansas after seeing his sons safely to Iowa, commanded one unit of twenty-eight or twenty-nine men that included the peace-loving Jason. Even to repel an assault on the town that housed his family and friends, Jason had no more wish to take a life than he ever had. But all summer he had regretted his harsh rebuke to his father after Pottawatomie, and Jason was determined to stand with him now. Captain James Cline commanded the smaller detachment of volunteers. Other Free State companies that might have been available for the defense of Osawatomie had been called to Lawrence, which was bracing for attack by another division of the proslavery force that no one expected Acting Governor Woodson would stop. Cattle theft and crop destruction in the night, common harassment tactics of both pro- and antislavery partisans, had been rampant in the area for weeks, but the rumored full-scale invasion had not occurred. If it did, Osawatomie's defenders thought, it would come from the east. But early in the morning of August 30, General Reid led his army of more than three hundred up Pottawatomie Creek, approaching Osawatomie from the southwest.

Many of the residents of the town had fled days before, and, with the exception of Florilla Adair, almost all the women. Florilla had remained, with her missionary husband and two young sons, in their home on Osawatomie's western edge, as had a cousin, David Garrison, and Frederick Brown, who had insisted on returning to Kansas with his father. Fred had arisen early that morning and was walking down the road toward his uncle's cabin when he saw a party of horsemen approach. They were the advance scouts for Reid's army, but, because of the distance, Fred could not tell their identity. He held up a hand in greeting as the leader wheeled to a stop, then lowered it as he brought the horseman's features into focus. "I think I know you," he said.

Martin White could tell a Brown when he saw one as well. "I know you, and we are foes" he replied, as he shot Frederick through the heart.

David Garrison and Samuel Adair both heard the gunshot and rushed outside to see what had happened. The Missourians spotted Garrison and gunned him down as he tried to flee. Adair managed to sound the alarm to other neighbors, who quickly spread word of the attack throughout the settlement, and to Brown and his men on its other side, before taking to the woods.

The Free State companies moved quickly west, crossed the river, and took cover in the timber along its southern bank. The Missourians had delayed while Reid received White's report, and some minutes passed before they appeared in force on the crest of a hill above the town. Brown's and Cline's men were well positioned and concealed when the enemy drew within range of their fire. The first Free State volley blunted the attackers' advance, but the Missourians quickly regrouped, responding with rifle fire into the trees and blasts from the cannon that they had transported for use on abolitionist blockhouses. Cannonballs shattered tree limbs above the heads of the crouching Free State fighters, as Brown paced back and forth behind their line, urging them to stay low and keep firing. Captain Cline disagreed. Perceiving the odds to be hopeless, he instructed his company to retreat. Reid soon recognized his overwhelmingly superior numbers, and ordered his men to charge the tree line on foot. Brown's fighters pulled back only when their position had been nearly overrun. Scattering into the river, they clambered back to the north side, some crossing on logs collected for the sawmill, others diving and swimming underwater to escape the bullets that skimmed across its surface. Satisfied with this rout, the Missourians turned to the business at hand. Proceeding house to house through the deserted town, they smeared an incendiary agent on the walls of each and then applied the flame. Lying on their bellies on a hill across the river, Brown and Jason watched Osawatomie burn. When Jason looked over at his father, tears were streaming down the old man's face. "God sees it," Brown said.

When the Missourians had gone, they returned to the smoldering town. Only four Free State men had been killed, and the same number injured. Reid's casualties were almost ten times as high. The Missourians had plundered the Adairs' house but spared it upon discovering Florilla inside, and treated her considerately except to say that they would be obliged to hang her husband if they found him. Not until after dark did Adair venture to return safely from hiding with his young sons Charles and Mike. Brown's men built a coffin for Frederick, and Brown presided at the burial service. The son he had most wished to protect, the son least equipped to protect himself, was the one he had led to destruction. Brown would arrange to share his tombstone.

Ten days later, Governor Geary arrived in the Territory, just as the proslavery forces gathered for a final attack on Lawrence. This time, Free State militia companies had also massed in and around Lawrence and were ready for a fight. Geary promptly mobilized his federal troops and interceded, preventing a bloodbath. Brown had been on the first line of the town's defense, but when the battle failed to materialize he resolved to leave Kansas with Jason and John Jr. and let the new governor attempt to restore order without his inflammatory presence. Wealthy and Ellen, the families had decided, would be safe enough traveling east with their young children through Missouri. The Brown men, however, would have to take the much longer and more arduous northern route. Owen, who had convalesced in the Quaker town of Tabor in southwestern Iowa, and decided to stay on there, returned to Kansas to accompany his father and older brothers on the trip back to the free states.

Off active military duty for the first time in four months, John Brown's body broke down. He lay ill in Tabor for some weeks, nursed by Owen, after Jason and John Jr. had returned by rail to their wives in Ohio. When he had regained his strength, he continued to Iowa City and then by train to Chicago. The crime against Kansas had touched the nerves and opened the pockets of wealthy and influential men in the east. That crime was ongoing and unresolved, and more funds and arms were required to combat it. Brown's experience and reputation were irrefutable credentials that he would use to raise these funds and arms and control them. Once gathered, the resources would not be devoted to the abolition of the crime against Kansas alone. That, after all, was merely the rotten fruit of a far more evil tree.

In Chicago, Brown learned that he had crossed paths with his son Watson. Accompanied by his brother Salmon, Watson was headed west to Tabor, with the intention of continuing into Kansas Territory. He had found out from a newspaper story that a proslavery preacher named Martin White was boasting of having personally shot Frederick

Brown dead in the street on the morning of the Battle of Osawatomie. Relieved of his solitary management of the North Elba farm by Oliver's and Henry Thompson's return, Watson had set out for Kansas himself to kill White. Brown sent word to Owen that he was returning to Tabor and that Watson was to be detained there until he arrived. When he did, Brown greeted the son he had not seen in more than a year, the only son of his who had not done or suffered violence in Kansas.

We have no interest in revenge, Brown told him. What we do is for a principle.

CHAPTER TEN

Bringing Forth a New Nation

"A very few, as heroes, patriots, martyrs, reformers in the great sense, and men, serve the State with their consciences also, and so necessarily resist it for the most part; and they are commonly treated by it as enemies."
–Henry David Thoreau

W HEN JOHN BROWN came back east at the end of 1856, New England intellectuals and social reformers—at least the ones who happened to be male—were in a state of psychological crisis. The crisis had been coming on for more than a quarter century, but now it was full-blown: a crisis of confidence, of status, of masculinity. It had begun around the time that the last members of the Revolutionary generation, John Adams and Thomas Jefferson, died on July 4, 1826, the fiftieth anniversary of the Declaration of Independence. How, wondered newspaper editors and lyceum lecturers, were the sons and grandsons of this generation to measure up to the standard of virtue and achievement set by the Founding Fathers? The most common answer was that those who had inherited the nation that the founders had brought forth were bound to secure and strengthen it, to make it grow and prosper. Though this service could not equal the winning of American independence and the formation of the Republic itself, it was a way to honor that patrimony and bequeath it with interest to future generations.

Land development, the creation and expansion of markets and industries, and wealth production in general became a patriotic duty. Americans responded energetically, so much so that a national type was born. The American, as figured in both U.S. and European popular imagination during the middle years of the nineteenth century, was a maker and a man on the make. To an American, the world was a storehouse of tools and resources for the realization of his designs.

During his two terms in office, Andrew Jackson gave presidential embodiment to the figure of the entrepreneurial common man. The first president who did not hail from Virginia or Massachusetts, Jackson also represented the movement of American economic activity and potential toward the south and west, regions in which Indian land was a prime resource and African slave labor a prime tool for growth. The New England industrialists and merchants who established America's textile industry, processing slave-grown cotton and flax to meet an exploding domestic and foreign demand for manufactured clothing, were hardly excluded from the national economy that took shape during these years. Yet New England and the northeast were also home to a class whose occupations and values were neither agrarian nor commercial, an intellectual and professional class made up of ministers, educators, writers, physicians, scholar-lawyers, and the occasional philanthropic and reform-minded industrialist. For these men, many of them descendants of Revolutionary families, the United States had not been founded for the sake of economic opportunity and material progress alone. The fact that it was developing as if it had such origins was a situation that they witnessed with a multitude of unsettling feelings: distress, alienation, anger, guilt, condescension, and inadequacy.

The Founding Fathers had been men of property and action but also men of thought, letters, and principle. There was Jefferson, the planter-philosopher; Franklin, the businessman, scientist, and writer; Hancock, the merchant-statesman and strategist. But the synthesis of man's active and practical functions with his intellectual and moral ones that such leaders had represented seemed to have died with them. Sometime between the beginning and the middle of the nineteenth century, these functions had been split. At least this was how many thinking men in the northeast perceived it. Americans, they believed, had come to value only those pursuits that yielded immediate material results. This left intellectuals sidelined, emasculated.

"The so-called 'practical men' sneer at speculative men," Ralph Waldo Emerson told the members of the Phi Beta Kappa Society at Harvard in 1837, the year Jackson left office, "as if, because they speculate or *see*, they could do nothing. I have heard it said that the clergy,— who are always, more universally than any other class, the scholars of their day,—are addressed as women; that the rough, spontaneous conversation of men they do not hear." To recover the capacity for rough, spontaneous living that he felt he and hypercivilized New Englanders were in danger of losing by lack of use, Henry David Thoreau borrowed an axe and, in 1845, built himself a solitary cabin on Walden Pond, where he lived by his own exertions and fantasized about eating woodchucks raw to possess their wildness. Nathaniel Hawthorne's three great novels of the early 1850s all pair imaginative, indecisive, talking men with driven and cruel men of action whom the former admire and fear. And *Moby-Dick*, Herman Melville's 1851 masterpiece, is narrated by a neurotic ex-schoolmaster who only lives to tell his tale because he falls out of the boat in which the larger-than-life Captain Ahab, who would "strike the sun if it insulted me," is racing to his final confrontation with the indestructible white whale.

It had seemed for a while that abolitionism was the arena in which intellectual men could act again, reclaiming the country for its founding principles. But Garrison's mighty rhetoric had proved mighty in rhetoric alone. Twenty years of abolitionist speeches and organizing had not prevented the passage of the Fugitive Slave Law in 1850, and neither Harriet Beecher Stowe's 1852 bestseller *Uncle Tom's Cabin* nor her 1854 petition, signed by more than three thousand ministers, had stopped the Kansas-Nebraska Act from overturning the Missouri Compromise and permitting slavery's expansion into the west. In that same year, Massachusetts reformers had encountered the power and reach of the slave system more intimately than ever before. Anthony Burns, an escaped Virginia slave living peacefully in Boston, was pursued and discovered there by his owner, who directed city constables to arrest him and hold him for a remand hearing under the Fugitive Slave Law. A tense confrontation over Burns's fate played itself out in the courts and streets of Boston throughout the last week in May. On one side was the slave power, supported by federal law and duly served by local law enforcement officers, elected officials, and members of the Massachusetts judiciary. On the other was the Boston Vigilance Committee, comprised of some of the commonwealth's leading intellectuals and civic activists, and dedicated to preventing Boston's moral pollution by southern "bloodhounds" seeking to extradite negroes from the very "cradle of liberty." When that crisis came to a head, the slave power held firm while the reformers blinked.

At the first news of Burns's arrest, the Vigilance committee had met and taken a strong resolution. If its attorneys could not win a prompt dismissal of the petition to return the fugitive to bondage, it would rally the people of Boston to free him by force. "The man shall not go out into slavery, but over our bodies," pronounced the committee's founder, Samuel Gridley Howe, a prominent Boston physician. Handbills were published announcing a mass demonstration at Faneuil Hall, across Court Square from the courthouse in which armed guards held Burns. Reverend Theodore Parker, the current chair of the Vigilance Committee and Boston's most radical minister, would preside at that demonstration. A magnetic orator and intellectual celebrity who regularly preached to thousands in services held at the Boston Music Hall, Parker was the man to rally his listeners to march on the courthouse, where an advance guard of liberators would be waiting with axes and a battering ram. Thomas Wentworth Higginson, a bold young minister and reformer who also served as a Vigilance Committee officer, was ready and eager to lead the charge. Alone among his colleagues, Higginson had already realized and accepted the fact that violent resistance would be required to bring American slavery to an end. Where better to strike the first blow and ignite a new revolutionary spirit than in Boston?

On the night of Friday, May 26, 1854, at the appointed hour, Higginson and a few companions prepared to batter down the west side door of the courthouse the moment they perceived the inflamed throng from Parker's Faneuil Hall rally surging around the corner. But, looking out over the audience that he had whipped into a fighting frenzy, Parker had flinched at the thought of what might ensue. So, rather than send them out into the street at the peak of their outrage and courage, he hesitated, hedged, rambled, and finally dismissed them with no clear marching orders. The anticipated throng never materialized. Higginson's men, losing patience, smashed in the door anyway. Howe was in the square not far behind them, but, observing the plan's disintegration, thought of the effect of his injury or arrest on his fragile, pregnant wife, and stayed where he was. The assailants were beaten back by Boston police and the building was secured. Higginson went home with his face gashed. A week later, after a far more extensive legal proceeding than the Fugitive Slave Law required, but with no further popular resistance, Anthony Burns walked the length of Boston's main street to a ship waiting in the harbor. He was flanked by columns of special deputies and United States troops: a solitary black man at the center of a guard detail of two hundred and sixty-five whites. Anthony Burns was reenslaved.

With his son Watson and a single mule, John Brown traveled back across Iowa from Tabor, a distance of two hundred and fifty miles. Brown was fifty-six years old and as poor as he had ever been. But he was not a failure now. He had commenced to answer the end of his being, and only that end's achievement or his death would turn him aside. The bullet that he had fired into the forehead of the slain James Doyle had been his private solemnizing ritual—an initiation, a symbolic consummation. The war on slavery had begun. There would be no diversions and no retreats.

Iowa in the 1850s was in the midst of a population explosion that would increase its citizenry from less than 200,000 at the beginning of the decade to almost 700,000 at its end. Quakers had been among the first white Iowa settlers on lands purchased from Black Hawk tribal leaders in the late 1830s, and Iowa's political climate continued to reflect their strong antislavery sentiments. Towns such as Tabor in the state's western region and Springdale, east of Iowa City, were small but thriving communities, sustained by Quaker traditions of diligent and cooperative labor and by the mild self-governance of monthly general meetings at which collections might be taken up for a newcomer's stove or a committee might be appointed to admonish a young man "for getting in a passion and using unbecoming language." Most Iowa Quakers had emigrated from Indiana or western Ohio. Early in the century, though, many of their families had lived in the south. Their emigration was launched by an ominous vision revealed in a South Carolina meetinghouse in 1803. Zachariah Dicks had told of a horrific "internecine war" that the sin of slavery would one day visit upon America. Quakers in the south had responded by selling their farms and moving away from the trouble. Fifty years later, to their annoyance and dismay, Iowa Quakers found that the trouble had followed them in the form of Missouri slave catchers, on the prowl for fugitives.

Late in November of 1856, Brown rode his exhausted mule into the eastern Iowa village of West Branch, a few miles from Springdale, and stopped outside of a small tavern and inn, the Traveler's Rest. James Townsend, the Quaker proprietor, greeted him at the door. In physique and disposition, the plump and genial Townsend was the antithesis of the stranger before him, whose leanness and severity were accentuated by his long journey and virtual penilessness. To the innkeeper's polite request for an introduction, Brown replied: "Have you ever heard of John Brown of Kansas?" Townsend looked at him a moment, then dug in a pocket and removed a piece of chalk, took Brown's hat from his hand and marked the inside of its brim. Brown would never pay for a meal or a bed at the Traveler's Rest.

His name had had the same effect that August in Chicago, where his son-in-law Henry had stopped on his way back to North Elba. Still suffering pain from the rifle ball pressed against his spine, Henry had seen a surgeon there, who said the bullet needed to come out and asked where he had received it. When Henry told him he had suffered the wound at Black Jack, fighting with John Brown, the doctor replied that it would be his honor to perform the operation without charge.

The newspapers had done their work well. Lionized or demonized, he was "Old Brown" now, "Osawatomie Brown," the scourge of the proslavery forces in Kansas. It was as that man, Brown understood, that he would finally get what he needed, what he had earned. To that man, at last, would be given the money, the arms, and the companions to complete his work. For what other reason had God guided him to Kansas and preserved him there than to prepare him for that work? There was strategic importance in making Kansas a free white state, but no higher value. Any self-interested or fearful man whose wealth did not reside in slaves might approve a defensive fight to keep slavery out of a place where it was not yet established. Brown had fought that lesser fight, he now realized, to win the recognition and approval of men who would recoil at the greater one: a siege on slavery at a place where it thrived, an attack on its roots where it was most deeply rooted. His plan and purpose now was to exploit his reputation and the still uncertain outcome of the approved Free State struggle in Kansas to gain the resources he required to make all the states free.

The first necessity was to gather a cache of weapons. For this, the situation in Kansas was ideal. Guns there were both plentiful and insecure, changing hands so often that no one could hope to keep track of their whereabouts. Ruffian militias looted U.S. government storehouses in Missouri, or were secretly supplied by them. When Free State raids on proslavery camps or towns succeeded, these guns passed over to the other side. At the same time, the caravans of Free State settlers streaming into Kansas often lost their weapons to ruffian ambushes or had them confiscated by government troops. Brown had carried guns out of Kansas on both of his recent wagon treks into Iowa. A safer and more reliable weapon supply, however, were the shipments purchased by the newly organized National Kansas Committee, or its more aggressive Massachusetts chapter. These weapons awaited transport from the railroad depot in Iowa City. Visiting the National Committee's Chicago headquarters before continuing east, Brown impressed on several of its officers that the prompt delivery of guns to Kansas was of no use if they were entrusted to men who were likely to lose them. His son Owen, a veteran fighter like himself, was established in the supportive Iowa community of Tabor, from whence the supplies could be taken in swiftly and expertly as needed. Tabor was a logical place to train fighters and store arms. For the present, no one need know that the battle Brown was planning was nowhere near Kansas.

On the second day of the new year, 1857, wearing a new suit of clothes that admiring National Committee members had insisted on purchasing for him during his stay in Chicago, Brown strode into the small Boston office of the Massachusetts Kansas Committee. To the young man at the desk, he handed several letters of reference. The gangly twenty-five-year-old who accepted them was Franklin Benjamin Sanborn. A descendant of the Pilgrims, Sanborn had grown up as a bookish boy in a small New Hampshire town, dreaming of one day rubbing shoulders with great men and taking part in the great affairs of New England's metropolis. Upon passing the Harvard admissions examination, he eagerly moved to Cambridge and became a devotee of the Transcendentalist writers and preachers, whose faith in the world-transforming power of human intellect and moral instinct fired his idealism and ambition. Sanborn took long walks to Concord, hoping to chance upon Emerson or Thoreau as they strolled the woods. But it was Theodore Parker whom he selected as his intellectual and personal mentor. Sanborn sat riveted, Sunday after Sunday, beneath the cascade of spiritual inspiration and political incitement that fell from the abolitionist minister's lips. "How we mistake. Men think if they can but get wickedness dignified into a statute, enrolled in the Capitol, signed by the magistrates, and popular with the people, that all is secure," Parker had intoned, in a famous sermon on the function of conscience. "But the still small voice of justice will whisper in the human heart, will be trumpet-tongued in history to teach you that you cannot vote down God."

In 1855, Emerson had offered the new Harvard graduate a position teaching school in Concord. But over the next year, the growing Kansas crisis drew Sanborn out of the classroom and into antislavery work, first as a member of the Middlesex County Kansas Committee and, in the fall of 1856, as the secretary of the Massachusetts Kansas Committee. The Massachusetts' Committee chairman who appointed Sanborn, George Luther Stearns, was another scion of one of Massachusetts' first families and admirer of Emerson. A wealthy industrialist who had recently turned his time and talents to philanthropy and abolition, Stearns presided over the most active of the state committees that had arisen throughout the north to help bring victory to antislavery Kansans in both the population race and the armed conflict. Over the last five months of 1856, Stearns, Sanborn, and their colleagues had raised forty-eight thousand dollars for the Free State cause. A share of that money had purchased two hundred new Sharps rifles, which had been shipped to the National Committee headquarters in Chicago for transport through Iowa to equip new northern emigrants and replenish the firepower of the antislavery leaders already operating in Kansas Territory. Sanborn scarcely needed to read the letters presented to him to familiarize himself with the person of John Brown.

Brown's account of the facts on the ground in Kansas enthralled the young secretary, both by its intimate detail and by the boldness of the old soldier's analysis. When Brown wrapped his ideas and arguments in the literal language of Scripture, as it seemed he could not help but do, Sanborn was reminded of the sober spiritual zeal of the New England patriarchs who considered themselves bound in covenant to convert a howling wilderness into a city upon a hill. Brown, too, had consecrated his life to a higher cause, yet he was no mere idealist. He shrewdly assessed the danger that the incoming Buchanan administration posed to the Free State cause in Kansas and outlined a plan for an elite defense force, comprised of a well-armed and well-trained cavalry of one hundred men, that would serve as the front line against ruffian aggression anywhere in the Territory. Brown was prepared to gather and lead this force, if the Massachusetts friends of freedom would supply him. The funds he required would be spent entirely on weapons and other essential supplies, travel and training expenses, and the humblest maintenance of his recruits and his unsupported wife and daughters in North Elba. He would take no pay nor any men who required payment to fight for principle.

The conversation between the young Massachusetts secretary and the old Kansas veteran continued over several days. By January 5, Frank Sanborn had a new hero.

On that day, Sanborn arranged for Brown to meet the other influential members of the Massachusetts Committee at the home of Theodore Parker. In addition to Parker and the chairman, Mr. Stearns, these leaders included William Lloyd Garrison, Reverend Higginson, and Dr. Howe. Garrison and Brown soon squared off in a polite but heated debate about the teachings of Christianity and the permissibility of violence. Blows struck in anger, *The Liberator*'s editor contended, yielded blows of retribution, compounding the world's store of pain and sin. What would be the worth of victory in Kansas if, to win it, antislavery men must become more brutal than the Missourians? No, Garrison argued, true victory would be won by the Free State settlers' patient perseverance in the right and by the moral outrage at their unmerited sufferings that was already converting thousands to their cause. Brown struggled to mute his contempt. How much greater and longer, he challenged, had been the unmerited sufferings of millions of slaves, and what victory for them had moral outrage achieved? There had been a time when the others would have stood with Garrison, but that time was past.

On January 9, the Massachusetts Kansas Committee voted to reclaim from the National Committee its two hundred Sharps rifles and entrust them to Brown for use in defense of freedom in the Territory. It also voted him five hundred dollars for expenses, with the promise of more. On the 11th, Brown dined with the Stearns family in their Medford mansion. Mary Preston Stearns had ambitions for her husband

Patriotic Treason

JOHN BROWN'S NORTHERN SUPPORTERS

Harpers Ferry backers–later known as the Secret Six–included two ministers, a physician, an industrialist, an educator, and a philanthropist. From upper left to lower right, they are: George Luther Stearns, Gerrit Smith, Franklin Sanborn, Reverend Thomas Wentworth Higginson, Reverend Theodore Parker, and Dr. Samuel Gridley Howe.
(WEST VIRGINIA STATE ARCHIVES)

that he had not satisfied. Despite his wealth, he had not attained the public stature that she felt was his due. Mrs. Stearns suspected, too, that the time he devoted to his philanthropies, the Kansas Committee included, could be more profitably spent. But if he were going to bring home national celebrities like Captain Brown, she was willing to be persuaded otherwise.

Brown regaled the charmed Mrs. Stearns and her two young sons with his exploits. Detecting, in an offhanded remark, his hostess's resentment of the many hours her husband spent away from home on various public projects, Brown cemented Stearns's friendship by paying tribute to his own self-sacrificing wife, the knowledge of whose devotion and support during his long absences gave him strength to do his necessary work. Before Brown left, twelve-year-old Henry Stearns insisted on giving him the contents of his savings, for the relief of some poor boy in Kansas whose things the Missourians had stolen or home they had burned. He asked the abolitionist hero to write him a letter describing the kind of boy he had been, and Brown promised he would.

Leaving Boston, Brown traveled with the Massachusetts delegation to attend the National Kansas Committee meeting at the Astor House in New York on January 24. There, Sanborn moved that five thousand dollars be allocated Brown to organize and drill military companies in Kansas, but the national leaders were more cautious than Brown's Massachusetts friends. Suspicious of Brown's ultraabolitionist principles, they interrogated him about his plans and asked him to swear that any money or arms provided would be used only in Kansas and not to invade any slave state. He replied that he would not disclose his precise intentions or make any limiting promises. If the gentlemen of the committee could not support him on the basis of his proven character and achievements, he advised them to grant him nothing.

After much discussion, a divided National Kansas Committee at last approved the allocation, earmarking the money for "defensive measures" and restricting Brown from arming more than one hundred men. But the funds it promised needed to be raised before they could be turned over to Brown. The committee's treasury was empty and little energy had been expended to refill it. Governor Geary had restored relative calm to Kansas over the past four months. Public sentiment in the north had cooled, and donations had diminished. It seemed possible to hope that Kansas was on the path to free statehood without the further services of men like John Brown.

For the next three months, Brown fought northern complacency and the northeastern winter, traveling ceaselessly across Massachusetts, Connecticut, New York, and Pennsylvania, staying in one place only long enough to tell his tale and ask for money before moving on to repeat the routine at the next. After consultations with Frederick Douglass and Gerrit Smith and a brief stay with his family in North Elba in early February, he was back in Boston by mid-month, where he addressed a committee of the Massachusetts legislature that was considering a grant of state funds for Kansas relief. Sanborn gave a florid introduction in which he spoke of the "best blood of the Mayflower" running through Brown's veins, and pronounced him "eminently qualified either to represent Massachusetts in Kansas or Kansas in Massachusetts." Brown held up the trace-chains that Pierce's and Shannon's federal officers had used to bind his eldest son's ankles when they ran him before their horses like a slave being taught a lesson for seeking freedom. He recounted the boasts of the Missourians that the men of the north were too timid to fight, and that one southerner could lick a dozen of them. And, to a senator's question about the kind of emigrants Kansas most needed now, he responded: "We want good men, industrious and honest, who respect themselves, and act only from principle, from the dictates of conscience; men who fear God too much to fear anything human."

Brown's speeches and accounts of the Kansas struggle were regularly reported in the press, but yielded little ready cash. In early March, he tried a public service advertisement in the *New York Tribune*. Titled "To the Friends of Freedom," the ad called upon "all honest lovers of liberty and human rights, both male and female, to hold up my hands by contributions of pecuniary aid, either as counties, cities, towns, villages, societies, churches, or individuals." It further pledged that Brown would "endeavor to make a judicious and faithful application" of any funds he received. Outside of a few modest donations from people he knew personally, the appeal was ineffective.

In the second week of March, Brown spoke on three consecutive nights to audiences in Canton, Connecticut, his parents' childhood home. More valuable to him than the eighty dollars he raised there was his discovery of the abandoned gravestone of his grandfather, Captain

John Brown, which he arranged to have shipped to North Elba. The confidence that had surged within him since he came out of Kansas the previous fall had begun to ebb in the face of his difficulty obtaining adequate resources to advance his plan. To come across this granite testament to his namesake's Revolutionary service and to take it into his possession buoyed him. He wrote immediately to tell his wife and children the news. The stone was large enough for additional inscriptions, and he meant for it to be "faced and inscribed in memory of our poor Frederick, who sleeps in Kansas. I prize it very highly, and the family all will, I think," he added, concluding that he wished to see them all very much but could not tell when he would be able to return to North Elba. In the meantime, he hoped they would write to him soon.

The letter he received from Mary in reply was not the one he had hoped for. In twenty months, including the six since he had left Kansas, Brown had spent less than two weeks at home. Though he wrote regularly and affectionately and sent money when he could, he had left the care and support of his family to his teenage sons. Under these circumstances, the boys had responded less than enthusiastically to the prospect that the marker of the dead Captain John Brown would soon grace the home in which the live one so rarely appeared. And in case the project that their father was away financing included them, as they presumed it did, they had asked their mother to inform him that they planned to "learn and practice war no more." The implied accusation gave Brown pain, but his response was firm and unapologetic. With respect to the boys' resolution, he wrote back, through Mary, to remind them "that it was not at my solicitation that they engaged in it at the first, & that while I may *perhaps* feel no more love of the business than they do, still I think there may be *possibly* in their day that which is more to be dreaded: if such things *do not now exist.*"

As early as February, Brown had approached his new Massachusetts associates about a subscription to provide for his wife and children during his antislavery military service and in the event of his death. Though he reserved the right to define the terms and tactics of that service, Brown regarded himself as an agent of the "friends of freedom" and felt justified in asking them to help support his family at home while he traveled. After reading reports of his speech to the Massachusetts legislature, New England Emigrant Aid Society treasurer Amos Lawrence had sent Brown seventy dollars for that purpose, along with a note advising him not to expect that the National Kansas Committee would fulfill its pledge. In a subsequent letter, Lawrence professed himself unable to do anything more at the moment, but assured Brown that "your wife and children shall be cared for more liberally than you now propose" in case "anything should occur, while you are engaged in a great and good cause, to shorten your life." Brown continued to press Sanborn, Stearns, Howe, Gerrit Smith, and other antislavery activists and financiers to raise or donate funds sufficient to ease his wife's immediate burdens and anxieties for the future. At times, his evident sense of entitlement to this support came close to alienating these men. Yet, to Brown, the basis of that entitlement was clear. He would never have suggested that others should share responsibility for his family's welfare, he wrote to Sanborn, were he not conscious of "performing that service which is equally the duty of millions who need not forego a single hearty dinner by efforts they are called to make."

Overtly self-interested and coolly strategic in its attempt to play on class guilt, Brown's argument nonetheless expressed a radical principle sharply at odds with the emerging national ethos. The United States in the nineteenth century was rapidly enshrining possessive individualism as its cultural norm. A man was responsible for, and most appropriately concerned with, his personal conduct, his private property, his immediate family. A few small utopian communities on the society's fringes attempted to chart an alternative course. But Brown's notion of the duty of millions for millions did not derive from any of the European or homegrown socialisms of the day, though he followed and applauded the midcentury revolutionary struggles across the ocean. It had developed slowly in him, gaining force in reaction to the disappointments of his early career in speculation and ambition for personal wealth. But its roots lay in an earlier moment—not even so much an achieved moment as a spiritual understanding—of Protestant congregationalism.

In this understanding, notably set forth by future colonial Governor John Winthrop in his 1630 shipboard sermon "A Model of Christian Charity," each individual's first relation and responsibility was to the social body as a whole, rather than to his restricted personal domain. The reason for this priority was simple: the social body was Christ's body. Illustrating his lesson with verse after biblical verse, Winthrop reminded the first colonists of Massachusetts Bay on their way to the New World that "when He is pleased to call for His right in anything we have, our own interest we have must stand aside till His turn be served." And He calls, Winthrop continued, when the neediest members of his body call: "if thy brother be in want and thou canst help him, thou needst not make doubt what thou shouldst do; if thou lovest God thou must help him." Accordingly, Brown's assertion that he had always intended to provide for his family as best he could harbored a silent qualification that Mary understood and accepted. He would do his best under the constraints imposed by his commitment to answer his antislavery call; he would no longer sacrifice or moderate that commitment in order to do better.

With the March 31 letter, in which he told his sons that there were things more dreadful than war, Brown sent a Bible for his two-and-a-half-year-old daughter. The inscription bid his "dearly beloved daughter Ellen Brown" to carefully preserve the book "in remembrance of her father (of whose care she was deprived in her infancy), he being absent in the territory of Kansas," and "to incline your heart" toward "Him in whose care I leave you." The gesture was Brown's indirect response to the rebuke he felt he had received from Mary and his sons for his willingness to sacrifice his family life and his family's interests to the cause of the slaves. He was guilty of the charge, but the gift and message for the toddler were his way of telling the others—and reassuring himself—that his chosen absence did not cancel his love.

The language of the inscription also suggests a final farewell. Death was indeed on Brown's mind as March passed into April. With his fundraising campaign foundering, he brooded again that his time on earth would pass before his purpose was fulfilled. Jason had also written from Ohio to warn his father that federal marshals were back on his trail, this time in the eastern states, with a warrant to arrest him and extradite him to Kansas. Efforts were under way to compel John Jr., too, to return to Kansas and stand trial. Hearing that his eldest son was resisting this pressure, with the help of the family's Ohio allies, Brown wrote to him encouragingly: "If any of us are hereafter to be tried in Kansas, I would much rather it should be with Irons in rather than upon our hands." To thwart the latter outcome in his own case, Brown spread false information in the Boston press that he had returned to the Territory, while he sequestered himself on the third floor of the suburban West Newton home of Massachusetts Superior Court Judge Thomas Russell and his wife. There, he shocked Mrs. Russell by a display of the concealed weapons that he had brought down to dinner, and charmed her by apologizing in advance for ruining her carpet in case a marshal barged through the door.

Beneath his bravado, Brown acknowledged to John Jr. that discouragement and depression were his close companions during the ten days he spent in near isolation at the Russells' house. He had two hundred rifles waiting at Tabor, and the Massachusetts Committee had recently authorized him to sell half of them to entering Free State settlers to generate funds for other supplies. But otherwise he had acquired only a thousand dollars in cash, far less than he needed to execute his plan to recruit and train an army to attack slavery in the south, and he had watched the northeastern abolitionist community and Kansas committees falter in their resolution to raise thousands more. Unwilling to reveal his true intentions, he also recognized that he was expected to return to the Territory soon to put the weapons and money he had received to use. This he at last decided to do, but not before giving vent to his anger in a stinging public letter accusing the present generation of Americans of betraying their Revolutionary heritage.

"Old Brown's Farewell to the Plymouth Rocks, the Bunker Hill Monuments, Charter Oaks, and Uncle Tom's Cabins" announces his departure for Kansas and stipulates that "he leaves the States, with a feeling of deepest sadness" at its citizens' failure to suitably equip "his regular Minute men." There follows a litany of the sufferings of his sons and volunteers–hunger, cold, sickness, imprisonment, torture, death– that builds to an outraged conclusion: "that after all this, in order to sustain a cause which every citizen in this *glorious Republic* is under equal moral obligation to do, *and for the neglect of which he will be held accountable by God,* a cause in which every man, woman, and child of the *entire human family* has a *deep* and *awful* interest, that when no wages are asked or expected, he cannot secure, amidst all the wealth, luxury, and extravagance of this 'Heaven exalted' people even the necessary supplies of the common soldier. 'How are the mighty fallen?'" So enraptured or conscience-stricken by this indictment was Mary Stearns, whom Brown had favored with an advance copy of his text, that her husband sought Brown out at the Russells' and authorized him to draw up to seven thousand dollars from his personal bank account for any emergency funds he required once he returned to the field.

In mid-May, after a two-week stay with his family at North Elba, Brown set out again for Kansas with less certainty of his immediate course than hope that it would be revealed to him in due time. His consolation, as he wrote to his half brother Jeremiah, "was in the assurance that 'God reigns,'" and in his belief that "'God will not deliver me into the hand of the wicked,' and that he will still 'guide me and hold my hand,' though I have not known him at all as I ought." His reliance on God notwithstanding, Brown had made several arrangements to augment his security. In March, during the trip to Connecticut that had led him to his grandfather's gravestone, Brown had contracted with blacksmith Charles Blair to produce one thousand spears, each with an iron blade affixed by screws to a sturdy six-foot-long wooden handle. That same month, he had also secured the services of Colonel Hugh Forbes, an English merchant turned military field commander who had served under Giuseppi Garibaldi during the recent revolutionary struggles in Europe. Abandoning the comforts of his civilian life in Florence, Forbes had parlayed a talent for military strategy into a leadership role in the fight to defend the short-lived Roman Republic against vastly superior forces. Now he was lecturing in New York on the theory and practice of popular insurrection against tyranny, the subject of his nearly completed pamphlet titled *Manual of the Patriotic Volunteer*.

Seeing in Forbes a man of principle like himself, a man who had chosen to embrace a liberation struggle and was willing to take up arms for it, Brown hired him to come to Tabor and drill his volunteer militia in the latest strategies and techniques of guerrilla warfare. He could hardly protest when Forbes demanded that his six-hundred-dollar fee for six months of training be paid in advance, so that his wife and daughter—whom he had installed in France after the family fled Italy—would not starve.

The spears and the guerrilla training, for which together Brown advanced nearly all the money he had collected, were not for the defense of Kansas but for the attack on Virginia. Yet the situation in the Territory was sufficiently unsettled in the spring of 1857 to provide a plausible pretext for Brown's contracts. In March, John Geary had resigned after six months as governor of Kansas Territory, disgusted by the violence and corruption he had witnessed there. The Pierce administration had used him, putting him forward as an evenhanded peacemaker in September and then pressuring him to force slavery on an unwilling populace, once Buchanan's election was secured. "I have learned more of the depravity of my fellow man than I ever before knew," Geary wrote as he departed.

In May, Mississippi politician Robert J. Walker arrived in the Territory as its fourth governor in two and a half years. Territorial laws would be enforced and taxes collected to support its current government, Walker insisted, but the fall election of a new legislature would be fair. Though the most recent census, predictably dubbed "bogus" by Free State residents, heavily favored proslavery counties in its apportionment of seats, the eastern backers of the Free State cause urged their clients in Kansas to participate in the election and refocused their fundraising on the political campaign. Brown followed these developments from Ohio in June and from Iowa beginning in July. For long stretches during the summer and early fall, he lay disabled by severe bouts of ague, the chills, fever, and general bodily weakness to which he seemed especially susceptible when he did not know what to do.

Hugh Forbes dallied so long in New York after agreeing to conclude his affairs there and present himself for service in Iowa, that Brown wrote to him in late June to demand that he either come west at once or return the six hundred dollars he had been paid. But when Forbes joined Brown in Tabor in August, bearing copies of his *Manual of the Patriotic Volunteer* to use in the professional training of an abolitionist fighting force, Brown had just arrived himself, and he and Owen were the only patriotic volunteers on hand. From the outset, the strong wills and imperious personalities of Captain Brown and Colonel Forbes collided. The more Brown revealed to Forbes about his plan in Virginia, the more Forbes doubted the older man's military acumen and urged the substitution of a plan of his own. The two revolutionaries agreed on the tactic of lightning liberation raids as a way to undermine the security and the economics of slavery in the region of operation. But Forbes wanted to restrict that operation to slavery's northern border areas, where the raiders would be safer and transport of the freed slaves to Canada would be easier. In his view, Brown's insistence on penetrating more deeply into slave states and setting up bases in the mountains introduced unnecessary risks. As for Brown's idea of attacking a federal arsenal and arming the slaves who he was confident would flock to assist the invaders, Forbes considered it downright foolhardy.

Clashing strategies and egos alone, however, did not doom the partnership. The fact that Forbes had no one to drill, that he had spent the money he'd received, and that Brown could pay him nothing more soured the Englishman on the whole arrangement. Forbes had counted on the deep pockets of Brown's friends in the east to be a source of continuing income for himself. But when the October 5 Kansas election passed without incident, and Free State candidates won thirty-three of the fifty-two seats in the territorial legislature, Forbes concluded that no further support for Brown's military company would be forthcoming. A few weeks later, he packed up and returned to New York.

Throughout August and September, antislavery militia leaders in the Territory and Kansas Committee members in Massachusetts had implored Brown to leave Tabor and bring the two hundred Sharps rifles in his possession into Kansas for use. In numerous equivocating letters, Brown deflected their appeals. Illness and lack of funds for the weapons' transport were his stated reasons for delay, but at bottom he was unwilling to risk or share the rifles unless new hostilities produced an immediate demand for them. And inquiries he made of Samuel Adair and other friends in Kansas confirmed that no new crisis threatened. After the October elections, George Luther Stearns reached the same conclusion and wrote both to Brown and to E. B. Whitman, the territorial agent of the Massachusetts Kansas Committee, to close the seven-thousand-dollar line of credit that he had opened to Brown and personally guaranteed in April. Brown had not drawn on Stearns's account, and wrote to his benefactor on November 16 that he "had fully determined not to do it unless driven to the last extremity." To this letter he added a postscript about the cache of weapons with which the committee had entrusted him: "If I do not use the Arms & Ammunition in *actual service*, I intend to restore them unharmed; but you *must not* flatter yourself on that score *too soon*."

Brown wrote to Stearns from Topeka. He had entered Kansas quietly in early November, not for the purpose of bringing antislavery weapons in but of leading antislavery militants out. In a series of private meetings over the course of two weeks, Brown persuaded nine men to return with him to Tabor to train for a new and secret assignment. The group included one escaped Missouri slave, Richard Richardson, and eight white men. Five of these eight would remain with Brown over the next two years and go with him to Harpers Ferry. Twenty-seven-year-old John Edwin Cook—slight, sandy-haired, and romantic—was the son of a wealthy Connecticut family and had studied law in New York before deciding to emigrate to Kansas. He had met Brown shortly after Black Jack, and served in his militia unit during the rest of the summer of 1856. Eighteen-year-old William Leeman had worked at a shoe factory in Haverhill, Massachusetts, since the age of fourteen, but left it a year earlier, and arrived in Kansas just in time to fight with Brown at Osawatomie. Twenty-three-year-old Charles Tidd was a poor, idealistic, quick-tempered Kansas settler who had emigrated from Maine.

Twenty-six-year-old Aaron Dwight Stevens, a descendant like Brown of a Revolutionary War captain, had run away at sixteen from his genteel, threadbare Massachusetts home, where his father and older brother were music teachers and choirmasters. After serving in a volunteer regiment that fought in the Mexican War, Stevens enlisted in a company of United States Dragoons, where he assaulted an abusive superior officer and was sentenced to three years hard labor at the Fort Leavenworth brig. Escaping from military prison, the dashing, black-eyed, six-foot-two-inch Stevens remained in the Territory, adopted a pseudonym, and became the commanding officer of the Second Kansas Free State Militia. Twenty-two-year-old John Henry Kagi, the self-educated son of an Ohio blacksmith, came to Kansas after being fired as the schoolteacher and run out of Hawkinstown, Virginia, for making disparaging remarks about slavery. In Kansas, Kagi became a leading correspondent for eastern newspapers, fought with Stevens's militia unit, and served several months in jail for his antislavery activities.

Brown's new recruits at first assumed that the mission he had in mind was in Kansas or along its Missouri border. In Tabor, he told them their destination was Virginia.

Some of the young men argued with their leader as the eleven unpaid foot soldiers made their way east across the frigid Iowa plains, walking for twenty-four days in December beside two horse-drawn wagons crammed with a hundred Sharps rifles and a hundred revolvers each. In his journal, Owen Brown described the "hot discussion." At least it helped keep the blood from freezing in their veins. At thirty-three, Owen had learned from long experience what Cook and Tidd and Leeman were just finding out, yet still he marveled at it: you could neither change the old man nor leave him. The volunteers discussed the Bible's position on warfare, and the effects of abolishing slavery on the character and economy of the north and the south and on civilization generally. They exchanged views on what caused prejudice against color. And, huddled at night around campfires in the woods, they sang hymns and ballads and negro spirituals, Stevens's rich, beautiful baritone anchoring and elevating the efforts of the rest. As much as the cause itself, it was the thinking, the conversation, and the camaraderie that the cause inspired that bound them together.

On the 27th of January in 1858, Brown appeared at the home of Frederick Douglass in Rochester, New York, and asked if Douglass could house him for several weeks. When his friend readily agreed, Brown declared that he would only stay if he were permitted to pay for his board. Reluctantly, Douglass acceded to this condition, and, over the next three weeks, Brown spared the writer further awkwardness by remitting his weekly three dollars to Anna Douglass or to the couple's oldest daughter, Rosetta. He had left his Kansas recruits training under Stevens's direction in Springdale. The weapons had been shipped to John Jr. in Ohio, who had arranged for a safe place to hide them until they were needed over the border in western Virginia. Brown had left Kansas, crossed Iowa, and come east discreetly. He had not yet been home or contacted his family at North Elba. During his residence with the Douglasses, however, Brown wrote letters to Sanborn, Stearns, Smith, Howe, Higginson, and Parker, and to a larger network of black abolitionist friends and contacts in Philadelphia, New York, Providence, Syracuse, Chicago, and Chatham, Ontario. Within a month, he informed both sets of colleagues, he wished to meet with them in person on a matter of great importance. In the meantime, they should address any return mail to Mr. Nelson Hawkins, care of Frederick Douglass, in Rochester.

Douglass's thirteen-year-old son Charles was enlisted to post and retrieve letters for the family's boarder. Brown stayed inside composing the document that would anchor and solemnize the initiative he was about to unveil and commence. The document was a new constitution for the people of the United States who wished to pledge allegiance to their country's founding principles and defiance to its oppressive racial practices. Its purpose was first to provide an administrative and moral framework for the egalitarian, interracial provisional state that Brown planned to establish in the Appalachians; in two or three years, after slavery had been dismantled and the outlaw government dissolved, it would serve as a model charter for the free and reunited nation as a whole.

Like most of Brown's antislavery utterances and actions, "Provisional Constitution and Ordinance for the People of the United States," written by a white guest in the home of America's most famous runaway slave, combined a practical and a symbolic dimension. As well as any radical reformer before or since, Brown understood that both the institutional and the attitudinal expressions of prejudice and inequality must be attacked together. Slavery was rooted in law, economics, and physical force, but also in imagination, psychology, and ideology. Since these material and conceptual roots intertwined and reinforced one another, both must be pulled up at once. This was the reason why Brown, Douglass, and many other radical abolitionists, black and white, believed it was important for slaves to have an opportunity to fight for their freedom rather than passively receive it. Brown's audacious and remarkable document—part mundane procedural manual and part grand moral design—was founded on the same double logic. More than just a legal framework for the people who might choose to follow Brown to the mountains and join together in an extended struggle against slavery, it offered a vision of how the Constitution should be understood, and who The People of the United States truly were.

Brown's verdict on these questions stood in explicit opposition to the one that the Supreme Court had handed down eleven months earlier. A slave named Dred Scott, who had lived with his master for some years in the free state of Illinois and the free territory of Wisconsin before being taken back to Missouri, petitioned for his freedom. During his residences in Illinois and Wisconsin territory, Scott argued, he had become free under their laws and gained entitlement to the protections of citizenship. Lower courts had vacillated on the case, but when it was appealed to the Supreme Court, in which justices from slaveholding families predominated, the result was decisive and dramatic. Scott had no standing to bring a suit in a federal court and no claim to U.S. citizenship, the Court ruled. Moreover, no black person–slave or free, living or yet unborn–could ever obtain the protections of citizenship, whatever state laws might say, because a state "cannot introduce any person, or description of persons, who were not intended to be embraced in this new political family, which the Constitution brought into existence, but were intended to be excluded from it." Writing for the majority, Chief Justice Roger Taney explained that "the words 'people of the United States' and 'citizens' are synonymous terms," neither of which the founders ever meant to encompass negroes. On the contrary, blacks were regarded "as beings of an inferior order, and altogether unfit to associate with the white race, either in social or political relations; and so far inferior, that they had no rights which the white man was bound to respect; and that the negro might justly and lawfully be reduced to slavery for his benefit." Obviously then, Taney continued, when the Constitution or the Declaration of Independence used such phrases as "the rights of man and the rights of the people," it did not intend "to include them or to give to them or their posterity the benefit of any of its provisions." As far as federal law was concerned, then, blacks as property were protected anywhere in America, while black people were protected nowhere–in fact, they did not exist as bearers of any human rights at all.

The preamble of Brown's "Provisional Constitution and Ordinance for the People of the United States" announces its interpretation of America's political legacy and constituents to be the antithesis of the chief justice's. "Whereas, slavery throughout its entire existence in the United States is none other than a most barbarous, unprovoked, and unjustifiable war of one portion of its citizens upon another portion, the only conditions of which are perpetual imprisonment and hopeless servitude or absolute extermination; in utter disregard of those eternal and self-evident truths set forth in our Declaration of Independence: Therefore, We, citizens of the United States, and the Oppressed People, who, by a recent decision of the Supreme Court are declared to have no rights which the White Man is bound to respect; together with all other people degraded by the laws thereof, Do for the time being ordain and establish ourselves the following PROVISIONAL CONSTI-

TUTION and ORDINANCES, the better to protect our Persons, Property, Lives, and Liberties; and to govern our actions."

Forty-eight articles follow, beginning with the extension of citizenship to "all persons of mature age," without respect to race or sex, "who shall agree to sustain and enforce the Provisional Constitution and Ordinance." Many of the articles that follow prescribe a structure of government—complete with legislative, executive, and judicial branches—or concern the relationship between its military and its civic functions. Article twenty-five specifies that "no person connected with this organization shall be entitled to any salary, pay, or emolument, other than a competent support of himself and family." Article thirty-three pledges friendship and active protection of person and property to all slaveholders who voluntarily free their slaves. Article thirty-nine stipulates that all members of the organization "shall be held as under obligation to labor in some way for the general good." Article forty-two prescribes that "the marriage relation shall be at all times respected; and families kept together as far as possible; and broken families encouraged to reunite," and then goes on to designate the Sabbath as a day of rest and religious instruction, "unless in extremely urgent cases." Article forty-three states that all persons "of good character, and of sound mind and suitable age, who are connected with this organization, whether male or female, shall be encouraged to carry arms openly." And article forty-six reads: "The foregoing Articles shall not be construed so as in any way to encourage the overthrow of any State Government of the United States: and look to no dissolution of the Union, but simply to Amendment and Repeal. And our flag shall be the same that our Fathers fought under in the Revolution." The project, as Brown saw it, was not to destroy or divide the Union but to force it to unify and heal.

For days, he worked on his Provisional Constitution from dawn to long after dark with a single-minded earnestness that his host found both impressive and maddening. As it neared completion, he arranged for a week's visit at the end of February with Reverend James Newton Gloucester and his wife Elizabeth, a rare and successful businesswoman, both imposing figures in New York's black community. In early March he would stay with Reverend Stephen Smith, Gloucester's counterpart in Philadelphia, and meet with other black leaders there, including a veteran slave rescuer and longtime linchpin of the Underground Railroad movement, William Still. From these communities and from the large enclave of escaped slaves across the Canadian border in Chatham, Brown planned to recruit the black volunteers who would join the white men waiting at Springdale, and any of his sons who were willing to stand with him again, in the march on Virginia. With eight hundred dollars, he calculated, he could go into "Rail Road business on a *somewhat extended* scale," as he impishly described his project to Higginson, before the summer.

The action for which he sought support, Brown promised the Worcester minister, was "BY FAR the most *important* undertaking of my whole life." It would also be "my last effort in the begging line." Along with the other members of the Massachusetts Kansas Committee to whom Brown appealed, Higginson was skeptical. Brown would not reveal in his correspondence exactly what he had in mind, and he refused to come to Boston for a meeting because he feared he would be recognized there. He was generally believed to be still in the west, he said, and wished to preserve that misapprehension. Proposing to outline his plan to his Massachusetts supporters in a more out-of-the-way venue, he urged them to meet him at Gerrit Smith's estate in Peterboro, New York. No one was enthusiastic about making the trip. After all, the Free State party seemed to have matters under control in Kansas. There was nothing urgent to do there now and no need to stir things up by some ill-advised border raid. Besides, several of the committee members had received shocking and disturbing letters from Colonel Forbes, claiming that they owed him money and threatening to reveal to the authorities everything he knew about John Brown and his Massachusetts conspirators if he were not paid.

On February 18, Brown arrived at the radical New York land baron's provincial mansion. More than any white abolitionist save Brown himself, Gerrit Smith had formed close personal relationships with black activists and intellectuals. He had long shared the view of men like Douglass and Loguen that blacks would never gain white America's respect, or fully regain their own, until they had fought for their freedom. The Dred Scott decision, moreover, had reconfirmed his belief that slavery would not be dislodged except by violent insurrection. After several intense conversations, Brown persuaded Smith that the time for such insurrection had arrived and that his plan to spark and lead it, and to prevent it from spiraling into anarchy and indiscriminate slaughter, was worthy of Smith's backing. Whatever the odds of its success, Smith reasoned, there was no other plan and no other leader on offer.

Edwin Morton, a former classmate of Sanborn's and the resident tutor to Gerrit Smith's children, was party to these discussions between the sponsor of the Timbucto colony and its sole white colonist. "This is news," Morton reported to his college friend. "He 'expects to overthrow slavery' in a large part of the country." When Morton added that Smith was prepared to support the enterprise, Sanborn decided to go to Peterboro after all and hear more. In Morton's bedroom on the third floor of Smith's house, Brown paced back and forth as he rehearsed the details of the operation to the two young men: how his handpicked raiders, men fighting for principle not for pay, would infiltrate the south in western Virginia and begin to stage a series of hit-and-run liberation raids; how word of these raids would spread both in the press and through the secret communications networks that blacks had established from plantation to plantation, prompting massive slave desertions; how they would establish a chain of hidden bases in the mountains and send most of the escaped and rescued slaves north, via Brown's extensive Underground Railroad contacts; how they would retain the bravest and most able-bodied of the young fugitives to serve in the liberation force, and arm them by seizing the weapons at the lightly guarded federal armory at Harpers Ferry, when they judged the time was right and their strength sufficient to do so; how they would move farther and farther south down the Appalachian range, destabilizing and impoverishing the slave system until it finally collapsed or the South's leaders agreed to give it up.

Sanborn and Morton peppered him with practical questions and objections about supply and communication lines, the insurgents' prospects for evading or surviving the massive force that southern militias, slave patrols, and the federal government would bring to bear against them; the willingness of large numbers of slaves to risk attempting to escape; and those slaves' ability to find, assist, and be governed by Brown if they did. Patiently, Brown addressed each concern. When his interrogators were unsatisfied with his answers and pressed him for better ones, he replied simply that no good cause could fail if God wished it to succeed.

After two days, Sanborn returned to Boston, committed again to be Brown's ambassador in Massachusetts. With many men or few, with sufficient funds or none, Brown had resolved to carry out his design, leaving Sanborn and Smith "only the alternatives of betrayal, desertion, or support," as Sanborn later wrote. In the end, both found the first two options unacceptable. Jubilant, Brown composed a letter, within hours of Sanborn's departure, to thank his young friend and cement his active allegiance. The "successful cultivation" of the field in which they labored, Brown predicted, would yield a "rich harvest which not only this entire country but the whole world during the present and future generations may reap." Compared to this expectation, he continued, "how very little we can possibly lose! Certainly the cause is enough to live for, if not to _____ for." As for himself, he anticipated "nothing but to 'endure hardness'; but I expect to effect a mighty conquest, even though it be like the last victory of Samson."

That evening, Brown strolled in silence with Morton on Smith's estate. A fresh snow was falling, and the white fields were lit by a rising, clouded moon. Brown walked stiffly, hands clasped behind his back. He appeared smaller now than he had the day before, when his caged energy and high, insistent voice filled the attic room. That day, after everyone's tolerance for political conversation but Brown's had been exhausted, Smith had asked Morton to play for them at the piano in the parlor. Morton had obliged, beginning with some light concert music and then providing his own vocal accompaniment to several popular airs. Midway through Schubert's *Serenade*, he had become aware of Brown, across the room, singing softly along with him in surprisingly melodious tones. Turning his head to acknowledge his fellow singer, he found himself transfixed by the tears streaming down Brown's face. Now, lost in his own thoughts, Morton discovered that he had outstripped his companion. Brown had stopped some distance behind and turned to survey the course they had covered. Morton walked back toward him. Brown did not pivot to face him, but said as he approached, in a voice that Morton could never confidently assign either to conversation or to soliloquy: "I like to see my tracks behind me."

CHAPTER ELEVEN

An Extended Family

"In John Brown's house, and in John Brown's presence, men from widely different parts of the continent met and united into one company, wherein no hateful prejudice dared intrude its ugly self–no ghost of a distinction found space to enter. . . . I thank God that I have been permitted to realize to its furthest, fullest extent, the moral, mental, physical, social harmony of an Anti-Slavery family."
    –Osborne P. Anderson

Leaving Gerrit Smith's Peterboro mansion for James and Elizabeth Gloucester's house on Bridge Street in Brooklyn felt like coming home. Over the past year, the expensively appointed parlors and dining rooms of men such as Smith, George Luther Stearns, and Thomas Russell had been Brown's theater. On these stages, Captain John Brown had performed his stirring role and spoken his sounding lines before audiences of genteel reformers, philanthropic capitalists, poets and scholars, graduates of Harvard. These performances were for pay, or, rather, they were auditions for a far grander one that he needed underwriters to produce.

No such division between performer and audience marked the conversations at the Gloucesters' at the end of February in 1858, or at William Still's house in Philadelphia in March. The plan Brown shared with his black friends and associates might be endorsed or criticized by them, but for none of them—no more than for the solitary white man with whom they discussed it—was it a spectatorial drama, remote from their daily lives. To the black men and women who gathered with him in the Gloucesters' kitchen to pray and contemplate revolution, Brown was not an exotic, an outlaw, a Puritan throwback, or even a political extremist. He was an ally in a struggle whose urgency was self-evident and whose moral demand on them and on the nation was inescapable, whatever arguments from prejudice, interest, or timidity whites might make to the contrary. Intellectually and emotionally, Brown's orientation toward this struggle more closely resembled the orientation of black activists in the north than it did that of his white antislavery colleagues. The gulf of race, he had discovered, was easier to cross than the gulf of respectability, security, and privilege.

There was another divide that Brown's black associates warned him about, when they heard his Virginia plan, and it was one he was determined to discount. The enslaved masses, most free black leaders believed, would be far more difficult to mobilize for collective desertion and resistance than Brown supposed. As individuals, slaves desired freedom and sometimes made bold efforts to escape. But, the slave population in general–whether from suspicion, resignation, ignorance, fear, or simple inexperience in self-directed action–was likely to greet Brown's initiative with confusion and paralysis. Douglass, Gloucester, and Henry Highland Garnet all expressed this reservation to Brown. "The *masses* suffer from want of intelligence and it is difficult to reach them in a manner like you propose," James Gloucester bluntly asserted in one 1858 letter. "They are like a bark at sea without a *commander* or *rudder* ready to catch port–or no port as it may be–and it is so difficult to strike a line to meet them." Nonetheless, Gloucester concluded, "I do not despair, I only note it as it may form part of the history of your understanding and that it may not otherwise damp ardor."

Despite their concerns, his black confidantes echoed Gloucester and gave Brown their qualified encouragement. Desperate times required desperate measures. The year 1857 had brought both the Dred Scott decision and the worst economic depression since the 1837 panic. Black community leaders in the northern states and Canada were gathering to consider more seriously than ever before an array of Central American, South American, West Indian, and African colonization schemes. Chief among the black colonizationists was Martin Delany, formerly a Pittsburgh physician and negro suffrage campaigner who had qualified for admission to Harvard Medical School and studied there for one semester before the rest of the student body refused to attend class with him and insisted that he be dismissed. In 1856, Delany organized the Niger Valley Exploring Party and began to seek funds and colonists for the establishment of a free-labor settlement in Africa. In the meantime, he joined the growing number of American blacks, escaped slaves and freedmen, who had taken up residence in Canada. A formidable intellect and powerful writer and orator, Delany was a man whose career illustrated the bitter point of James Gloucester's second 1858 letter to Brown. Professing himself "more and more convinced that now the day and now the hour, and that the proper mode is at last suggested," the minister enclosed twenty-five dollars to support the insurrection that he had come to see as the best hope not only for slaves but for blacks throughout the country. "There is in truth no black man, north or south of Mason and Dixon Line," wrote Gloucester, who qualifies as "a freeman, whatever be his wealth, position, or worth to the world."

Brown believed that the slaves were similarly desperate and that they would fight when supplied with aid, arms, and leadership from the north. He bristled at a white abolitionist friend whose argument to the contrary invoked the racial stereotype of innate negro passivity and good-natured tolerance of injustice and pain. "You have not studied them right, and you have not studied them long enough," Brown countered. "Human nature is the same everywhere."

His own personal study, however, had been limited to an unrepresentative sample of the black population, consisting mainly of the north's most militant black intellectuals and boldest Underground Railroad conductors. Yet he had also seen, and helped organize, the determination of common laborers in Springfield, Massachusetts, to resist the enforcement of the Fugitive Slave Law in their community, by deadly violence if necessary. And he had supplemented and confirmed his firsthand observation by reading.

Even when he was bankrupt, Brown had managed to save or borrow small sums of money to keep up his subscriptions to abolitionist newspapers: the *National Era*, the *Anti-Slavery Standard*, *The Liberator*, *Frederick Douglass's Paper*, and other shorter-lived journals such as *The Ram's Horn*. Year after year, these publications had reported the countless acts of resistance by which slaves defied the authority of their masters, and the horrific punishments that regularly followed such acts yet failed to deter them. The well-known deeds of Nat Turner, Madison Washington, and Cinque also proved the willingness of slaves to rise up against their oppressors when leaders and opportunities presented themselves. But the most eloquent testimony to black revolutionary potential was the career of Toussaint L'Ouverture, the George Washington of Haiti.

Brown had read everything he could find on Toussaint, the subject of several popular biographies and published lectures that appeared in the early 1850s to mark the fiftieth anniversary of Haiti's successful slave revolution. In the representations of his nineteenth-century biographers, Toussaint, the grandson of an African king, was a deeply spiritual and principled man, and an avid self-taught reader, who thrilled to the ideals of human liberty, equality, and fraternity that he discovered in the literature of his French enslavers. Though he died in a French prison, the middle-aged Toussaint was the master strategist who guided half a million slaves to eventual victory in a many-sided, decade-long war of liberation. Brown believed that other Toussaints lived today. As obscure as the Santo Domingo revolutionary had been before his moment arrived, these potential slave leaders labored on Virginia tobacco farms or Louisiana cotton plantations while they awaited theirs. American slaves craved freedom no less than Haitian ones had. Human nature was the same everywhere.

Brown's conversations with James Redpath buttressed his conviction. Redpath, the journalist and radical abolitionist who wandered into his camp a few days after Pottawatomie, had left Kansas at about the time Brown did and remained a close associate. During two tours of the south, the journalist conducted discreet interviews with slaves, whom he reported to be "already ripe for a rebellion." Redpath's account of his conversations, *The Roving Editor; or, Talks with Slaves in the Southern States*, also included a description of "the extraordinary facilities possessed by the slaves in communicating with each other," an Underground Telegraph by means of which, at the appropriate hour, a signal to revolt could "spread southward, and reach, in the silent hours of the night, thousands of eager souls now awaiting, in trembling anxiety, for the terrible day of deliverance."

Brown's consultations with black leaders in Philadelphia concluded in mid-March. Douglass arranged for him to stop in Rochester two weeks later on his way to Canada to meet with the legendary slave rescuer Harriet Tubman. Jermaine Loguen would join Brown at Douglass's house and accompany him on the trip north as a liaison to Tubman and a guide to the vibrant and radical black communities of St. Catherines and Chatham in Canada. There, Brown meant to hold a convention to unveil his Provisional Constitution and enlist black officers for the fighting force that he would take to Virginia and administrators for the revolutionary state that would form in the mountains as slaves heard about the plantation raids and flocked to join their rescuers. Brown planned to send for Owen and the others in Iowa, bring them together with his black recruits from Canada and the northeastern states, and infiltrate the south by summer.

Between his Philadelphia and Canada trips, Brown went home. It had been nearly eleven months since he had seen his family in North Elba, and, in his recent correspondence, he had allowed himself to feel and acknowledge the strain of this long, solitary absence. "The anxiety I feel to see my wife and children once more I am unable to describe," he had written from Rochester at the end of January. But his strongest emotional commitment and sense of obligation now frankly attached to a more distant and extended family, and he made no promises to his immediate dependents. "The cries of my poor, sorrow-stricken despairing children, whose 'tears on their cheeks' are ever in my eyes, and whose sighs are ever in my ears, may however prevent my enjoying the happiness I so much desire," he added. He was particularly eager to hold his new grandchild, Ruth and Henry's youngest, whom he had not met, and his own baby daughter Ellen, now three-and-a-half, who he feared had forgotten him again. She had perched on his lap each day of his last visit, as he read aloud from her Bible, the one he had inscribed and mailed to her along with his response to Mary's news that their sons planned to study war no more. But he had stayed less than two weeks before setting off again for Kansas. This time the reunion would be even shorter. Nor was family reunion Brown's entire purpose in making the trip, unless reunion included the rededication of his sons to their father's war.

In the moment he gave the signal outside the Doyles' cabin, heard the quicksilver whistle in the hilts of Owen's and Salmon's sabers, and watched dark stains spread on the nightclothes of two of the Doyles as they fell, Brown had completed the sacrifice of his own family as well to the cause for which he fought. Or he had completed their identification with it. Like other men, he would continue to entertain personal longings and regrets, but he would not indulge them. There was no more private sphere for him; family feeling and family welfare were encompassed in a larger circle of empathy and obligation. If the wife and children that he left at home understood themselves to be diminished in his affections or esteem, they expressed no sense of betrayal. As for the sons who stood with him in battle, they understood and accepted that he loved them as fellow soldiers and volunteers. So long as they chose to fight, their lives belonged to the cause, whose life was more important than theirs, as it was than his. That was his other purpose for returning to North Elba. His sons and son-in-law were the most tested and altruistic fighters against slavery he knew, and the ones he most trusted. Brown needed them back.

He had made this desire clear well in advance of his arrival. The letter he wrote to his family from Douglass's home at the end of January had touted the qualifications of Salmon, Oliver, Watson, and even Jason for the project he was organizing, but it appealed particularly to Ruth for the further services of her husband: "O my daughter Ruth! could any plan be devised whereby you could let Henry go 'to school' (as you expressed it in your letter to him while in Kansas), I would rather have him 'for another term' than to have a hundred average scholars." Brown's request produced in both Ruth and Henry an intense ethical and emotional struggle, one that reveals the depth of the entire Brown family's commitment to personal sacrifice in aid of the slaves. "Dear father," Ruth wrote back, "you have asked me rather of a hard question. I want to answer you wisely, but hardly know how. I cannot bear the thought of Henry leaving me again; yet I know I am selfish. When I think of my poor despised sisters, that are deprived of both husband and children, I feel deeply for them; and were it not for my little children, I would go almost anywhere with Henry, if by going I could do them any good."

Brown spent nine days with his family. By Oliver's wedding day on April 7, he was well on his way to Canada. Oliver had romanced the daughter of a nearby farmer named Brewster who despised abolitionists and washed his hands of his child Martha when she married into the Brown family. But the teenage Martha Brown promptly embraced her husband's principles and accepted his recommitment, confirmed during Brown's visit, to fight slavery with his father when he was called.

Watson, who had set off for Kansas to kill Martin White within days of his marriage to Henry Thompson's sister Isabella in the fall of 1856, also announced himself ready to join the Virginia expedition. Only Salmon appeared inclined to remain a noncombatant, in deference to his wife of five months, Abbie Hinckley, who adamantly opposed his return to service with Brown and vexed the other Brown women by her stance.

Ruth and Henry agonized over their competing responsibilities throughout Brown's stay in North Elba. At some point in their discussions with the man whom both called "father," they concluded that those who went south with Brown were likely to die there. Still, Henry and Ruth were equivocal. Finally, three weeks after Brown's departure, Henry wrote to him in Canada to say that he had decided to remain behind. "If I thought the success of the enterprise depended on my going, I should go at once. *Nothing* but three little helpless children keeps me at home," he explained, adding that, even for his family, it was "hard to give it up, my whole heart is in the work."

Brown passed the middle weeks of April in Canada's two largest and most active settlements of American fugitive slaves. In St. Catherines, across the Niagara River from Buffalo and a principal destination of the Underground Railroad line that ran through Philadelphia and New York, he spent several days conversing with Harriet Tubman, the most famous and daring fugitive slave conductor of the 1850s. Beyond her prodigious energy and courage, Tubman possessed an unerring instinct for danger and a brilliant array of deceptions, disguises, communication codes, and navigational strategies. More than fifteen times, since her own 1849 escape from a plantation on Maryland's Eastern Shore, the former field slave had returned to Dorchester County, often disguised as an elderly woman or man, and rescued groups of family and friends. Arranging for Saturday night departures, so that the next newspaper in which one could print fugitive announcements would not appear until Monday, and employing free blacks to follow a distance behind slave catchers and tear down the runaway notices they posted, Tubman managed to convey more than seventy slaves to freedom without having to fire the large pistol that she always carried as a last means of defense.

Harriet Tubman's willingness to go back to the site of her bondage and confront slavery on its own ground made her a crucial ally in

Brown's view. She could gather and inspire large numbers of black recruits for him if anyone could, he thought, and her Railroad experience and contacts in Maryland and eastern Pennsylvania could help him establish a passageway wide and secure enough for the transport north of the large numbers of slaves that his raids would liberate or encourage to flee. Sitting with Tubman and some of the men and women she had liberated, Brown considered whether he had ever encountered anyone he admired more. This diminutive, illiterate woman, who suffered from chronic poverty and intermittent seizures stemming from a near fatal blow to her head with an iron weight, regularly defied and defeated the slave power, relying often, as she told him, on directions intuited from her sense of God's mysterious presence and will. "He (Harriet) is the most of a man, naturally, that I ever met," Brown wrote exuberantly to John Jr.

From St. Catherines, Brown traveled west to Chatham, the center of black political and cultural life in Canada. Due east of Detroit on the opposite bank of Lake St. Clair, Chatham was home to more than one thousand fugitive slaves and free black emigrants from the United States. The town's black residents made up nearly a third of its total population and, by the mid-1850s, had attained a public visibility and a communal solidarity that prompted blacks on both sides of the border to speak of Chatham in tones of awe, pride, and envy. Chatham's black community created and sustained its own cultural institutions, including not only three churches, which had merged into the single large First Baptist Congregation of Chatham by the time of Brown's visit in 1858, but also Canada's first black public school; a Vigilance Committee that rivaled Springfield's League of Gileadites in its militancy and effectiveness; two black newspapers, the *Voice of the Fugitive* and the *Provincial Freeman;* and several benevolent societies, literary circles, and lecture series organized by two noted women intellectuals and activists, Amelia Freeman Shadd and Mary Ann Shadd Cary.

In spite of its vibrancy and cohesiveness, the black community in Chatham, like black communities elsewhere in Canada and the United States, was uncertain of its future. Some of its leaders believed that the best hope for Canada's blacks lay in affirming their identity and loyalty as black Anglo-Canadians. Canadian blacks encountered hostility less violent and pervasive than their counterparts in northern cities below the border, but they also faced mounting prejudice and restrictions as their numbers increased. These circumstances, combined with the never-ending risk of recapture for fugitives and their families, pushed other leaders, such as Dr. Martin Delany, toward the last resort of African colonization. When Captain John Brown of Kansas appeared unannounced at the door of Delany's house in Chatham and asked the doctor to organize and host a general convention to plan the armed overthrow of slavery in the American south, Delany was already immersed in his preparation for the third National Emigration Convention, which was scheduled to take place in Chatham that summer.

Though he held out little hope for a viable future for blacks in North America, Delany was attracted by the sheer vitality and immediacy of Brown's intention, and flattered by his fierce insistence that only Delany had the credibility to bring large numbers of militant blacks together to consider its enactment. As a rule, Delany had little faith in white antislavery leaders and less interest in working for them, but he signed on to recruit delegates to Brown's constitutional convention and to chair the proceedings. Only violent revolt against the masters, he believed, could bring self-respect and manhood to blacks in America. Besides, Brown proposed to begin his invasion near Harpers Ferry in Jefferson County, Virginia–Delany's birthplace.

While Delany made the arrangements in Canada, Brown traveled back across the border and took the train from Detroit to Chicago to the one-street Quaker village of Springdale, Iowa. There, he would gather his sequestered Kansas fighters and bring them east. With the convention scheduled for the second week in May, Brown thought he might just be able to consolidate his black and white recruits, get the promised funds from his friends in Boston and New York, and have his weapons delivered to a safe house near the point of attack in time for the midsummer launch of his operation. Harriet Tubman had proposed the Fourth of July as a fine date for the second American Revolution, and he had smiled and nodded at the suggestion. That two people of different sexes, races, and origins should independently seize on the same idea delighted Brown. All were indeed equal under God, and united in Him.

If violence, chaos, and hardship had made Kansas seem like hell to the idealistic young men who followed Brown out of the Territory in the last weeks of 1857, in Springdale, Iowa, they found a kind of heaven. Order and quiet reigned on the town's broad thoroughfare, lined with neat frame houses set in spacious yards. The simple dress of their Quaker hosts, their frank and respectful manners, and the aura of sacredness that their quaint "thee's" and "thou's" imparted to those with whom they conversed bathed Brown's men in calm. Everyone understood that their residence was only temporary and that they were combatants. Yet the visitors received affectionate welcome from this wholesome, serious-minded community, and experienced the town's embrace as a benediction on the course they had elected to pursue.

Not all was silence and spirit for Brown's little company during their four-month bivouac among the Quakers. They were there to train. Sharing their visitors' antislavery zeal, Springdale's Quaker householders nonetheless preferred not to shelter carnal weapons under their roofs or to provide the actual grounds for the military exercises. So the men lodged three miles northeast of the village at the farmhouse of William Maxson, who was not a member of the Society of Friends, and performed daily military exercises and physical conditioning drills in the east yard by a thick stand of evergreens. Aaron Stevens served as trainer, leading his fellows in mock tactical maneuvers, target practice, and swordplay with wooden sabers. By the commencement of their physical training at ten each morning, the men had already devoted three or four hours to book study in the large Maxson sitting room. Though Colonel Forbes himself had abandoned them, his *Manual of the Patriotic Volunteer* was pored over and discussed. And Brown had had Frank Sanborn solicit from his friends' ample libraries used copies of other books to instruct and inspire his volunteers as they awaited their call: Plutarch's *Lives*, Irving's *Life of Washington*, biographies of Napoleon and other great or bold leaders, and books that provided maps and statistics of the various regions of the United States.

On Tuesday and Friday evenings, Brown's men met in one of the rooms of the district school building to conduct formal debates on political and moral topics. After a while, they hit upon the idea of convening a mock legislature and followed up their policy debates by drafting and passing appropriate laws for their ideal "State of Topeka." Increasingly, these biweekly forensic efforts were witnessed and joined by local young men and women, who found the evenings both entertaining and intellectually stimulating. To the small village of Springdale, this curious, exuberant band of antislavery soldiers, journalists, and moral philosophers had brought the wide world. For their part, the collection of bachelors, outcasts, loners, and runaways who made up the company found in each other and in the town the closest family and most sustaining home that many of them had ever known.

Several of the men quickly established affectionate sibling relationships with the young women of the town. The intimacy of these bonds was permitted and protected by a common understanding that, under the circumstances, romantic attachments were not to be pursued or contemplated. In the eyes of their "sisters," and in their own, the visitors' acceptance of chastity as the only course consistent with honor ennobled their cause and sanctified their zeal in it. That cause, and the appeal of its devotees, attracted the young men of Springdale as well. By the time Brown returned for his troops, two Quaker brothers, Barclay and Edwin Coppoc, had decided that helping bring slavery to an end more truly expressed the spirit of their religion than preserving its traditional practice of pacifism.

On the morning of April 27, each of Mr. Maxson's ten boarders wrote his name in pencil on the parlor wall near the door. A crowd accompanied the young men to the station. Tears flowed freely at their departure. Few in Springdale knew the particulars of the mission on which their friends were embarking, but most had gleaned enough to share the pessimism of Dr. H. C. Gill, a leading citizen of the town whom Brown had taken into his confidence. "I did my best to convince him that the probabilities were that all would be killed," Dr. Gill later wrote. Specifically, he recalled warning Brown: "You and your handful of men cannot cope with the whole South." Brown only shrugged, and replied: "I tell you, Doctor, it will be the beginning of the end of slavery."

The constitutional convention was called to order on Saturday, May 8, at Chatham's negro schoolhouse on Princess Street. In the preceding ten days, Brown had mailed several dozen requests for attendance at "a very quiet convention" to radical abolitionists, black and white, across New England, New York, and Pennsylvania. To those possessed of slender means, he offered to pay travel expenses to Canada. No one accepted the invitation. Martin Delany's recruitment efforts, on the other hand, yielded thirty-four black delegates. Though residents of Chatham and surrounding Canadian settlements predominated, this group also included several activist ministers, vigilance committee heads, and Underground Railroad station masters from Detroit and northern Ohio.

The only whites in attendance were Brown and the men he had brought from Iowa. Strolling the streets of the negro district of Chatham, these volunteers at first struck the town's black residents as mere oddities, but, like their leader, soon won general affection and trust. They were not like any white men anyone had ever seen before. In the first week of May, Osborne Anderson, the only Chatham black who would participate in the Harpers Ferry raid seventeen months later, had worked with several members of Brown's band on the convention's final arrangements. Anderson, a Pennsylvania native and student of the printing trade in Canada, was drawn to these men from the start by the love of words and ideas that they seemed positively to radiate. As much as their conversation, it was the men's appearance that distinguished them as intellectuals and radicals in Anderson's eyes. John Kagi, who had emerged as Brown's most energetic and trusted lieutenant, typified the personal style of the group. Tall, angular, and slightly stoop-shouldered, Kagi could appear awkward and bashful until he began to speak. Then, it was as if his logic and passionate eloquence unified all the ill-assorted parts, including his haphazard clothing and his unbrushed hair. To varying degrees, the other young men in the "surveying party," as they referred to themselves, shared this combination of insouciance and underlying intensity. Both expressed the bond that joined them. To Anderson, watching them "sallying forth arm in arm, unshaven, unshorn, and altogether indifferent about it," Brown's surveyors signified freedom.

The first order of business conducted by the delegates to the convention was the election of Reverend William Monroe, rector of St. Matthew's Protestant Episcopal Mission in Detroit, to serve as presiding officer. Monroe was a longtime member of the Michigan Anti-Slavery Society and a tireless campaigner for black voting rights. Fifteen years earlier, he had attended the National Convention of Colored Citizens in Buffalo and heard Henry Highland Garnet's shocking "Address to the Slaves of the United States of America" with its tribute to "the patriotic Nathaniel Turner" and its overt call for rebellion: "Rather die freemen, than live to be slaves." Monroe had voted with the minority, and against Douglass, to publish Garnet's speech and include reference to it in the convention's minutes. That was in 1843, before the Fugitive Slave Law, the Dred Scott decision, the admission to the Union of the slave state of Texas, and the continuing efforts of slaveholders and their representatives in Congress and the White House to create new slave states in the western territories. Garnet had appeared rash and impatient to many of Monroe's colleagues then. Now Garnet's way, John Brown's way, seemed to Monroe the only hope for blacks in America.

To disguise the purpose of this conspicuous gathering, Delany had dropped hints around town about the formation of a Masonic lodge. The rumors did not allay suspicion so much as they generated intrigue. By midmorning, so many curious townspeople hovered outside the schoolhouse windows that Monroe's first executive decision was to move the proceedings to the more cloistered interior of Chatham's black firehouse. Returning to business, the delegates chose John Kagi as convention secretary. Then Delany rose to introduce Brown himself and request that he explain the objectives of the action he proposed and how he hoped to achieve them. Fastidious in his grooming, Brown had gone clean-shaven throughout his life, before letting his beard grow out over the last few months. It had come in white and full and unruly, so that the man who stood to address the assembled black abolitionists in the engine house of Volunteer Fire Company No. 3 looked like an Italian painter's image of an Old Testament prophet. Brown spoke, however, more like a professor than a prophet. Enumerating the precedents for slave revolt and successful popular insurgency, and citing lessons gleaned from his readings in military history and his survey of Napoleonic battlefields, he outlined his plan to destabilize and eventually defeat slavery by a series of plantation raids, retreats to a network of secure mountain fortresses, and gradual assimilation of ever larger numbers of liberated and escaping slaves into his fighting force.

No one objected to a direct, armed attack on slavery in the south. For at least some of the delegates, the matter was not an ethical or a tactical one so much as a question of whether any reunion with family left behind might be possible in their lifetime. The discussion that followed Brown's speech focused on the prospects of fulfilling two necessary conditions for the plan's success: the ability of the insurgents to evade or defeat the army and slave patrol search teams that would be sent into the mountains to destroy them, and the willingness of slaves to risk rising up en masse and bearing arms against their former masters. Brown had heard the objections before and argued strenuously that both conditions could be met. When Chatham gunsmith and Oberlin graduate James Monroe Jones expressed the same doubt about the aggressiveness of the average Virginia slave that Douglass, Gloucester, and even Garnet had previously voiced, Brown defused the debate by begging "Friend Jones" to keep that idea to himself, since, after all, it had so many other champions. The delegates laughed. How could anyone truly know whether the slaves would revolt until they were provided with adequate means and a promising occasion to do so?

The convention proceeded to the reading of the Provisional Constitution and Ordinance for the People of the United States. Following an oath of secrecy administered by Delany, the secretary began to read the document aloud. Kagi's rich, clear voice and his four months of Tuesday and Friday evening oratorical training in Iowa were not wasted. In his mouth, the words of Brown's preamble exploded into the stillness like cannon fire.

Authorized by "those eternal and self-evident truths set forth in our Declaration of Independence," the new nation would be established on land taken by force from the existing United States. Exactly who would make up the citizenry of this provisional and combatant nation, what territory it would occupy, and where and how the proposed executive, legislative, and judicial branches of its government would function were details on which its constitution was necessarily silent. But these details were of small concern to the delegates crowded into the firehouse. Uncertainty and improvisation were too familiar in their lives to disturb them. They well understood that the union conceived in this document might never be realized, yet they endorsed it because it was the same one that each had dreamed.

Listening to Kagi, they heard that union articulated for the first time, not as a religious or utopian ideal but as an immediate political demand and commitment. Eligible citizens, as the constitution's first article defined them, consisted of "all persons of mature age, whether Proscribed, oppressed, and enslaved Citizens, or of the Proscribed and oppressed races of the United States." All were equally "the People of the United States" in whose name Brown had written, all shared the distortion of their humanity by slavery, and all, by the terms of this Provisional Constitution, were equally entitled to vote, to bear arms, to own nonhuman property, to hold office, to pursue happiness.

Only one article drew resistance and debate. Article XLVI stipulated that the Provisional Constitution called for no overthrow of any state government and no dissolution of the Union. "And our flag," the paragraph concluded, "shall be the same that our Fathers fought under in the Revolution." It was this embrace of the Stars and Stripes as their standard at which several of the black delegates balked. Too many of them, James Monroe Jones grimly observed, already carried America's stripes on their backs. But several influential black delegates, including Delany and Monroe, urged that the flag be retained as a symbol of the revolutionary principles to which they held true, and of their right to liberty in the land of their birth and labor. Opposition began to crumble. In the end, the constitution was unanimously approved, and each black man and white in turn affixed his signature to the document.

On Sunday morning, May 9, his fifty-eighth birthday, Brown worshipped with the black population of Chatham at their First Baptist Church. The previous evening forty-five men, three quarters of them former slaves or descendants of slaves, had ratified his blueprint for a second American Revolution and a new American nation that would fulfill the betrayed promise of the old. The act of bringing that nation forth would soon begin.

On Monday, the convention moved to the church for its concluding session: the election of the officers of the new provisional government. After some discussion, it was resolved that the election of a president and vice president would be deferred. Two black delegates, Alfred Ellsworth and Osborne Anderson, were elected as congressmen and agreed at an appropriate future date to join Brown and several members of his militia in selecting the initial appointees to offices unfilled by the convention. Balloting for cabinet positions essential to the impending military campaign returned four of Brown's Kansas volunteers, who would immediately accompany him south. Kagi was to be secretary of war. Earlier, by acclamation, Brown had been appointed army commander in chief.

Osborne Anderson, a journeyman printer who emigrated to Canada from Pennsylvania, was selected at the Chatham convention to hold the office of congressman under Brown's Provisional Constitution. Anderson was the only Canadian black to participate in the raid on Harpers Ferry. (WEST VIRGINIA STATE ARCHIVES)

Brown's experience of triumph and his men's anticipation of moving swiftly "onward to the chosen field of our labor" were short-lived. Throughout the spring of 1858, while Brown sought funds and men for his southern campaign and planned the Chatham convention, an aggrieved Colonel Hugh Forbes was mailing threatening letters to the "humanitarians"–as he sarcastically addressed the officers of the Massachusetts Kansas Committee–who were starving his children. Forbes had received from Brown and Gerrit Smith more than the six-month salary he had demanded, and had spent less than three months in Iowa, where he trained no one. Yet he contended that he had been promised a year's employment and was owed the balance. Scorn for Brown's invasion scheme, for which his own superior plan and military judgment had been spurned, compounded Forbes's anger. Though he did not know the identities of all of Brown's Massachusetts backers, or the extent of their knowledge of Brown's intentions, Forbes understood that prominent members of the Kansas Committee had given Brown money and weapons earmarked for Kansas's defense that the old man planned to use offensively elsewhere.

When his ranting letters to Sanborn and Howe failed to produce a satisfactory response, Forbes began to drop hints to elected officials of a brewing conspiracy. Finally, he appeared in Washington, where he managed to buttonhole Massachusetts Senator Henry Wilson to ask whether the senator knew that some of his most prominent constituents were involved in a plot to misappropriate state Kansas Committee resources in support of a wild attack on the south. Sanborn had planned to attend the convention in Chatham and deliver the six hundred dollars that Brown claimed he needed to pay his men's bills in Canada and transport them to Virginia. Instead, in the first week of May, he found himself huddling frantically with Howe, Stearns, Parker, and Higginson to determine how to respond to Wilson's demand for answers, how to deflect or discredit Forbes, and what to do with Brown.

On May 12, Dr. Samuel G. Howe wrote to assure his friend Senator Wilson that "no countenance has been given to Brown for any operations outside of Kansas," whatever Wilson might have heard to the contrary from a certain "disappointed and malicious man, working with all the activity which hate and revenge can inspire." Two days later George Stearns posted to Chatham an icy letter, addressed "Dear Sir" and signed "Chairman Mass. State Kansas Committee," that officially warned Brown not to use the Kansas Committee's arms in his possession for any purpose besides the defense of Kansas. Both Howe's and Stearns's letters were smokescreens, saved by technicalities from being outright lies. It was not the state Kansas Committee but a second private committee, composed of the chairman and several other prominent members of the first, that had authorized Brown to fight slavery outside of Kansas. As for the weapons, they had been quietly purchased from the Kansas Committee and re-entrusted to Brown without conditions by Stearns himself. By this time, moreover, the rifles in question were nowhere near Kansas but in a furniture warehouse in Ashtabula County, Ohio, where an abolitionist associate of John Brown Jr.'s had agreed to store them beneath his inventory of ready-made coffins.

Brown's men also proceeded to eastern Ohio to await further instructions, while Brown remained in Canada, awaiting funds from Boston with which to pay the remainder of his Chatham expenses and provide passage south for new black recruits who could not afford their own transport. The money that arrived barely covered his debts for the convention and was accompanied by an urgent summons to Boston to discuss postponement of the surveying expedition. Gerrit Smith joined Stearns, Howe, Parker, and Sanborn for two days of meetings with Brown in his room at the American House, where the financiers of the Virginia campaign agreed that it should be postponed. Promising Brown two to three thousand dollars to revive the initiative at some point in the future, his sponsors instructed him to return to Kansas for a few months in order to undermine Forbes's credibility and dispel any alarm or suspicion that he may have aroused. In his characteristically embarrassed financial circumstances, Brown had no choice but to comply. On his way back west, he stopped in Cleveland to rally his dispirited troops. It was clear now that the Chatham convention would not significantly increase their numbers. There was no money to pay for the travel of black recruits and nowhere for them to go. To his original surveyors Brown preached patience and courage.

The 1857 depression had not yet lifted. Two thousand men were out of work in Cleveland alone, and the best a placeless man could hope for was ten hours of daily farm work in exchange for a dry bed and enough food to live on. Forced to scatter, the company of volunteers resolved to keep in touch by letter, in order to retain their mutual bond and assure their prompt reunion when their moment finally arrived. "It is in times of difficulty that men show what they are," one of Brown's letters encouraged. "Are our difficulties sufficient to make us give up one of the noblest enterprises in which men were ever engaged?" The men were young and glory was not unappealing. Yet it was not glory or moral nobility that was their watchword, but duty. This was the term that circulated among themselves and that they offered to family and friends, often without fanfare or adornment, to explain the unpromising chosen field of their labor. Cook spoke for most when he wrote to his adopted "sisters" in Springdale that, although time hung heavily, there was "one thing that keeps me from being absolutely unhappy, and that is the consciousness that I am in the path of duty."

Kagi and Tidd accompanied Brown to Kansas. With Iowa native George Gill, Aaron Dwight Stevens went back to Iowa to look for jobs there. They rejoined Brown later in the summer. Owen found farm work for a time with a tyrannical employer whom he soon left to lodge with Jason in Akron. For the escaped Missouri slave, Richard Richardson, migratory day labor in the United States was both unpromising and perilous. He returned to Canada, where he experienced a religious conversion and dedicated himself to missionary work. Richard Realf, a British-born journalist who had embraced Brown's cause and methods in Kansas, was dispatched to New York to try to talk reason to Forbes. Before Realf left Canada, he too sought to rally his colleagues, reminding them that "it is natural that men who have cut themselves loose from all other associations, purposely to devote themselves to a great and worthy end, should be chafed by difficulties and delays." But in the end, he affirmed, God "will not let his work go unfinished. Much love of all to all." John Cook alone proceeded to Harpers Ferry. Though Brown had reservations about the discretion of his most sociable and loquacious follower, Cook convinced him that these very qualities would help him assimilate naturally into the community and acquaint himself with its inhabitants and their routines. Once he was no longer a stranger, Cook would discreetly survey the surrounding estates and assess the disposition of their slaves.

On Friday evening, June 25, 1858, an old man with a formal bearing and a flowing gray beard took a seat at the long public table of a Lawrence hotel dining room. He attracted stares from the other patrons, many of whom thought he looked familiar. A few whispered to their companions that they believed the man was John Brown, in disguise. To his Kansas friends, Brown seemed somewhat more agitated than he had been during the height of the troubles, two summers before. Yet he still sufficiently commanded his emotions, or at least their expression, that the agitation rarely surfaced in any overt form. "Patience is the hardest lesson to learn," he told Richard Hinton, an abolitionist comrade. "I have waited for twenty years to accomplish my purpose." Though Kansas no longer figured in that purpose, a grisly incident in a Free State settlement along its southeastern border gave Brown something to do there besides wait.

On May 19, a proslavery party of close to thirty men, led by a Georgian named Charles Hamilton, had crossed the Missouri border into Linn County in Kansas and abducted eleven leading citizens, including the local minister, from their homes, businesses, and farms in and around the village of Trading Post. The captives were marched to a ravine a half mile from the Missouri line, where they were shot by firing squad. All the victims fell, and those who were not mortally wounded remained motionless as the executioners hastily inspected the bodies, shooting one of the Kansans again in the head at point-blank range.

Kansas's governor, the state of Missouri, and the Buchanan administration, which had recently been rebuffed in one final attempt to bribe the population of Kansas Territory to accept a proslavery constitution, all declined to pursue or prosecute the killers. To help calm the settlers of Linn County and Bourbon County to its south, some of whom had fled their claims in the aftermath of the executions, Brown traveled to the region shortly after his arrival in Kansas. Under the name Shubel Morgan, he organized fifteen men into a military defense force and camped for a month on a hill that commanded a panoramic view of the surrounding countryside, including a portion of the Missouri line. In spite of his alias and altered appearance, the news soon spread that John Brown was back in the field. Free State homes were reoccupied, and a belated diplomatic intervention by Governor Denver yielded a fragile truce between the area's belligerent factions that strengthened as the summer passed without further violence. When this crisis had lifted, Brown fell ill with as debilitating and sustained a bout of fever and chills as he had ever had.

For several weeks he remained in camp, where heavy morning dews, daily heat, and occasional squalls of rain in the evenings brought him to the point of delirium. His men transported him in early August to Osawatomie, where he lay for a month longer in the corner of the Adairs' parlor, nursed by Kagi. By mid-September, he was strong enough to hold a pencil and clear-headed enough to write to his family. By early November, he was able to travel back to Linn County and rejoin his men.

Six months had passed since the ratification of the Provisional Constitution that had been meant to launch the operation in Virginia. To Stevens, the impetuous former U.S. Dragoon and Springdale drillmaster who had returned with Gill to Kansas, the delay seemed interminable. Brown's standard assurance that no good cause could fail in the end if God wished it to succeed had long since ceased to placate him. "If God controls all things, and dislikes the institution of slavery," Stevens finally shot back at his captain, "why does He allow it to exist?" Brown started to search his repertoire for a ready Bible verse to parry this challenge. Then he paused, looked into Stevens's clouded black eyes, and replied softly: "Well, that is one question I cannot answer."

When the secret committee members had written to Brown in May to report Forbes's disclosures and urge him to do nothing rash while suspicion fastened on them all, the individual letters he sent them in response contained the same phrase: "It is an invariable rule with me to be governed by circumstances, or, in other words, not to do anything while I do not know what to do." In early December he scrawled a postscript to a short, otherwise uninformative letter to John Jr. and Jason in Ohio: "Am still preparing for my other journey." Yet little in these preparations suggested that Brown yet knew what to do to reactivate his plan.

Three weeks later, circumstances—or God, as Brown saw it—presented him with an opportunity.

Near dark on December 19, as he patrolled the Missouri line, George Gill was approached by a mulatto slave selling brooms. After engaging Gill in a brief conversation and determining his politics, the slave, Jim Daniels, begged him for help. He had discovered that he, his wife, and his children were to be sold by their owner Mr. Hicklan before Christmas and would likely be sent to the deep south. Several other slaves on neighboring farms, Daniels reported, faced the same imminent fate. Could Gill help them escape?

From the moment Brown received Gill's report, his course was clear. Late the next night, he and Stevens each took command of a small band of men and crossed into Missouri. Along with Tidd and Kagi, the raiding force included two new recruits and recent immigrants to Kansas: Indiana native Jeremiah Goldsmith Anderson, and Pennsylvanian Albert Hazlett. Both would fight and die with Brown in Virginia.

Brown's contingent forced Hicklan's door and held him at gunpoint while they liberated the Daniels family of five. The intruders also ransacked Hicklan's home for small articles of personal property that could be transported and sold or exchanged en route to Canada for provisions for the fugitives and themselves. Guided by Jim Daniels, Brown and his men quickly covered the three quarters of a mile to the home of Hicklan's neighbor, John Larue, where five more slaves were freed and Larue and a guest taken hostage. Larue owned a large covered wagon, which was appropriated for transport, along with a yoke of oxen to pull it and several horses. Along with the ten blacks, the wagon was loaded with food staples from Larue's storeroom and an ample quantity of bedding. Numbering more than twenty with the freed slaves and the two white hostages, Brown's party rumbled back toward Kansas.

Hicklan's and Larue's slaves had been rescued without opposition or injury. A few miles away, the raid by Stevens's unit on the home of David Cruise had not gone as smoothly. Its object was a single slave, a young woman named Jane, whose husband, Sam Harper, was the property of Larue. Stevens chose to gain admittance to Cruise's home by guile rather than force. Keeping his men out of sight, he knocked on the door, posing as a solitary and friendly traveler. Cruise answered and politely invited him in. Once inside, Stevens announced that he had come to free Jane Harper and told Cruise to produce her. Expecting no resistance from a rich and stately gentleman considerably older and smaller than himself, Stevens also failed to notice the pistol on a table by the door until Cruise grabbed and began to raise it. Pulling his revolver from his belt, Stevens fired first, killing the property owner. He would brood on the incident until his execution in Virginia, fifteen months later. During the dead time at the Kennedy farm before the Harpers Ferry raid, his fellows once induced him to speak of it. "You might call it a case of self-defense," he reflected, "or you might say that I had no business in there, and that the old man was right."

The latter verdict was nearly unanimous on both sides of the Kansas-Missouri border. Yet it was not only the shooting but the entire raid that most Free State newspapers and officials roundly condemned. The majority of Free State settlers in Kansas wished to outlaw slavery there for the same reason the slave power wished to establish it: economic self-interest. Now that the political tide had turned decisively in their favor, these Kansans had nothing to gain by antagonizing their slaveholding neighbors. The *Leavenworth Herald* spoke the common wisdom when it editorialized that "in the present state of affairs, the people of Kansas owe it to themselves, to the country, and to justice and right to put down these outlaws and preserve the peace. There is no earthly excuse for their invasion of Missouri." The citizens of Linn and Bourbon counties reasonably feared a wave of retaliation. But in Kansas and elsewhere, many avowed opponents of slavery whom Brown's action had placed in no personal danger also repudiated it. It was one thing to disapprove human bondage or even to help along a poor fugitive who had fled his master of his own accord. It was quite another, Brown's antislavery critics fumed, to invade a man's home and rob him of his property. This was lawlessness; it threatened the property rights and domestic tranquility of all householders. This was where all but the most radical abolitionists drew the line.

Even when the theft of the slaveholders' human property was approved, few justified Brown in taking livestock, wagons, and supplies to accommodate the slaves' escape. For Brown, the measure was both necessary and appropriate. If one believed that blacks were unjustly enslaved and approved their liberation, then how could one logically oppose the practical means to achieve it? If one believed that slavery was unjust in part because it forcibly extracted labor from unrecompensed laborers, then how could one logically object to the recovery of a fraction of a slave's lifelong unpaid wages to support him in his severance of the relationship? On his way back east, after seeing the fugitives safely onto the Canada ferry at Detroit, eighty-two frigid days and eleven hundred contested miles after the initial rescue, Brown was challenged again on this subject in a Cleveland restaurant. Upon what biblical principle, demanded the indignant stranger who had recognized him as he sat with Kagi at dinner, had he ransacked the Missourians' homes? "Upon what principle?" Brown shouted, rattling the dishware by the crack of his fist on the table. "Upon the same upon which Moses spoiled the Egyptians!"

The consternation of the raid's white analysts was contrasted by the pure joy of its black beneficiaries. After a day spent well hidden in a thick woods, the party of fugitives and rescuers pushed on at night into the Territory's interior. Releasing the two hostages along the way, Brown directed his men to a house two miles past Mound City, the home of Augustus Wattles, a member of the defense force that he had organized as "Shubel Morgan" and a trusted friend. Arriving after midnight on December 22, the freed slaves could give vent to their emotions for the first time as they huddled around the Wattles's stove. Their laughter and excited conversation woke James Montgomery, southern Kansas's most notorious abolitionist militant aside from Brown, who was lodging in the Wattles's loft and came down to see what the commotion was about. Wattles' daughter Emma, who had been awakened to help her mother prepare some supper for their unexpected guests, recalled years later how Brown turned to address Montgomery on the staircase, waved his hat in a sweeping circular motion to indicate the crescent of black men, women, and children who had fallen silent around him, and pronounced: "Allow me to introduce to you a part of my family. Observe, I have carried the war into Africa."

The next night, some of Brown's men pushed on with the fugitives to Osawatomie and found shelter with the Adairs. Brown himself led the remainder of the company back to the border, where they joined Montgomery and his militia in preparing for a retaliatory attack from

Missouri. Though southeastern Kansas swarmed with posses intent on recapturing the slaves and claiming the three thousand dollar reward that the governor of Missouri had offered for Brown's apprehension, no organized assault on the citizens of the region ensued. For a month, guarded by a cordon of sentries, the eleven blacks hid in an abandoned cabin in the middle of a patch of frozen prairie a few miles from the often-searched underbrush and timber stands along Pottawatomie Creek.

At the end of the third week in January, Brown judged that it was safe enough to begin the trek north. He and George Gill piloted the runaways alone on the first leg of the journey to a Railroad stop near Lawrence. Driving the oxen forty miles over the frozen earth while the slaves lay concealed in the wagon, both white men suffered from frostbite by the time they reached their destination. They stopped only long enough to send an ally into town to sell the wagon, the ox team, and other items stolen from the slaveholders, and purchase horses and two new wagons with the proceeds. Gill's health failed under the strain of the pace and the harshness of the elements; replaced by Stevens at Topeka, he promised to rejoin the effort in a few days. To him, Brown's endurance seemed almost preternatural. He could not fathom how a man thirty years his senior, who had been too weak to lift his head a few months before and still suffered from intermittent fits of uncontrollable shaking, could push himself so relentlessly and not simply collapse.

At Holton, thirty-five miles from the Nebraska border, a heavy snowstorm forced the caravan to take refuge at a tavern. When eleven blacks piled out of the wagons and into the warmth, it was impossible to disguise the identity of the entourage. Within a day, the whereabouts of John Brown and his stolen negroes and other property had been broadcast widely. At Atchison, twenty-five miles to the northeast, near the Missouri border, Deputy Marshal J. N. Wood assembled a large posse, which rode hard to reach the swollen north bank of Spring Creek before Brown and his party were able to ford it. Forced to delay their crossing until the high water had subsided, Brown anticipated that he would face resistance there. A scouting expedition by Stevens confirmed that dozens of Missourians had positioned themselves on the creek's far bank. Brown's call for reinforcements from a Free State militia company in Topeka yielded a fifteen-man bodyguard. The black adults, male and female, were given rifles and instructed in their use. Outnumbered three or four to one by the enemy blocking their path, Brown also expected that troops from Fort Leavenworth would soon be approaching from behind with warrants for their arrest. He gave the order to advance, relying, as was his habit, on the principles for which his men fought to give them courage that their antagonists lacked. He also relied on the mystique of Osawatomie Brown in the minds of the proslavery men, on their superstition that he was invincible.

Brown's men marched double file toward the creek, leading the wagons behind them. On the opposite bank, Wood hesitated. Was this frontal assault a ruse? Were other, larger abolitionist forces concealed on his flanks, waiting to catch him in a crossfire the moment he concentrated his effort on the company that now approached the stream? Wood had not yet given an order when the first of the advancing party charged into the stream and his posse panicked and broke. Some clambered onto nearby horses. Others simply ran. While Brown and his followers pulled the wagons across the creek with ropes, several of the Topeka men mounted the Missourians' abandoned horses and captured a few retreating stragglers. "The Battle of the Spurs," as Brown's last Kansas campaign came to be known, was a bloodless rout. Its prisoners were made to join the march for two days before being sent home on foot from the Nebraska line. One of them conceded later that they had been treated well and fed the same fare their captors ate, though it was humiliating to have to sit down to a meal with "damned niggers."

On February 4, 1859, Brown's party entered Iowa, "through the great mercy of God," as he wrote to his family several days later. Full of his success and renewed notoriety, Brown expected a hero's welcome in the town of Tabor, where he had recuperated after his Kansas campaigns in the summer of 1856. But the town's residents, though solidly antislavery, were repelled by the violent circumstances of this particular slave rescue and by the lawless appropriation of property that had accompanied the relief of oppressed people. When Brown strode into the church of his friend Reverend John Todd on the Sunday after his arrival and requested that the minister offer a public thanksgiving for God's preservation of the fugitives and their liberators, the gesture seemed to many of Todd's parishioners more imperious than pious. Brown's petition was deferred until a meeting could be held to discuss it. The result was not a public thanksgiving but a public rebuke: "While we sympathize with the oppressed, and will do all that we conscientiously can to help them in their efforts for freedom," the people of Tabor formally resolved, "we have no sympathy with those who go to slave states, to entice away slaves, and take property or life when necessary to attain that end."

Two weeks later, the citizens of Grinnell in central Iowa gave Brown and his company the reception he was hoping for. He recorded each expression of their approval—loud cheers, free housing, clothing for captives, cakes baked and packed for travel, public thanksgiving—as if it were an inventory item, and sent the list back to Tabor as a point of information and rebuke. With the assistance of other friends in Iowa City and then in Chicago, he secured uninspected boxcars in which the slave stealers and stolen slaves traveled the final five hundred miles of their odyssey together. On March 12, he and Kagi, who had joined the procession en route, stood on the dock in Detroit and watched the Canada ferry recede on the horizon, carrying those they had brought out of bondage. In fact, it carried one more. Mrs. Daniels had been seven months pregnant at the time of her rescue. During the journey, she safely delivered a son and named him John Brown.

CHAPTER TWELVE

ABOLISHING SLAVERY IN VIRGINIA

"Now we must be magnanimous to the South. Slavery cannot be extended. Whether it can ever be got rid of in this country is doubtful. It is a curse imposed by the sins of our ancestors, and we must bear it patiently."
–Amos Lawrence

"HE HAS BEGUN THE WORK IN EARNEST," Sanborn wrote to Higginson, as newspapers in the east followed the unfolding drama of Brown's delivery of his twelve Missouri fugitives to freedom in Canada. Brown, too, regarded the achieved rescue and his evasion of capture as a demonstration to the Virginia plan's skittish supporters that he was equal to its grand ambition, that its time had come. After seeing the escaped slaves to safety, he stayed two days in Detroit, where he met with Douglass and several of the Chatham delegates who were in town for a gathering of black abolitionists. He spent a few weeks giving speeches and consulting with family and antislavery colleagues in Ohio, where law enforcement officials ignored wanted posters affixed to the walls of the very establishments in which he dined and boarded. In the second week of April 1859, he arrived at the home of his most influential co-conspirator, Gerrit Smith.

In the northeast, financing for antislavery activities had all but dried up. This was partly due to the lingering effects of the 1857 recession on northern business. But diminished contributions to the antislavery cause proceeded from a changed political climate as much as an economic one. Amos Lawrence, treasurer of the New England Emigrant Aid Company, captured the sentiments of most antislavery northerners when he expressed his satisfaction with the prevention of slavery's expansion into Kansas and his view that, as a matter of both magnanimity to the south and practical realism, the institution should be left alone in the states where it already existed. This was the platform of the Republican Party in 1859, and the policy of its congressional delegation and leading presidential candidates. Looking forward to the 1860 election, the Republican political establishment was busy presenting itself to free-soil, free-labor constituencies in the north and west as the only party that could be relied upon to guard these antislavery principles as the nation completed its march across the continent. At the same time, Republicans were busy assuring an anxious, volatile south that they were antislavery only in principle and in respect to the addition of new slave states; if they came to power, they proposed no harm to the economy or social system of the southern states.

Born of the Kansas-Nebraska Act, the five-year-old Republican Party had effectively consolidated practical antislavery politics in the United States. Yet it was not practically antislavery. While some abolitionists in the Republican ranks hoped that a Republican administration would become an agent for rapid emancipation, the party's mainstream simply wanted slavery contained and otherwise favored any accommodation with the south that might yield peace on that basis. For this reason, radical abolitionists such as James Redpath and John Brown feared that a victory for the "antislavery" party in 1860 would weaken the antislavery cause, diminishing any hope of relief for America's four million slaves in the present generation. The excitement on both sides at the prospect of a Republican takeover would, as the writer Lydia Maria Child put it, "settle down into a miserable mush of concession, leaving the country in a worse state than it found it." Black activists feared the same thing. Gerrit Smith, whose associations with black leaders were close and extensive, reported their mood in a grim public letter. "Intelligent black men in the States and Canada," he wrote, "are brought to the conclusion that no resource is left to them but in God and insurrections."

Smith himself had come to share that view. Of his own race, he remarked: "So debauched are the white people by slavery that there is not virtue enough left in them to put it down." John Brown, in his eyes, was the exception that proved the rule. When Brown came to Peterboro to renew his initiative of the previous year, Smith was prepared this time to embrace it enthusiastically. Brown's plan properly depended on slaves rallying to help win their own freedom. It invited insurrection of a sort, but not the anarchy and wanton slaughter of the spontaneous and desperate uprisings that Smith believed were likely to commence soon if no more promising emancipation campaign were undertaken. Brown mentioned to his host that, during his recent visit to Detroit, he had been shocked by a proposal by one of their black friends that had reflected just such desperation. George DeBaptiste, a well-known Underground Railroad operator and the head of Detroit's Colored Vigilance Committee, had recommended that gunpowder be planted in fifteen prominent southern churches and detonated on a designated Sunday as an example to the south of what lay in store if it refused to free its slaves. Brown rejected such tactics. His goal, he told Smith, was to liberate the slaves without any such vindictive brutality and with as little bloodshed as possible.

With four hundred dollars from Smith in his pocket, Brown traveled to Boston in May. Sanborn arranged for him to lecture again in Concord, where Emerson, Thoreau, and the educational reformer Bronson Alcott were among the crowd who came to the town hall to hear him. The appearance yielded Brown much praise—including a long, rhapsodic diary entry by Alcott, pronouncing him "the manliest man I have ever seen, the type and synonym of the Just"—but only modest contributions, until George Luther Stearns greeted him with a personal bank draft for twelve hundred dollars. In gratitude, Brown paid public tribute to his chief sponsor at a meeting of the Bird Club, a social organization of Massachusetts political, business, and cultural leaders that gathered regularly for dinner at Boston's Parker House. Presenting Stearns with the large, pearl-handled bowie knife that he had taken from Henry Clay Pate at Black Jack, Brown toasted his friend, adding that he supposed the two of them would "never meet again in this world."

Stearns understood the private significance of Brown's remark, and it disturbed him. Certainly the Virginia project was dangerous, but hadn't Brown shown in Missouri his ability to free slaves in lightning raids and evade capture? Brushing his concerns aside, Stearns attributed Brown's intimation that he expected to die to the old veteran's flair for the dramatic. Brown's thoughts, however, had begun to register the reality of his changing plan.

Slaveholders held slaves. They were morally accountable for the inhumanity of their practice. However, they were not the ones who sanctioned and sustained the institution of slavery. That institution was a national crime. The United States government was slavery's prime source of authority and protection. It would be the target of Brown's first attack.

Brown had long intended to raid the arsenal at Harpers Ferry so as to arm the legions of slaves he expected to rally to his support. But there was no practical reason to attack the Ferry until he had gathered to him a force large enough to begin his greater campaign. Now, though, he began to contemplate the dramatic effect of making such an attack the first strike of his campaign—a strike to free the slaves, yes, but also to transform America, to restore its revolutionary commitments and Christian principles. An assault on the U.S. armory would surely bring government troops into the field against him, but he had eluded them in Kansas and would trust that he could do so again. If not, he did not doubt that, by God's providence, his defeat and death would yield another kind of victory.

In mid-June, Brown returned to North Elba to spend a week with his wife, children, and grandchildren. The family's emotions at this reunion were characteristically restrained. Mary expressed her concern that, as far as she could recall, the plight of the slaves had been mentioned only twice in four years in the local church services that her husband's letters so earnestly bid them attend during his absences. Brown agreed that it might not be entirely proper to attend Sunday services such as those. Oliver prepared to leave his seventeen-year-old wife Martha and go south with his father. Watson would meet them in a month. His wife, Isabella, Henry Thompson's young sister, was near to term with their first child, and Watson wanted to be present at the delivery. Salmon, who like Henry had suffered a serious wound at Black Jack, declined again to join the new campaign. Henry had wrestled mightily with his conscience before resolving, the previous year, to stay with Ruth and their young children rather than resuming his Kansas role as his father-in-law's readiest "scholar." But his younger brother William, who in 1856 had hurried to Kansas when he learned that Henry had been shot, now volunteered to join the class when Watson did. William held firm to this intention in spite of his wife Mary's terrible, tearful premonitions of his death. "Oh Mary," Ruth once heard him rebuke her, "you do not think of anything but self! What is my life in comparison to thousands of poor slaves in bondage?"

A slight western detour on their way to Harpers Ferry took Brown and Oliver to Akron, where they met up with Owen at Jason and Ellen's home. Jason walked with them through his orchard, pointing out the hybrid specimens that had been especially difficult to cultivate and in which he took the greatest pride. The men feasted on his Morella cherries, which had ripened early. One night Brown sat up alone with his second son, Dianthe's favorite, and invited him to take up the cause again with his father and brothers. "I cannot," Jason replied. "I have such a horror of war. Once already I have lost all I had. I have a family to care for. And I cannot bear to kill anything." John Jr., permanently weakened in body and spirit by his imprisonment and abuse in Kansas, also knew that he was unfit for combat, but volunteered to handle weapons transports and to recruit additional raiders.

From Ohio, Brown, Owen, and Oliver continued on to Chambersburg, Pennsylvania, fifteen miles from the Maryland state line and fifty miles due north of Harpers Ferry. There they stayed for several days, registering at the hotel as "I. Smith and sons." Chambersburg was the railway depot to which John Jr. would ship the rifles, pistols, and pikes that would then be transported at night by covered wagon to the headquarters near the Ferry. Joined by the young Indianan, Jeremiah Anderson, who had been Brown's companion and bodyguard during his tour of the east that spring and had developed a deep filial affection and loyalty toward him, Brown and his sons traveled by train to Harpers Ferry and took lodgings in a village a mile away on the Maryland side of the Potomac.

Surveying the countryside the next day, July 4, they encountered a local resident whom Brown asked about land prices and farms for sale in the area. The man directed them to the heirs of the recently deceased Dr. Booth Kennedy, who wished to sell the property that the old physician had left. The ramshackle Kennedy farmhouse sat on high ground five miles to the northeast of Harpers Ferry. Set well back from the road, the house contained a basement storeroom, a living room and two small bedrooms on its main floor, and a spacious attic that occupied the entire floor above. There was also a cabin on the property, several hundred yards from the main house. The elder Mr. Smith negotiated an eight-month rental, to give him time to assess his business prospects and determine whether to send for his wife and daughters before he made a purchase. Thirty-five dollars entitled him to the use of both structures, a pasture, and firewood for the duration of the lease.

A day later, Brown dispatched Oliver back to North Elba. His men would soon be gathering at the Kennedy house, where circumstances might compel them to remain for weeks before the campaign began. Even if most came at night and remained indoors all day, they could not expect entirely to escape notice. Without the visible presence of women, the party would be sure to arouse suspicion. As I. Smith, Brown wrote to Mary and asked her to come with fifteen-year-old Anne for a stay of several weeks. Oliver would accompany them. In as many ways as he could think of in his short letter, Brown implored Mary to grant his request. Now that the plan was in motion, he was momentarily frantic that it would be derailed by something as trivial as a suspicious or overly friendly neighbor. "It will be likely to prove the most valuable service you can ever render to the world," his final persuasive effort grandly pronounced. But he knew that she would be reluctant to leave four-year-old Ellen and twelve-year-old Sarah or the mountain cabin where he had left her with almost nothing four years ago, and where she had managed to make a life. So he gave her a second option: "If you cannot come, I would be glad to have Martha and Anne come on." After her tearful parting with Oliver less than a month before, Martha was delighted to share a few weeks with him in Virginia, and soon started back with him and the vivacious, adventuresome Annie.

In mid-July, Isabella gave birth to a boy. She and Watson named their son Freddy, after the brother whose murder Watson had been prevented from avenging. Two weeks later, Watson kissed his wife and infant and backed out of the room in his mother's house where they slept, closing the door softly behind him. Then he leaned his forehead against the door frame and sobbed so deeply and long that it seemed to the house's other hushed occupants that its log walls were vibrant with his grief. He left a little while later with William and another young Thompson, a bashful twenty-one-year-old named Dauphin who admired Annie Brown and decided to accompany his brother and brother-in-law to Virginia after she had gone on with Martha and

Oliver. On the journey south, Watson carried in his pocket a copy of the poem "Bury Me in a Free Land," by the black poet Frances Harper, a Brown family favorite. The poem began:

> Make me a grave where'er you will.
> In a lowly plain, or a lofty hill;
> Make it among earth's humblest graves,
> But not in a land where men are slaves.

It was in his pocket still when he was killed, along with both his brothers-in-law, at Harpers Ferry.

Martha and Annie brought an aura of serenity and domestic routine to the Kennedy farmhouse that was not wholly a camouflage. They sewed the strips of coarse unbleached sheeting that Brown had bought into bedticks and filled them with hay. As the raiders arrived, singly or in groups of two or three, the young women presented each man with bedding to carry up to a free spot on the floor of the attic. Rolled coats or duffel bags served as pillows. In the mornings, when the men came downstairs to the big room for the prayer and Bible chapter reading that Brown insisted begin each day, they were greeted by the smiles and playful jibes of "sisters," not by the solemn fervor of "Uncle," as they called their leader, alone.

Annie took to calling the men "my invisibles" and the farm "headquarters: war department" in all her conversations with its inhabitants. She persisted in this conspiratorial manner of speaking despite her father's disapproval, laughing off his anxiety that she might slip one day and use the labels in public. On the contrary, she and Martha both proved adept at disarming the women of the surrounding farm families. They prepared the meat from the calves and hogs that Brown butchered, and delivered gifts of veal and salted pork to their new neighbors, after the country custom. And they plausibly answered or skillfully deflected the queries of the overly curious, and managed unannounced neighborly visits to minimize the chance of anyone discovering or suspecting that, in the still, clammy attic above, upwards of a dozen men, several of them black, sat silently on the floor with their backs against the walls, amidst a crated arsenal of weapons, waiting.

Most of the company had orders to remain indoors and out of sight during daylight hours. The men worked leather into belts and holsters, read, exercised, played cards and checkers, and talked about their mission, keeping their spirits up. At night, Brown allowed them to sing or to gather in front of the hearth downstairs and pose a topic for general debate. The skeptical Aaron Stevens had brought to the farm a copy of Thomas Paine's *Age of Reason*, which circulated among the men. Paine's rejection of biblical revelation, in particular the "wretched contrivance" of the miracles of Jesus's birth and resurrection, and his declaration that the only true church was a man's own mind, sparked a lively discussion. Though the prevailing opinion in the room inclined toward Paine and away from himself, Brown enjoyed the contest and congratulated the young men who had expressed themselves most thoughtfully and independently on the questions that the pamphlet raised. Spirited argument was one form of release for his concealed and immobile volunteers, exceeded only by the occasional late-night summer storm that allowed all the men to race out into the rain to leap, dance, and shout under cover of darkness and thunder.

Watson Brown, the Thompson brothers, and Jeremiah Anderson slept in the cabin on the Kennedy property, located across the road from the farmhouse. Invisible to passersby by virtue of the thick grove of trees that surrounded it, the cabin made for an excellent lookout post. Eight other men who had trained in Springdale–Owen, Kagi, Stevens, Tidd, Hazlett, Leeman, and the Quaker brothers, Edwin and Barclay Coppoc–slept in the attic loft. They were joined later in August by Stewart Taylor, a white Canadian and friend of George Gill's who had met Brown in the spring of 1858, and by two black recruits: Shields Green, a fugitive slave who had settled in Rochester, New York, and found work as an assistant to Frederick Douglass; and Dangerfield Newby, the only raider over forty besides Brown himself. Manumitted in Ohio shortly before his father-master's death, Newby had encountered Brown that summer in Oberlin, where Brown and his sons had tried to recruit additional funds and fighters on their way south. Newby had resolved to return to Virginia with the raiders to attempt to free his wife and children from the plantation thirty miles from Harpers Ferry where they were enslaved. His wife feared that she would be sold further south and had written to tell him that, unless he could somehow raise money enough to buy their freedom, the family would soon be parted forever. "Oh, Dear Dangerfield," urged the letter that was found at Harpers Ferry on his mutilated corpse, "come this fall without fail, money or no money I want to see you so much: that is one bright hope I have before me." Newby's personal stake and motive in their operation colored Watson Brown's profound response to an incident that occurred nearby in early September. "Oh Bell," Watson wrote to his wife, "I do want to see you and the little fellow very much but must wait. There was a slave near where we live whose wife was sold to go south the other day and he was found hanging in Thomas Kennedy's orchard, dead, the next morning. I cannot come home as long as such things are done here."

Martha was the chief cook. When one or another of "the invisibles" found the tedium of the attic unbearable, he would creep down to the kitchen to sit with her while she worked. Amused by the men's reliance on the maternal care that Oliver's child bride offered them, and by the fact that twenty-year-old Oliver–the second youngest man present–was the only visible family man among them, Tidd began to call the pair "mother and father." Martha handled the teasing with matronly tolerance and grace, as she did her sister-in-law's demand to know what in the world she and Oliver were doing on nights when Annie was awakened by sounds of agitation from across the room: "We are just trying to stir a little soft into our bed," Martha would say.

John Cook, who had come to Harpers Ferry to spy the previous summer, lived in town with the young wife he had married in April and their newborn child. Cook supported the revised plan that Brown announced to the men in mid-August, of raiding the Harpers Ferry armory as the opening move of their campaign. The facility was lightly guarded and easily taken, he argued. And the effect of their appropriation of U.S. government arms to defeat the institution that the government was doing everything in its power to protect would be electric. The trick would be to gather the weapons and escape with them before local militias could take up positions on the hills above the town and block the narrow bridges across the Shenandoah and Potomac rivers, thus cutting off any avenue of escape. Cook believed that their surprise attack would create enough panic and confusion to give them the time they needed. Kagi agreed. Stevens, Leeman, and Jeremiah Anderson were willing to go along. But most of the others, including Brown's sons and the Thompsons, had grave doubts. And some, who had understood the Virginia operation to be a larger-scale version of the successful Missouri raid, felt they had been misled.

For several days, the armory plan was fiercely contested. Tidd led the opposition, doggedly repeating: "We shall be caught in a pen." When Annie Brown ventured to concur, her brother Owen sharply rebuked her disloyalty to their father. But all the Browns, including Owen, were caught between filial devotion and their own reasoned doubts. Wounded by the challenges hurled at him from all sides, even by his children, Brown offered to resign as the provisional army's commander in chief and follow the orders of any other man whom the company might elect to lead it. The room fell heavily silent as the men took in this unthinkable notion. It was Brown's vision, Brown's exploits, Brown's energy, Brown's certitude that had brought and held them together. Could their commitment and their faith survive his displacement from their center? More terrible now than the failure and fatality of their enterprise was the prospect of its dissipation. Brown strode out onto the porch and left the others to caucus and decide. After a while, Owen was delegated to deliver to him written notice of the collective will. "Dear Sir," the statement read: "We have all agreed to sustain your decisions, until you have *proved incompetent*, & many of us will adhere to your decisions as long as you will. Your Friend, Owen Smith." Tidd was so overwrought that he left the farmhouse to cool off for a few days as a guest of Cook's at Harpers Ferry. But neither he nor any of the other men walked away. As Owen's letter emphasized, Brown's tactics as a guerrilla leader had never yet *proved* incompetent. And even if they did this time, the men who had come so far were too attached to his vision or his person or both to abandon him. So they persuaded themselves that the plan would work and Brown would prevail again. Or they made a version of the resolution that Oliver voiced to his brothers: "We must not let our father die alone."

As the weeks passed, it became clear to everyone in the Kennedy farmhouse that the force that marched on Harpers Ferry would be small. The weapons arrived in Chambersburg, where Kagi had been stationed to receive them, but no new recruits reported. In fact, the nucleus of Brown's force–the men who had trained in Iowa, traveled with him to Chatham, or joined in the Missouri slave rescue–had diminished. George Gill had grown fearful and remained in Iowa. Luke Parsons and C. W. Moffet had also drifted away. Richard Realf, selected at Chatham as secretary of state under the Provisional Constitution, had been summoned to the bedside of his dying mother in England. As for the black Chatham delegates, however intently they had committed themselves to Brown's plan in May 1858, most had lost faith in it or him by August 1859. For some, such as Richard Richardson, their lives had simply unfolded in other directions. Delany, continuing with his West African emigration scheme, had set sail for Liberia in May. Harriet Tubman was ill and unable to provide assistance. Of the Canadian blacks, only Osborne Anderson reported for military service. Financing his own travel to Virginia, Anderson arrived in mid-September. J. H. Harris, a Cleveland activist who had attended the convention, wrote to Brown to apologize for his own defection and that of the others. He was disgusted with himself, Harris added, "and the whole Negro set, ____ ____ 'em."

Psychologically and practically, however, it was more difficult for blacks than for whites to throw in with Brown. It was not only a matter of the leader's color. To Brown's young white idealists, freedom was an unmerited privilege and a moral burden in a land where their race and their representatives kept four million blacks in bondage. For them, even a failed assault on the institution of slavery was a powerful symbolic repudiation of that privilege and a successful release from that burden. Free blacks, on the other hand, had earned or stolen their freedom; they earned and stole it anew every day, and still it was not secure. Blacks had no guilt or national sin to expiate. For them, the parameters of victory were narrower and more concrete, and few had illusions that the enemy would submit without a savage fight. If they fought and lost, moreover, they understood that they would be doomed not just to death but to savagery.

In mid-August, Frederick Douglass received an urgent message from Brown. The Virginia campaign would commence soon, Brown told him, but he still needed money. More than that, he needed to see Douglass before he went forward. Douglass must meet him at an old quarry near Chambersburg, Pennsylvania. A local barber, Henry Watson, would direct him to the place once he arrived in town. Brown asked Douglass to come with Shields Green, whom he had met during his stay in Rochester in January 1858, and to bring any funds he could gather. Douglass immediately complied. The men had been close friends for more than a decade, and Brown believed that Douglass, who had known and approved his plan as long as anyone, would join him in it. If he did, his presence might still inspire more northern and Canadian blacks to volunteer. And once the revolt had begun, Douglass's eloquence and force of personality would help Brown secure the cooperation of the slaves whom they freed or who fled to them.

Accompanied by Kagi, Brown reached the quarry before sunrise on the morning of Friday, August 19. That afternoon, Douglass and Green approached the site of the rendezvous. On the bank of a nearby stream, Douglass observed a leather-faced old white man standing with his fishing tackle and staring suspiciously from under a storm-beaten hat. It was Brown, looking "every way like a man of the neighborhood" in his fisherman's disguise. Inside the quarry, shadowed by the rocks and flanked by their seconds, the pair of abolitionists sat and talked. Brown outlined his final plan. Douglass opposed it. Running off slaves from their masters was one thing, Douglass argued. But an attack on the federal government, beyond its certain doom for any who attempted it, would startle the nation and unite public sentiment against their cause.

Brown heard him out. "It seems to me, Frederick," he replied, "that something startling is just what the nation needs."

"It's a perfect steel trap, John," Douglass pronounced, changing tacks. Each consonant exploded from his lips, as if spring-loaded. "Once in, you will never get out alive."

"Remember the trumpets of Jericho? Harpers Ferry will be mine. The news of its capture will be the trumpet blast that will rally slaves to my standard from miles around. Join me, Frederick. Together we will bring slavery down."

"Not this way. It is you and your men who will be surrounded. Nothing will be easier for the local militia than to cut off your escape routes. And when you are captured or killed it will be worse for those in bondage than it was before."

"You forget that I have some experience with southern militias,"

Brown retorted. "They are cowards, and if their slaves come to me they will be even less eager to fight in Virginia than they were in Kansas. But should the worst happen and they hem us in, I have planned for that. We will take captives, the best citizens in the neighborhood, the descendants of presidents. If we cannot cut our way out, we will use our hostages to dictate the terms of our release."

Douglass looked at him in astonishment. He had often felt with Brown what he felt now—split down the middle, divided against himself. Part of him seemed to look down on his friend from a great height, as if he himself were the older man, the man of experience, and Brown a perpetual innocent despite his years. The other part seemed to shrink and dim in this man's presence, his own antislavery passion the "taper light," as he would later put it, to Brown's "burning sun." *I am willing to live for the slave, but he is willing to die for him,* Douglass thought. He said something different.

"You forget, John, that I have some experience with the south." Douglass paused to let the authority of his statement resonate. "Virginia will blow you and your hostages sky-high rather than let you hold Harpers Ferry for an hour."

Neither man could bring the other over, and neither could let the other go. In the furrow of their difference grew seeds of doubt. If Brown could not make Douglass believe in him, how could he hope to command the confidence of slaves? If Douglass could not turn Brown from his course, and the old man died in it, how could he be sure afterward that reason and not fear had kept him away? They broke off the conversation without resolution, agreeing to resume it the next day. Douglass went back to Chambersburg to make good on his promise to give the citizens there an abolition lecture. On Saturday morning he returned to the quarry and they continued the debate. Douglass urged Brown to return to his original idea of staging a series of surprise raids, liberating a few slaves in each, and hastily retreating to mountain hideouts. Brown would not give up on his plan to make the federal arsenal at Harpers Ferry his first dramatic target. Still Douglass did not start for home. On Sunday morning, without hope of victory on either side, the two men rehearsed their familiar arguments and counterarguments for the last time. Finally, Douglass told Shields Green he was ready to go. As the stately black man rose and turned, Brown leapt to his feet, took a long stride forward, and threw his arms around Douglass's neck, clutching him to his chest as a parent his long-lost child or a shipwreck a saving spar of wood.

"Come with me, Douglass," he whispered. "I will defend you with my life. I want you for a special purpose. When I strike, the bees will begin to swarm, and I shall want you to help hive them."

Douglass could only shake his head as he extricated himself from the embrace. "What do you wish to do?" he asked Green.

For nearly three days Green had observed and listened, scarcely uttering a word. "I b'leve I'll go wid de ole man," he answered.

Douglass nodded and departed. Events would prove him right about the steel trap, wrong about the consequence of Brown's attack and capture for the future lives of slaves. But it was not who had been right or wrong so much as the conversations with Brown themselves that remained important for Douglass later on—important for their earnestness, their intimacy, and the possibilities they had dared to presume. "To have been acquainted with John Brown, shared his counsels, enjoyed his confidence, sympathized with the great objects of his life and death," wrote Douglass, six months after his friend was hanged, "I esteem as among the highest privileges of my life."

As Douglass pleaded with Brown to abandon his suicidal plan to attack Harpers Ferry, an Iowa Quaker was writing to the U.S. secretary of war to expose it. Several of Brown's men, over the long, lonely weeks at Kennedy Farm, had found the magnitude of what they were about to attempt—and the burden of its secrecy—to be too much to bear in silence. They had written incautiously to family and friends at home, some of whom had voiced their fears to others. David Gue learned of the plot in Springdale. In consultation with several others, he decided that the brave young men who had trained in the town and been embraced by its inhabitants must be saved from the destruction that their noble folly would bring down upon their heads. The means Gue seized upon to preserve the attackers was to alert Secretary of War John B. Floyd to the plot. Floyd, Gue assumed, would deploy a large detachment of troops to protect the armory; Brown's scout in the armory town would witness the buildup, and Brown would have no choice but to abort the raid.

The anonymous letter that Secretary Floyd received on August 25 identified "Old John Brown, late of Kansas" as the leader of an association of black and white abolitionists who were about to attempt "the liberation of the slaves at the South by a general insurrection." Brown's company, Gue wrote, would "enter Virginia at Harpers Ferry," and distribute to slaves "a large quantity of arms" that they either already possessed or planned to obtain from "an armory in Maryland" that "one of their leading men (a white man)" had infiltrated. Gue's elaborate account of Brown's design was inaccurate in only one detail: the armory was not in Maryland but just across the Potomac at Harpers Ferry itself. Floyd, formerly the governor of Virginia and later a brigadier general in the Confederate army, dismissed the letter as a fantasy or a hoax. There was no armory in Maryland. Besides, as he testified afterward: "I was satisfied in my own mind that a scheme of such wickedness and outrage could not be entertained by any citizens of the United States."

Though Brown never learned of Gue's letter, he feared discovery or betrayal from other quarters. Hundreds of people throughout the United States and Canada knew at least the rough outline of his intentions, many of them from his own lips. By carelessness or ill will, any one of them might expose him. And, nearer at hand, his headquarters at the Kennedy Farm had proved too close to the road and in too inquisitive a community for his liking. Martha and Annie established routines that allowed them to keep nearly constant vigil on the porch or at one of the windows as they went about their daily chores. Still, more than once at mealtime the men had had to scramble up the stairs to the attic, their plates clattering and food spilling inside the tablecloth that they knew to scoop up by its corners and take with them, to avoid detection by a sociable or needy neighbor. Tiny barefoot Mrs. Huffmaster, who had rented a garden on the Kennedy grounds before Brown arrived, was the most incorrigible offender—"a worse plague than fleas," in Annie's account. Trailing her four barefoot children behind her, Mrs. Huffmaster took every opportunity that the pretext of weeding her garden presented to snoop around the house of the mysterious, odd-mannered Isaac Smith family. Though the Brown women took care not to leave washed clothes to dry a moment longer than necessary, the volume of laundry did not escape Mrs. Huffmaster's attention. "Your men folks has a right smart lot of shirts," she once remarked to Annie. After the day in late September when she spied Shields Green sitting at the table in the living room, Brown realized that, ready or not, he could not wait much longer to begin the campaign.

Brown's financial situation, a familiar nemesis, also dictated that he attack soon. The expenses of travel, arms shipments, and board for twenty people over several months had depleted his funds. In late August, he wrote to John Jr. that, though he had "endeavored to economize in every possible way," he found himself with only "a trifle over one hundred and eighty dollars on hand" and outstanding bills to pay. By October 10, six days before the raid, the men holed up in the Kennedy farmhouse had five dollars between them and a rapidly diminishing store of food. Two weeks earlier, Oliver had escorted the women to Chambersburg, and from there by train and wagon back to North Elba. The evening before they left, Annie had brought Mrs. Huffmaster a crock of bacon grease along with the news that she and Martha were going to Pennsylvania for a few weeks to visit relatives and that their neighbor could keep the pot until they returned.

With the women gone, the men at the Kennedy Farm quickly settled into a mood of quiet introspection and grim resolve. A conscious shadow of death draped the sentences of their letters home. But, in letter after letter and from man to man, these sentences were also radiant with a selflessness in the service of the nation's most wronged and despised others that only these few, among millions, had summoned the conscience—or succumbed to the fanaticism—to achieve. "I am now in a Southern slave state, and before I leave it, it will be a free state, and so will every other one in the South," twenty-year-old William Leeman informed his mother. "I am in a good cause and I am not afraid. I know my mother will not object. You have a generous heart. I know you will sacrifice something for your fellow beings in bondage." To his wife Isabella, Watson Brown confided: "I sometimes feel as though I could not make the sacrifice, but what would I want others to do, were I in their place?" And, describing the impending campaign in a letter to his brother, Jeremiah Anderson reflected: "Millions of fellow beings require it of us; their cries for help go out to the universe daily and hourly. Whose duty is it to help them? Is it yours, is it mine? It is every man's; but how few there are to help. But there are a few who dare to answer this call, and dare to answer it in a manner that will make this land of Liberty and Equality shake to the center. If my life is sacrificed, it can't be lost in a better cause."

Oliver and Martha Brown were the only husband and wife who lived together at the Kennedy farmhouse as Brown and his followers prepared for the Harpers Ferry raid. (LIBRARY OF CONGRESS)

On Saturday, October 15, three final recruits, two black men and a white, found their way to Kennedy Farm, the first new arrivals in a month. The two blacks were residents of Oberlin, Ohio, the abolitionist and integrationist hub with whose community and college the Brown family had been involved for twenty-five years. Lewis Sheridan Leary, the son of an Irish immigrant father and a half-black, half Indian mother, was a saddler and harness maker who left his wife and small child to join Brown's force. His nephew John Copeland Jr., a student preparing for admission to Oberlin and a man in his mid-twenties like his uncle, had earlier served time in a Cleveland prison for his part in the rescue of a captive fugitive awaiting transport back to his master. The white man, twenty-one-year-old Francis Jackson Merriam, was the physically feeble and emotionally volatile grandson of an early president of the American Anti-Slavery Society. Well known and lightly regarded by Sanborn and Brown's other supporters in Boston, Merriam finally persuaded them to tell him where Brown was by pledging his recent inheritance of six hundred dollars in gold to the cause in exchange for a place in the old man's company. With Merriam's money in reserve for the uncertain days and weeks ahead, and with a force that now numbered twenty-two including himself, Brown resolved to set the plan in motion the next evening.

Sunday morning had scarcely dawned when Brown gathered his soldiers and read aloud the fifty-eighth chapter of the book of Isaiah: "Is not this the fast that I have chosen? to loose the bands of wickedness, to undo the heavy burdens, and to let the oppressed go free, and that ye break every yoke? Is it not to deal thy bread to the hungry, and that thou bring the poor that are cast out to thy house? when thou seest the naked, that thou cover him; and that thou hide not thyself from thine own flesh?" At ten o'clock, after a formal roll call, Brown convened a council before the fire. Seven of the company—the Coppoc brothers, Dangerfield Newby, Shields Green, Merriam, Copeland, and Leary—had not yet heard or read the Provisional Constitution or sworn the oath to abide by its ordinances that Article XLVIII required. Stevens's rich voice was commissioned for a reading of the document that, from this evening until slavery was abolished, would govern the men in the room and all the men and women who joined them or whom they liberated.

The new recruits listened as Stevens rehearsed the founding principles of a society unknown to them all, one in which every person of mature age, of whatever sex or race, was an equal citizen with equal rights and an equal responsibility to labor for the benefit of the whole. In the struggle ahead, Article XXXII stipulated, when prisoners are taken, "it shall be the duty of all persons, male and female, connected herewith, at all times and under all circumstances, to treat all such prisoners with every degree of respect and kindness the nature of the circumstances will admit of." And though this was a wartime constitution, Article XLII spoke to the familial, educational, and religious commitments and institutions that were to be sustained so far as possible. "The marriage relation shall be at all times respected," Stevens intoned, as choked emotion surged up into Newby's throat and several other men blinked back tears, "and broken families encouraged to reunite, and intelligence offices established for that purpose." After the reading concluded and the oaths had been sworn, Brown detained the company for a moment longer to reemphasize the requirement of their Provisional Constitution that antislavery fighters pursue their single objective with as little violence as possible. "And now, gentlemen, let me press this one thing on your minds. You all know how dear life is to you, and how dear your lives are to your friends; and, in remembering that, consider that the lives of others are as dear to them as yours are to you. Do not, therefore, take the life of anyone if you can possibly avoid it, but if it is necessary to take life in order to save your own, then make sure work of it."

Brown spent the afternoon reviewing and neatly arranging the documents in his possession that pertained to the raid. These included copies of the Provisional Constitution; maps of the southern states annotated with estimates of local slave populations and markings of prospective attack sites and mountain hideouts; the minutes of the Chatham Convention; a rewriting of the Declaration of Independence, closely paralleling Jefferson's composition in style and structure, entitled "A Declaration of Liberty by the Representatives of the Slave Population of the United States of America"; and a sheaf of letters from Brown's friends and sponsors. Brown had long ago admitted to himself–though, for practical reasons, he claimed otherwise–that he could not entirely predict or control the events of his campaign, once it was begun. But what he felt he could control, or at least strongly shape, was its representation.

The power of representation had fascinated and drawn him from his youth. Every public antislavery action, from the afternoon in Franklin when he walked his family to the back of the church and returned to usher negroes to his pew in front, had combined a practical and a representative or symbolic dimension. The Harpers Ferry raid was no exception. Even if its military action should fail, its dramatic representation, properly managed, might in the end suffice to realize its objectives. Leaving incriminating letters from leading citizens of the north among his papers was a part of Brown's representational strategy, a version of the tactic that he had recommended to the League of Gileadites nearly ten years before. He would commit as many to the struggle as possible, willing or not.

Night fell, damp, cold, and starless. At last, Brown broke the nervous tension that had been gathering throughout the day: "Men, get on your arms. We will proceed to the Ferry." Merriam and Barclay Coppoc, among the youngest of Brown's volunteers and the least experienced, were assigned to remain at the farm under Owen Brown's command. Their job was to guard the crates of Sharps rifles, revolvers, and pikes, which were to be moved in the morning to a schoolhouse just across the Potomac from Harpers Ferry and made available for distribution to those who rallied to join the insurgency. Brown's eighteen other followers wrapped themselves in gray woolen blankets. Each carried a knife, a revolver, a rifle, and forty to fifty rounds of ammunition. Two by two, they walked the five and a half miles along the Maryland Heights to the covered bridge over the Potomac that emptied into the town of Harpers Ferry, Virginia, situated at the tip of the peninsula formed by the convergence of the Potomac and Shenandoah rivers. John Cook, who was known, liked, and unsuspected in the region, and Charles Tidd, who had gone to stay with Cook and his wife in August to let his anger over Brown's plan cool, led the procession. Between them and the next pair of raiders, Brown rode alone in the horse-drawn farm wagon, its bed loaded with several additional Sharps rifles, some of the speared pikes, a sledgehammer, a crowbar, and a few pine-knot torches. The company encountered no one on the road; but for the creaking of the wagon, silence reigned for more than an hour. It was broken by the whistle of the westbound Baltimore and Ohio passenger train as it prepared to cross into Virginia over the bridge that Brown's men would reach a mile farther on.

They stopped some yards short of the river and waited for Cook and Tidd to steal down the embankment, climb a pole beneath the bridge's northern abutment, and cut the telegraph wires. Then Kagi and Stevens led the others onto the carriage and pedestrian passageway that ran alongside the railroad tracks. William Williams, the night watchman, suspected a practical joke when Brown's second and third in command walked up and told him he was under arrest. Lifting their shawls to expose their weapons, the fighters convinced him otherwise. With Williams as their first hostage, Brown and his men proceeded into Harpers Ferry, leaving Stewart Taylor and Watson with orders to guard the bridge and detain anyone who attempted to cross. The first building in town, at the Point, where the bridge emptied, was the Wager House, a hotel and restaurant that also served as the railroad depot. A few yards to the left stood the Galt House saloon. No one emerged from either of Harpers Ferry's two most prominent public establishments or noticed as Brown's party passed between them to the gate of the armory, fifty yards down Potomac Street. The employees of the federal armory–managers, clerks, skilled gunsmiths, and factory workers–were all civilians, and the facility was lightly guarded by watchmen whose main job was to see that the fires in the plant's forges were properly extinguished for the night. The watchman on duty, Daniel Whelan, sat inside the padlocked armory gate, which he approached as the wagon stopped before it. One of the raiders reached over the fence and grabbed Whelan's coat, while another put a pistol to the guard's chest and ordered him to quietly relinquish the key. When Whelan claimed not to have a key, the crowbar was retrieved from Brown's wagon and the lock was forced.

Two short rows of facing buildings across a central courtyard made up the armory complex. But the most important sites of weapons production and storage lay outside its gates. Back toward the saloon, at the mouth of Shenandoah Street, which ran nearly perpendicular to Potomac Street along the other river, lay the arsenal. Brown dispatched Albert Hazlett and Edwin Coppoc to enter and hold the unguarded building where most of the finished weapons were stored. Hall's Rifle

Newspaper illustration of Harpers Ferry, Virginia, as viewed from the Maryland side of the railroad bridge over the Potomac that Brown and his men crossed in launching their invasion. (WEST VIRGINIA STATE ARCHIVES)

U.S. armory at Harpers Ferry at the time of Brown's raid. The engine house in which Brown was trapped is the first building inside the gate on the left. (MADISON BAY COMPANY)

Works, where the government rifles were produced, was located half a mile down Shenandoah Street. Kagi and Copeland proceeded to that building, and captured without a fight a small night detail of ordnance workers. When William Thompson and Oliver Brown took up their post on the bridge across the Shenandoah, the raiders controlled the two principal thoroughfares in and out of Harpers Ferry and all of the important government buildings. It was not yet midnight, and not a shot had been fired.

The first building to the left inside the armory grounds was a squat brick structure consisting of two separate units, without interior access to each other. One section, which Brown took for his headquarters, was the engine house, where fire equipment was stored. In the other, the watch house, Brown installed his hostages, Williams and Whelan, and later the workers taken by Kagi and Copeland at the Rifle Works. With the Ferry secured, Brown turned to the practical pursuit and symbolic declaration of liberty for the slave population of the United States. Colonel Lewis Washington, the area's most distinguished citizen and the great-grandnephew of the first president, lived on his plantation five miles south of town. To the homes of Washington and another prominent slaveholder, John Allstadt, Brown sent a six-man delegation, three black and three white, with orders to take the men of these households hostage and bring their adult male slaves to the Ferry to be freed and armed. The black women whom Washington and Allstadt owned were to be told that an army of liberation had arrived, and that they should spread the word through the night to the slaves in the area that all who wished to be free would receive weapons and direction at Harpers Ferry. Brown's written instructions to Stevens, the leader of this operation, also required that he stage a piece of political theater in Washington's home. Washington owned a pair of antique pistols presented to his great-granduncle by the Marquis de Lafayette, and a sword reputedly sent the president by Frederick the Great of Prussia. Stevens was to compel the planter to hand these national heirlooms over to black Chatham delegate and provisional government representative Osborne Anderson. "Anderson being a colored man, and colored men being only *things* in the South," Brown's orders read, "it is proper that the South be taught a lesson on this point."

The orders were successfully executed. Washington, Allstadt, and

Allstadt's adult son were taken prisoner, Washington's pistols and sword relinquished to Anderson, and the slave women informed of the raid's meaning. By 3:30 A.M., five of Brown's fighters, along with the Allstadts and ten of Washington's and Allstadt's black men, were riding back to the Ferry in a large four-horse wagon that had been appropriated for this purpose from Washington's barn. Washington, escorted by the sixth raider, had been permitted to make the journey in his carriage. But in town the raid's smooth, bloodless course had begun to alter. Between midnight and 1:00 A.M., Patrick Higgins, the relief railroad watchman, arrived at the Wager House depot. Failing to find William Williams, Higgins walked onto the covered bridge over the Potomac and was apprehended by Watson Brown and Stewart Taylor when he reached the Maryland side. Higgins stood for a moment, mystified by the men's demand that he surrender. Then he responded with a sudden staggering blow to the side of Watson's head, whirled, and began to run back into the bridge's darkness. Taylor shouted "Halt." Higgins kept running, ignoring the order—as he always claimed, in his many retellings of the story—because "I knew no more about the word than a hog knows about a holiday." Taylor's bullet creased the watchman's scalp, but Higgins reached the Wager House with only a flesh wound and reported to the duty clerk that two train robbers or worse were lurking on the bridge.

At 1:25 A.M. the eastbound train to Baltimore arrived at the Wager House station. Its conductor, A. J. Phelps, was alerted to the trouble on the bridge, and advised not to attempt to continue. The train's engineer and baggage master took lanterns and walked up the tracks to investigate Higgins's incredible report. The station's negro baggage man, a popular and longtime Harpers Ferry resident named Shephard Hayward, also advanced toward the bridge. The railroad men saw the glint of rifle barrels, just as a voice from the shadows demanded that they halt and surrender. They ran, instead, and, the raiders fired. A bullet entered Hayward's back and passed through his chest. The free black man collapsed on the station platform, the first casualty of Brown's campaign to free the south's slaves. Meanwhile, the others had regained the safety of the Wager House. The train was backed away a hundred feet and its coal-oil lamps extinguished. Some passengers sat terrified in the dark. A few rushed onto the tracks with pistols and began to fire in the direction of the sentries on the dark bridge. Most hurried into the Wager House, where Hayward was carried and attended soon afterward by a physician, John Starry, who lived close by the station and had been awakened by the gunfire.

In spite of the commotion among the Baltimore travelers and the shooting of Hayward, no general alarm was sounded in the town. George Chambers, the proprietor of the Galt House, walked across to the depot to discuss matters with the train passengers, surmised that the negro porter must have been the victim of some sort of railroad strike, and went home to bed. The hours between two and four in the morning passed quietly. A few late-retiring or early rising citizens, noticing unusual activity around the Point, approached the armory gate, where they were apprehended and placed in the watch house. Others, including Starry, roamed the streets and observed the raiders' movements unmolested. During these hours, Brown and Phelps communicated several times through an intermediary. Brown acquainted the B&O conductor with the intent of his mission and told him the train could continue on its route but that it was the last he would allow to pass. Fearing that the insurgents might have weakened or mined the bridge, however, Phelps refused to leave the station until daylight.

Shortly after 4:00 A.M. Lewis Washington's carriage entered the armory yard, followed by his wagon, with its closely packed black and white cargo of slave owners, slaves, and abolitionists. Brown greeted his prisoners politely and assured them they would be released in due time, perhaps in a hostage exchange for black men. Some of Washington's and Allstadt's slaves were given pikes and assigned to stand guard over their former masters. Brown instructed Cook, Tidd, and Leeman to take four or five others back over the Potomac bridge to the Kennedy farm. There, with Owen, Merriam, and Barclay Coppoc, they were to load the rest of the weapons into Washington's wagon and move them to the schoolhouse a mile from the Ferry. Along the way, Cook's party encountered Maryland slaveowner Terence Byrne, who had gotten an early start on an errand in Harpers Ferry. A near neighbor of Brown's during his residence at the Kennedy Farm, Byrne was stunned when Cook stopped him and proposed that he voluntarily give up his slaves in exchange for protection of his person and the rest of his property.

When Byrne refused, he was taken prisoner and delivered to the engine house later that morning.

Dr. Starry watched the arrival and departure of Washington's wagon and the arming of his slaves and decided to act. Mounting a horse, he rode up into the hills, where many of Harpers Ferry's citizens lived in homes overlooking the business district, and roused the armory's acting superintendent, A. M. Kitzmiller. Neighbors and other government employees were quickly awakened and began to gather the few serviceable weapons in town that were not housed at the arsenal. Starry continued his climb up Bolivar Heights, enlisting the Lutheran minister to sound a general alarm by the continuous ringing of his church bell. Emissaries were dispatched to alert militia units in Shepherdstown and Martinsburg, and Starry himself galloped to the nearby county seat of Charlestown, home of the Jefferson Guards. By 7:00 A.M. the Guards were beginning to mobilize.

A few minutes later, the delayed Wheeling-Baltimore night express arrived at the station at Monocacy in western Maryland, where Conductor Phelps was able to send a telegram to William Prescott Smith, the B&O master of transportation in Baltimore, reporting that armed abolitionists controlled the U.S. armory and the town of Harpers Ferry and were determined to stop further train passage in either direction. At the next station, Phelps had a return telegram accusing him of exaggeration and hysteria, and asking "Why should our train be stopped by Abolitionists and how do you know they are such?" Smith's condescension outraged Phelps. He had not relayed the wild and otherwise unsubstantiated report of one of his subordinates, who had been captured and briefly held in the armory yard, that five or six hundred armed negroes and half that many whites had already congregated inside the government compound. From Ellicott Mills, the conductor fired off a second bulletin: "My dispatch is not exaggerated. I have not made it half as bad as it is. The captain expects a reinforcement of 1500 men to liberate the slaves." Soon afterward, the president of the B&O line, John W. Garrett, contacted the White House.

The fifteen hundred men that Brown hoped to inspire to join his revolution were not all black. Transplanted northerners made up a sizeable portion of the white population of Harpers Ferry, especially of armory employees, and many of the farm families of northern Virginia owned no slaves and harbored little love for slavery. At the least, Brown assumed that few of the white citizens of the region would be zealous enough in slavery's defense to take up arms against him. His greeting of General Washington's great-grandnephew in the armory yard reflected that assumption: "My particular reason for taking you first," Brown explained to the honorary colonel, "was that, as the aid to the Governor of Virginia, I knew you would endeavor to perform your duty, and perhaps you would have been a troublesome customer to me; and, apart from that, I wanted you particularly for the moral effect it would give our cause having one of your name, as a prisoner." As a member of the local land- and slave-owning aristocracy and a figure in state government, Washington was bound to offer vigorous opposition to Brown's assault on slavery in Virginia; men less invested in both power structures, Brown believed, would not.

In fact, some local whites sympathized with the raiders even as the raid was taking place. John Cook—who could not get back to the Ferry from Maryland that afternoon once two companies of Charlestown militia had arrived and driven Brown's sentries off the bridges—received food, information, and concern for his welfare from several area residents to whom he acknowledged his part in the attack. But passive sympathy is not revolutionary activism. Between the two yawns a chasm of caution, obedience, and routine, as less committed and less categorical antislavery crusaders than Brown and his followers might easily have understood.

Brown had long since crossed this chasm, and looked on the crossing as an obligation and a measure of moral integrity for all people of right convictions. He never accurately assessed or fully appreciated how difficult it was for others. Nine months earlier, arguing the case for radical action with his more prudent Kansas friend, W. A. Phillips, Brown had cut off the debate by remarking: "When your household gods are broken, as mine have been, you will see all this more clearly." It was not just Fred's assassination or the deaths of so many of his younger children or his own business failures and humiliations that had alienated Brown from the common satisfactions of home and hearth that restrain ordinary men and women from embracing all-consuming causes or taking wild risks. It was that these experiences, combined with his religious and political commitments and his associations with blacks, had produced in him a vision of such satisfactions as idols. Most people parcel their devotion among several gods, in this way checking and balancing the extremity of any single god's demands. But for Brown, everything sacred had come to be concentrated into the principle of justice for "the least of these," and slavery, "that 'sum of all villainies,'" filled the category of the profane.

For the white men who began to fire down on Brown's position from the hills above the armory or to march on Harpers Ferry from Charlestown and Martinsburg, there were other villainies. Invading a sovereign state; terrorizing an unsuspecting population; jeopardizing lives and livelihoods—these actions counted as villainous to the men who took up arms against Brown, even those among them who owned no slaves and considered slavery to be wrong. Brown was too much the moral monopolist, or monotheist, to have anticipated this response. Viewing slavery in the abstract as the sum of all villainies also prevented him from recognizing its different practical degrees of evil. Even had there been time for the area's slaves to learn about his strike on their behalf and determine that it was genuine, they would still have had to calculate whether the prospective reward of joining Brown at the Ferry outweighed the action's mortal risk. The relative harshness or lenity of their particular form of enslavement, and the degree of their desperation for relief, would have figured heavily in their calculations. Slavery was slavery for Brown, but slaves knew better, or knew differently, and there were much worse places to be a slave than along the Blue Ridge of northern Virginia.

Monday morning, October 17, 1859. A hard rain fell and subsided and fell again. Government employees who had slept peacefully through the night were stopped on the street or at the armory gate by small clusters of men who pulled back gray ponchos to reveal their Sharps rifles and herded the workers into the watch house. News that the armory was under siege, punctuated by intermittent rifle reports, spread quickly through the awakening town. Acting superintendent Kitzmiller and another high-ranking armory official, paymaster J. E. P. Daingerfield, were captured and joined Washington and the Allstadts under the guard of black men with pikes. A few of the bolder Harpers Ferry residents armed themselves with shotguns and crept down side streets toward the armory, looking to position themselves for a clear shot at the invaders. At a little past seven, Thomas Boerly gained a favorable vantage point only to be cut down by a sentry's bullet as he took aim at the abolitionists around the gate. After Boerly's death, local resistance that morning confined itself to shots fired from cover in the hillside homes above the town's center and to threatening conversation among the crowd of citizens who congregated, speculated, and drank in the Galt House saloon. Meanwhile, Brown sent a hostage to the Wager House to request that breakfast be delivered for his prisoners and men. He dispatched Newby to reinforce the guard detail on the Shenandoah bridge, Osborne Anderson to relieve Coppoc at the arsenal, and Leary to join Kagi and Copeland at the rifle works. And he conversed companionably with his distinguished captives, assuring Washington that "if you knew my heart and history, you would not think evil of me," and predicting to the paymaster Daingerfield, as he had to Conductor Phelps seven hours before, that "by noon there will be fifteen hundred men with us, ready armed."

Half a mile away at the rifle works, Kagi observed the growing number of armed defenders in the hills above the town and the buildings around it, and the increasing volume of their fire. He concluded, and communicated by messenger to Brown, that the little company of raiders should reunite, gather what weapons they could carry, and retreat across the Potomac to await whatever reinforcements might arrive. Otherwise, he warned, they risked losing control of both the town and its escape routes. Brown ignored the entreaties of his second in command. To some of the hostages and raiders at the engine house, the man of action seemed strangely paralyzed. A year and a half earlier, when Hugh Forbes's revelations had forced a postponement of his Virginia campaign, Brown had assured his panicky Boston sponsors that he would not act rashly, but only as circumstances dictated and clarified his course. Now, as the minutes ticked toward noon on a rainy Monday morning, and the cold and wet penetrated Brown's garments, the circumstances and what they demanded remained unclear to him.

Though bullets occasionally whistmed by his ear, Brown's principal emotion was relief. His obstructed, uncertain, circuitous path to a dramatic act of practical abolitionism had reached its destination. Brown did not feel paralyzed, but he had expended an extraordinary psychological and physical effort over many years to arrive at this place, and with his arrival that expenditure began to take its delayed toll on his reserve of energy and initiative. As he assessed the situation, he had occupied the town for twelve hours without yet losing a single man. The fire from the hills was more vigorous than he had anticipated—the townspeople had found and distributed a cache of government weapons that had been in storage on high ground outside the armory complex—but it remained ineffectual. If he ordered his volunteers to evacuate now, what would they have to show for their efforts? Without Washington's large wagon, still ferrying arms from the farmhouse to the school in Maryland, they could take only a few of the guns in the arsenal. And without a visible outpouring of slaves to arm, the raid's objectives would be sure to be vilified as mere lawlessness and larceny. Better to wait for a while longer. The slaves, Brown continued to believe, would arrive.

The assumption that slaves would rush to his aid was a mistake that John Brown shared with many southerners and much of the national press. Dispatches received by the Associated Press office in Washington and disseminated throughout the day to newspapers around the country announced a "stampede of Negroes" from Maryland. A 2:00 P.M. report from Baltimore pronounced, "Harpers Ferry is in possession of the Negroes, who arrest everyone they can catch and imprison them." The facts were otherwise. By noon, hundreds of armed and outraged Virginians, including the Jefferson Guards and a second large "irregular" militia from Charlestown, had surrounded the town. Crossing the Potomac at low water and coming around from the Maryland side, a hundred Guards marched on the railroad bridge, forcing Watson and Taylor to abandon their post and fall back to the armory. The Charlestown irregulars took up shooting positions on the hillside as another contingent of the Guard charged the Shenandoah bridge, flushing Oliver, William Thompson, and Dangerfield Newby out onto the open ground between the Galt House, the Wager House, and the armory gate. From above, a militia man took aim at the negro with a musket he had loaded with a six-inch iron spike. The missile entered Newby's throat and slit it from ear to ear.

The fire into the armory grounds had grown so intense that many of Brown's prisoners feared they would be killed by their own friends and neighbors. Brown had earlier moved the ten most prominent hostages into the engine house and instructed them to take cover on the floor or behind the fire engine, away from the windows. The other captives sat unguarded in the watch house but were too afraid of the bullets that shattered the window glass and pocked the exterior walls to open the door and attempt an escape. Resin Cross, one of the prisoners in the engine house, and William Thompson volunteered to go out together under a flag of truce to try to negotiate a cease-fire with local leaders and the commanders of the Charlestown units. The guns went silent as they walked together into the square and approached the Wager House. But in a moment a mob of townspeople converged on the pair, grabbed Thompson, and dragged him into the hotel.

The consternation and anger of Brown's hostages, as they watched this peace effort thwarted, was as great as their captor's own. In addition to their risk of being shot alongside the raiders, they feared they would be the victims of Brown's retaliation once he realized that he and his men were doomed. As the armory's chief administrator on the scene, Kitzmiller assumed the responsibility of bringing the violence to an end. Brown accepted his offer to personally arrange for a cease-fire and sent Watson and Stevens with him, under a second white flag, to see to the terms. This time the peace delegation took only a few steps before firing began. Watson fell first. Critically wounded by a bullet to the stomach, he crawled back to the engine house and was pulled inside. Stevens's massive body was ripped by two lead slugs fired from the second-floor window of the Galt House by saloonkeeper George Chambers. Kitzmiller scampered to safety. Frederick Douglass had been right, and not only about the steel trap. Rather than let Brown hold the Harpers Ferry armory for a few more hours, Virginia was prepared to blow him and his hostages sky-high.

Witnessing the fate of Watson and Stevens, twenty-year-old William Leeman was overcome by terror. When he saw the combatants and spectators diverted by the brave and merciful act of a citizen who carried Stevens into the Wager House for medical attention, Leeman crept across the armory enclosure to the edge of the Potomac, climbed the fence, crossed the railroad tracks, and scrambled for the Maryland shore. Halfway across he was spotted and immobilized by the bullets that splashed and skipped in the water all around him. In the middle of the stream, he crouched and shivered on a protruding rock. A group of townsmen waded out to him. One put his pistol to his head and pulled the trigger. A little later, George Turner, a former West Point graduate and army artillery officer, was killed as he prepared to fire into the armory from the doorway of a nearby residence. Fontaine Beckham, Harpers Ferry's longtime B&O railroad agent and current mayor, ignored the advice of his friends in the Galt House and ventured out to assess the situation. Peeking out from behind a water tank from which the raiders had taken steady fire since early in the day, Beckham incautiously exposed his head to view, and was killed by Edwin Coppoc. Soon after that, Oliver Brown, having relieved Coppoc on guard duty at the engine house door, observed a sniper behind the stone trestle at the near end of the Maryland bridge. As he raised his rifle, the militiaman's bullet exploded in his chest, driving his body backward toward his pacing father.

With the mounting deaths and evident desperation of the invaders, terror gave way to carnival in the town. Some of the drinkers in the Galt House passed the afternoon shooting at Newby's corpse a few yards away. Discovering that it lay outside the line of fire from the engine house, they walked out and kicked it for a while. Someone decided he could use the black man's cowhide boots, and yanked them off. Then two men stooped over the body and cut off its ears for mementos. From the Potomac bridge, others practiced their marksmanship on Leeman's body, stiffening on its rock pedestal in the river. Reports of the mayor's death prompted a new wave of rage that demanded a living target for retaliation. At the Wager House, a self-appointed posse burst into the room where a bound William Thompson sat under armed guard. They dragged him to his feet and out toward the bridge. "Though you may take my life, eighty thousand will arise to avenge me and give liberty to the slaves," Thompson shouted, a moment before he was shot in the head and tumbled over the railing into the river.

Dr. Starry disdained the cowardly shooting of prisoners and corpses. Braver defenders of the town, he challenged, would reclaim Hall's Rifle Works from the small detachment of raiders that occupied it. Starry enlisted forty men to attack the rifle works from three sides, maintaining a steady barrage of fire at each of its windows. Half a mile down Shenandoah Street from their remaining allies in the engine house, Kagi, Copeland, and Leary could do little but take cover behind machinery. When their sanctuary was breached from an adjoining building, the three leapt through a window and managed to reach the Shenandoah. But as they began to swim, dozens of Virginians poised on the opposite bank opened fire. Within a few seconds, Kagi and Leary were floating face down on the water. Copeland, miraculously unhit, turned back toward the town. A citizen waded out to execute him, but his gun was wet and failed to fire. Shouts of "Lynch him" arose from the shore, and the black invader was dragged up onto the bank to await a rope. But Starry, riding up on horseback, intervened and prevailed on his followers to imprison Copeland and preserve him for legal prosecution.

In the evening, before the midnight arrival of Robert E. Lee and the marine company from Washington, Virginia Governor Henry Wise instructed Colonel Robert Baylor of the 3rd Regiment Cavalry to take general command of the various military units on the scene. Baylor sent a surrender ultimatum to Brown, who replied that he would only peacefully relinquish the armory if all his men, living and dead, were returned to him and allowed to cross the Potomac with the eight hostages whom they still held in the engine house. Once they had gained safe passage into Maryland, he pledged, the hostages would be released unharmed. Baylor rejected these terms, as J. E. B. Stuart would do the next morning. Sometime during the night, Albert Hazlett and Osborne Anderson, who had lain undetected throughout the day in a room on the second floor of the arsenal building, slipped out of town and across the river. Cook, Tidd, Merriam, Barclay Coppoc, and Owen Brown–the five raiders who were in Maryland when the Jefferson Guard cut off access to the Ferry–also reluctantly abandoned their comrades when it became clear that they could do nothing to help them. Hazlett and Cook were apprehended within a week of their escape and returned to Virginia for trial and execution.

In the engine house, Watson and Oliver Brown lay dying and in pain. Stewart Taylor cracked the door to stare out into the darkness and was instantly shot dead. Brown paced the twenty-foot-square compartment, offering an occasional word of encouragement to the four

Patriotic Treason

John Brown and sixteen of the eighteen men whom he led into Virginia on October 16, 1859, died there: ten of wounds suffered during the raid, and seven by execution.

John Brown
(WEST VIRGINIA STATE ARCHIVES)

Jeremiah Anderson
(LIBRARY OF CONGRESS)

Oliver Brown
(LIBRARY OF CONGRESS)

Watson Brown
(LIBRARY OF CONGRESS)

John Cook
(LIBRARY OF CONGRESS)

John Copeland
(LIBRARY OF CONGRESS)

Edwin Coppoc
(LIBRARY OF CONGRESS)

Shields Green
(WEST VIRGINIA STATE ARCHIVES)

Albert Hazlett
(LIBRARY OF CONGRESS)

John Kagi
(LIBRARY OF CONGRESS)

Lewis Leary
(WEST VIRGINIA STATE ARCHIVES)

William Leeman
(LIBRARY OF CONGRESS)

Dangerfield Newby
(WEST VIRGINIA STATE ARCHIVES)

Aaron Stevens
(LIBRARY OF CONGRESS)

Stewart Taylor
(LIBRARY OF CONGRESS)

Dauphin Thompson
(LIBRARY OF CONGRESS)

William Thompson
(LIBRARY OF CONGRESS)

able-bodied volunteers who remained to him—Edwin Coppoc, Shields Green, Dauphin Thompson, and Jeremiah Anderson—and an occasional complaint to Washington and the other local representatives about the gross violations of the rules of war that his men had suffered under flags of truce. Oliver begged his father to shoot him. "No, my son, have patience," Terence Byrne recalled Brown responding. "I think you will get well; if you die, you die in a glorious cause, fighting for liberty." Again and again, Oliver pleaded for death, a mercy his father would not provide. Finally, according to the younger Allstadt, Brown advised his youngest son, "If you must die, die like a man." Oliver became quiet, and when Brown called his name a few minutes later he was gone.

Neither then, nor at any other moment during the siege, did Brown or any of his men threaten or harm their prisoners, as Daingerfield, the armory paymaster, remarked with gratitude and wonder after his release: "When his sons were shot down beside him, almost any other man similarly situated would have exacted life for life."

At dawn on Tuesday, with Lee looking on, J. E. B. Stuart delivered the final surrender offer. When it was rejected, the marine detail battered down the engine house door. One marine was killed in the assault, as were Thompson and Anderson. Coppoc and Green were able to surrender.

Two slaves, one belonging to Washington and one to Allstadt, sought freedom during the raid. One was shot trying to cross the river; the other died in jail of pneumonia a few days after his master was released. Other slaves—perhaps as few as a handful, perhaps several dozen—actively assisted their would-be liberators or tried to join them before abandoning the effort as hopeless. When they returned to their homes and owners, these local blacks claimed that any service to the raiders that could be charged against them had been extracted by force and terror. Whether such claims were believed or not, the story of slaves remaining faithful to their masters was the one southern leaders wanted told, and it quickly became the official one.

As a military mission, the raid had been a fiasco. Not a single slave had been freed. But Brown had always believed that, somehow, the effects of his action would far exceed what he might physically accomplish. By the end of the forty-five days that remained to him, after he survived Israel Green's saber thrust, it was clear to some that this faith would be vindicated. Against the many voices that dismissed the invasion as an utter failure and the work of a madman, abolitionist orator Wendell Phillips stood at Brown's graveside and delivered a different and ultimately more accurate assessment:

"He has abolished slavery in Virginia. . . . True, the slave is still there. So, when the tempest uproots a pine on your hills, it looks green for months—a year or two. Still, it is timber, not a tree. John Brown has loosened the roots of the slave system; it only breathes,—it does not live,—hereafter."

CHAPTER THIRTEEN

A Settlement of the Question

"I wish to say, furthermore, that you had better–all you people at the South–prepare yourselves for a settlement of that question that must come up for settlement sooner than you are prepared for it. The sooner you are prepared the better. You may dispose of me very easily; I am nearly disposed of now; but this question is still to be settled–this Negro question I mean– the end of that is not yet."
–John Brown, October 18, 1859

Watson Brown lay on the grass beneath the flagpole in the Harpers Ferry armory yard, struggling for breath. He could not remember being carried outside–just listening to Oliver die, then feeling his father kneel beside him in the engine house and hold his wrist, then the sound of a crash. The assault was over in minutes. Afterward, Colonel Lee instructed that the hostages be cared for and released, the captured insurgents secured in the watch house, and the dead carried out onto the grass. Watson sensed that he lay in a line of corpses. Soon, he knew, he would also die. Figures in uniform hovered above him and scuffled by his head and outstretched feet. Someone knelt and said "this one's still alive," and Watson felt himself being lifted and carried out of the light, then lowered onto some burlap sacks or blankets. Time passed.

He woke to a warm touch. A hand cupped the back of his neck, raised his head, and placed something soft beneath it. He opened his eyes. A fair young man in a clean suit crouched above him. "Can I bring you some water?" he asked. Watson nodded. C. W. Tayleure, a native South Carolinian who wrote for a Baltimore newspaper, had just arrived on the scene. Tayleure raised Watson's head again and held a cup to his lips. As the dying raider drank, the reporter studied his face. "What brought you here?" he asked. It took Watson Brown some time to clear his throat. "Duty, sir," he replied.

When Colonel Lee was informed that the insurrection's leader would live, he ordered Brown moved to a bedtick on the floor of the paymaster's office, where his wounds were cleaned and bandaged. Stevens was also brought from the Wager House and placed next to his chief. Within a few hours, Brown's bedside had become a magnet for Virginia's social, political, legal, and military elite. Governor Wise, Senator James Mason, Congressman Charles James Faulkner, and attorney Andrew Hunter, who would be appointed special state prosecutor of the cases against the invaders, had joined Lee, Stuart, and Washington on the scene. Ohio Congressman C. L. Vallandigham had also rushed down from Washington, frantic to vindicate his state and clear his constituents of involvement in the raid or its planning, and fearful that the facts would prove otherwise. Reporters from the *New York Herald* and the *Baltimore American,* along with several local bystanders, also crowded the room when Lee asked Brown if he would oblige the governor and the other distinguished gentlemen who had come to speak with him.

Brown's face and clothes were streaked and his hair was clotted with blood. He had not eaten in two days. Except for the morning's cycle of fitful dozes and awakenings in pain, he had not slept in almost three. But he found that his head was clear. In fact, though defeated, he felt powerful. Error, regret, unworthiness, indecision were all behind him. There were only words, selected, stored, and rehearsed over a lifetime, and he knew that whichever ones he spoke would be right. It was to speak them that he had been preserved. Lee offered to clear all but a handful of dignitaries from the room if Brown were unsettled or pained by the throng, but Brown declined the proposal. He wanted an audience.

The interrogation lasted three hours. Repeatedly, Brown was pressed and refused to reveal the names of his conspirators and the numbers and locations of his supporters. "Mr. Brown, who sent you here?" Congressman Vallandigham demanded. "No man sent me here,"

Brown replied. "It was my own prompting and that of my Maker, or that of the devil, whichever you choose to ascribe it to." Failing to elicit the identities of the raid's sponsors, the officials probed its motives and intentions. Again and again, they challenged the insurrectionist to justify his actions. "I think, my friend," Brown answered Senator Mason, "you are guilty of a great wrong against God and humanity—I say it without wishing to be offensive—and it would be perfectly right in any one to interfere with you so far as to free those you willfully and wickedly hold in bondage." Asked to provide a principle for his opinion, Brown three times cited the Golden Rule: "I want you to understand that I respect the rights of the poorest and weakest of colored people, oppressed by the slave system, just as much as I do those of the most wealthy and powerful. That is the idea that has moved me, and that alone. We expect no reward, except the satisfaction of endeavoring to do for those in distress and greatly oppressed, as we would be done by."

Mason questioned Brown about his men's compensation. Surely he offered them wages. "None," Brown replied, to which Stuart muttered, "'The wages of sin is death.'" Brown turned his head to regard the lieutenant. "I would not have made such a remark to you, if you had been a prisoner and wounded in my hands," he said. Not for the first time in the past thirty-six hours, Lewis Washington wondered that a man who had just committed a murderous, unprovoked, and unapologetic assault on a peaceable community should still feel himself entitled to be spoken to as a gentleman.

"Brown," someone in the crowd shouted out, "suppose you had every nigger in the United States. What would you do with them?"

"Set them free."

"To set them free would sacrifice the life of every man in this community," another bystander interjected.

"I do not think so."

The *Herald* correspondent asked Brown if he had anything further to say for the record. The people of the south, Brown responded, should prepare themselves for a settlement of the negro question, the question of perpetual human bondage and oppression. It was due to be settled soon, he predicted, sooner than they anticipated. "You may dispose of me very easily; I am nearly disposed of now; but this question is still to be settled—this Negro question I mean—the end of that is not yet."

Governor Wise frankly admired the old man's pluck, but he was weary of his self-righteous moral instruction. "Mr. Brown, the silver of your hair is reddened by the blood of crime," Wise reminded him. As a religious man, the governor continued, Brown would be well advised to stop casting blame upon others "and think upon eternity."

The reporters present transcribed and published Brown's answer: "Governor, I have, from all appearances, not more than fifteen or twenty years the start of you in the journey to that eternity of which you so kindly warn me; and whether my tenure here shall be fifteen months, or fifteen days, or fifteen hours, I am equally prepared to go. There is an eternity behind, and an eternity before, and the little speck in the center, however long, is but comparatively a minute. The difference between your tenure and mine is trifling and I want to therefore tell you to be prepared. I am prepared. You all have a heavy responsibility, and it behooves you to prepare more than it does me."

On Wednesday morning, October 18, the prisoners were transferred to Charlestown by train. A heavily guarded wagon carried Stevens and Brown the short distance to the station, while Green, Copeland, and Coppoc walked, enclosed by a cordon of soldiers and trailed by a mob screaming "Lynch them!" The Jefferson County jail, diagonally across the street from Charlestown's stately, pillared courthouse, offered more secure confinement for Brown and his associates while authorities decided where and by whom they would be prosecuted. The raiders had captured a U.S. government installation in the state of Virginia in a campaign aimed against the southern institution of slavery. Which jurisdiction would try them?

Some journalists and politicians on both sides of the Mason-Dixon line advocated a federal prosecution. To convict and execute Brown not only for murder but for treason to the United States, these leaders argued, would decisively signify that any criminal assault on the institutions of a single state or section was an intolerable attack against the nation as a whole. Of more immediate concern to Governor Wise, however, was the honor, outrage, and vindication of the state of Virginia. On the evening after Brown's defeat, the governor had publicly chastised his throng of constituents in the Wager House for their failure to dispatch the abolitionist invaders on their own. Virginia should not have required troops from Washington to arrest the disturbers of its peace and polluters of its sanctity; it would not now require Washington's help to punish them. Besides, a federal trial would entail delay and the transport of Brown and his cohorts out of state. Virginians, and southerners generally, wanted swift retribution delivered by the representatives of the people most aggrieved.

The editors of the *Richmond Whig* and the *Fredericksburg Herald* spoke for many when they urged that that retribution be summary and savage. "Immediate shooting or hanging without trial is the punishment they merit," the *Whig* editorialized. "In regard to such offenders, the just and safe principle is–'hang them first, and try them afterwards.'" In the view of the *Herald,* such deaths as these were more compassionate than the terrorists deserved. "The wheel nor the rack is a whit too hard for them. Shooting is a mercy they should be denied." But the governor was determined that Virginia justice show itself to be lawful and civilized, in pointed contrast to the anarchic barbarism that Brown and his conspirators in Boston and New York had unleashed upon the south. Wise's position was a difficult one. To him fell the task of both representing and containing the south's anger. It was his challenge, too, to deal with the perpetrators of the Harpers Ferry outrage in a manner commensurate with the public trauma it had produced, while communicating that the situation was under control and offered no cause for general alarm. These contradictory demands on Virginia's chief executive were rooted in the deeper contradictions of the community he served.

The *New York Times* remarked on what it saw as the incoherence and irrationality of the southern response to the raid in an editorial that ran in its Saturday, October 22, edition. Like other papers throughout the North, the *Times*–once the early reports of negro stampedes and takeovers that it had printed unquestioningly proved false–dismissed the incident as "practically a very harmless affair." For the *New York Tribune,* Harpers Ferry was "the work of a madman"; the *Cleveland Leader* judged that, but for its unfortunate though minimal toll on civilian lives, "the whole thing would be positively ridiculous, and it is fast becoming so even with the frightened chivalry themselves." Some southern publications did join in minimizing the raid's significance. This event, wrote the *Charleston Daily Courier,* "only demonstrates the impregnable safety of the South, when awakened to her own defense"; for another South Carolina paper, the *Edgefield Advertiser,* it was nothing but "a harebrained demonstration by a pack of crazy fanatics and poor deluded slaves." Yet, the *Times* charged, in spite of the evident failure and inconsequentiality of Brown's operation, many southern journals insisted on "making the whole South ring with the most absurd and extravagant exaggerations."

The *Times'* own commentary on the significance of Harpers Ferry, however, was as self-contradictory and extravagant as the southern response it criticized. The very same column that scolded the south for overreacting to the Harpers Ferry threat went on to justify that reaction by depicting the threat as mortal and perpetual. Governor Wise was wrong to call local citizens cowards for failing to put down the insurrection themselves, said the *Times,* since any citizenry would flinch when confronted by the "peculiar peril of Southern life." Southerners, the paper explained, "are in the power of the slaves who surround them. They live in constant and abiding dread of conspiracy and insurrection among them. They know that if any such movement should be made, the lives of their wives and children would be at the mercy of an ignorant and degraded race. What wonder, then, that they should be keenly sensitive to every hint of danger, and even irrationally suspicious of everything that indicates the approach of the peril they fear."

In a letter to a friend from prison, John Brown wrote: "Before I began my work at Harpers Ferry, I felt assured that in the worst event it would certainly pay. I often expressed that belief; and I can see no possible cause to alter my mind." Brown's work began to pay immediately by forcing to the surface the moral and psychological fissures in the foundation of southern society. Far from "harmless," the raid had activated explosive contradictions that shattered the political status quo, which had depended on their dormancy and suppression. Chief among these was the contradiction between the south's asserted pride in its benign and paternalistic tradition of labor and social relations between the races–a far more humane and civilized system, it was argued, than the impersonal "wage slavery" of the north–and its unspoken terror of murderous revolt by its black millions.

In the raid's aftermath, Wise and others struggled to prop up the pride and restore the complacency about black allegiance to their masters by trumpeting the voluntary return of Allstadt's and Washington's slaves to their homes. Virginia's slaves, they insisted, had given Brown no support. On the other hand, the hysterical eyewitness reports by railroad employees and passengers that converted five or six armed black men into five or six hundred, and the immediate and universal credence that those reports received, belied all assertions of confidence in the contentment of the servant class, let alone in "the impregnable safety of the South." Either the people whose self-emancipation was capable of producing such extravagant fear among white southerners were indeed subhuman beasts controllable by relentless force alone, or the south was, as Brown charged, "guilty of a great wrong against God and humanity," and its vision of murderous black revolt was the specter of self-punishment that its afflicted conscience placed before its eyes.

The Harpers Ferry raid proved effective not in any military or emancipatory goals that it achieved, but in the experience that it triggered. It was this experience that was registered by the southern journals that the *New York Times* so coolly rebuked for the extremism of their response. What the south experienced was betrayal. Northern communities made rich by manufactures and commerce based on southern agricultural production had allowed, and even supported, the south's invasion by radical abolitionists intent on destroying its essential social and economic institution. But the experience was also one of exposure. The attack had revealed a society whose mechanisms of control masked a fundamental uncontrol, whose civilization was founded on barbarism, and whose moral outrage at external disturbance was fueled by moral guilt for its internal routines.

Of course, this experience could not be admitted or even fully recognized by those whom it gripped. One avenue of relief was to displace the source of threat and corruption onto others and to separate from them. Before the raid, the *Richmond Enquirer* reported, talk of southern secession "had almost died out in Virginia." But Harpers Ferry "advanced the cause of Disunion more than any other event that has happened since the formation of the Government; it has rallied to that standard men who formerly looked upon it with horror; it has revived with tenfold strength the desires of a Southern Confederacy." However "harebrained" and "ridiculous" the invasion might have been, however overwhelming its condemnation by northern politicians or categorical

Scoffing at Brown's abortive attempt to free the slaves, *Harper's Weekly* embraced the defensive southern stereotypes of blacks as too simple, contented, or loyal to seek freedom. The mockery of the captions, however, barely suppresses the fearful hint of violent racial revolution in each of these three images of blacks brandishing weapons. (LIBRARY OF CONGRESS)

the assurances of northern newspapers that "there is not a handful of men in the North so base as to approve of the John Brown conspiracy," the south now found itself driven by a powerful psychological motive and impetus to secede.

In the north, too, Harpers Ferry exposed contradictions, brought suppressed possibilities and evasions to the surface, and pressured people in the uncommitted middle to move toward the extremes. As he had done in Kansas, as he had urged on the Gileadites, Brown's raid diminished the space of neutrality or the option of moderation on the question of slavery. For southern slaveholders and defenders of slavery, the shock of white men in league with blacks, ready to kill and die for the sake of slaves, accentuated the likelihood of the revolution they feared and deepened the trauma of its contemplation. For antislavery northerners, the same spectacle removed the protective buffer between themselves and their abstract principles. Though it had not succeeded at the Harpers Ferry armory, practical abolitionism was conceivable. There were white men willing to give their lives to the effort–whites, moreover, who regarded blacks not merely as objects of polite condescension in the north and of distant pity in the south but as familiar associates and equals. Confronted with this vision, some northern whites, such as Massachusetts senator and staunch unionist Edward Everett, heaped scorn on Brown and the "half-caste Republic" that actions like his promoted, while others, such as *New York Independent* managing editor Theodore Tilton, demanded: "What was his crime? Guilty of what? Guilty of loving his fellow man too well."

In both sections of the country, Brown had made white men feel personally challenged, personally threatened, personally judged, personally implicated by the negro question and its as yet undetermined settlement. "Christ told me to remember them that are in bonds, as *bound with them,* to do towards them as I would wish them to do towards me in similar circumstances," Brown wrote from prison to a stranger who had written sympathetically to him. In this synthesis of the two biblical verses upon which he had always most deeply relied, Brown captured the essence of his raid's radical effect. It had reminded whites, north and south, that their fates were bound up with the fates of slaves, and it had forced them to imagine themselves in the circumstances of others, and others in their own, across the divide of race.

Manacled to Edwin Coppoc, Brown appeared on October 25 before a court of examination whose charge was to conduct a preliminary evidentiary hearing prior to the submission of the case against the insurgents to the grand jury. The magistrates duly found cause to seek an indictment, which the grand jury handed down at noon the next day. Brown and his surviving men would stand trial on three counts: treason to the commonwealth of Virginia, conspiring with slaves to commit treason, and murder. Beyond enumerating the official charges, the indictment described the accused as "not having the fear of God before their eyes, but being moved and seduced by the false and malignant counsel of other evil and traitorous persons and the instigations of the devil."

In Massachusetts and New York, most of the "other evil and traitorous persons" to whom the Virginia grand jury alluded were panicking. The names of Sanborn, Howe, Stearns, Douglass, and Smith had all appeared in documents seized by government troops at the Kennedy farmhouse. Fearing arrest and extradition to Virginia to stand trial as Brown's co-conspirators, Sanborn, Howe, and Stearns fled to Canada. Douglass also quietly crossed the border and a few days later sailed to England to commence a lecture tour. In response to the shock and stress of Brown's capture and his own demonization in the press, the delicately constituted Gerrit Smith either had or feigned a nervous breakdown. His family committed him to a month's rest and psychological care at the Utica Asylum in upstate New York. Another of Brown's secret committee members, Theodore Parker, was dying of tuberculosis in Rome. Only the pugnacious Higginson remained at large in the United States, defying the authorities to come after him, raging against the personal cowardice of his abolitionist colleagues, and plotting a raid of his own on the Charlestown jail.

To discuss the idea of a jailbreak attempt with Mary Brown and to offer emotional and financial support to the decimated Brown family, Higginson traveled to North Elba at the beginning of November. Mail was delivered only once a week in the small, struggling Adirondack village, so it was not until some days after the conclusion of the Harpers Ferry affair that the family had learned of its occurrence and its toll. A neighbor had come to the cabin with a copy of the *New York Times*. The Browns assembled in the kitchen—Mary and her young daughters; Salmon and his wife; Watson's wife Isabella and their baby; Martha, carrying Oliver's unborn child; Ruth and Henry Thompson and their children—and listened as Annie, the family's fastest reader, read its account of the raid aloud. There were no shrieks or sobs of anguish as the deaths of Watson, Oliver, and both Thompson brothers, and the wounding and capture of Brown were revealed, just "a grief too deep and hard to find expression in words or even tears," as Annie later described the response. By the time Higginson arrived, that grief had had a week to settle into quiet fortitude.

The Browns had not yet received a letter from the head of their family and took a mournful delight in Higginson's reading from the newspaper transcript of Brown's instantly famous interview in the paymaster's office, where he had informed the assembly of national political and military leaders that he had come to Virginia under the auspices of John Brown. "That sounds just like father," Ruth and Annie chimed together. After supper, Higginson perused a small collection of family daguerreotypes as he sat with the women while they silently sewed. Contemplating an image of a beardless young man with a soft chin and dreamy eyes, he was startled by a girl's voice from the chair next to him that pronounced simply: "This is Oliver, one of those who were killed at Harpers Ferry." Higginson looked up and noticed that Martha did not quiver and continued to draw her thread while she identified her dead husband. Like the rest of the Browns, he thought, she asked for no pity and made no excuses or recriminations. What mattered to them now, and the question they wished to discuss with him, was whether freedom would gain or lose by the raid, the deaths of their young men, and the impending execution of their old one. "I have had thirteen children, and only four are left," Mary told him, "but if I am to see the ruin of my house, I cannot but hope that Providence may bring out of it some benefit to the poor slaves." The Worcester minister returned from his visit with a feeling akin to awe. Never before had he encountered or imagined a family so thoroughly and unanimously trained "on this one principle, and for this one special project." While some would argue that the Browns' vision was narrowed and impoverished by such a single-minded focus, Higginson disagreed. "It has given them a wider perspective than the Adirondacks," he wrote, adding: "Nothing short of knowing them can be called a liberal education."

The plan to attempt Brown's rescue was quickly put to rest by Brown himself. As the letters and newspapers that he received in his cell documented the passions that his deed, words, sacrifices, and impending execution were stirring throughout the country, he had come to recognize "that I am worth inconceivably more to hang than for any other purpose." His letters to his wife and children encouraged them to bear strongly and faithfully "the heavy tidings of our disaster." He assured them, too, of his kind treatment by his jailer, Captain Avis, and of his cheerful conviction "that for me at this time to seal my testimony for God and humanity with my blood will do vastly more toward advancing the cause I have earnestly endeavored to promote than all I have done in my life before."

The death sentence had been pronounced by Judge Richard Parker on November 2, after a four-day trial and a forty-five-minute deliberation by the jury on the three counts of the indictment. Early in the trial, one of Brown's court-appointed attorneys had sought to mitigate the charges by reading into evidence a telegram from a well-meaning Ohio relative stating that madness ran in the Brown family. Brown rejected this tactic, and no insanity defense was mounted, but the press took up the debate about Brown's mental balance and the inquiry into his family history. If her husband was insane, Mary Brown commented wryly to Higginson, he had been consistent in his insanity since the moment she met him. In response to prosecution witnesses' testimony to the facts of the invasion, the defense simply sought to establish that Brown had intended no violence against unarmed citizens, that he treated his prisoners kindly, and that, while he had ample opportunity to wantonly take life and destroy property in the first twelve hours of the raid, he had not done so. Hiram Griswold, a Cleveland lawyer belatedly added to Brown's defense team, pled in closing that Brown could not be guilty of treason against the commonwealth of Virginia since he was not a citizen of the state and owed it no allegiance. But the jury ignored this technicality and returned guilty verdicts on all charges.

Before the reading of the sentence, the court clerk asked the defendant if he had anything he wished to say. Still recovering from his wounds, Brown had spent most of the trial lying on a cot behind the attorneys' table and beneath the curious and hostile stares of the packed gallery. For this opportunity to address the court and the world, he rose. He began by reaffirming that his sole purpose had been to free the slaves. Though he acknowledged that his accusers spoke the truth about his actions in Virginia, he contended that, had he done the same to rescue the rich and the powerful from oppression, "this Court would have deemed it an act worthy of reward rather than punishment." He was satisfied with the respectful treatment that Virginia officials had accorded him since his capture, and with the fairness of his trial, he said, but he felt no consciousness of guilt.

"I see a book kissed, which I suppose to be the Bible, or at least the New Testament, which teaches me that all things whatsoever I would that men should do to me, I should do even so to them. It teaches me, further, to remember them that are in bonds as bound with them. I endeavored to act up to that instruction. I say I am yet too young to understand that God is any respecter of persons. I believe that to have interfered as I have done, as I have always freely admitted I have done, in behalf of His despised poor, I did no wrong, but right. Now, if it is deemed necessary that I should forfeit my life for the furtherance of the ends of justice, and mingle my blood further with the blood of my children and with the blood of millions in this slave country whose rights are disregarded by wicked, cruel, and unjust enactments, I say, let it be done."

Brown's public hanging was set for Friday, December 2, one month away. During these weeks, he read the Bible and marked the passages that showed God's declaration and demand of human equality. He received and answered dozens of letters from family members, abolitionist colleagues, and strangers. And he welcomed a stream of visitors from the north, who were allowed entrance to his cell by John Avis, the Jefferson County deputy sheriff and jailer, with whom Brown had formed a bond of mutual respect. In exchange for liberal visitation privileges, Avis had asked him to promise on his honor that he would attempt no escape, and Brown had willingly done so. As his death approached, he became increasingly confident that, by God's design more than his own, the Harpers Ferry enterprise had unfolded in such a way as to bring about, before much longer, the fulfillment of his highest hopes. He only needed to die for the result to be secured, and almost wished he could seize the chance more quickly to prevent its somehow being lost. He expressed these sentiments to a cousin, writing, "when I think how easily I might be left to spoil all I have done or suffered in the cause of freedom, I hardly dare wish another voyage, even if I had the opportunity."

It was fear of spoiling the effect of his brave deeds and words, and embarrassing his cause by a breakdown on the gallows, that prompted him to ask Mary not to come to Virginia. "I feel assured," he wrote on November 8, "for us to meet under such dreadful circumstances would only add to our distress." Mary felt differently, and had already begun her journey south in the company of her husband's abolitionist friends, though she let him know that she would not enter Virginia until she received his approval. On November 16, Brown wrote to her at the New Jersey home of Rebecca Spring, a longtime abolitionist who had visited the Charlestown jail within a few days of the raid's conclusion to minister to Stevens's and Brown's wounds. He still opposed Mary's visit but would not forbid it: "If you feel sure that you can endure the trials and the shock, which will be *unavoidable* (if you come), I should be most glad to see you once more; but when I think of your being insulted on the road, and perhaps *while here,* and of only seeing your wretchedness made complete, I *shrink* from it." Brown had earlier confessed to his lawyers that a visit from his grief-stricken wife was likely to unman him, but, in truth, this was not the only prospect from which he shrank. To Mary, he had written that "the sacrifices you & I have been called to make in behalf of the *cause we love, the cause of God, & of humanity,* do not seem to me as at all too great." But this was easier for him to say and feel in a letter than face to face with the mother of the children who had died for him or whom the cause had led him to abandon.

Still, Mary persisted. "My dear and beloved husband," she responded in mid-November: "I am here with Mrs. Spring, the kind lady who came to see you and ministered to your wants, as I am deprived of doing. You have nursed and taken care of me a great deal; but I cannot even come and look at you." She assured him that she did not wish to do or say anything to disturb his peace of mind. Yet she found it very hard to part without seeing him once more. "When you were at home last June I did not think that I took your hand for the last time." Finally, Brown relented. "I will close this," he wrote on November 26, "by saying that if you *now feel* that you are *equal* to the undertaking do *exactly as you* FEEL *disposed to do* about coming to see me before I suffer. *I am entirely willing.*"

While he waited for Mary and thought, alternately, about the cause that would be advanced and the family that would be forsaken by his death, Brown intensified the pace of his letter-writing. On his children he urged religious faith and composure. Several times, his letters to family speak of his hope, and affirm his belief, that the time would soon come when they would not be embarrassed to acknowledge their relation to him. Of friends and well-wishers, he requested financial assistance for his stigmatized and impoverished family. In response to a supportive letter from the writer and abolitionist Lydia Maria Child, Brown asked if she might initiate a relief fund for his wife and daughters by pledging fifty cents per year and urging as many of her friends as possible to do the same. To Mrs. Spring, he wrote about his anxiety for the welfare of his gentle second son, and his wish to help him relocate and find employment in a new and supportive community.

"His name is Jason; he is about thirty-six years old; has a wife and one little boy. He is a very laborious, ingenious, temperate, honest, and truthful man. He is very expert as a gardener, vine-dresser, and manager of fruit-trees, but does not pride himself on account of his skill in anything; always has underrated himself; is bashful and retiring in his habits; is not (like his father) too much inclined to assume and dictate; is too conscientious in his dealings and too tender of people's feelings to get from them his just deserts, and is very poor. He suffered almost everything on the way to and while in Kansas but death, and returned to Ohio not a spoiled but next to a ruined man. He never quarrels, and yet I know that he is both morally and physically brave." Like the seedlings he had managed to sustain throughout the ordeal of his voyage across Missouri, Jason required a quality of attention and nurture that his father had never provided. Now, Brown was asking a stranger to help him compensate for that deficiency: "Could I know that he was located with a population who were disposed to encourage him, without expecting him to pay too dearly in the end for it, I should feel greatly relieved."

Beyond his concerns for his family's future, Brown's equanimity in his final weeks was disturbed only by the occasional appearance of southern clergymen who wished to pray for or with him. The ministerial overtures of such men were rejected in a manner neither reverent nor meek. To an Ohio minister who had written to ask about his access to spiritual counsel, Brown replied: "It would be a great pleasure to me to have some one better qualified than myself to lead my mind in prayer and meditation, now that my time is so near a close. You may wonder, are there no ministers of the gospel here? I answer, No. There are no ministers of *Christ* here. These ministers who profess to be Christian, and hold slaves or advocate slavery, I cannot abide them. My knees will not bend in prayer with them while their hands are stained with the blood of souls."

On November 30, the day before Mary visited him in his cell, Brown composed his last letter to his family at North Elba. He enclosed a bank draft for a hundred dollars that a friend from Rhode Island had made over for the Brown family's use. He once more assured his survivors "that our seeming *disaster* will ultimately result in the most *glorious success*" and urged his "dear shattered & broken family" to be of good cheer and trust in God. He asked them to love and stick by one another, but, typically, this injunction to family affection and unity soon gave way to an affirmation of the Browns' commitment to a much larger family, even at the expense of their private lives: "And let me entreat you all to love *the whole remnant* of our once great family 'with a pure *heart fervently.*' Try to build again your broken walls & to make the *utmost* of every *stone* that is left. Nothing can so make life a blessing as the consciousness that you love & *are beloved*: & 'love ye the stranger' *still*. It is ground of the utmost comfort to *my mind* to know that so many of you as have had the *opportunity* have given full proof of your fidelity to the great family of man. *Be faithful* unto *death*." Brown's own radical humanitarianism had originated in religious conviction; now, he implored the skeptics among his children to cultivate religious conviction on the ground of their radical humanitarianism. "From the exercise of habitual love to man, *it cannot* be very *hard* to *learn* to *love* his *maker*." Finally, he requested that his children live contentedly with moderate means, that they teach their children and grandchildren not to measure happiness by riches, and that they "abhor with undying hatred, also, that 'sum of all villainies,' Slavery."

In Philadelphia, Mary did not receive the telegram from Governor Wise authorizing her visit to her husband until two days before the execution. She and her chaperones were told to go immediately by train to Harpers Ferry. From there, she would be taken alone to Charlestown by a military guard on the afternoon of December 1. The governor also required that she return from Charlestown to the Wager House that evening. John Brown's body would be delivered to her for transport and burial in the north on the afternoon of the following day. With Philadelphia abolitionist J. Miller McKim and his wife, and an attorney, Hector Tyndale, Mary traveled to Harpers Ferry on November 30, as instructed. Early the following afternoon, a cavalry captain called for her at the hotel. The captain ushered her into a carriage and got in beside her. Mounted soldiers took up positions in front, in back, and on either side of the vehicle, and so accompanied it on the eight-mile trip to Charlestown.

The Fauquier Cavalry made up only a few of the several thousand troops in full regalia that patrolled the surrounding towns and countryside. Passenger trains into the area had been stopped in an effort to keep everyone besides local residents and military personnel away from the site of Brown's execution. Governor Wise and Major General William Taliaferro, the commander of the military forces on the scene, had issued proclamations that urged Virginians to remain in their homes and guard their property on the day of the hanging. Fires of mysterious origin had illuminated the Charlestown nights throughout the month of November, and the barns and stockyards of several of the jurors in the Brown case had been among the properties burned. Perhaps the rash of fires had been coincidental, perhaps the work of negroes or northern infiltrators. Whatever the case might be, the authorities believed that anything could happen on the day that Brown was hanged, and they had placed the military and the citizenry alike on high alert.

Mary Brown reached the square in Charlestown at 3:30 P.M. John Avis escorted her through his residence, which adjoined the prison unit, to his office. Her husband was there, his leg shackles removed in deference to his wife's sensibilities and the solemnity of the occasion. The couple embraced without speaking. Both broke down in tears as

Avis turned away. They talked of their daughters' education, Brown's will, the health and futures of Oliver's and Watson's widows. Most of the subjects of their conversation had passed between them in letters over the last month. There was little new to say. Brown wished to hear the current details of their farm life, the condition of the house and the livestock. Mary told him that his speech to the court was talked of and preached on everywhere. She knew it would do much good. She also knew of the great disappointment of her husband's youth, long before she met him, almost before she was born. He had confessed to her that he had once planned to attend college and study for the ministry but had failed. So she added now that, if he had become a minister and delivered ten lives' worth of sermons, he could never have won more souls to grace than he had done with those few words.

As evening fell, Avis invited the Browns to have supper in his quarters with his family and himself. For an hour, both lost themselves in the strange yet well-remembered pleasure of a family meal, then paid for the simulation of normalcy when it was time for Mary to go. Brown briefly lost his practiced composure. He wept and pleaded with the helpless jailer to let his wife sit with him on his last night on earth, then began to rage at the arbitrariness and cruelty of the order requiring her to leave. Just as quickly, he regained control and dignity. He blessed his wife, embraced her one last time, commended her to God, and let her go.

The next morning, December 2, Colonel J. T. L. Preston of the Virginia Military Institute marched his corps of cadets to a large field at the southeast edge of Charlestown. There, workmen had constructed a gallows the day before on a stretch of raised ground that commanded a broad view of the Shenandoah Valley and the Blue Ridge Mountains arrayed in the distance. Preston's cadets, uniformed in red flannel shirts for the occasion, had been assigned a prime position immediately behind the gibbet on which Brown would hang. They were flanked by members of an artillery company commanded by one of Preston's VMI colleagues, Major Thomas J. Jackson, not yet hailed as "Stonewall." These troops from the military institute in Lexington shared the honor and duty of securing the execution site with militia units and guard details from cities and towns throughout Virginia, including two elite corps from the capital: the Richmond Grays and Company F. Among them, having borrowed a uniform to gain admission to the spectacle, stood a twenty-one-year-old aspiring actor named John Wilkes Booth. Rings of infantry, dragoons, and cavalry surrounded the small wooden platform at the center of the field, sealing it from public access for a distance of a quarter mile. Nearly one thousand men in arms patrolled the scene, and another five hundred stood their posts at the jail, around the town, or along the short route that Brown would travel from his cell to his hanging.

At a little before 11:00 A.M., deputy sheriff Avis, joined by several guards, led Brown out onto the jail's porch. The prisoner wore a wrinkled black suit, a white open shirt, and loose-fitting carpet slippers. His arms were pinioned to his side at the elbows. The short walk took Brown and his attendants along a corridor past the cells of the other condemned raiders, who wept as their leader shuffled by. "God bless you, my men," Brown said, meeting in turn the gazes of Stevens, Coppoc, Copeland, and Green. "May we all meet in Heaven." At the street, Avis was met by Sheriff John Campbell. The two men flanked their charge and waited. In a moment, a farm wagon, pulled by two large white horses, drew up in front of them. A large poplar box filled the center of the wagon bed. Inside of that lay a black walnut coffin. Brown climbed into the wagon and sat on the forward end of the box. Avis and Campbell stood in the bed beside him. The driver snapped the reins and the vehicle lurched ahead, falling in behind three companies of infantry. Two additional infantry companies and a mounted militia unit brought up the rear. General Taliaferro and his staff rode at the head of the procession. It was a clear, temperate early winter day.

As they neared their destination, Brown broke the silence. The majesty of God's creation–the peace and perfection of sky, cloud, fields, and mountains–had once delighted and inspired him. That vision had had to be obscured for a time by another. Now, he could let it return: "This is a beautiful country," he said to Avis. "I never had the pleasure of seeing it before."

The soldiers at the field's periphery opened a path and the wagon rolled to a stop at the foot of the platform. Brown ascended the steps quickly and without assistance, and stood in the center of the trap door that Sheriff Campbell would release by a hatchet stroke to the rope that held it in place. No clergy attended the condemned man, and no additional opportunity to speak was afforded him. John Brown had already had his say by the state's indulgence and at its expense. As Campbell

A magazine illustration of the spectacle of Brown's December 2, 1859, execution on a scaffold constructed in a field near Charlestown, Virginia (LIBRARY OF CONGRESS)

and Avis arranged the noose and drew a white hood over his face, Brown bid them goodbye. Campbell asked him if he would like to be given a signal before the rope was cut and his body dropped. His voice was calm and audible through the cloth to the troops around the gallows' base: "It does not matter to me, as long as you will not keep me too long waiting." Though Brown was ready, several of the guard units were out of their assigned positions. For more than ten minutes, he stood blindfolded while officers barked commands and soldiers rearranged themselves. Colonel Preston, standing below and behind Brown, watched him closely, as he wrote in his account of the event, "to see if I could detect any signs of shrinking or trembling in his person, but there was none. Once I thought I saw his knees tremble, but it was only the wind blowing his loose trousers." Finally, the overseer of the execution's military detail, Colonel F. H. Smith, announced to Sheriff Campbell that the troops were ready. Momentarily distracted or lost in thought, Campbell did not respond, and Smith repeated his statement loudly. Leaving Brown's side, the sheriff descended the stairs, and chopped at the trap door's support. Brown fell three feet and the noose jerked. But for a clenching of the hands, the body remained rigid. In a few minutes it relaxed, and began to sway gently in a sudden breath of wind.

No one cheered or spoke. Not until Colonel Preston turned to face the crowd was the silence broken. "So perish all such enemies of Virginia!" he intoned. "All such enemies of the Union! All such foes of the human race!"

Blacks proclaimed December 2 "Martyr Day." Antislavery clergy rang church bells and led packed prayer services for Brown. Abolitionists held large public rallies in cities and towns throughout the north. In the days that followed, however, counterdemonstrations in these same communities were even larger. Reporting on the impressive size and vehemence of the crowd of respectable Bostonians who turned out to hear speaker after speaker condemn Brown's motives and methods, one prominent Republican remarked with satisfaction: "I have never in my life seen a fuller or more enthusiastic demonstration of public sentiment, especially in reprobation of the attempt of John Brown at Harpers Ferry." Brown's only sympathizers, he added, were "ultra-philanthropists and fanatical clergymen." Such clerical fanatics, a New York religious journal estimated, were themselves a small fringe in the Christian community: "Of the *five hundred* pulpits of this city we believe that not *five* uttered a word of approbation of the John Brown invasion of Virginia." Another New York paper assured its readers that the great mass of northerners remained "as uncorrupted with Negro equality doctrines as ever." And a third predicted a general backlash from Harpers Ferry that would soon produce "such a coming together from all places and parties as has never before been witnessed. Many are eager for an occasion of this sort that the power of those men who uphold the Constitution may be felt at this time, immediately succeeding the infamous attempt of the Abolitionists upon the rights of a sovereign State."

No such statistics or assurances from the north, however, could calm the fears and passions Brown had aroused, or heal the psychic wound he had exposed within both sections and between them. "No, gentlemen," Mississippi Senator Albert Gallatin Brown declaimed on the Senate floor, rebuffing the conciliatory overtures of his northern

An artist's rendering of John Brown's burial in North Elba, New York. Brown's farmhouse is depicted in the background, with Whiteface Mountain looming behind it. (WEST VIRGINIA STATE ARCHIVES)

colleagues, "disguise it as you will, there is throughout all the non-slaveholding States of this Union a secret, deep-rooted sympathy with the object which this man had in view."

Long-standing southern secessionists such as Virginia's Edmund Ruffin immediately recognized Brown's raid as a bonanza for their languishing cause. "Such a practical exercise of abolition principles is needed to stir the sluggish blood of the South," Ruffin wrote in his journal on October 19. To be sure that blood was stirred well, Ruffin managed to acquire some of the spear-headed pikes that were captured at the schoolhouse near the Ferry and sent one to each southern governor with the message, "Sample of the favors designed for us by our Northern Brethren." As the election year of 1860 approached, it began to appear likely that a victory by the "'Black Republican, free love, free Nigger' party," as southern polemicists termed it, would lead to disunion. Many political observers, however, expected that Brown's action would undermine Republican support in the north precisely by the opportunity it offered the party's opponents to associate it with dangerous fanaticism on the subject of slavery. And this opportunity was taken up, both by the Democrats and by the newly formed Constitutional Union Party, which blamed both the Democratic and the Republican leaderships for exploiting and inflaming the slavery issue since 1854, and offered itself as a healing alternative on the basis of a return to Henry Clay's Compromise of 1850 and under the slogan "The Union, the Constitution, and the enforcement of the Laws."

But the Democratic Party split at its national convention, when its northern and southern factions failed to agree either on a platform or on a candidate, and the Constitutional Union Party's campaign was disorganized and ineffective. In a four-man race, Lincoln was elected with 40 percent of the popular vote, almost none of it in the south. The Republicans had done what they could to distance themselves from John Brown, practical abolitionism, and any reasonable suspicion that they planned to interfere with the internal policies of the slave states. Brown deserved to die, Lincoln had stated on the day of his execution. Opposition to slavery on principle, he continued, "cannot excuse violence, bloodshed, and treason." In a speech the next February, Lincoln returned to the subject of Harpers Ferry, mocking Brown's action as "so absurd that the slaves, with all their ignorance, saw plainly enough it could not succeed." John Brown was no Republican, he insisted, and those who pretended otherwise out of malice or political opportunism had "failed to implicate a single Republican in his Harpers Ferry enterprise." At the May nominating convention in Chicago, Republicans passed a unanimous resolution endorsing "the maintenance inviolate of the rights of States, and especially the right of each State to order and control its own domestic institutions according to its own judgment exclusively." In case the resolution's message was unclear, they passed another that condemned "the lawless invasion by armed force of the soil of any state or territory, no matter under what pretext, as among the gravest of crimes." And, in the opening sentences of his inaugural address, President Lincoln solemnly promised: "I have no purpose, directly or indirectly, to interfere with the institution of slavery in the States where it exists. I believe I have no lawful right to do so, and I have no inclination to do so."

For southerners, however, nothing the Republicans might say could neutralize what Brown had done. The raid had decisively tipped the balance of power and influence in the south in favor of the fire-eating secessionists, who had persuaded their constituents that, sooner or later, the Republican administration would allow or even encourage legions of John Browns to descend upon them. In fact, as many of the fire-eaters themselves recognized, John Brown was not legion in the north. Several years of recruitment in the free states, the territories, and Canada had netted Brown fifteen men, outside of his immediate family, willing to take up arms against slavery in the south. But southern leaders did not require fear of an actual attack as a trigger. The expression of sympathy or admiration for Brown by a vocal minority of northerners was insult, judgment, and provocation enough. Lincoln's election only confirmed what the *New Orleans Daily Picayune* had called "the fanaticism of hatred against slavery which the event had shown to exist throughout the North."

Anthony W. Dillard, a close associate of Alabama governor John Anthony Winston and a delegate to the divisive 1860 Democratic Convention in Charleston, was convinced of Brown's decisive role in bringing about the Confederacy. "But for John Brown's insane attack upon Harpers Ferry," Dillard later wrote, "it is very questionable whether any of the Southern States could have been screwed up and egged on to secede, purely because of the election of Mr. Lincoln. They would have waited for some overt attack to be made on slavery, which would not have happened during Mr. Lincoln's term, as he would have conformed to and respected the platform upon which he had been elected." Dillard long lamented what Stephen A. Douglas, the losing northern Democratic presidential candidate, and many historians after him regarded as the needless war.

The Civil War took more than six hundred thousand American lives and left scars on the forcibly reunited nation that have not fully healed a hundred and forty years later. No war in U.S. history has exacted a greater domestic toll. Yet Brown, had he lived to see it, would have insisted on asking a question that few whites of his era or later ones cared to confront: needless for whom? There were opportunities to avert the war and opportunities to end it quickly that were not seized. Had leaders seized them, hundreds of thousands of Americans would have been spared. But four million other Americans—along

A Settlement of the Question

Around the turn of the twentieth century, a freedman reads a pamphlet that tells the story of Harpers Ferry. (LIBRARY OF CONGRESS)

with millions more of their descendants for perhaps many years to come—would also have remained enslaved.

In his Second Inaugural Address, after four years of slaughter, Lincoln proposed that the terrible war be understood as an act of divine retribution and accepted as a rite of national expiation for the sin of slavery. "If we shall suppose that American slavery is one of those offenses which, in the providence of God, must needs come, but which, having continued through His appointed time, He now wills to remove, and that He gives to both North and South this terrible war as the woe due to those by whom the offense came, shall we discern therein any departure from those divine attributes which the believers in a living God always ascribe to Him? Fondly do we hope, fervently do we pray, that this mighty scourge of war may speedily pass away. Yet, if God wills that it continue until all the wealth piled by the bondsman's two hundred and fifty years of unrequited toil shall be sunk, and until every drop of blood drawn with the lash shall be paid by another drawn with the sword, as was said three thousand years ago, so still it must be said 'the judgments of the Lord are true and righteous altogether.'"

John Brown, for all his religious fervor, never embraced so apocalyptic a vision or wished for so punitive an occasion of slavery's demise. But, on the day of his death, his last written words predicted both the suffering and the redemption that Lincoln's oratory would later struggle to sanctify. As he exited the Charlestown jail, he handed one of his guards a note:

"I John Brown, am now quite *certain* that the crimes of this *guilty land* will never be purged *away,* but with Blood. I had *as I now think vainly* flattered myself that without *very much* bloodshed it might be done."

EPILOGUE

THE UNFINISHED AMERICAN REVOLUTION

> *"You know what John Brown did? He went to war. He was a white man who went to war against white people to help free slaves.... And any white man who is ready and willing to shed blood for your freedom—in the sight of other whites, he's nuts."*
> –Malcolm X

During the eighteen months in which most of my waking hours outside of my day job were spent writing *Patriotic Treason*, I sometimes had occasion to mention to a colleague, family friend, airplane seatmate, or fellow party guest that I was working on a book about John Brown. My conversation partners were typically well-educated Americans who recognized Brown's name from a college class they had taken or a PBS series or History Channel feature about the Civil War they had seen. Most recalled that he was an abolitionist; some remembered that he led the raid on Harpers Ferry. But many of those who knew these things about him also thought that he was black.

The people who knew John Brown was a white man—a group that included several professors of history—tended also to have retained the information that he was mentally unbalanced, a religious fanatic, a violent sociopath, or all three. This was what most of the American historical establishment, including several of its preeminent figures, taught and wrote about Brown until well into the 1970s and beyond. Brown was "ignorant, narrow-minded, fanatically prejudiced" and "subject to extravagant religious fixations," declared Alan Nevins in 1950; "a brutal murderer if ever there was one," pronounced Bruce Catton in 1961; " a grim, terrible man," chimed David Donald in 1969; "a madman," judged Monroe Lee Billington in 1971; "so deranged" that it would have been more appropriate for Governor Wise "just to have committed him to an asylum," concurred John Garraty in 1974; "fanatical, millenarian, and possibly mad," reiterated Eugene D. Genovese in the same year; "a pitiful failure" and an "incompetent revolutionary," concluded Charles Joyner in 1995.

Academic historians of the middle and late twentieth century were hobbled by and hostile to John Brown for a number of reasons. Some were simply southern partisans, but more were working within a framework of professional assumptions and purposes that Brown threatened. Proper historical inquiry into watershed events such as the Civil War was supposed to focus on complex intersections of economic and social conditions and elite actors (presidents, diplomats, financiers, generals). Private citizens agitating on single issues were not the preferred engines of history. Linked to this framing assumption about historical complexity was the general predisposition of mainstream historians of the war to serve as agents of national reconciliation by taking a dispassionate and equalizing view of the claims, motives, interests, and miscalculations of both the north and the south. Such a purpose cannot accommodate a heroic, or even a tolerable, John Brown.

Brown also offended the historians' sensibilities by the nature and intensity of the personal commitments that he derived from Christian teachings and from America's racial order and revolutionary heritage. His experience of religion, race, and revolution fell outside the acceptable boundaries set by a modern, moderate, rationalistic, white professional guild; therefore it was relegated to the domain of the pathological. Finally, the story of the Civil War had its tragic heroes and reluctant warriors in Lee and Lincoln; what it needed was a reckless villain. Though historians minimized his causal role, Brown was nonetheless linked with, and blamed for, the polarization and savagery that resulted in the deaths of the six hundred and eighteen thousand.

These reasons for the historians' dislike and defamation of Brown might have remained in force had Brown been black. But had Brown been an escaped slave or a free northern black man who acted and spoke exactly as the historical John Brown did, professional historians of the last fifty years would not have labeled him mad. Radical, militant, enraged, desperate, impatient, self-aggrandizing, perhaps—but not crazy. The historical misconception of Brown as a madman and the popular misconception of him as a black man proceed from a common source: the stunted moral imagination and the incomplete embrace of democratic principles of the society that shapes the conventional assumptions of its historians and its ordinary citizens alike. A man who lived, went to war, and died to help win black people's rights to life, liberty, and the pursuit of happiness must have been black. A white man who did these things must have been deranged or fanatical. One hundred and fifty years ago, Brown's extended abolitionist family achieved a practical and empathetic crossing of the color line that set them apart from the vast majority of white Americans. Today, as our received misconceptions of Brown attest, that crossing is still hard for us to imagine.

It is difficult, in part, because of the way we have become accustomed to viewing the cultural and political landscape of both the United States and the world: as a patchwork of competing interest groups, ethnic and religious communities, or other sorts of collectives defined by their members' common mode of self-identification. There are many good reasons, of course, for people to claim and cultivate special connections with others who share their important experiences and commitments. Yet the logics of "identity politics" and multiculturalism may also condition us to accept the idea that human knowledge, feeling, and responsibility are particular to and bounded by clan. From the undeniable assertion that different communal histories and cultural pathways produce different social visions and values, it is a short, yet mistaken, step to the cynical relativism that claims there are as many truths and moralities as there are identity groups, and that human beings from different groups are capable of no deep and broad consensus about what they are obligated to believe or to do.

Not long before the raid on Harpers Ferry, Jeremiah Anderson offered a simple and direct explanation of why he was going to join it: "Millions of fellow beings require it of us; their cries for help go out to the universe daily and hourly. Whose duty is it to help them? Is it yours, is it mine? It is every man's." If the strong claims for ethnic, cultural, or interest-based particularism and relativism were true, then Anderson's words would scarcely be comprehensible, let alone resonant, to anyone besides slaves or blacks. If we truly believed such claims, we would be hard pressed to explain how Anderson, who was white and free, ever felt the feelings or thought the thoughts that led him to pose his questions and answer. We would also have trouble explaining the extraordinary psychological effect on the south of Brown's unsuccessful military action and unachieved slave uprising. Far more traumatic than the suppressed danger that the raid exposed was the suppressed guilt. It was in the south's interest to believe that slavery was not just necessary but right, and for thirty years the region's writers, teachers, preachers, and politicians had been spinning out arguments to prove it. But to no avail. Southern whites could defend against Brown, but not—when his words and action probed them—against their own consciousness of wrong.

Better than anyone, Henry David Thoreau understood Brown's raid to be an incursion into the consciousness of the north as well, a radical operation meant to stimulate moral recovery. In a speech at the Concord Town Hall, two Sundays after Brown's volunteers crossed the Potomac bridge into Harpers Ferry, Thoreau called the raid "the best news that America has ever heard. It has already quickened the feeble pulse of the North, and infused more and more generous blood into her veins and heart than any number of years of what is called commercial and political prosperity could. How many a man who was lately contemplating suicide has now something to live for!"

Thoreau's figure of the pre–Harpers Ferry north as bloodless and even suicidal echoed the imagery he had used in his essay on civil disobedience, written more than a decade before: "Is there not a sort of blood shed when the conscience is wounded? Through this wound a man's real manhood and immortality flow out, and he bleeds to an everlasting death. I see this blood flowing now." In characteristically vivid language, Thoreau expresses in these passages an idea that is central to many religious traditions, Christianity prominent among them. It is that individuals and societies may live, even prosper, in a way that is spirit-killing.

For Thoreau, the most spiritually corrosive life is lived by relatively privileged members of democratic societies who know in their hearts that their elected government is doing great wrong in their names, who derive personal and national benefit from that wrong, and who—out of convenience, conformity, cynicism, or despair—do nothing to stop or correct it. As the United States was completing the imposition of its will on Mexico, Thoreau observed that most of his Concord neighbors heartily disapproved of the attack on a foreign nation for material gain under a flimsy pretense of self-defense, and the legal oppression and exploitation of blacks that the war promised to extend. Yet they remained obedient citizens, paid for the war with their tax dollars, and resignedly pocketed their share of the national wealth that imperialism and slavery produced. "Thus, under the name of order and civil government," he concluded, "we are all made at last to pay homage to our meanness. After the first blush of sin, comes its indifference; and from immoral it becomes, as it were, unmoral, and not quite unnecessary to that life which we have made."

In January of 1859, en route to Canada with the eleven slaves he had stolen from their Missouri owners, John Brown met quietly in Lawrence, Kansas, with the *New York Tribune* correspondent William Addison Phillips. Phillips shared Brown's abolitionist sentiments but disapproved of his increasingly radical methods. He argued that, in spite of the blot of slavery, there was virtue enough in the American people to bring an end to it in time through normal political processes. Brown doubted that the people could access that virtue without some galvanizing shock. "They have compromised so long," he said, "that they think principles of right and wrong have no more any power on this earth." What Thoreau found spiritually lifesaving in Brown's raid was its demonstration that such principles retained some motivational power. Here was his theory of civil disobedience fulfilled: "Action from principle,–the perception and performance of right,–changes things and relations; it is essentially revolutionary, and does not consist wholly with any thing which was."

Many of the radical abolitionists of Brown's day regarded the American Revolution as an event that was "essentially revolutionary." The founders' action from principle, they believed, had not only established a new nation but forever changed and raised the prevailing standards for human relations in the political sphere. Patriotism and the highest moral and social ideals were united and mutually supporting. As Brown remarked to Franklin Sanborn: "I believe in the Golden Rule and the Declaration of Independence. I think they mean the same thing." The continuation and expansion of slavery, and its entrenchment in the country's political, economic, and legal framework, shattered this synthesis of patriotism and principle. For Thoreau, those "patriots"–as he insisted on calling them–who still wished to "serve the State with their consciences" would have to "resist it for the most part" and accept being "treated by it as enemies." The force of their example, he hoped, or the shame of their suppression, would confront others with their own spiritual bleeding and inspire them to take action to staunch it.

No great insight is required to see this blood flowing now. The egalitarian ideals and justice-seeking aspirations of the Declaration of Independence hold little interest, except as tokens to be spun, for those who currently define—and would enforce—American patriotism. The Christianity that is invoked in our national halls of power has nothing in common with the teachings that Brown understood to be at the heart of the faith: Remember them that are in bonds, as bound with them. Do unto others as you would that others should do unto you. Inasmuch as ye did it not to one of the least of these, ye did it not to me.

"Whose duty is it to help them? Is it yours? Is it mine? It is every man's, but how few there are to help. But there are a few who dare to answer this call, and dare to answer it in a manner that will make this land of liberty and equality shake to its center." There are never likely, at any given moment, to be more than a few. Most of us have unbroken "household gods" to serve—gods that circumscribe our obligations and our risks, but also, at their best, deepen the human meaning of our lives and are worthy of reverence. Those who answer Brown's or Thoreau's call with immoderate passion and abandon will always be controversial, always be extreme. But their "madness" and "treason" remain necessary. At the least, such radical actors and actions force "sanity" and "patriotism" to define themselves rather than stand exempt from examination and debate. At the most, they reduce suicide, and sustain—perhaps even advance—the hope of fulfilling our revolutionary potential.

SOURCE NOTES

Full bibliographical information for each of the printed sources cited in these notes is provided in the first reference to each source. Previously quoted sources are identified by the author's last name, the book or article title, and the page number. The notes also specify the author, recipient, and date of each of the many letters by John Brown, his family, and his associates that I quote. To reduce the distraction of unconventional punctuation and occasional misspellings (both areas in which American writing was less rule-bound in the early nineteenth century, especially for self-taught writers like Brown), I have standardized the spelling and removed unnecessary commas, dashes, and colons in the quoted correspondence, without changing any of the words or meanings.

The sources for *Patriotic Treason* include archival materials as well as published ones. Archival sources are identified in the first instance by name and subsequently by the following abbreviations: OGV indicates the Oswald Garrison Villard collection of John Brown materials at the Columbia University Library, one of the most extensive John Brown collections in the country; STUT indicates the Boyd Stutler Collection at the West Virginia State Archive; RWL indicates the Robert Woodruff Library at Atlanta University, which houses a collection of Brown's early business letters; OHS indicates the Ohio Historical Society; and BPL indicates the Boston Public Library.

Author's Note

ix *"the stone in the historians' shoe":* Truman Nelson, "John Brown Revisited," *The Nation*, Aug. 31, 1957, 88.

ix *"He was a stone":* Stephen Vincent Benet, *John Brown's Body* (1928; reprint, Chicago: Ivan R. Dee, 1990), 56.

ix *"God's stone in the pool of slavery":* Stephen B. Oates, *Our Fiery Trial: Abraham Lincoln, John Brown, and the Civil War Era* (Amherst: University of Massachusetts Press, 1979), 9.

xi *"Even suppose blood should flow":* Henry David Thoreau, "Civil Disobedience," *Collected Essays and Poems* (New York: Library of America, 2001), 214.

xi *"Of all the men who were said":* Thoreau, "The Last Days of John Brown," *Collected Essays and Poems,* 428.

Prologue: The Dawn's Early Light

1 *"Was John Brown simply an episode?":* W. E. B. Du Bois, *John Brown* (Philadelphia, George W. Jacobs & Co., 1909), 374.

2 *Stuart estimated:* J. E. B. Stuart to mother, January 1860, quoted in H. B. McClellan, *I Rode with Jeb Stuart* (Bloomington: Indiana University Press, 1958), 29.

3 *As Chief Justice Roger Taney wrote:* Quoted in John Elliott Cairnes, *The Slave Power* (1862; reprint, New York: Harper & Row, 1969), 250.

5 *"Colonel Lee represents":* Quoted in Oswald Garrison Villard, *John Brown* (1910; reprint, Gloucester, Mass.: Peter Smith, 1965), 451.

6 *Stuart knew him:* J. E. B. Stuart to mother, January 1860, quoted in McClellan, *I Rode with Jeb Stuart,* 29.

9 *Brown had greeted him pleasantly:* Lewis Washington testimony to U.S. Senate Select Committee on the Harpers Ferry Invasion, 36th Congress, *Senate Report* No. 278, 34

9 *"You will get over it":* John Allstadt statement, quoted in Villard, *John Brown,* 448.

11 *Sometimes he even posed the question to himself:* JB to Henry Stearns, July 15, 1857, Louis Ruchames, ed., *A John Brown Reader* (London: Abelard-Schuman, 1959), 38.

12 *"This is Osawatomie":* quoted in Villard, *John Brown,* 453.

Chapter 1: Founding Fathers

13 *"If a tax on tea":* Quoted in Daniel C. Littlefield, "Blacks, John Brown, and a Theory of Manhood," *His Soul Goes Marching On: Responses to John Brown and the Harpers Ferry Raid,* ed. Paul Finkelman (Charlottesville: University Press of Virginia, 1995), 70.

14 *Now," he asked:* 36th Congress, *Senate Report No. 278,* 241–42.

15 *"I should have disapproved of it":* Ibid., 242.

16 *"Americans!":* Quoted in George Forgie, *Patricide in the House Divided* (New York: W. W. Norton & Co., 1979), 38.

16 *"That stone":* JB, March 1837, as quoted by H. N. Rust in Franklin Sanborn, *The Life and Letters of John Brown* (Boston: Roberts Bros., 1885), 376.

17 *"Is life so dear, or peace so sweet":* David A. McCants, *Patrick Henry, The Orator* (Westport, Conn.: Greenwood Press, 1990), 125.

17 *"To contend for liberty":* Quoted in Leon Litwack, *North of Slavery* (Chicago: University of Chicago Press, 1961), 7.

17 *"It always appeared a most iniquitous Scheme":* Quoted in David McCullough, *John Adams* (New York: Simon & Schuster, 2001), 104.

18 *how an American could "inflict on his fellow men":* Thomas Jefferson, *The Complete Jefferson,* ed. Saul K. Padover (New York: Duell, Sloan, & Pearce, 1943), 73.

19 *"The prejudice of race":* Quoted in Litwack, *North of Slavery,* 65.

20 *"the real distinctions which nature has made":* Jefferson, *Complete Jefferson,* 661.

20 *"Will not a lover":* Ibid., 665.

21 *"their interest must be viewed as one":* Jonathan Edwards, *Basic Writings* (New York: Signet, 1966), 239–40.

23 *"Should we be willing":* Jonathan Edwards Jr., *The Injustice and Impolicy of the Slave Trade and the Slavery of the Africans* (1791; reprint, New Haven, Conn.: New Haven Anti-Slavery Society, 1833), 4.

23 *"a duty which we owe to mankind":* Ibid., 28.

23 *"I believe in the Golden Rule":* Quoted in Sanborn, *Life and Letters,* 122.

23 *"My life has been of little worth":* Quoted in Villard, *John Brown,* 11.

24 *"give an account of the souls":* Quoted in David E. Stannard, "Death and the Puritan Child," *Puritan New England: Essays on Religion, Society, and Culture,* ed. Alden T. Vaughan and Francis J. Bremer (New York: St. Martin's Press, 1977), 237.

24 *"he that spareth his rod":* Proverbs 13:24, King James Version. Subsequent biblical references are to this version.

24 *"earthly treasures"* to *"course of discipline":* JB to Henry Stearns, July 15, 1857, Ruchames, *John Brown Reader,* 36–37.

26 *"the beginning of days with me":* Quoted in Villard, *John Brown,* 12.

26 *"All my earthly prospects":* Ibid., 13.

27 *the phrase "delightful child" had been mistakenly carved:* Lora Case, *Hudson of Long Ago* (1897; reprint, Hudson, Ohio: Hudson Library and Historical Society, 1963), 49.

28 *"was complete & permanent":* JB to Henry Stearns, July 15, 1857, Ruchames, *John Brown Reader,* 38.

28 *"the wretched, hopeless condition":* Ibid., 38.

30 *"If any man say"* and following verses: 1 John 4:20; Deuteronomy 1:17; Matthew 25:45.

31 *One afternoon, spying a strip of Brown's sheepskin:* Reminiscence of Heman Hallock, 1859, in Sanborn, *Life and Letters,* 32.

Chapter 2: A Firm Foothold at Home

33 *"It is a source"*: JB to sons John Jr., Jason, Frederick, and daughters-in-law, Dec. 4, 1850, Sanborn, *Life and Letters*, 76–77.

34 *"eighteen-hundred-and-froze-to-death"*: Quoted in Louis A. DeCaro Jr., *"Fire from the Midst of You": A Religious Life of John Brown* (New York: New York University Press, 2002), 64.

34 *"if Salmon had done the thing"*: J. H. Vaill to Franklin Sanborn, April 11, 1885, quoted in ibid., 62–63.

35 *"May you ever prove yourself"*: JB to Lora Case, Dec. 2, 1859, Case, *Hudson of Long Ago*, 52.

35 *young Lora Case's perfect memorization:* Ibid., 14.

35 *"Children, obey your parents"*: Ephesians 6:1.

37 *Brown thought these things:* JB to Henry Stearns, July 15, 1857, Ruchames, *John Brown Reader*, 38.

37 *quiet, industrious, and "remarkably plain"*: Ibid., 40.

37 *"tasty," or fastidious, in his own dress:* Milton Lusk, quoted in Sanborn, *Life and Letters*, 34.

38 *"Blow ye the trumpet"*: Charles Wesley, 1750; quoted in DeCaro, *"Fire from the Midst of You"*, 67.

38 *"And ye shall hallow"*: Leviticus, 25:10.

39 *Milton called her "my guardian angel"*: Quoted in Sanborn, *Life and Letters*, 33.

39 *"You see that needle"*: W. A. Phillips, "Three Interviews with Old John Brown," 1879, Ruchames, *John Brown Reader*, 214.

40 *staccato "Tut! Tut!"*: Ruth Brown Thompson, quoted in Sanborn, *Life and Letters*, 93.

41 *"rather opposed to good order"*: James Foreman to James Redpath, Dec. 28, 1859, Ruchames, *John Brown Reader*, 163.

42 *"I think a worse punishment"*: Ibid., 164.

42 *"'crock' me, like mother's kettle"*: Quoted in Sanborn, *Life and Letters*, 35.

44 *"I wonder that any roof timbers"*: Quoted in Eric Ledell Smith, "John Brown in Crawford County: The Making of a Radical Abolitionist," *Journal of Erie Studies* (Fall 2001), 42.

45 *Brown wished to know three things:* Foreman to Redpath, Dec. 28, 1859, Ruchames, *John Brown Reader*, 167.

46 *"Christianity is not a sedentary profession"*: Richard Baxter, *The Saint's Everlasting Rest* (abridged, 1759; reprint, Philadelphia: Presbyterian Board of Publication, 1847), 9-10.

46 *"What you intend to be tomorrow"*: JB to John Brown Jr., March 24, 1846, Sanborn, *Life and Letters*, 62.

46 *"my babies":* Oswald Garrison Villard/John Brown Archive (OGV) at Columbia University, Annie Brown Adams Folder, Box 1A.

46 *the couplet that he taught them all:* Ibid., Box 6, Mrs. John and Family Folder.

46 *"as enterprising and honest as John Brown":* Foreman to Redpath, Dec. 28, 1859, Ruchames, *John Brown Reader,* 166.

47 *"Business is not brisk":* JB to Owen Brown, June 16, 1830, Ernest C. Miller, *John Brown: Pennsylvania Citizen* (State College: Pennsylvania State University Press, 1952), 10–11.

47 *"I trust that getting or losing money":* JB to Owen Brown, Dec. 2, 1847, Sanborn, *Life and Letters,* 23.

47 *"The general aspect of our worldly affairs":* JB to John Brown Jr., June 22, 1844, ibid., 61.

47 *"We have in this part of the country":* JB to Owen Brown, Feb. 5, 1849, ibid., 25.

48 *"I feel that I ought to expect God's judgment":* JB to Owen Brown, June 16, 1830, Miller, *John Brown: Pennsylvania Citizen,* 11.

50 *In the latter stages of the audit:* Sanborn, *Life and Letters,* 92.

50 *"When you know that I suffer":* Reminiscence of Ruth Brown Thompson, quoted in Lou V. Chapin, "The Last Days of Old John Brown," *Overland Monthly* 33, (April 1899), 325.

51 *"Harder! harder! harder!":* John Brown Jr., quoted in Sanborn, *Life and Letters,* 92.

51 *"After that," John Jr. concluded:* Eleanor Atkinson, "The Soul of John Brown: Recollections of the Great Abolitionist by his Son," *America Magazine,* October 1909, 635.

Chapter 3: The Great and Foul Stain

53 *"Slavery is the great and foul stain":* Diary entry for Feb. 24, 1820, quoted in Richard O. Boyer, *The Legend of John Brown* (New York: Alfred A. Knopf, 1973), 294.

54 *"I determined, at every hazard":* The Liberator, Jan. 1, 1831.

55 *"unconstitutional and wicked":* Quoted in Leonard L. Richards, *The Slave Power: The Free North and Southern Domination, 1780–1860* (Baton Rouge: Louisiana State University Press, 2000), 129.

55 *Emancipation would come about: The Liberator,* July 31, 1831.

56 *"The more you improve":* Quoted in David Walker's "Appeal, in Four Articles, together with a Preamble, to the Colored Citizens of the World," 1829, reprinted in Herbert Aptheker, ed. *One Continual Cry* (New York: Humanities Press, 1971), 116.

56 *"they would be in the midst":* Henry Clay, *The Life, Correspondence, and Speeches of Henry Clay,* ed. Calvin Colton (New York: A. S. Barnes, 1857), vol. 5, 331.

56 *"a peculiar, a moral fitness":* Quoted in Aptheker, *One Continual Cry,* 110.

57 *Beginning with the three thousand:* Litwack, *North of Slavery,* 24-25; other statistics and conditions of slavery in the North cited in the following five paragraphs are also drawn from Litwack, 14, 75, 114-15, 93-94, 100, 73, 66, 24.

62 *Mississippi, Alabama, and Georgia:* Richards, *The Slave Power,* 125.

63 *One Sunday afternoon:* Jason Brown's reminiscences are the source of the episode described in the following two paragraphs. OGV, Box 2, Jason Brown Folder.

64 *"I am most sure":* OGV, Box 2, Jason Brown Folder.

65 *"I thought I might go to rest":* JB to Owen Brown, Aug. 11, 1832, Ruchames, *John Brown Reader,* 42.

65 *"Remember now thy Creator":* Ecclesiastes, 12:1.

65 *Once, John Jr. wandered past:* Chapin, "The Last Days of Old John Brown," 325.

66 *"we (colored people of these United States)":* Aptheker, *One Continual Cry,* 63

66 *"Let our enemies go on":* Ibid., 78.

67 *By 1831, Virginia's security force:* Howard Zinn, *A People's History of the United States* (New York: Harper & Row, 1980), 170.

67 *"We do not preach rebellion":* The Liberator, Jan. 8, 1831.

68 *"a positive good":* "On the Reception of Abolition Petitions," *Speeches of John C. Calhoun,* ed. Richard K. Crallé (New York: D. Appleton and Co., 1864), 631.

68 *"I tremble for my country":* The Complete Jefferson, 677.

68 *Thomas R. Dew patronizingly observed:* Review of the Debate in the Virginia Legislature of 1831 and 1832 (Richmond, Va.: T. W. White, 1832), 112.

68 *"We have no hesitation in affirming":* Ibid., 111.

69 *"There is and always has been":* Calhoun, "On the Reception of Abolition Petitions," 632.

Chapter 4: Going Down to Tarshish

71 *"Now the word of the Lord came unto Jonah":* Jonah 1:1-3.

72 *"I feel justly condemned":* JB to Owen Brown, Dec. 10, 1846, Sanborn, *Life and Letters,* 22.

72 *"He that hath a bountiful eye":* Proverbs, 22:9.

72-73 *"The slaves have risen":* Quoted in Sanborn, *Life and Letters,* 34.

74 *"Dear Brother":* JB to Frederick Brown, Nov. 21, 1834; Ruchames, *John Brown Reader,* 42–43.

75 *"When the molten rock":* Robert H. Abzug, *Passionate Liberator: Theodore Dwight Weld and and the Dilemma of Reform* (New York: Oxford University Press, 1980), 86.

75 *"What would be said":* Ibid., 138.

75 *"no powerful opposition influence":* Ruchames, *John Brown Reader,* 43.

75 *The Quaker schoolmistress:* The following account of the Prudence Crandall controversy draws on details and quotations in Litwack, *North of Slavery,* 126–31.

76 *The business relationship with Kent:* Boyer, *The Legend of John Brown,* 266–70.

79 *Many years later:* Atkinson, "The Soul of John Brown," 636.

79 *"Cast ye up, cast ye up":* Isaiah 57:14.

80 *"A discrimination has been made":* John Brown Jr., quoted in Sanborn, *Life and Letters,* 52.

80 *"Brown saw everything large":* Quoted in Boyer, *The Legend of John Brown,* 273.

82 *he stood "prepared freely to offer up my all":* Quoted in ibid., 310.

82 *"The crisis has come":* Quoted in DeCaro, *"Fire from the Midst of You,"* 122.

82 *"I pledge myself, with God's help":* Quoted in Case, *Hudson of Long Ago,* 53–54.

82 *"Here before God":* Quoted in Boyer, *The Legend of John Brown,* 314.

83 *"scarcely a dozen men":* Quoted in Stauffer, *The Black Hearts of Men: Radical Abolitionists and the Transformation of Race* (Cambridge, Mass.: Harvard University Press, 2002), 115.

84 *"the rich plunder":* American Anti-Slavery, *Fourth Annual Report* (New York: The Society, 1837), 50–51.

84 *"I would rather be a convict":* quoted in Stauffer, *Black Hearts of Men,* 115.

86 *"Oh that I were as in months past":* Job 29:1–3, 11–13, 16–17.

87 *Who among you":* Recollection of John Brown Jr., in Villard, *John Brown,* 45–46.

CHAPTER 5: CROSSING THE LINE

89 *"The most interesting part of my visit":* "Editorial Correspondence," *The North Star,* Feb. 11, 1848.

90 *"I am now somewhat in fear":* JB to wife and children, June 12, 1839, Ruchames, *John Brown Reader,* 44–45.

90 *"I have left no stone unturned":* JB to wife and children, June 19, 1839, ibid., 45.

91 *his "abuse of the confidence":* JB to George Kellogg, Aug, 27, 1839, ibid., 46.

91 *Brown wrote again to Kellogg:* JB to George Kellogg, Sept. 20, 1839, quoted in Boyer, *The Legend of John Brown,* 330.

91 *one of the postdated promissory notes:* JB to Seth Thompson, Feb. 18, 1840 and Mar. 4, 1841, RWL, John Brown Collection, Box 1, Folders 67 and 69.

92 *"In our sore affliction":* JB to John Jr., Sept. 25, 1843, Ruchames, *John Brown Reader,* 50.

92 *"As soon as circumstances":* JB to Henry Stearns, July 15, 1857, Ruchames, *John Brown Reader,* 41.

93 *the shepherd's life:* JB to John Jr., Aug. 27, 1846 and Jan 11, 1844, Sanborn, *Life and Letters,* 62, 59.

94 *Four hundred of the four hundred and fifty subscribers:* Charles H. Wesley, "The Negroes of New York in the Emancipation Movement, " *Journal of Negro History* 24, no.1 (January 1939): 76.

95 *"I have no more hope from him":* Elizur Wright to Beriah Green, Oct. 17, 1837; quoted in Jane H. Pease and William H. Pease, *Bound with Them in Chains* (Westport, Conn.: Greenwood Press, 1972), 230.

95 *"Prejudice must be killed":* Quoted in Gerald Sorin, *Abolitionism: A New Interpretation* (New York: Praeger, 1972), 108.

96 *"to hang out our own shingle":* Quoted in C. Peter Ripley, ed., *Black Abolitionist Papers,* vol. 3 (Chapel Hill: University of North Carolina Press, 1991), 24.

96 *"In speaking of him, " Douglass recalled:* Frederick Douglass, *Autobiographies* (New York: Library of America, 1994), 715.

97 *"to the slaves of the United States of America":* Henry Highland Garnet, "An Address to the Slaves of the United States of America," 1843, in Ripley, ed., *Black Abolitionist Papers,* vol. 3, 408–10.

98 *he had been watching and waiting for "some true men":* Reported in *The North Star,* Feb. 11, 1848.

99 *to worship and sometimes preach at its black church:* DeCaro, *"Fire from the Midst of You",* 149–50.

99 *"trust in God and keep their powder dry":* JB to wife, Nov. 28, 1850, Ruchames, *John Brown Reader,* 72.

99 *"three of whom were but recently in Akron jail":* JB to John Jr., Jan. 11, 1844, ibid., 53.

99 *"Mr. Brown's wool has ever been of the highest":* Quoted in Boyd Stutler, "The Shepherd and the Wool Dealer," Stutler archive (STUT), West Virginia Memory Project, http://www.wvculture.org.

100 *"with the exception of Messrs. Perkins & Brown's":* Quoted in ibid.

100 *Between 1845 and 1848, no fewer than fourteen articles:* Boyer, *The Legend of John Brown*, 600 n. 48.

100 *"He was always concerning himself with Negroes":* Quoted in ibid., 354.

101 *"He had a consuming idea in life":* Quoted in ibid., 354.

101 *"the same calling that the old patriarchs followed":* JB to sons, Dec. 4, 1850, Sanborn, *Life and Letters*, 75.

101 *He could tell every sheep:* Brown quoted by Simon Perkins, in ibid., 57.

102 *"for receiving wool of growers and holders":* Quoted in ibid., 63.

102 *"Their calls are incessant":* Quoted in Stutler, "The Shepherd and the Wool Dealer," STUT.

104 *For good measure, they bribed a man named Flint:* Ibid.

105 *Thomas accepted Brown's offer:* Sanborn, *Life and Letters*, 133.

106 *"My Dear Afflicted Wife and Children":* JB to family, Nov. 8, 1846, Ruchames, *John Brown Reader*, 56.

106 *Brown wrote again to Mary alone:* JB to wife, Nov. 29, 1846, ibid., 57–58.

107 *Douglass's knees shook:* Douglass, *Autobiographies*, 660.

107 *"Have we been listening to a thing":* Quoted in Boyer, *The Legend of John Brown*, 368.

108 *"Tell your story, Frederick":* Douglass, *Autobiographies*, 662–63.

108 *There was "a peculiar music":* JB to wife, March 7, 1847, Ruchames, *John Brown Reader*, 59.

109 *The character of the inhabitants was also surprising:* Douglass, *Autobiographies*, 715.

109 *They were evidently used to it":* Ibid., 716.

109 *"His arguments":* Ibid.

110 *"Perhaps we might convert the slaveholder":* Ibid., 719.

111 *"the white man who expected to succeed in whipping":* Ibid., 65.

111 *"I felt as I never felt before":* Ibid.

112 *"My utterances became more and more tinged":* Ibid., 719.

Chapter 6: The Slave Law of the Land

113 *"This filthy enactment":* July–October 1851 journal entry; in *Emerson's Prose and Poetry*, ed. Joel Porte and Saundra Morris (New York, W. W. Norton & Co., 2001), 522.

114 *"but little inferior to some of the whites":* "Sambo's Mistakes," in Ruchames, *John Brown Reader*, 61.

114 *another "small mistake":* Ibid., 61–63.

114 *"Another trifling error of my life":* Ibid., 63.

116 *"Smith niggers":* DeCaro, *"Fire from the Midst of You,"* 167.
116 *"I am something of a pioneer":* Quoted in Sanborn, *Life and Letters,* 97.
117 *To Mary he had confessed:* JB to wife, March 7, 1847, Ruchames, *John Brown Reader,* 59.
118 *"I like to live in a country":* Quoted in DeCaro, *"Fire from the Midst of You,"* 176.
118 *"Father's New Palestine":* Jason Brown, quoted in ibid., 210.
118 *he urged them to remember "the vast importance":* JB to Willis Hodges, Jan. 22, 1849, quoted in Villard, *John Brown,* 72–73.
120 *"It is small," Brown admitted:* Quoted in Sanborn, *Life and Letters,* 99.
120 *he restored a land deed:* DeCaro, *"Fire from the Midst of You,"* 173.
120 *Brown enjoyed visiting his neighbor:* Ibid., 178–79.
122 *"Mr. and Mrs. Brown, and their large family":* Richard Henry Dana, "How We Met John Brown," *Atlantic Monthly* 28 (July 1871), 7.
123 *"We found him well informed":* Ibid., 6–7.
123 *"Horses, as seen at Liverpool":* JB to John Jr., Aug. 29, 1849, Ruchames, *John Brown Reader,* 69–70.
124 *"Gentlemen, if you have":* Quoted in James Redpath, *The Public Life of Captain John Brown* (London: Thickbroom & Stapleton, 1860), 57.
126 *"myriads of enterprising Americans":* Quoted in Zinn, *A People's History,* 152.
126 *It was "our manifest destiny":* Ibid., 149.
126 *"We must march from Texas":* Ibid., p. 153.
128 *Sacramento storekeeper Sam Brannan:* Howard Dewitt, "The Gold Rush and California Statehood," http://online.ohlone.cc.ca.us/english/eng163/GoldRush.html.
128 *the* California Star *had written:* Rockwell D. Hunt, "How California Came to Be Admitted," http://www.sfmuseum.org/hist5/caladmit.html.
128 *"The causes which exclude slavery":* Walter Colton, quoted in ibid.
129 *Roanoke, Virginia, representative John Randolph:* Richards, *The Slave Power,* 85.
129 *"They were scared":* Ibid., 85.
132 *"His wonderful organization":* Emerson, Aug. 17, 1843, diary entry, quoted in Boyer, *Legend of John Brown,* 428.
132 *"Mr. President," he began:* http://www.dartmouth.edu/~dwebster/speeches/seventh-march.html.
132 *"Webster is a fallen star!":* Mary Mann, *Life of Horace Mann, By His Wife* (Boston: Lee & Shepard, 1891), 293.
133 *"The word* liberty*":* *Emerson's Prose and Poetry,* 519.
134 *"the beginning of a reign of terror":* Harriet Jacobs, *Incidents in the Life of*

a Slave Girl (1860; reprint, Cambridge, Mass.: Harvard University Press, 1987), 191.

134 *"I want all my family"*: JB to wife, Jan. 17, 1851, Ruchames, *John Brown Reader*, 75.

134 *"It now seems," he wrote*: JB to wife, Nov. 28, 1850, ibid., 72.

134 *At Springfield's Free Church*: DeCaro, *"Fire from the Midst of You,"* 190.

134 *"Trust in God and keep your powder dry"*: JB to wife, Nov. 28, 1850, Ruchames, *John Brown Reader*, 72.

135 *In 1854, according to one report*: Account of William Wells Brown, in DeCaro, *"Fire from the Midst of You,"* 196.

135 *"Nothing so charms the American people"*: Sanborn, *Life and Letters*, 124.

Chapter 7: To Answer the End of My Being

139 *"Dear Wife and Children, All"*: JB to family, Sept. 4, 1855, ibid., 199–200.

139 *the second he had received from his father that week*: JB to John Jr., Dec. 4 and Dec. 6, 1850, ibid., 75–79.

139 *"I think the situation"*: JB to John Jr., Jan. 18, 1841, Ruchames, *John Brown Reader*, 48.

140 *"He is a most noble-spirited man"*: JB to John Jr., Dec. 4, 1850, Sanborn, *Life and Letters*, 76.

141 *his father had returned to this theme*: JB to John Jr., Dec. 6, 1850, ibid., 79.

141 *a "slavery of the soul"*: John Brown Jr., quoted in DeCaro, *"Fire from the Midst of You,"* 206.

141 *"Indeed, your letter throughout"*: JB to John Jr., Dec. 6, 1850, Sanborn, *Life and Letters*, 78.

142 *"The book has been sealed"*: Quoted in ibid., 78.

142 *"You are very active"*: O. S. Fowler's phrenological reading of John Brown, Feb. 27, 1847, typescript in John Brown Jr. Papers, Ohio Historical Society (OHS).

143 *"the same calling that the old patriarchs followed"*: JB to sons, Dec. 4, 1850, Sanborn, *Life and Letters*, 75.

143 *"We don't like to ask people"*: OGV, Box 5, Ohio Interviews Folder.

144 *"You have been very kind"*: JB to Ruth and Henry Thompson, Jan 23, 1852, Ruchames, *John Brown Reader*, 80.

144 *"an accumulation of blood on the brain"*: Quoted in Stephen B. Oates, *To Purge This Land With Blood* (Amherst: University of Massachusetts Press, 1970, 1984), 64.

144 *"Should my Frederick be with you any":* JB to Owen Brown, May 23, 1850, OGV, Box 4, Letters Through 1854 Folder.

144 *"the largest and strongest boy":* JB to Ruth and Henry Thompson, May 14, 1852, Sanborn, *Life and Letters,* 149.

145 *according to an appalled Mrs. Perkins:* OGV, Box 5, Ohio Interviews Folder.

145 *"My affections are too deep-rooted":* JB to John Jr., Aug. 6, 1852, Sanborn, *Life and Letters,* 151.

145 *"After THOROUGH AND CANDID investigation":* Ibid., 46.

145 *"brought hundreds of Negroes":* OGV, Box 4, JB in Hudson, Franklin, Etc. Folder.

145 *"Cross?" Lambert pronounced:* Quoted in DeCaro, *"Fire from the Midst of You,"* 211-12.

147 *"The tide of emigration":* Quoted in Nicole Etcheson, *Bleeding Kansas: Contested Liberty in the Civil War Era* (Lawrence: University Press of Kansas, 2004), 9.

148 *"all questions pertaining to Slavery":* Ibid., 14.

149 *"peculiarly healthy to the negro":* Ibid., 30.

150 *"Come on, then, gentlemen":* Quoted in William A. Phillips, *The Conquest of Kansas by Missouri and Her Allies* (Boston: Phillips, Sampson, & Co., 1856), 21.

150 *North Elba, he thought, was the place:* Brown's sentiments are reported in John Brown Jr.'s account of the Brown brothers' emigration to Kansas, John Brown Jr. Papers, OHS.

150 *"I would like to have all my children":* JB to John Jr., April 3, 1854, Sanborn, *Life and Letters,* 157.

151 *"The Climate is mild":* Nyle H. Miller et al., *Kansas: A Pictorial History* (Topeka: Kansas State Historical Society, 1961), 20.

151 *"As I volunteered":* JB to Ruth and Henry Thompson, Sept. 30, 1854, Ruchames, *John Brown Reader,* 86.

152 *"the actual dwelling or inhabiting":* Quoted in Etcheson, *Bleeding Kansas,* 53.

152 *the detaining of a Massachusetts emigrant:* Ibid., 33.

152 *"We will have difficulty":* Quoted in Boyer, *The Legend of John Brown,* 491.

153 *"I tell you to mark every scoundrel":* Quoted in Phillips, *The Conquest of Kansas,* 47.

155 *"laws more efficient to protect slave-property":* Quoted in Sanborn, *Life and Letters,* 176.

156 *"Kansas has been invaded":* Quoted in Boyer, *The Legend of John Brown,* 503.

Source Notes

157 *"We have nothing for you":* John Brown Jr.'s account is quoted in Sanborn, *Life and Letters*, 190.

157 *"Her lovely prairies":* Ibid., 190.

157 *"We are Free State":* OGV, Box 2, Jason Brown Folder

158 *The Browns were better armed:* John Brown Jr. to JB, May 20–24, 1855, quoted in Boyer, *The Legend of John Brown*, 525.

158 *He described the prairie:* Ibid., 524. The following quotations from John Jr.'s letter appear on pages 524–25.

164 *she would cut out the lines:* OGV, Box 4, Ohio Interviews Folder.

166 *"Where are you going?":* Henry Thompson to Katherine Mayo, OGV, Box 17, Henry and Ruth Brown Thompson Folder.

Chapter 8: Blood and Remission

167 *"I never had much doubt":* Quoted in Sanborn, *Life and Letters*, 171.

169 *"I can cook a meal":* Ellen Brown to Mary Brown, Nov. 25, 1855, quoted in Villard, *John Brown*, 112.

169 *"in that miserable Frosty region":* JB to wife and children, Nov. 2, 1855, Sanborn, *Life and Letters*, 204.

170 *"Whosoever will come after me":* Mark 8:34–35.

170 *Brown "felt a great deal troubled":* JB to wife and children, Nov. 23, 1855, John Brown Collection, Boston Public Library (BPL).

170 *"I think much, too":* Ibid.

170 *"something of a warlike spirit":* Owen Brown to Samuel Adair, Aug. 8, 1855, quoted in DeCaro, *"Fire from the Midst of You,"* 225.

173 *"Let them shoot and be damned":* J. R. Kennedy affidavit, quoted in Sanborn, *Life and Letters*, 208.

176 *"Christ says, 'If a man smites thee'":* Charles B. Stearns, *Practical Christian*, Jan. 26, 1856, quoted in Lewis Perry, *Radical Abolitionism: Anarchy and the Government of God in Antislavery Thought* (Ithaca, N.Y.: Cornell University Press, 1973), 240–41.

177 *"As for law here":* Samuel Adair to Owen Brown, Jan. 31, 1856, quoted in DeCaro, *"Fire from the Midst of You,"* 227.

177 *the "fanatical devotion" of some northerners:* Quoted in Boyer, *Legend of John Brown*, 470.

178 *"Look here, old man":* Henry Thompson's account, OGV, Box 17, Henry and Ruth Brown Thompson folder.

179 *"insurrectionary combinations":* Quoted in William Elsey Connelley, *John Brown* (Topeka, Kans.: Crane & Co., 1900), 133.

180 *"those damned Browns":* OGV, Box 17, Henry and Ruth Brown Thompson Folder.

Source Notes

181 *"unlawful, and before unheard-of organization":* Quoted in Phillips, *The Conquest of Kansas,* 267.

182 *jury foreman Owen C. Stewart reported:* Ibid., 268.

182 *"The law-abiding citizens of the territory":* Ibid., 276.

182 *"the legally constituted posse":* Ibid., p. 278.

183 *"This is the happiest day of my life":* Quoted in Samuel A. Johnson, *The Battle Cry of Freedom* (Lawrence: University Press of Kansas, 1954), 159.

183 *"a little company by ourselves":* JB to wife and children, June 1856, Ruchames, *John Brown Reader,* 94.

184 *"the rape of a virgin territory":* Charles Sumner, "The Crime Against Kansas," May 19–20, 1856, www.sewanee.edu/faculty/Willis/Civil_War/documents/Crime.html.

184 *"It seemed to be the finishing, decisive touch":* Quoted in Villard, *John Brown,* 154

185 *"Something is going to be done now":* Recollection of Jason Brown, quoted in ibid., 151.

185 *"those Hellish enactments":* JB to Joshua R. Giddings, Feb. 20, 1856, quoted in ibid., 131.

185 *a "supply of men and arms and money":* J. R. Giddings to John Brown, March 17, 1856, quoted in Sanborn, *Life and Letters,* 224.

185 *"only half right in regard to slavery":* JB to Owen Brown, Jan. 19, 1856, OGV, Box 6, Letters 1855–58 Folder.

186 *their toes cracked and black from frostbite?:* Ibid.

186 *"calculated to unman me":* JB to wife and children, Feb. 1, 1856, ibid.

186 *"It is a great trial to stay away":* Henry Thompson to Ruth Brown Thompson, April 16, 1856, OGV, Box 17, Henry and Ruth Brown Thompson Folder

186 *"my heart is sorely grieved at your trials":* JB to wife and children, April 17, 1856, John Brown Collection, BPL.

186 *"Such a state of things":* Samuel Adair to Owen Brown, May 16, 1856, OGV, Box 1A, Adair Family Folder.

187 *"And almost all things":* Hebrews 9:22.

188 *"Father, I object":* George and Henry Grant, "The Potawatomie Tragedy," *Lawrence Daily Journal,* Dec. 5, 1879, reprinted in Ruchames, *John Brown Reader,* 205.

188 *a more avid reader than Brown himself:* OGV, Box 6, Sarah Brown Folder.

191 *"Hush, mother, hush":* OGV, Box 17, Henry and Ruth Brown Thompson Folder.

191 *Oliver had been unable to strike:* Years after the murders, statements

by Salmon Brown and Henry Thompson suggested that Salmon and Owen were responsible for the Doyle killings, while Henry and Theodore Weiner were the team that killed Wilkinson and Sherman. Several pieces of testimony confirm that Frederick Brown and Townsley stood guard and committed no violence. Oliver appears to have been with his father and two brothers when they marched the three Doyles out of their cabin, but Salmon's account specifies that Owen killed one of the Doyle brothers while "another of the Browns" [himself] killed James Doyle and his other boy. On the basis of these statements, and of the nature of Drury Doyle's wounds and the distance of his body from the others, I infer that Oliver was the assigned captor and executioner of the youngest Doyle but could not strike. Accounts of the Pottawatomie incident and its surrounding circumstances by Salmon Brown, James Townsley, and George and Henry Grant (who lived on Pottawatomie Creek in 1856 and served in John Brown Jr.'s Pottawatomie Rifle Company) are reprinted in Ruchames, *John Brown Reader*, 189–208.

193 *"There shall be no more work such as that"*: Townsley statement, 1879, quoted in Oates, *To Purge This Land with Blood*, 137.

CHAPTER 9: MARKED MEN

195 *"If murder and assassination"*: *The Leavenworth Herald*, June 4, 1856, quoted in James C. Malin, *John Brown and the Legend of Fifty-Six* (Philadelphia: American Philosophical Society, 1942), 57.

196 *"We give you just one hour"*: Jason Brown provided the account of his brother's ill-fated slave rescue and its aftermath; his statement is the source of the quotations that follow. OGV, Box 2, Jason Brown Folder.

198 *"I think it was an uncalled for, wicked act"*: Quoted in Villard, *John Brown*, 165.

198 *"Can't keep you here"*: Quoted in Ibid., 166.

199 *"Get away," he shouted*: Quoted in Ibid., 167.

200 *"You are one of the very men"*: OGV, Box 2, Black Jack Folder

200 *"My name is Jason Brown"*: Ibid.

200 *"Swing him up"*: Ibid.

201 *"changed my whole mind and life"*: Ibid.

202 *"who feigns to be crazy"*: Quoted in Malin, *John Brown and the Legend of Fifty-Six*, 55.

202 *Governor Shannon reported to President Pierce*: OGV, Box 2, Black Jack Folder.

203 *"Hitherto, murder had been"*: Quoted in Connelley, *John Brown*, 242.

203 *"Hundreds of the Free State men"*: OGV, Box 2, Black Jack Folder.

203 *the "body of good citizens":* Ibid.
204 *"oppose all men who are so ultra":* Quoted in Connelley, *John Brown*, 220.
204 *"as desirous of peace":* Quoted in Ibid., 237.
205 *"even the Pro-Slavery men":* Quoted in Ibid., 231.
205 *To each man, Brown rationed:* OGV, Box 2, Bondi Folder.
205 *"Father, have you ever":* OGV, Box 3, Anecdotes Folder.
205 *Once, Salmon awoke in the night:* Ibid.
206 *"Don't fear," said Frederick Brown:* Redpath, *The Public Life of Captain John Brown*, 111.
207 *"Give me men of good principles":* Ibid., 114.
207 *"They were not earnest":* Ibid.
207 *"ideas, suspicions, and memories":* August Bondi; quoted in Sanborn, *Life and Letters*, 298.
210 *"Then stay with me":* Quoted in ibid., 299.
211 *"for one of those lately arrested":* Quoted in Villard, *John Brown*, 207.
213 *"commanding all persons":* Quoted in Sanborn, *Life and Letters*, 303.
213 *"at the head of an unauthorized company":* Quoted in Villard, *John Brown*, 211.
215 *The symmetry and harmony:* W. A. Phillips, "Three Interviews," in Ruchames, *John Brown Reader*, 212.
215 *the "sum all of villainies":* Ibid.
215 *"In his ordinary moods":* Ibid., 212, 210.
216 *"Old Captain Brown":* OGV, Box 2, Jason Brown Folder.
217 *"the Abolition fort and town of Osawatomie":* J. W. Reid correspondence, Aug. 31, 1856, quoted in Villard, *John Brown*, 246.
217 *"I think I know you":* Quoted in Oates, *To Purge This Land with Blood*, 169.
218 *"God sees it":* OGV, Box 17, Henry and Ruth Brown Thompson Folder.
218 *treated her considerately:* OGV, Box 1A, Adair Folder.

Chapter 10: Bringing Forth a New Nation

221 *"A very few, as heroes, patriots":* Thoreau, "Civil Disobedience," *Collected Essays and Poems*, 205.
222 *"The so-called 'practical men'":* Emerson, "American Scholar," *Emerson's Prose and Poetry*, 61.
223 *"strike the sun if it insulted me":* Herman Melville, *Moby-Dick* (New York: W. W. Norton & Co., 1967), 144.
224 *"The man shall not go out into slavery":* Samuel Gridley Howe to Theodore Parker, May 25, 1854, quoted in Albert J. Von Frank, *The Trials of Anthony Burns* (Cambridge, Mass.: Harvard University Press, 1998), 11.

224 *Howe was in the square:* Ibid., 69.

225 *to admonish a young man "for getting in a passion":* Louis Thomas Jones, *The Quakers of Iowa* (Iowa City: State Historical Society of Iowa, 1914), 45.

225 *Zachariah Dicks had told:* Quoted in ibid., 37.

226 *"Have you ever heard of John Brown of Kansas?":* Quoted in Richard Hinton, *John Brown and His Men* (1894; reprint, New York: Arno Press, 1968), 118.

227 *Sanborn took long walks to Concord:* Jeffery Rossbach, *Ambivalent Conspirators: John Brown, the Secret Six, and a Theory of Slave Violence* (Philadelphia: University of Pennsylvania Press, 1982), 47.

228 *"How we mistake":* Theodore Parker, "Sermon for the Times," Sept. 22, 1850, in *Works: Centenary Edition* (Boston: American Unitarian Association, 1911), vol. 11, 312.

231 *"defensive measures":* National Kansas Committee, Resolution No. 1, Jan. 24, 1857, cited in Sanborn, *Life and Letters,* 359.

232 *"best blood of the Mayflower":* Franklin Sanborn to Massachusetts legislature, Feb. 18, 1857, quoted in ibid., 371.

232 *"We want good men":* Quoted in ibid., 372.

232 *"To the Friends of Freedom":* Ruchames, *John Brown Reader,* 102.

233 *"faced and inscribed in memory":* JB to wife and children, March 12, 1857, Sanborn, *Life and Letters,* 375.

233 *"learn and practice war no more":* quoted in JB to wife and children, March 12, 1857, Ruchames, *John Brown Reader,* 103.

233 *"that it was not at my solicitation":* Ibid., 103.

234 *"your wife and children shall be cared for":* Amos Lawrence to JB, March 20, 1857, Sanborn, *Life and Letters,* 374.

234 *"performing that service which is equally":* JB to Franklin Sanborn, May 15, 1857, quoted in Rossbach, *Ambivalent Conspirators,* 117.

235 *"when He is pleased to call for His right":* John Winthrop, "A Model of Christian Charity," in *Norton Anthology of American Literature,* shorter 5th edition (New York: W. W. Norton & Co., 1999), 110.

235 *"dearly beloved daughter Ellen Brown":* JB to wife, March 31, 1857, Ruchames, *John Brown Reader,* 103.

235 *"If any of us are hereafter":* JB to John Jr., April 15, 1857; ibid., 104–5.

236 *"he leaves the States, with a feeling of deepest sadness":* "Old Brown's Farewell," ibid., 106.

237 *"'God will not deliver me into the hand of the wicked'":* JB to Jeremiah Brown, April 15, 1857, OGV, Box 5, Letters: 1855–1858 Folder.

238 *"I have learned more of the depravity":* Geary to brother, Feb. 25, 1857, quoted in Etcheson, *Bleeding Kansas,* 143.

239 *"If I do not use the Arms & Ammunition":* JB to George Luther Stearns, Nov. 16, 1857, Villard, *John Brown,* 305.

241 *the "hot discussion":* Quoted in ibid., 311.

243 *a state "cannot introduce any person":* *A Legal Review of the Case of Dred Scott* (Boston: Crosby, Nichols, & Co., 1857), 18. Subsequent quotations from Chief Justice Taney's opinion appear on pages 17, 19, and 20.

243 *"Whereas, slavery throughout its entire existence":* John Brown, "Provisional Constitution and Ordinance for the People of the United States," in Hinton, *John Brown and his Men,* 619–20.

245 *"Rail Road business on a* somewhat extended*":* JB to Thomas Wentworth Higginson, Feb. 12, 1858, quoted in Oates, *To Purge This Land with Blood,* 227.

245 *"BY FAR the most* important *undertaking":* JB to Thomas Wentworth Higginson, Feb. 2, 1858, quoted in Villard, *John Brown,* 320.

246 *"This is news":* Quoted in Oates, *To Purge this Land with Blood,* 227.

247 *"only the alternatives of betrayal, desertion, or support":* F. B. Sanborn, *Recollections of Seventy Years* (Boston: Gorham Press, 1909), vol. 1, 147.

247 *The "successful cultivation":* JB to Sanborn, Feb. 24, 1858, ibid., 150.

247 *"I like to see my tracks behind me":* OGV, Box 3, Anecdotes Folder.

CHAPTER 11: AN EXTENDED FAMILY

249 *"In John Brown's house":* Osborne P. Anderson, *A Voice From Harpers Ferry,* (Boston, 1861), 23–24.

250 *"The* masses *suffer":* James Newton Gloucester to JB, Feb. 19, 1858, in Benjamin Quarles, ed., *Blacks on John Brown* (Urbana: University of Illinois Press, 1972), 4.

251 *"more and more convinced":* James Newton Gloucester to JB, March 9, 1858, Quarles, *Blacks on John Brown,* 4–5.

251 *"You have not studied them right":* Phillips, "Three Interviews with Old John Brown," Ruchames, *John Brown Reader,* 218.

252 *an avid self-taught reader:* William Wells Brown, *St. Domingo: Its Revolutions and its Patriots* (Boston: Bella Marsh, 1855), 12–13.

252 *"already ripe for a rebellion":* James Redpath, *The Roving Editor; or, Talks with Slaves in the Southern States* (New York: A. B. Burdick, 1859), 52. Subsequent quotations in this paragraph are from pages 284–86 and 287.

253 *"The anxiety I feel to see my wife":* JB to wife and family, Jan. 30. 1858, Sanborn, *Life and Letters,* 441.

254 *"O my daughter Ruth!":* Ibid., 441.

254 *"Dear father,"* Ruth wrote back: Ruth Brown Thompson to JB, Feb. 20, 1858, Sanborn, *Life and Letters,* 442.

255 *"If I thought the success":* Henry Thompson to JB, April 21, 1858, OGV, Box 17, Henry and Ruth Brown Thompson Folder.

256 *"He (Harriet) is the most of a man":* JB to John Jr., April 8, 1858, quoted in Benjamin Quarles, *Allies for Freedom* (New York: Oxford University Press, 1974), 42.

259 *Tears flowed freely:* Irving B. Richman, *John Brown Among the Quakers, and Other Sketches* (Des Moines: Historical Department of Iowa, 1894), 31.

259 *"I did my best to convince him":* Quoted in ibid., 29.

259 *attendance at "a very quiet convention":* statement by John Edwin Cook, Nov. 1859, in Hinton, *John Brown and His Men,* 703.

260 *"sallying forth arm in arm":* Anderson, *A Voice from Harpers Ferry,* 14.

260 *"the patriotic Nathaniel Turner":* Garnet, "An Address to the Slaves of the United States of America," 1843, in *Black Abolitionist Papers,* vol. 3, 409.

262 *Brown defused the debate:* Quarles, *Allies for Freedom,* 47.

262 *"those eternal and self-evident truths":* "Provisional Constitution and Ordinance for the People of the United States," in Hinton, *John Brown and His Men,* 619–20. The following quotations from this document appear on pages 620 and 633.

263 *Too many of them, James Monroe Jones grimly observed:* Quarles, *Allies for Freedom,* 48.

265 *"onward to the chosen field":* John Cook to "My Dear Sisters," June 6, 1858, Richman, *John Brown Among the Quakers,* 42.

265 *"no countenance has been given":* S. G. Howe to Henry Wilson, May 12, 1858, Sanborn, *Life and Letters,* 462.

266 *George Stearns posted to Chatham:* G. L. Stearns to JB, May 14, 1858, ibid., 461.

267 *"It is in times of difficulty":* JB to Owen et al., May 21, 1858, Richman, *John Brown Among the Quakers,* 41.

267 *"one thing that keeps me":* John Cook to "My Dear Sisters," May 6, 1858, ibid., 36.

267 *"it is natural that men":* Richard Realf to Owen et al., May 18, 1858, ibid., 40.

268 *"Patience is the hardest lesson":* Quoted in Sanborn, *Life and Letters,* 472.

269 *"If God controls all things":* Quoted in Villard, *John Brown,* 364.

269 *"It is an invariable rule with me":* JB to Franklin Sanborn, May 14, 1858, Sanborn, *Life and Letters,* 456.

269 *"Am still preparing":* JB to children, Dec. 2, 1858, ibid., 481.

271 *"You might call it a case of self-defense":* Quoted in Villard, *John Brown,* 369.

271 *"in the present state of affairs":* Leavenworth Herald, Jan. 29, 1859, quoted in ibid., 370.

272 *"Upon what principle?":* Quoted in DeCaro, *"Fire from the Midst of You,"* 256.

272 *"Allow me to introduce":* Mrs. Emma Wattles Morse, quoted in Villard, *John Brown,* 371.

274 *"damned niggers":* Quoted in Sanborn, *Life and Letters,* 485.

274 *"through the great mercy of God":* JB to wife and children, Feb. 10, 1859, ibid., 490.

275 *"While we sympathize with the oppressed":* Tabor citizens' resolution, Feb. 7, 1859, in Villard, *John Brown,* 385.

CHAPTER 12: ABOLISHING SLAVERY IN VIRGINIA

277 *"Now we must be magnanimous":* Amos Lawrence to Rev. E. Nute, July 18, 1857, quoted in Malin, *John Brown and the Legend of Fifty-Six,* 695–96.

277 *"He has begun the work in earnest":* Franklin Sanborn to T. W. Higginson, Jan. 19, 1859, quoted in DeCaro, *"Fire from the Midst of You,"* 256.

278 *"settle down into a miserable mush":* Quoted in Albert Fried, *John Brown's Journey* (Garden City, N.Y.: Anchor Press, 1978), 206.

278 *"Intelligent black men in the States":* Gerrit Smith to John Thomas, Aug. 27, 1859, quoted in Stauffer, *Black Hearts of Men,* 241.

278 *"So debauched are the white people":* Ibid., 241.

279 *"the manliest man I have ever seen":* Bronson Alcott diary, May 8, 1859, quoted in Sanborn, *Life and Letters,* 505.

279 *"never meet again in this world":* Quoted in Rossbach, *Ambivalent Conspirators,* 204.

281 *"Oh Mary,"* Ruth once heard him: OGV, Box 17, Henry and Ruth Brown Thompson Folder.

281 *"I cannot," Jason replied:* OGV, Box 2, Jason Brown Folder.

282 *"It will be likely to prove":* JB to wife, July 5, 1859, Villard, *John Brown,* 405.

283 *"Make me a grave":* Frances E. W. Harper, "Bury Me in a Free Land," *Complete Poems of Frances E. W. Harper,* ed. Maryemma Graham (New York: Oxford University Press, 1988), 93.

283 *"my invisibles":* OGV, Box 1A, Anne Brown Adams Folder.

284 the *"wretched contrivance":* Thomas Paine, *Age of Reason,* in *Basic Writings of Thomas Paine* (New York: Willey Book Co., 1942), 12.

285 *"Oh, Dear Dangerfield":* Quoted in Villard, *John Brown,* 415.

285 *"Oh Bell," Watson!wrote:* Quoted in ibid., 416.

285 *"mother and father":* OGV, Box 1A, Anne Brown Adams Folder.

285 *"We are just trying to stir":* Ibid.
286 *"We shall be caught in a pen":* Ibid.
286 *"Dear Sir," the statement read:* Villard, *John Brown*, 416.
286 *"We must not let our father die alone":* Quoted in Hinton, *John Brown and His Men*, 259.
286 *"and the whole Negro set":* Quoted in Villard, *John Brown*, 413.
287 looking *"every way like a man of the neighborhood":* Douglass, *Autobiographies*, 758.
288 *"perfect steel trap":* Ibid., 759.
288 *the "taper light," as he would later put it:* Frederick Douglass, "John Brown," 1881, in Ruchames, *John Brown Reader,* 315.
289 I am willing to live for the slave: Ibid., 315.
290 *"Come with me, Douglass":* Ibid., 320.
290 *"I b'leve I'll go wid de ole man":* Ibid., 320.
290 *"To have been acquainted with John Brown":* Quoted in Stauffer, *Black Hearts of Men*, 251.
291 *"Old John Brown, late of Kansas":* David J. Gue to John B. Floyd, Aug. 20, 1859, in Villard, *John Brown,* 410.
291 *"I was satisfied in my own mind":* Quoted in ibid., 410.
291 *"a worse plague than fleas":* OGV, Box 1A, Annie Brown Adams Folder.
291 "Your men folks has a right smart lot of shirts": Ibid.
292 *"a trifle over one hundred and eighty dollars":* JB to John Jr., August, 1859, Sanborn, *Life and Letters,* 536.
292 *"I am now in a Southern slave state":* Quoted in Barrie Stavis, *John Brown: The Sword and the Word* (Cranbury, N.J.: A. S. Barnes & Co., 1970), 104.
292 *"I sometimes feel as though I could not make the sacrifice":* Quoted in Sanborn, *Life and Letters,* 549.
292 *"Millions of fellow beings require it":* Quoted in Villard, *John Brown,* 682.
294 *"Is not this the fast":* Isaiah 58:6–7.
295 *"it shall be the duty of all persons, male and female":* "Provisional Constitution and Ordinances," in Hinton, *John Brown and His Men,* 629, 631.
295 *"And now, gentlemen":* Statement by John Edwin Cook, in ibid., 708.
296 *"Men, get on your arms":* Quoted in Villard, *John Brown,* 426.
299 *The black women whom Washington and Allstadt owned:* D. E. Henderson testimony, RWL, John Brown Collection, Box 2, Folder 3.
299 *"Anderson being a colored man":* Quoted in Stavis, *The Sword and the Word,* 126.
300 *"I knew no more about the word":* Quoted in Allan Keller, *Thunder at Harper's Ferry* (Englewood Cliffs, N.J.: Prentice-Hall, 1958), 43.

302 *"Why should our train be stopped":* William Prescott Smith to Andrew Phelps, Oct. 17, 1859, in Jules Abels, *Man on Fire: John Brown and the Cause of Liberty* (New York: Macmillan, 1971), 174.

302 *"My dispatch is not exaggerated":* Andrew Phelps to William Prescott Smith, Oct. 17, 1859, ibid., 174.

302 *"My particular reason for taking you":* Lewis W. Washington testimony, 36th Congress, *Senate Report No. 278,* 34.

303 *"When your household gods are broken":* "Three Interviews," Ruchames, *John Brown Reader,* 218.

303 *"that 'sum of all villainies'":* JB to wife and children, Nov. 30, 1859, ibid., 158.

305 *"if you knew my heart and history":* Quoted in Keller, *Thunder at Harper's Ferry,* 75.

305 *"by noon there will be fifteen hundred men":* Ibid., 60.

306 *"Harpers Ferry is in possession of the Negroes":* Ibid., 132.

308 *"Though you may take my life":* Harry Hunter testimony, quoted in Villard, *John Brown,* 442.

312 *"No, my son, have patience":* Terence Byrne testimony, 36th Congress, *Senate Report No. 278,* 19.

312 *"If you must die, die like a man":* J. T. Allstadt testimony, quoted in Villard, *John Brown,* 448.

312 *"When his sons were shot down":* Quoted in ibid., 443.

313 *"He has abolished slavery in Virginia":* Quoted in ibid., 562.

Chapter 13: A Settlement of the Question

315 *"I wish to say, furthermore":* JB interview with Senator Mason et al., October 18, 1859, Ruchames, *John Brown Reader,* 124.

316 *"What brought you here?":* Quoted in Villard, *John Brown,* 455.

316 *"Mr. Brown, who sent you here?":* Oct. 18, 1859 interview, Ruchames, *John Brown Reader,* 118. The quotations from the interview that follow appear on pages 119, 122, 120, and 125.

318 *"Mr. Brown, the silver of your hair":* Quoted in Villard, *John Brown,* 463.

319 *"Immediate shooting or hanging without trial":* Quoted in the *New York Times,* Oct. 22, 1859.

319 *"The wheel nor the rack":* Ibid.

319 *"the work of a madman":* Quoted in Villard, *John Brown,* 472.

319 *"the whole thing would be positively ridiculous":* Ibid., 472.

319 *"only demonstrates the impregnable safety":* Quoted in Charles Joyner, "'Guilty of Holiest Crime': The Passion of John Brown," in Finkelman, ed., *His Soul Goes Marching On,* 302.

320 *"a harebrained demonstration":* quoted in ibid., 302.

320 *"making the whole South ring": New York Times,* Oct. 22, 1859.

320 *the "peculiar peril of Southern life":* Ibid.

320 *"Before I began my work":* JB to Reverend H. L. Vaill, Nov. 15, 1859, Sanborn, *Life and Letters,* 590.

321 *Harpers Ferry "advanced the cause of Disunion":* Quoted in Villard, *John Brown,* 476.

323 *"there is not a handful of men in the North": New York Observer,* quoted in Washington *National Intelligencer,* Dec. 6, 1859.

323 *the "half-caste Republic":* Quoted in Merrill D. Peterson, *John Brown: The Legend Revisited* (Charlottesville: University of Virginia Press, 2002), 29.

323 *"What was his crime?":* Quoted in Joyner, "'Guilty of Holiest Crime,'" in Finkelman ed., *His Soul Goes Marching On,* 316.

323 *"Christ told me to remember":* JB to Reverend James W. McFarland, Nov. 23, 1859, Ruchames, *John Brown Reader,* 146.

324 *"not having the fear of God":* Quoted in Villard, *John Brown,* 488.

325 *"a grief too deep and hard":* OGV, Box 1A, Annie Brown Adams Folder.

326 *"That sounds just like father":* Higginson, "A Visit to John Brown's Household in 1859," in Ruchames, *John Brown Reader,* 227. Subsequent quotations from Higginson's essay appear on pages 225, 226, and 222-23.

326 *"that I am worth inconceivably more":* JB to Jeremiah Brown, Nov. 12, 1859, Ruchames, *John Brown Reader,* 134.

326 *"the heavy tidings of our disaster":* JB to John Jr. & Jason and families, Nov. 22, 1859, Sanborn, *Life and Letters,* 597.

327 *"that for me at this time":* JB to wife and children, Nov. 8, 1859, Ruchames, *John Brown Reader,* 132.

327 *"this Court would have deemed it":* Brown's speech to the court, Nov. 2, 1859, ibid., 126.

328 *"when I think how easily":* JB to Luther Humphrey, Nov. 19, 1859, Sanborn, *Life and Letters,* 595.

328 *"I feel assured":* JB to wife and children, Nov. 8, 1859, Ruchames, *John Brown Reader,* 133.

328 *"If you feel sure":* JB to wife, Nov. 16, 1859, ibid., 138.

328 *"the sacrifices you & I have been called to make":* JB to wife, Nov. 10, 1859, Villard, *John Brown,* 540.

328 *"I am here with Mrs. Spring":* Mary Brown to JB, Nov. 13, 1859, OGV, Box 6, Mrs. John Brown & Family Folder.

329 *"I will close this":* JB to wife, Nov. 26, 1859, Ruchames, *John Brown Reader,* 152.

329 *"His name is Jason"*: JB to Rebecca Spring, Nov. 24, 1859, ibid., 148.

330 *"It would be a great pleasure to me"*: JB to Reverend James W. McFarland, Nov. 23, 1859, ibid., 146.

330 *"that our seeming disaster"*: JB to wife, sons, and daughters, Nov. 30, 1859, ibid., 156.

330 *"And let me entreat you all"*: Ibid., 157.

333 *"God bless you, my men:* Quoted in Villard, *John Brown,* 554.

333 *"This is a beautiful country"*: Ibid., 555.

334 *"to see if I could detect any signs"*: Col. J. T. L. Preston, "The Execution of John Brown," STUT.

335 *"So perish all such enemies of Virginia!"*: Ibid.

335 *"I have never in my life"*: Nathan Appleton to John Crittendon, Dec. 17, 1859, OGV, Box 3, John Brown: Individual Estimates Folder.

335 *"Of the* five hundred *pulpits"*: *New York Observer,* Quoted in *National Intelligencer,* Dec. 6, 1859.

335 *"as uncorrupted with Negro equality doctrines"*: Quoted in Joyner, "'Guilty of Holiest Crime,'" in Finkelman ed., *His Soul Goes Marching On,* 317.

335 *"such a coming together from all places"*: *New York Journal of Commerce,* quoted in *National Intelligencer,* Dec. 6, 1859.

335 *"No, gentlemen"*: Quoted in Peter Wallenstein, "Incendiaries All: Southern Politics and the Harpers Ferry Raid," in Finkelman, ed., *His Soul Goes Marching On,* 161.

336 *"Such a practical exercise of abolition principles"*: Quoted in ibid., 153.

336 *"Sample of the favors designed for us"*: Peter Huber, "Edmund Ruffin Fires First Shot of Civil War," http://www.oldnewspublishing.com/edmunt.htm.

336 the *"Black Republican, free love, free Nigger' party"*: Oates, *Our Fiery Trial,* 72.

337 *"The Union, the Constitution"*: Peter Knupfer, "A Crisis in Conservatism: Northern Unionism and the Harpers Ferry Raid," in Finkelman, ed., *His Soul Goes Marching On,* 128.

337 *"cannot excuse violence"*: Quoted in Villard, *John Brown,* 564.

337 *"so absurd that the slaves"*: Abraham Lincoln, *Speeches and Writings, 1859–1865* (New York: Library of America, 1989), 125.

337 *"I have no purpose, directly or indirectly"*: Ibid., 215.

338 *"the fanaticism of hatred against slavery"*: *New Orleans Daily Picayune,* Dec. 2, 1859, quoted in Joyner, "Guilty of Holiest Crime," in Finkelman, ed., *His Soul Goes Marching On,* 320.

338 *"But for John Brown's insane attack"*: Anthony W. Dillard, "William Lowndes Yancey: The Sincere and Unfaltering Advocate of Southern Rights," *Southern Historical Society Papers,* vol. 21, 1893, 153.

340 *"If we shall suppose that American slavery":* Lincoln, *Speeches and Writings, 1859–1865,* 687.

340 *"I John Brown":* Ruchames, *John Brown Reader,* 159.

Epilogue: The Unfinished American Revolution

341 *"You know what John Brown did?":* Malcolm X, *By Any Means Necessary: Speeches, Interviews, and a Letter* (New York: Pathfinder Press, 1970, 1985), 81–82.

341 *most of the American historical establishment:* The judgments that follow are culled from Fried, *John Brown's Journey,* 8–9; Peterson, *John Brown,* 148; Oates, *Our Fiery Trial,* 40–41; and Finkelman, ed., *His Soul Goes Marching On,* 299.

344 *"the best news that America has ever heard":* Thoreau, "A Plea for Captain John Brown," *Collected Essays and Poems,* 414.

345 *"Thus, under the name of order":* "Civil Disobedience," ibid., 210.

345 *"They have compromised so long":* "Three Interviews," in Ruchames, *John Brown Reader,* 217.

345 *"Action from principle":* Thoreau, "Civil Disobedience," 210.

345 *"serve the State with their consciences":* Ibid., 205.

Acknowledgments

Robert Keith Sweitzer called me one day from California to say that he had been reading scripts for historical action pictures and was struck by how their stories paled in comparison with that of John Brown, whom he had studied in my class at the University of Texas at Austin. Keith suggested that I tell that story and energetically promoted the outline I produced. Without his initiative, for which I am very grateful, this book would not have been written.

For his confidence, sound advice, and excellent representation, I thank my agent, Alan Nevins. My editor at Free Press, Leslie Meredith, gave me encouragement, latitude, and valuable guidance in the final phases of the book's preparation—especially when it came to cutting the fat and the rhetorical indulgence from my manuscript. Leslie, her assistant Andrew Paulson, and the rest of her team were a pleasure to work with.

During the writing of this book, I pleasurably and profitably discussed many of its issues with my friend Ben Fischer, who also read parts of the manuscript and offered encouragement and thoughtful commentary. I benefited, too, from the exceptional contributions of Jill Anderson, my graduate student and research assistant, whose resourcefulness and efficiency in providing me with materials and historical research was matched by her astute and constructive comments on my ideas and my prose.

Janis Bergman-Carton—my most intimate partner in intellect and spirit, as well as in love—enriched this project long before I ever imagined it. Her passion and intelligence infuse it. Her provision of every kind of support I could have asked for, without my having to ask, enabled it. In every way, she has made this a better book, and continues to make me a better person, than would have been conceivable without her.

Acknowledgments

Among its more obvious concerns, *Patriotic Treason* is about families: about the legacies we receive from our parents and bequeath to our children. The optimism and humanity of my parents, Edwin and Lonnie Carton–along with the vitality and love of my sisters, Deborah Riemer and Paula Rossen–inform this book. So does my hope for my daughters, Jacqueline and Rebecca, to whom I have dedicated it.

INDEX

Abbott, J. B., 213
Abolitionism, 13–14, 22–23, 28–30, 223.
   See also Slavery
   blacks in movement, 95–98, 107–108, 113–115
   Brown's early convictions, 9–11, 28, 72–76, 79–80, 82–83, 86–87
   Brown's first public statement, 82–83
   education of free blacks, 59, 74–76
   Garrison and, 53–55, 65–67, 94–95
   in Ohio, 72–75
   Underground Railroad, 10, 30, 64, 100, 103, 145–146, 244, 246, 251, 255–256, 260, 279
Adair, Charles, 219
Adair, Florilla, 153–154, 159, 177, 187, 198, 217–219, 269, 272
Adair, Mike, 219
Adair, Samuel, 153–154, 159, 160, 177, 186–187, 198–199, 205, 217–219, 239, 269, 272
Adams, Abigail, 17
Adams, John, 17, 18, 221
Adams, John Quincy, 45, 53
"Address to the Slaves of the United States of America" (Garnet), 260–261
Adirondack Mountains, 115, 116, 119
Aesop's *Fables,* 46
Age of Reason (Paine), 284

Akron, Ohio, 99, 102, 119, 143, 281
Alcott, Bronson, 279
Allstadt, John, 8, 9, 299–300, 304, 312, 321
Alton, Illinois, 81–82
Amalek, 98–99
American and Foreign Anti-Slavery Society, 97
American Anti-Slavery Society, 55, 73, 84, 94, 96, 97, 108
American Colonization Society, 56–57, 60–61
American Indians, 21, 24, 61–63, 146, 149, 154, 180
American Shepherd (Morrell), 100
Amistad mutiny, 96, 97, 135
Anderson, Jeremiah Goldsmith, 11, 270, 281, 283, 285, 292, 310, 312, 343
Anderson, Osborne P., 249, 260, 263, 264, 287, 299, 300, 305, 309
Anti-Slavery Society in the Western Reserve, 73
Anti-Slavery Standard, 176, 251
Appalachian Mountains, 105, 110, 246
Appeal, in Four Articles, with a Preamble, to the Colored Citizens of the World, but in particular to Those of the U.S. (Walker), 66–68
Ashtabula County, Ohio, 266
Astor, John Jacob, 115

Index

Atchison, David, 147–149, 152–153, 172, 175
Austin, Moses, 127
Avery, Mr., 79, 80
Avis, John, 326, 327, 331–334

Bailey, Fred (*see* Douglass, Frederick)
Banks, Russell, x
Baptisteville, Kansas, 200–202
Barber, Thomas, 175, 176
Baxter, Richard, 46
Baylor, Robert, 309
Beckham, Fontaine, 308
Benet, Stephen Vincent, ix
Bethel Church, Philadelphia, 57
Bible, the, 29, 30, 34, 35, 45, 46, 49, 71, 86, 98–99, 134–135, 142, 143, 187, 294
Bierce, Lucius V., 168
Billington, Monroe Lee, 341
Black Hawk Indians, 225
Black Jack Springs, Battle of, 6, 203, 207–212, 214, 226, 279, 280
Black Laws (Ohio), 60
Blair, Charles, 237
Blakeslee, Levi, 10, 24, 25, 35–36, 38, 42
Blue Ridge Mountains, 1, 332
Boerly, Thomas, 305
Bolivar Heights, Virginia, 1, 8, 302
Bondi, August, 205, 207
Booth, John Wilkes, 333
Boston Vigilance Committee, 223–224
Bourbon County, Kansas, 268, 271
Brandywine Creek, Ohio, 25, 28
Brannan, Sam, 128
Branson, Jacob, 172–175, 181
Brisbane, Albert, 83
Brockett, W. B., 210, 211
Brooks, Preston, 184, 213
Brown, Abbie Hinckley, 255
Brown, Albert Gallatin, 335
Brown, Amelia ("Kitty"), 106, 116, 165
Brown, Anna, 24
Brown, Annie, 109–110, 119, 120, 164, 282, 283, 285, 286, 291, 292, 325
Brown, Austin, 92, 154, 156, 158, 165, 168, 186

Brown, Captain John (grandfather) 16, 22, 232–233
Brown, Charles, 84, 92
Brown, Dianthe Lusk, 36–40, 43, 46, 48, 53, 64–65, 71, 84, 165, 281
Brown, Edward, 82
Brown, Ellen (daughter), 119
Brown, Ellen (daughter), 164, 165, 235, 253, 282
Brown, Ellen (wife of Jason), 119, 154, 157, 158, 165, 168, 169, 198, 216, 219, 281
Brown, Freddy, 282
Brown, Frederick (brother), 24, 73–75, 78, 118
Brown, Frederick (son), 46, 48, 53, 65
Brown, Frederick (son), 16–17, 53, 80, 119, 141, 143, 144, 151–154, 157, 167, 188, 190–192, 198, 204, 206–207, 209–210, 216–220, 233
Brown, Isabella, 255, 280, 282, 285, 292, 325, 332
Brown, Jason, 40, 43, 49, 51, 63–65, 85–87, 102, 105, 106, 116, 118, 119, 141, 143, 151, 154, 155, 156–160, 163, 165, 169, 186, 188, 195–202, 211, 216–219, 235, 254, 269, 281, 329–330
Brown, John
  American origins of, 20
  arrest warrant for, 235–236
  attitude toward business, 47
  at battle of Black Jack Springs, 6, 203, 207–212, 226, 279
  at battle of Osawatomie, 218, 240
  at battle of the Spurs, 273–274
  Bible reading by, 29, 34, 35, 45, 46, 49, 86, 98, 143, 294
  birth of, 21, 24
  birth of children of, 40, 46, 48, 64–65, 71, 77, 84, 89, 106
  in Boston, 227–229, 231, 232, 235–236
  in Canada, 255–257, 260–263, 266
  as captain of Liberty Guards, 174, 175
  cattle drives made by, 10, 28, 85, 89
  at Chatham convention, 260–263, 266

376

childhood of, 24–27
children, relationship with, 40, 48–51, 139–144, 165, 329–330
death of children of, 53, 92, 119, 144, 219, 220
death of mother of, 10, 26–27, 65
death of wife (Dianthe) of, 65, 71
debate and, 45–46
Dianthe, relationship with, 37–38, 65
Douglass and, 89, 96–97, 107–112, 145, 241, 244, 287–290
early abolitionist convictions of, 9–11, 28, 72–76, 79–80, 82–83, 86–87
education of, 25, 27, 30–31, 33–34
employees, relationship with, 41–42
father, relationship with, 23, 25–28, 170
finances of, 47, 49, 78, 83–85, 89–92, 99, 101, 117, 133, 140, 233–234, 237, 266, 292
Fugitive Slave Law and, 134–135
fugitive slaves helped by, 6, 36, 42, 47, 93, 100, 122, 145–146, 270–275, 277
fundraising campaigns by, 227–229, 231–237, 249, 279
funeral and burial of, 15, 122, 313, 336
grandfather's gravestone and, 16–17, 219, 232–233
hanging of, 12, 34, 327, 333–335
Harpers Ferry raid and. *See* Harpers Ferry raid
health of, 48–49, 64, 117, 144, 219, 238, 269, 273
historical establishment on, 341–343
Indians and, 62, 63
interrogation of, 316–317
journalists and, 215, 252, 345
in Kansas, 6, 7, 45, 51, 160, 164–165, 167–171, 174–177, 179, 180, 183, 185–193, 197–199, 202–206, 211–219, 226, 239, 268–274
as land speculator, 78–79, 83
last meeting with wife, 331–332
last written words by, 340
letters from prison by, 34–35, 320, 323, 326–330
marriage of, 38–39

Mary, relationship with, 162, 164
Massachusetts Kansas Committee and, 227–229, 231, 233–234
mother, relationship with, 25–26, 37
names of, 5–7, 268
National Kansas Committee and, 231–232
newspapers read by, 251
North Elba settlement and, 116–120, 122, 123, 133, 150, 151, 162, 164, 170, 237, 253, 254, 280–281
personality and character of, 39–40, 123, 124, 140, 142–143, 162, 215–216
personal relationships with blacks, 93–94, 104–105, 108–112, 249–250, 253, 256, 260
photographs of, 103, 310
phrenology and, 141
physical appearance of, 6, 28, 37, 206, 261, 268, 316
Pottawatomie murders and, 6, 187–193, 197–199, 202–206, 211, 214, 253
prosecution and trial of, 135, 318–319, 324, 326–327
Provisional Constitution by, 242–244, 253, 262–263, 269, 287, 294–295
reading by, 28–29, 29, 34, 35, 45, 46, 49, 86, 98, 143, 294
Redpath biography of, 207
religiosity of, 20, 29, 30, 34, 35, 45–47, 49, 86, 98, 143, 145, 170, 187, 234–235, 237, 294
remarriage of, 71
on the run, 202–203, 205–206
"Sambo's Mistakes" article by, 114–115
sentence handed to, 326–327
as shepherd and wool merchant, 85, 92–93, 99–102, 104, 117–119, 123–125, 133–134, 140–141, 143, 150
singing and, 44, 247
sons' lack of faith and, 145, 162, 330
as Sunday school teacher, 30, 34, 35

Index

Brown, John *(cont.)*
  in tanning and cattle business, 27–28, 35–37, 40, 43, 49, 72, 76–77, 81
  travel to Europe by, 123–125, 140
  United States League of Gileadites formed by, 135–137
  women, attitude towards, 37, 244, 252
  wounding of, 12, 312
Brown, John, Jr., 36, 40, 42, 43, 49–51, 63, 65, 79, 80, 85–87, 99, 102, 105, 116, 117, 119, 123, 150, 154, 177, 201, 219, 269, 281, 292
Brown, Martha, 254, 280, 282, 283, 285, 291–293, 325, 332
Brown, Mary Ann Day, 15, 71, 77, 79, 80, 85–87, 89, 93, 102, 106–109, 116, 117, 119, 122, 134, 143, 144, 160–164, 169, 170, 186, 233, 235, 253, 254, 280–282, 324–326, 328–329, 331–332
Brown, Oliver (brother), 24
Brown, Oliver (son), 9, 11, 15, 84, 89, 106, 119, 120, 143, 145, 160, 165–169, 186, 188, 190–192, 205, 209, 215, 216, 220, 254, 280–283, 285, 286, 292, 293, 299, 306, 308–310, 312, 315, 325
Brown, Owen (father), 9, 10, 22–30, 34–36, 38, 42, 47, 48, 72–74, 82, 85–87, 145, 165, 170, 186–187
Brown, Owen (son), 40, 48, 49, 51, 63, 85, 116, 119, 120, 143, 151–154, 157, 163, 167, 168, 188, 190, 191, 193, 199, 205, 214, 216, 219, 220, 227, 241, 253, 267, 281, 296, 301, 309
Brown, Peter (Pilgrim), 20
Brown, Peter (son), 92
Brown, Ruth (daughter). *See* Thompson, Ruth Brown
Brown, Ruth (mother), 9, 24–27, 29, 37, 46, 47, 187
Brown, Sally Root, 27, 28
Brown, Salmon (brother), 24, 27, 30, 33, 34, 42
Brown, Salmon (son), 77, 84, 106, 119, 120, 143, 145, 151–154, 156, 157, 160, 163, 167–169, 179, 184, 186, 188, 190, 191, 193, 205, 209, 214, 216, 219, 253, 254, 255, 280, 325
Brown, Sarah (daughter), 71, 80, 84, 92
Brown, Sarah (daughter), 106, 119, 120, 164, 282
Brown, Watson, 8, 9, 11, 15, 84, 106, 119, 120, 143, 145, 164, 170, 219–220, 225, 254, 255, 280, 282–284, 292, 296, 300, 306, 307, 309, 310, 315–316, 325
Brown, Wealthy Hotchkiss, 140, 142, 154, 157, 168, 198, 214, 219
Brown's Station, Kansas, 158, 178, 197, 198, 207
Brunswick, Missouri, 165
Buchanan, James, 2, 4, 7, 212, 214, 229, 238
Buford, Jefferson, 179–180, 189, 203
Bunyan, Paul, 46
Burns, Anthony, 122, 223–225
"Bury Me in a Free Land" (Harper), 283
Butler, A. P., 184
Byrne, Terence, 301–302, 312

Caldwell, Elias, 56, 57
Calhoun, John C., 68, 69
Calvin, John, 20
Calvinism, 20–21, 142
Campbell, John, 333–334
Canada, 7, 29, 36, 60, 100, 122, 134, 145, 245, 251, 253, 255–257, 259–260, 275, 324
Canterbury, Connecticut, 75–76
Canton, Connecticut, 232
Canton, Ohio, 16
Carpenter, O. A., 205, 208
Cary, Mary Ann Shadd, 256
Case, Lora, 34–35, 82
Cato, Sterling, 178–179, 200
Catton, Bruce, 341
Chamberlain, Amos, 91–92
Chambers, George, 301, 307
Chambersburg, Pennsylvania, 281, 286–289
Charlestown, Virginia, 34, 302, 306, 318, 324, 331–333

Index

Chatham, Canada, 256–257, 259–266, 295
Cherokee Indians, 61–62
Chickasaw Indians, 62
Child, Lydia Maria, 278, 329
Chippewa Indians, 24
Choctaw Indians, 62
Cincinnati, Ohio, 60
Cinque, 96, 251
Civil War, 338, 340, 342
Clay, Henry, 56, 129, 337
Cleveland, Ohio, 266, 267
Cline, James, 217, 218
Coffin, William C., 107
Coleman, Franklin, 172–173, 182
Collamer, Jacob, 13–15
Collective bargaining, 101–102
Collins, Samuel, 172
Colonization, 55–58, 60, 61, 250–251, 257, 287
Compromise of 1850, 129–130, 133, 146, 147, 337
Congregationalists, 22, 25, 30, 38, 63–64, 75, 82–83, 234–235
Constitutional Union party, 337
Constitution of the United States, 4, 15, 95, 242, 243
  preamble to, 17
Convention of the Free People of Color of 1843, 97
Cook, John Edwin, 240, 241, 267–268, 285, 286, 296, 297, 301, 303, 309, 310
Copeland, John, Jr., 294, 299, 305, 309, 310, 318, 333
Coppoc, Barclay, 259, 284, 294, 296, 301, 309
Coppoc, Edwin, 12, 259, 284, 294, 297, 305, 308, 310, 312, 318, 324, 333
Cotton economy, 3, 29, 60, 67
Cotton gin, invention of, 19
Covey, Edward, 111
Crandall, Prudence, 75–76
Crawford County, Pennsylvania, 43, 46, 62, 75, 76
Creek Indians, 62
Creole mutiny, 96, 97

Cromwell, Oliver, 28
Cross, Resin, 307
Cruise, David, 270–271
Cuyahoga River, 76, 77
Cyrus, 120, 135

Daingerfield, J. E. P., 304, 312
Dana, Richard Henry, Jr., 122–123
Daniels, Jim, 270
Daniels, John Brown, 275
Daniels, Mrs., 275
David, Donald, 341
Davis, Jefferson, 13, 14, 152–153, 179
Day, Charles, 71
DeBaptiste, George, 279
Declaration of Independence, 17, 19, 20, 23, 74, 221, 243, 262, 295, 345, 346
"Declaration of Liberty by the Representatives of the Slave Population of the United States of America, A" (Brown), 295
Delamater, Thomas, 45, 71
Delany, Martin, 250–251, 257, 259, 261–263, 287
Delaware Indians, 149
Democratic party, 337
Denver, Governor, 269
Depression of 1857, 250, 267
Detroit, Michigan, 145, 275, 277, 279
Dew, Thomas R., 68
Dillard, Anthony W., 338
Dodge, Augustus, 146–147
Donald, David, 341
Donaldson, I. B., 182, 210, 211
Doniphan, Kansas, 172
Doolittle, James, 13
Dorchester County, Maryland, 256
Douglas, Stephen A., 60, 61, 146–148, 338
Douglas County, Kansas, 172–173, 175
Douglass, Anna, 107, 241
Douglass, Charles, 241
Douglass, Frederick, 113, 115, 135, 151, 164, 215, 232, 250, 252, 261, 262, 277, 284, 307, 324
  Brown and, 89, 96–98, 107–112, 145, 241, 244, 287–290

Douglass, Frederick *(cont.)*
  education of, 107
  escape from slavery of, 111
  as orator, 107–108
  photograph of, 103
Douglass, Rosetta, 241
Dow, Charles, 172, 182
Doyle, Drury, 191
Doyle, James, 178–180, 189–191, 204, 225
Doyle, Mahala, 190–191, 201
Doyle, William, 179, 190, 191, 204
Dred Scott decision of 1857, 3–4, 242–243, 245, 250, 261
DuBois, W. E. B., 1
Dutch Henry's Crossing, Kansas, 178–179, 189–192

Edwards, Jonathan, 21, 46
Edwards, Jonathan (the younger), 22–23
Ellsworth, Alfred, 263
Emerson, Ralph Waldo, 113, 132, 133, 222–223, 227, 228, 279
Enlightenment, 19
Epps, Lyman, 120–122, 151
European immigrants, 3, 61
Everett, Edward, 61, 323
Exodus, 97, 98

Fast, John, 22
Faulkner, Charles James, 316
Fauquier Cavalry, 331
Fayette, John, 86
Fitch, Graham, 13
Fitzhugh, George, 69
Floyd, John B., 290–291
Forbes, Hugh, 237–239, 245, 258, 265–267, 269, 305
Foreman, James, 41–43, 46, 49, 65
Founding Fathers, 16–19, 221, 222
Fowler, Orson Squire, 141
Fowler and Wells, 142
Fox Indians, 149
Franklin, Benjamin, 29, 46, 47, 114, 222
Franklin, Ohio, 76–79, 84, 91
Franklin Congregational Church, 79–80
Franklin Land Company, 77, 78

Frederick Douglass's Paper, 251
Frederick the Great, 299
Free blacks
  abolitionism and, 95–98, 107–108, 113–115
  Adirondack experiment and, 115–116
  colonization and, 56–58, 60, 61, 250–251, 257, 287
  education and, 59, 74–76
  employment and, 59
  in Franklin, Ohio, 79–80
  resettlement of, 59–60
  voting rights and, 58–59, 97
Free Soil party, 122
Free State movement, 171–182, 185, 186, 203–204, 207–219, 227, 229, 238
Frémont, John C., 212
French Creek, Pennsylvania, 62, 63
Fugitive Slave Law of 1850, 3, 122, 130–134, 148, 223–225, 251, 261
Fugitive slaves, 6, 36, 42, 47, 93, 100, 122, 145–146, 270–275, 277

Garibaldi, Giuseppe, 237
Garnet, Henry Highland, 96–98, 113, 250, 260–262
Garraty, John, 342
Garrett, John W., 302
Garrison, David, 217, 218, 223
Garrison, William Lloyd, 13, 53–55, 65–67, 73, 75, 83, 86, 94–95, 97, 107–108, 215, 229
Gaylord, Daniel C., 91
Geary, John, 213, 216, 219, 231, 238
Genovese, Eugene D., 342
Giddings, Joshua R., 185
Gill, George, 267, 269, 270, 273, 284, 287
Gill, H. C., 259
Gloucester, Elizabeth, 244, 249
Gloucester, James Newton, 244, 249–251, 262
Gold rush, 125, 127, 128, 146
Graham, Dr., 210–211
Grant, Mary, 204
Greeley, Horace, 84

Green, Beriah, 73, 95
Green, Israel, 4, 11, 12, 312
Green, Shields, 12, 284, 288–291, 294, 310, 312, 318, 333
Griffing, Charles S. S., 100–101
Grinnell, Iowa, 275
Griswold, Hiram, 326
Guadalupe Hidalgo, Treaty of, 125
Gue, David, 290–291

Hallock, Heman, 31
Hallock, Jeremiah, 22, 23, 30, 187, 237
Hallock, Moses, 30, 31, 33
Hamilton, Charles, 268
Hancock, John, 222
Hanford, Mr., 30, 34
Hanway, James, 204
Harper, Frances, 283
Harper, Jane, 270–271
Harper, Sam, 270–271
Harpers Ferry raid, 1–2, 4–9, 11–12, 14–15, 135, 296–309, 312
  Brown family reaction to, 325–326
  Brown's travel to, 281
  documents pertaining to, 13, 295–296, 324
  execution of, 296–309
  journalistic response to, 319–323, 335
  Kennedy farmhouse base, 271, 281–285, 290–292
  Lincoln on, 337
  photographs of town, 298
  planning and training for, 237–241, 245–247, 249–250, 257–260, 266–268, 269, 277–280, 285–286, 288–290, 294, 295
  significance of, 320–321, 323, 326, 328, 337–338, 343–344
  white sympathy for, 304
Harris, J. H., 287
Harris, James, 192–193
Harvard Medical School, 250
Hawthorne, Nathaniel, 223
Haymaker, Frederick, 78, 84
Hayward, Shephard, 300–301
Hazlett, Albert, 270, 284, 297, 309, 310

Henry, Patrick, 17
Hicklan, Mr., 270
Hickok, Laurens, 82
Hickory Point, Kansas, 172
Higgins, Patrick, 300
Higginson, Thomas Wentworth, 224, 229, 230, 241, 245, 265, 277, 324–326
Hinton, Richard, 215, 268
Hodges, Willis, 113, 114
Howe, Samuel Gridley, 224, 229, 230, 234, 241, 265, 266, 324
Hudson, David, 26, 30, 39, 42
Hudson Township, Ohio, 3, 24, 25, 28, 64, 72, 81, 90–92, 165
Huffmaster, Mrs., 291, 292
Hunter, Andrew, 316

Illinois River, 128
Illinois State Anti-Slavery Society, 82
Incidents in the Life of a Slave Girl (Jacobs), 134
Indian Removal Act of 1830, 61, 62
"Injustice and Impolicy of the Slave Trade and of the Slavery of the Africans, The" (Edwards), 22–23
Iowa City, Iowa, 179

Jackson, Andrew, 55, 61, 62, 222
Jackson, Thomas J., 332
Jacobs, Harriet, 134
Jacobs, Judge, 201
Jay, John, 17, 18
Jefferson, Thomas, 18–20, 68, 98, 221, 222, 295
Jefferson, Thomas (teamster), 120, 122
Jefferson Guards, 302, 306, 309
Jones, James Monroe, 262, 263
Jones, Ottawa, 205
Jones, Samuel, 155, 173–176, 181, 183, 184, 212
Joyner, Charles, 342
Judson, Andrew T., 76

Kagi, John Henry, 240, 260–263, 267, 269, 270, 272, 275, 284–286, 288, 297, 299, 305, 309, 311

Index

Kansas City, Kansas, 179
Kansas-Nebraska Act of 1854, 147–149, 223, 278
Kansas River, 180
Keene Valley, 117
Kellogg, George, 89–91
Kennedy, Booth, 281
Kent, Marvin, 80
Kent, Zenas B., 76–78, 80
Kickapoo Indians, 149
Kitzmiller, A. M., 302, 304, 306

Lafayette, Marquis de, 299
Lambert, William, 145–146
Lane Seminary, Cincinnati, 73–74
Larue, John, 270, 271
Laughlin, Patrick, 172
Lawrence, Amos, 149, 234, 277
Lawrence, Kansas, 149, 153, 155, 158, 172–177, 180–186, 195–196, 217, 219, 268, 273
Lawrence, Samuel, 100
Lawrence Committee of Safety, 174
Leary, Lewis Sheridan, 294, 305, 309, 311
Leavenworth, Kansas, 174, 214
Lecompte, Samuel D., 171, 181–182, 211
Lee, Robert E., 2, 4–8, 11, 309, 312, 316, 342
Leeman, William, 240, 284, 285, 292, 301, 307–308, 311
Legate, James, 205
Liberator, The, 53–55, 65–67, 73, 94, 107, 251
Liberia, 56–58, 287
Liberty Guards, 174, 175
Life of Washington (Irving), 258
Life of Washington (Weems), 16, 29
Lincoln, Abraham, 337, 338, 340, 342
Linn County, Kansas, 268, 269, 271
Lives (Plutarch), 28, 258
Loguen, J. W., 96, 113, 115, 116, 245, 253
Louisiana Purchase, 128, 146
Lovejoy, Elijah, 81–83, 215
Lusk, Amos, 36, 37
Lusk, Edward, 153

Lusk, Milton, 38–39
Lusk, Mrs., 36, 39

Madison, James, 61
Malcolm X, 341
Mann, Horace, 133
Manual of the Patriotic Volunteer (Forbes), 237, 238, 258
Marais des Cygnes, Kansas, 202
Marion Rifles, 183
Mars, John, 134, 135
Marshall, John, 61
Maryland Heights, Virginia, 2, 296
Mason, James, 13–15, 131, 316, 317
Massachusetts Kansas Committee, 227–229, 231, 233–234, 236, 239, 245, 265, 266
Mather, Cotton, 24
Maxson, William, 258
McKeever, Matthew, 100
McKim, J. Miller, 331
Meadville, Pennsylvania, 43–45, 62–64
Mechanical Association of Ohio, 59
Melville, Herman, 223
Merriam, Francis Jackson, 294, 296, 301, 309
Metcalf, Emily, 82
Mexican War, 122, 125–127, 132, 146, 344
Middle Creek, Kansas, 178
Mills, Gideon, 25
Mills, Lucius, 216
Mississippi River, 128, 151, 154
Missouri Compromise of 1820, 3, 129, 147, 148, 149, 223
Missouri River, 128, 151, 156, 179
Moby Dick (Melville), 223
"Model for Christian Charity, A" (Winthrop), 234–235
Moffet, C. W., 287
Monroe, William, 260–261, 263
Monterey Constitutional Convention of 1849, 128
Montgomery, James, 272
Morrell, L. A., 100
Morris, Gouverneur, 16

Morris Academy, Litchfield, 33, 34
Morton, Edwin, 246–247
Moses, 98, 99, 272
Mount Vernon, 15
Mutinies, 96, 97, 135

Napoleon, Emperor, 123, 258
National Emigration Convention, 257
National Kansas Committee, 227, 229, 231–232, 234
Nat Turner revolt, 67, 69, 72–73, 251
Nelson, Truman, ix
Nevins, Alan, 341
New Bedford, Massachusetts, 107
Newby, Dangerfield, 284–285, 294, 295, 305, 306, 308, 311
New England Anti-Slavery Society, 55
New England Emigrant Aid Company, 149, 186, 277
New Lucy (steamer), 156
New York State Anti-Slavery Convention, 95–96
Niger Valley Exploring Party, 250
Northampton, Massachusetts, 162
North Elba (Timbucto) settlement, 16, 116–118, 143, 150, 151, 160, 162, 164, 169, 170, 186, 220, 232, 233, 237, 253, 254, 280–281, 324–325
North Star, The (newspaper), 108, 109, 115
Notes on the State of Virginia (Jefferson), 20
Nueces River, 126

Oates, Stephen, x
Oberlin Collegiate Institute, 23, 74, 294
Ohio-Lake Erie Canal, 77
Ohio River, 29, 100
"Old Brown's Farewell to the Plymouth Rocks, the Bunker Hill Monuments, Charter Oaks, and Uncle Tom's Cabin" (Brown), 236
Oregon Trail, 146
Organic Law of the territories. *See* Kansas-Nebraska Act of 1854
Osage River, 154, 176, 178, 217

Osawatomie, Battle of, 203, 217–220, 240
Osawatomie, Kansas, 154, 157, 159, 167–172, 174, 176–178, 180, 198, 199, 269, 272
O'Sullivan, John, 126
Otoe Indians, 149
Ottawa Creek, Kansas, 183, 184, 205, 206, 210, 214
Ottawa Indians, 24
Oviatt, Heman, 42, 84, 85, 92, 99, 100
Owen, John, 209

Paine, Thomas, 284
Palmyra, Kansas, 196
Panic of 1837, 81, 83, 250
Parker, Richard, 326
Parker, Theodore, 188, 224, 227–230, 241, 265, 266, 324
Parsons, Luke, 287
Pate, Henry Clay, 6, 201, 202, 207, 208, 210–213, 279
Pennsylvania-Ohio Canal, 77, 78, 84
Perkins, Mrs. Simon, 100, 141, 144
Perkins, Simon, 99–102, 104, 117, 119, 133–134, 140–141, 143, 151, 152
Perkins & Brown, 99–105, 118, 123–125, 133, 134, 140, 141
Peterboro, New York, 115, 245, 246, 249, 278
Phelps, A. J., 300–302, 305
Phillips, Wendell, 313
Phillips, William Addison, 215–216, 303, 345
Phrenology, 142
Pickersgill & Company, 119, 123, 125, 140
Pierce, Franklin, 148, 152, 156, 171, 174, 175, 177–180, 185, 186, 202, 211, 212, 232
Pilgrims, 20
Pilgrim's Progress (Bunyan), 46
Pittsburgh, Pennsylvania, 77
Plainfield Academy, Massachusetts, 30, 33
Plantation economy, 19, 29
Plutarch, 28, 258

Index

Plymouth Rock, 20
Polk, James, 126, 127
Pomeroy Guards, 183
Poor Richard's Almanac (Franklin), 29, 46
Potomac River, 1, 5, 285, 296, 305, 306, 309
Pottawatomie Creek, Kansas, 154, 167, 178, 183, 189, 190, 192, 193, 204, 216, 273
Pottawatomie murders, 6, 187–193, 197–199, 202–206, 211, 214, 253
Pottawatomie Rifles, 183, 187, 195, 197
Prairie City, Kansas, 205, 207, 211
Prairie City Rifles, 207
Presidential election of 1860, 278, 336–338
Preston, J. T. L., 332, 334, 335
Protestantism, 20–21
"Provisional Constitution and Ordinance for the People of the United States" (Brown), 242–244, 253, 262–263, 269, 287, 294–295
Puritans, 21, 22

Quakers, 22, 225–226, 258, 259

Ram's Horn, The (newspaper), 114, 251
Randolph, John, 129
Randolph Township, Pennsylvania, 43
Realf, Richard, 267, 287
Redpath, James, 206–207, 215, 252, 278
Reed, Mrs., 122
Reeder, Andrew, 152–156, 171
Reformation, 20
Reid, John W., 216–218
Republican party, 212, 278, 336–337
Review of the Debate in the Virginia Legislature (Dew), 68
Revolutionary War, 15, 16, 22, 23, 57–58, 98, 263
Reynolds, David, x
Richardson, Richard, 240, 267, 287
Richfield, Ohio, 92
Richmond Township, Pennsylvania, 43, 45–49, 62, 75, 76, 118
Robinson, Charles, 158, 167, 177

Rockford, Illinois, 160
Roving Editor, The; or, Talks with Slaves in the Southern States (Redpath), 252
Ruffin, Edmund, 336
Ruggles, Dr., 162, 164
Russell, Thomas, 236, 249

Sac Indians, 149
St. Louis, Missouri, 156, 179
Saint's Everlasting Rest, The (Baxter), 46
Salem, Massachusetts, 22
"Sambo's Mistakes" (Brown), 114–115
Sanborn, Franklin Benjamin, 227–232, 234, 241, 246–247, 258, 265, 277, 279, 294, 324, 345
Santa Fe Trail, 146, 196, 207
Scott, Dred, 242–243
Secret Six, 230
Sedgwick, John, 213
Seminole Indians, 62
Senate Committee on Territories, 146
Seneca Falls Convention, 109
Seneca Indians, 24
Sentinel Range, 117
Sermon on the Mount, 74
Seward, William, 61, 150
Shadd, Amelia Freeman, 256
Shannon, Wilson, 171, 173–177, 179, 180, 182, 185, 186, 202, 211–213, 216, 232
Shawnee Indians, 149
Shenandoah River, 1, 285, 296, 299
Shenandoah Valley, 1, 332
Sherman, "Dutch" Henry, 178, 188, 189, 192, 193, 204
Sherman, William, 178, 188, 189, 192, 204
Shore, Samuel, 207–212
Sierra Nevada, 127, 128
Silliman, Benjamin, 75
Slavery. *See also* Abolitionism; Brown, John
  Compromise of 1850 and, 129–130, 133, 146, 147, 337
  Dred Scott decision of 1857 and, 3–4, 242–243, 245, 250, 261

Fugitive Slave Law of 1850 and, 3, 122, 130–134, 148, 223–225, 251, 261
growth of population in, 2, 18
Jefferson and, 18–20, 68
John Quincy Adams quoted on, 53
Kansas-Nebraska Act of 1854 and, 147–149, 223, 278
Missouri Compromise of 1820 and, 3, 129, 147, 148, 149, 223
mutinies, 96, 97, 135
Nat Turner revolt, 67, 69, 72–73, 251
population in northern states, 58
proslavery theorists on, 68–69
Republican party and, 212, 278, 336–337
Walker's pamphlet and, 66–68
Slave trade, end of, 2, 18
Smith, F. H., 334
Smith, Gerrit, 115–117, 143, 151, 159, 164, 230, 232, 234, 241, 245–247, 249, 265, 266, 277–279, 324
Smith, Isaac, 5
Smith, Peter, 115
Smith, Stephen, 244
Smith, William Prescott, 302
Southampton County, Virginia, 67
Specie Circular, 81
Spring, Rebecca, 328, 329
Spring Creek, Kansas, 273–274
Springdale, Iowa, 225–226, 245, 257–259
Springfield, Massachusetts, 99, 102–106, 108, 109, 117, 118, 133–137, 251
Spurs, Battle of the, 273–274
Squatter Sovereignty Act. *See* Kansas-Nebraska Act of 1854
Starry, John, 301, 302, 308–309
Stars and Stripes flag, 263
Stearns, Charles B., 176
Stearns, George Luther, 13–15, 228–231, 234, 237, 239, 241, 249, 265, 266, 279, 324
Stearns, Henry, 14, 24, 25, 28, 92, 93, 231
Stearns, Mary Preston, 14, 15, 229, 231, 236–237

Stevens, Aaron Dwight, 240, 241, 258, 267, 269–271, 273, 284, 285, 294, 295, 297, 299, 307, 311, 316, 318, 328, 333
Stewart, Owen C., 182
Still, William, 244, 249
Stone, Lucy, 164
Storrs, Charles, 73
Stowe, Harriet Beecher, 223
Stringfellow, B. F., 149, 152, 153, 172, 181
Stuart, J. E. B., 1–2, 4–9, 11, 201, 213, 309, 312, 316, 317
Sumner, Charles, 171, 184, 213
Sumner, Edwin, 6, 174, 175, 213–214
Supreme Court of the United States, 3, 242–243

Tabor, Iowa, 219, 220, 227, 236, 237, 240, 274–275
Taliaferro, William, 331, 333
Taney, Roger, 3, 61, 243
Tayleure, C. W., 315–316
Taylor, Stewart, 284, 297, 300, 306, 309, 311
Taylor, Zachary, 126
Textile industry, 100–102, 104, 222
Thayer, Eli, 149
Thomas, Thomas, 103, 105, 107, 110, 113, 135
Thompson, Dauphin, 11, 282, 284, 286, 311, 312, 325
Thompson, Henry, 143, 144, 150–152, 160, 164–165, 167–169, 178, 179, 186, 188, 190–193, 208, 211, 214, 216, 220, 226, 253, 254, 280, 325
Thompson, Mary, 281
Thompson, Ruth Brown, 15, 46, 48, 80, 106, 109, 119, 122, 143, 144, 150–152, 162, 164–166, 186, 253, 254, 280, 325
Thompson, Seth, 43, 78, 81, 84, 85, 91
Thompson, William, 216, 280–282, 284, 286, 299, 306–308, 311, 325
Thomson, Estelle, 44
Thoreau, Henry David, xi, 127, 221, 223, 227, 279, 344–346

Thucydides, 28
Tidd, Charles, 240, 241, 267, 270, 284–286, 296, 297, 301, 309
Tilton, Theodore, 323
Tocqueville, Alexis de, 19
Todd, John, 274
Topeka, Kansas, 172, 177, 180, 214, 215, 217, 273
Torrington, Connecticut, 24, 30
Toussaint L'Ouverture, 252
Townsend, James, 226
Townsley, James, 189–193, 195
Trading Post, Kansas, 268
Truth, Sojourner, 164
Tubman, Harriet, 253, 255–257, 287
Turner, George, 308
Turner, Nat, 67, 69, 72, 260
Two Years Before the Mast (Dana), 122
Tyndale, Hector, 331

Uncle Tom's Cabin (Stowe), 223
Underground Railroad, 10, 30, 64, 100, 103, 145–146, 244, 246, 251, 255–256, 260, 279
Unitarians, 21, 98
United States League of Gileadites, 135–137, 256, 296, 323

Vallandigham, C. L., 316
Van Rennselaer, Thomas, 14, 89, 108, 113
Voting rights, 58–59, 97

Wadsworth, Tertius, 85, 90, 91
Wakarusa Creek, Kansas, 173, 174
Walker, David, 66–68
Walker, Robert J., 238
War of 1812, 18, 29, 58, 119
War of Independence, 15, 16, 22, 23, 57–58, 98, 263
Washington, Augustus, 89, 103, 108
Washington, George, 8, 15, 16, 299, 300

Washington, Lewis, 8–9, 12, 299–301, 303, 304, 312, 316, 317, 321
Washington, Madison, 96, 251
Washington County, Pennsylvania, 100

Waterloo, Battle of, 123
Watkins, William J., 96
Watson, Henry, 287–288
Wattles, Augustus, 272
Wattles, Emma, 272
Webster, Daniel, 60, 131–134
Weems, Mason Locke "Parson," 16, 29
Weiner, Theodore, 178, 188, 190, 192, 193, 207
Wellington, Duke of, 123
Wells, Joseph, 85, 90, 91
Western Reserve College, 23, 42, 73, 74, 82
Westlands farm, Ohio, 79, 84, 90–92
Westminster Catechism, 27, 40
Whelan, Daniel, 297, 299
White, Martin, 157, 200, 217–220, 255
Whiteface Mountain, 117–118
White supremacy, doctrine of, 61, 93
Whitfield, J. W., 152, 171, 213, 214
Whitman, E. B., 239
Whitman, Samuel, 85
Wilder, D. W., 203
Wilkinson, Allen, 178, 179, 189–192, 204
Williams, William, 297, 299, 300
Wilmot Proviso, 132
Wilson, Henry, 265–266
Winston, John Anthony, 338
Winthrop, John, 234–235
Wise, Henry, 309, 316, 318–320, 331, 341
Women's rights, 94, 109
Wood, J. N., 273, 274
Wood, Samuel, 173, 181
Wood, Thomas, 201, 202
Woodson, Daniel, 216, 217
Wright, Elizur, 73, 84, 95
Wright, Theodore S., 95